HUMAN DISEASES AND CONDITIONS

HUMAN DISEASES AND CONDITIONS

Neil Izenberg, M.D.
Editor in Chief

Published in Association with the
Center for Children's Health Media,
The Nemours Foundation

Volume 2

Ear Infections–Osteoporosis

Charles Scribner's Sons
An Imprint of The Gale Group
New York

The information in *Human Diseases and Conditions* is not intended to take the place of medical care by physicians and other health care professionals. This book does not contain diagnostic, treatment, or first aid recommendations. Readers should obtain professional advice in making all health care decisions.

Library of Congress Cataloging-in-Publication Data

Human diseases and conditions / Neil Izenberg, editor in chief.
p. cm.
"Published in association with the Center for Children's Health Media, the Nemours Foundation."
Contents: V. 1. Abscess-Dysrhythmia.
Includes bibliographical references and index.
Summary: Present articles dealing with all kinds of diseases and disorders, from acne and brain tumor to tobacco-related diseases and yellow fever.
ISBN 0-684-80543-X (set: alk. paper)—ISBN 0-684-80541-3 (v. 1 : alk. paper)
1. Medicine, Popular—Encyclopedias Juvenile. [1. Diseases—Encyclopedias. 2. Health—Encyclopedias.] I. Izenberg, Neil.

RC81.A2 H75 2000
616'.003—dc21

99-051442

ISBN 0-684-80542-1 (vol. 2)
ISBN 0-684-80621-5 (vol. 3)

3 5 7 9 11 13 15 17 19 20 18 16 14 12 10 8 6 4 2

Printed in the United States of America

The paper used in this publication meets the minimum requirements of the American National Standard for Information Sciences—Permanence of Paper for Printed Library Materials, ANSI Z39.48-1992.

Contents

Contents

Volume 3

Human Diseases and Conditions

E

E. coli *See* Diarrhea; Food Poisoning

Ear Infections

Ear infections are conditions in which bacteria or viruses invade the ear.

KEYWORDS
for searching the Internet and other reference sources

Earache

Eardrum

Hearing loss

Otitis media

Otolaryngology

Getting an Earful

When Bobby's little brother was still a baby, he started having one ear infection after another. At first, he was too young to tell anyone when his ear hurt, but he would tug at the ear and cry. Later, Bobby noticed that his brother always sat close to the television and sometimes did not seem to hear when other people spoke to him. The doctor said that Bobby's brother had fluid in the middle part of his ears that was interfering with his hearing. When the fluid did not go away within a few months, the doctor said that the boy needed to have tiny tubes put in his ears. It was a quick operation that the doctor was able to do without Bobby's brother needing to stay overnight in the hospital. With the fluid drained out of his ears, Bobby's brother was able to hear better.

What Are Ear Infections?

Ear infections are conditions in which bacteria* or viruses* invade the ear and cause problems. The human ear is divided into three main parts: the outer ear, the middle ear, and the inner ear. When people talk about an ear infection, they usually mean an infection of the middle ear, a disorder known as otitis media (o-TY-tis MEE-dee-a). Next to the common cold, this is the most frequent of all childhood illnesses. Most children have had otitis media at least once by the time they are 3 years old. It usually causes no lasting problems. However, if otitis media is not treated or if it occurs often, it can lead to hearing loss. In fact, otitis media is the most common cause of hearing loss in children.

* **bacteria** (bak-TEER-ee-a) are single-celled microorganisms, which typically reproduce by cell division. Some, but not all, types of bacteria can cause disease in humans.

* **viruses** are tiny infectious agents that lack an independent metabolism (me-TAB-o-liz-um) and can only reproduce within the cells they infect.

How Does the Ear Work?

To understand how an infection affects the ear, it helps to know how a healthy ear works. Sound travels through the air in invisible waves. These waves enter the body through the part of the outer ear that shows on the outside. They then travel through the ear canal until they strike the

Anatomy of the ear.

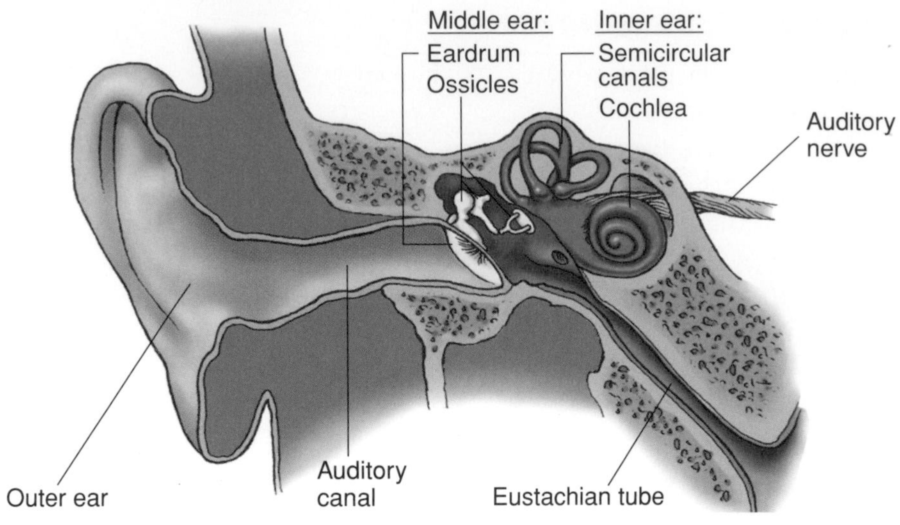

eardrum, a paper-thin membrane* that separates the outer ear and the middle ear. The middle ear is a pea-sized space containing three tiny, delicate bones. When sound waves hit the eardrum, it starts to vibrate, or move back and forth. These vibrations pass through the bones in the middle ear. They then are delivered to the inner ear, which changes them into nerve signals to be sent to the brain.

* **membrane** (MEM-brain) is a thin layer of tissue that covers a surface, lines a cavity, or divides a space or organ.

The middle ear is connected to the back of the nose by a narrow tube, known as the eustachian (u-STAY-kee-an) tube. This tube prevents too much pressure from building up inside the ear by letting air move into and out of the middle ear. Keeping a steady pressure inside the ear is important, so that the eardrum can work properly and does not get damaged. When a person yawns and hears a "pop," this is really the eustachian tube opening to make sure the air pressure is equal on both sides of the eardrum.

What Causes Ear Infections?

An ear infection often starts with a cold, another nose or throat infection, or an allergy* problem. The affected part of the body reacts by swelling and making fluid. Due to this swelling, the narrow eustachian tube can become blocked, trapping fluid in the middle ear. Bacteria or viruses can become trapped as well, thriving in the fluid. The buildup of fluid in the middle ear can cause earache and other symptoms. Since pressure from the fluid keeps the eardrum from moving back and forth properly, the buildup also can cause hearing loss. This is known as acute* otitis media.

* **allergy** (AL-uhr-jee) is a condition in which the body's immune system is overly sensitive to a particular substance.

* **acute** means sudden.

In some cases, the eardrum bursts, and pus drains out of the ear. In other cases, fluid remains in the middle ear, even after the infection has cleared up. Acute otitis media then turns into an ear problem known as otitis media with effusion*. The fluid buildup can last for weeks or months. This can lead to longer term hearing problems. It also may make the person more prone to new infections.

* **effusion** is the buildup of fluid in a tissue or body part.

Who Gets Ear Infections?

People of all ages get ear infections. However, such infections are especially common in young children. This is because the eustachian tubes of children under age five are very small and soft, and so they are easily blocked. Another reason that young children get ear infections is because of their adenoids (AD-e-noidz). The adenoids are lymph glands* in the top of the throat that help the body fight infections. Usually, the adenoids shrink as children grow older, until they have almost disappeared by puberty*. When the adenoids are infected, they sometimes swell until they block the eustachian tube.

*__lymph glands__ are masses of tissue that contain immune cells that filter out harmful microorganisms (my-kro-OR-gan-iz-um); they can become enlarged during infection.

*__puberty__ (PU-ber-te) is the period during which sexual maturity is attained.

What Are the Symptoms of Ear Infections?

The most common symptom of an ear infection is pain. Of course, babies are too young to explain when something hurts. However, they may tug or scratch at the infected ear. They also may have other symptoms, such as crying, crankiness, hearing problems, fever, vomiting, and drainage from the ear. Children, teenagers, and adults with an ear infection may have these symptoms:

- Earache
- Feeling of fullness or pressure in the ear
- Hearing problems
- Dizziness
- Loss of balance
- Fever
- Vomiting or nausea
- Drainage from the ear

Why Do Ear Infections Matter?

Most ear infections clear up without causing any lasting problems. However, they can be quite painful for a few days. In addition, they can lead to longer term hearing loss. In young children who are just learning to speak and understand language, even a mild hearing loss may make it harder to master these tasks. Another risk of ear infections is that they can spread to nearby structures in the head. In particular, an infection may spread to the mastoid (MAS-toid) process, the bone behind the ear. In rare cases, it can destroy this bone and attack other parts of the body.

How Are Ear Infections Diagnosed?

Doctors can view the inside of the ear with an otoscope (O-to-skope), a special tool, similar to a flashlight, with a light and a magnifying lens. Using this tool, doctors can look for redness in the ear and fluid behind the eardrum. Some otoscopes have a bulb attached that doctors can use to blow a puff of air onto the eardrum. This lets doctors see how well the

"Swimmer's Ear"

Another common ear infection is external otitis, better known as "swimmer's ear." This is an infection of the ear canal, the passage that carries sound from the outside part of the ear to the eardrum. It is caused by bacteria or fungi. When water gets into the ear, it can bring such germs with it. Usually the water runs out, the ear dries inside, and the germs do no harm. If the water stays for too long in the ear canal, though, the skin can get soggy, and the germs can grow and cause problems.

People usually get this kind of infection by swimming or diving for long periods in a dirty lake, river, or pond. However, even swimming in a pool can lead to infection, because pool water dries out the skin of the ear, making it easier for germs to invade. People who do not swim also can get this kind of infection by scratching the skin of the ear canal while trying to clean their ears with a sharp object, such as a hairpin.

The main symptom of external otitis is severe ear pain that gets worse when the outside part of the ear is touched or the head is moved. Other possible symptoms include itching, drainage of pus from the ear, hearing loss, and a mild fever. For treatment, doctors may clean the ear canal with a special probe or a suction device. Doctors also may prescribe medications to fight the infection and to relieve the itching and swelling.

eardrum moves. Other tests may be needed in some cases. Tympanometry (TIM-pa-NOM-e-tree) is a test in which a soft plug is placed in the ear. This plug is connected to a machine that makes a low sound and records how the eardrum reacts. The test is designed to find out if the eardrum is moving back and forth as it should. Audiometry (AW-dee-OM-e-tree) is a hearing test in which people listen to various sounds of different pitches. It is designed to find out if an ear problem has caused hearing loss.

How Are Ear Infections Treated?

* **antibiotics** (AN-tih-bi-OT-iks) are drugs that kill bacteria.

Antibiotics* often are used to treat ear infections. Such drugs usually make the earache go away quickly, but the infection may take longer to clear up. Therefore, it is important that all the antibiotic be taken just as the doctor prescribes. Many ear infections are caused by viruses, which are not killed by antibiotics. These infections are handled by the body's immune system. In addition, doctors may suggest a medicine to reduce the fever and pain. A warm heating pad or water bottle placed on the painful ear may help it feel better, too.

How Is Fluid in the Ear Treated?

Sometimes, fluid remains in the middle ear even after the infection is gone. For most children, this fluid goes away without treatment in 3 months or less. If the fluid persists, doctors may recommend additional courses of antibiotics. However, long-term antibiotic treatment can have unwanted effects, such as side effects of the drug, inconvenience, and cost. It may also play a role in the development of new strains of bacteria that are resistant to the drug. This means that the bacteria no longer are killed by it and so are harder to treat.

If fluid stays in the middle ear for longer than 3 months, and if it is causing a hearing loss, doctors may suggest an operation to insert tiny tubes through the eardrums. In this operation, a small slit is made in the eardrum, and the fluid in the middle ear is drained out. Then a tube is placed in the slit, letting air get into the middle ear and reducing the risk of future ear infections. Most such tubes come out of the eardrum on their own in a matter of months.

Labyrinthitis

The labyrinth (LAB-uh-rinth) is another name for the inner ear, which plays a key role in hearing and balance. An infection caused by bacteria or viruses in this part of the ear is known as labyrinthitis (LAB-uh-rin-THI-tis).

Symptoms include extreme loss of balance, dizziness, nausea, and vomiting. The eyes also may move slowly to one side, then flick back to the center. While these symptoms can be scary, they usually do not pose a serious threat if the person gets treatment.

Doctors may prescribe drugs to combat dizziness and nausea as well as antibiotics to fight bacteria. The person also may need to rest in bed for several days. The most severe symptoms usually pass within a week, although problems with balance can last for weeks or even months.

How Can Ear Infections Be Prevented?

Studies have shown that young children who live with smokers have more ear infections than other youngsters, and so it is smart to keep children away from cigarette smoke. Also, young children who spend time in group day care get more ear infections, probably because they are exposed to more colds and respiratory illnesses, and so it is a good idea to keep children away from playmates who are sick. In addition, babies who are bottle-fed, especially while they are lying down, get more ear infections than breast-fed babies, and so it is usually best if mothers breast-feed. If the baby is bottle-fed, it helps to hold the baby's head above his or her stomach level during feeding.

Resource

American Academy of Otolaryngology—Head and Neck Surgery, 1 Prince Street, Alexandria, VA 22314-3357. This group for doctors who specialize in treating ear, nose, and throat disorders has information about ear infections on its website.
Telephone 703-836-4444
http://www.entnet.org

▶ *See also*

Bacterial Infections
Deafness and Hearing Loss
Infection
Tonsillitis
Tinnitus
Vertigo
Viral Infections

Eating Disorders

Eating disorders are conditions in which a person's eating behaviors and food habits are so unbalanced that they cause physical and emotional problems.

KEYWORDS
for searching the Internet and other reference sources

Anorexia nervosa

Behavior

Binge eating disorder

Bulimia nervosa

Food and nutrition

Psychology

Psychiatry

Fear of Fat

Actress Tracy Gold appeared for six seasons in the television series *Growing Pains.* She had been diagnosed with anorexia at age 12, but went through psychotherapy and seemed fine for the next few years. At age 19, when she weighed 133 pounds, Tracy decided that she had to go on a diet of 500 calories per day to get down to 113 pounds. She did not stop at her target weight, however, but continued to lose weight. Her weight went down to 100 pounds, and then down to 90 pounds, and then down to 80 pounds. In January 1992, Tracy's fear that she was fat—when in fact she weighed only 80 pounds—forced her to leave the *Growing Pains* set to enter the hospital. Tracy's anorexia had returned.

What Are Eating Disorders?

The term "eating disorder" describes a wide range of eating and weight problems. At one end of the spectrum are anorexia nervosa (an-o-REK-see-a ner-VO sa) and bulimia (bu-LEEM-e-a) nervosa. Anorexia involves starving oneself to reduce body weight below a healthy minimum level. Bulimia involves binge eating followed by vomiting or other forms of purging and emptying the stomach. At the other end of the spectrum is excessive or binge eating without purging afterward to the point of severe ("morbid") obesity. Between the extremes are the much more common anorexic, bulimic, and binging behaviors that include body image distortions, "yo-yo" dieting (body weight going up and down like a yo-yo), too much or too little exercising, and feelings of anxiety and shame about food and body size.

The various eating disorders have distinct causes, origins, and symptoms, but the behaviors can be similar, and the less serious conditions sometimes may lead to more extreme ones.

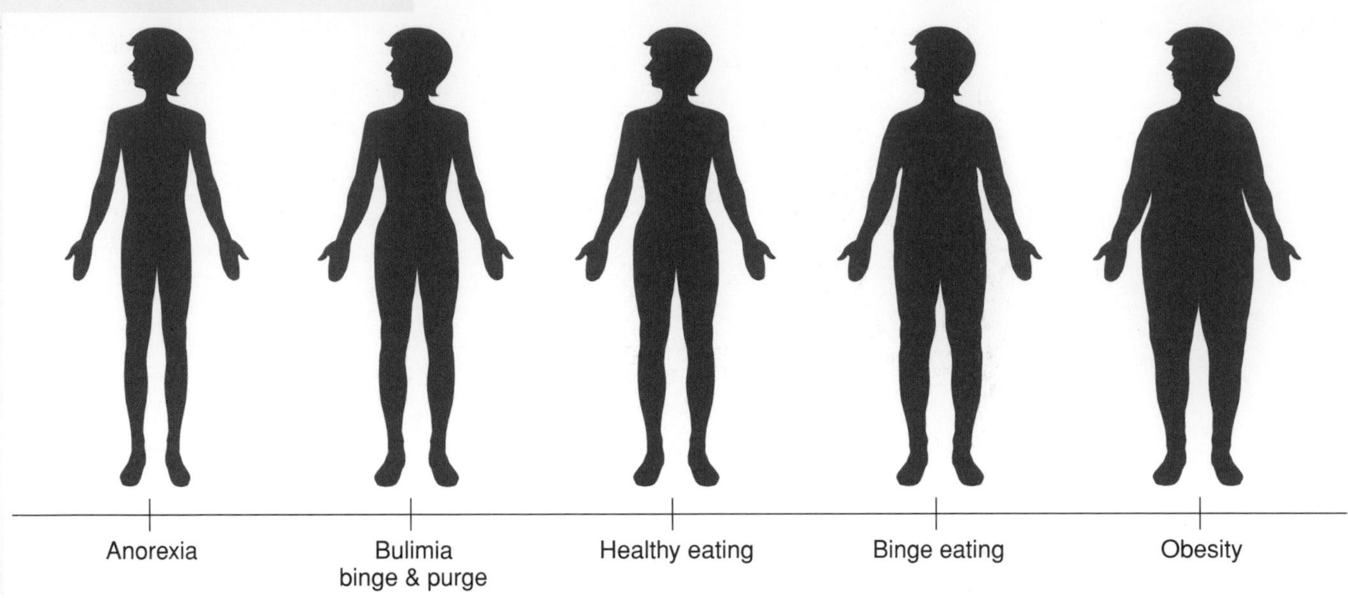

▲

Spectrum of eating disorders

In the United States today, pop culture figures discuss their current diets in all media. Bookstores carry racks of books recommending quick weight loss programs, strategies, and fad diets. Magazines and television carry advertisements for weight-loss drugs, diet foods, fat-burning supplements, remedies, and programs. In all, preoccupation with body size and weight loss have become public health issues, and eating disorders are having a profound impact on the physical and psychological health of people and society.

Anorexia Nervosa

Actresses and supermodels are admired as glamorous and superthin, but according to the American Anorexia/Bulimia Association, more than 1,000 women and girls die of anorexia each year. More than 90 percent of people with anorexia are girls, but it can affect boys too, especially boys who are active in sports that involve body image.

The primary characteristic of people with anorexia is a refusal to eat enough food to maintain a healthy minimum body weight. Starvation and weight loss may become severe enough to require hospitalization, but there are earlier warning signs too, which may include:

- a distorted body image, seeing themselves as fat in the mirror even when they are dangerously thin
- avoiding meals with others
- moving food around on a plate to hide a refusal to eat
- exercising too much or too frequently
- being a perfectionist
- feeling in control only when refusing to eat.

Medical complications Anorexia is a very serious disorder. When the body is not nourished properly, it responds to starvation by slowing down its metabolic processes. Complications may include anemia and other dietary deficiencies, drops in blood pressure and breathing rate, bone loss, loss of menstrual periods, loss of muscle mass and strength, dry skin, brittle hair and nails, constipation, and joint swelling. When people with anorexia lose the body fat they need to maintain a stable body temperature, they begin to feel cold all the time, and their skin may become covered with a baby-soft hair called lanugo (la-NOO-go). If starvation continues without treatment, anorexia may lead to heart failure and sometimes even to death.

Bulimia Nervosa

Bulimia is often called "binge and purge," and the term "bulimia" comes from Greek words that mean "ox-like hunger." People with bulimia eat huge quantities of food during binges, and then follow the binge with a purge to rid the body of the food they have eaten. Purging often involves self-induced vomiting, but people also use emetics (substances that cause vomiting), enemas, laxatives, and diuretics*.

*__diuretics__ (dy-u-RET-iks) are drugs that make people urinate.

Sometimes, bulimia results in visible weight fluctuations—the way anorexia and binge eating disorder do—but often it does not, and many people with bulimia are able to keep their eating disorder a secret for many years. The actress Jane Fonda reported that she had had bulimia for more than 20 years, at times binging and purging more than 20 times per day.

Bulimic behaviors may include:

- eating binges that continue to the point of abdominal pain
- frequent trips to the bathroom to vomit after eating
- trying to keep the vomiting a secret
- hiding laxatives, diuretics, and emetics
- exercising too much or too frequently
- abusing alcohol or street drugs
- acting impulsively* or recklessly
- frequently feeling out of control about the amount of food eaten.

*__impulsivity__ is behavior when people have trouble thinking through consequences before they act.

Medical complications People with bulimia may experience the same side effects of starvation that people with anorexia do. Purging behavior causes other serious health problems, including dehydration, fatigue, skin rashes, broken blood vessels in the eyes or face, and sometimes seizures. Constant vomiting damages the digestive system, especially the stomach, the esophagus*, and the mouth. Sometimes, a dentist will recognize the signs of bulimia even before a primary care doctor does because of the gum disease and tooth damage that can result from bulimia.

*__esophagus__ (e-SOF-a-gus) is the tube connecting the stomach and the throat.

Binge Eating Disorder

Binge eating disorder resembles bulimia nervosa, but without bulimia's purging and exercising behaviors. People with binge eating disorder frequently eat abnormally large amounts of food. They may call themselves "fast food addicts" or "compulsive overeaters." Binge eating is linked to depression, although researchers do not yet understand how the cause-and-effect linkage works. Characteristics of binge eating behavior may include:

- frequently feeling disgust or guilt after eating
- eating more rapidly than usual
- eating when not physically hungry
- eating to the point of abdominal pain
- eating alone out of shame
- frequently feeling out of control about the amount of food eaten.

Medical complications Binge eating often results in yo-yo dieting and in obesity, which in turn can lead to other health problems, including diabetes, heart disease, high blood pressure, and gallbladder disease. Experts estimate that approximately 15 percent of mildly obese people in weight loss programs have binge eating disorder, and that the percentage is much higher for people with severe ("morbid") obesity.

How Are Eating Disorders Treated?

Anorexia nervosa, if left untreated, may lead to severe malnutrition and medical emergencies that require hospitalization. Most people with eating disorders, however, can be treated by their family doctor and by a team of health care providers using a cross-disciplinary approach.

The doctor who diagnoses an eating disorder may prescribe medication for anxiety or depression, and probably will refer patients and their families to a nutritionist or dietician, to a counselor or family therapist, and to a support group. Long-term psychotherapy may be required for eating disorders that have continued for a long period of time before diagnosis. Because relapses may occur, as happened with Tracy Gold, ongoing support from family and friends remains an important part of treatment.

Resources

Book

Berg, Francie M., and Frances Berg. *Afraid to Eat: Children and Teens in Weight Crisis*. Hettinger, ND: Healthy Weight Journal, 1997.

Organizations

U.S. Food and Drug Administration (FDA) posts the fact sheet *On the Teen Scene: Eating Disorders Require Medical Attention* at its website.
http://www.fda.gov/opacom/catalog/eatdis.html

U.S. National Institute of Diabetes and Digestive and Kidney Diseases (NIDDK) posts the fact sheet *Binge Eating Disorders* at its website.
http://www.nidk.nih.gov/health/nutrit/pubs/binge.htm

KidsHealth.org from the Nemours Foundation posts the fact sheet *A Teen Guide to Eating Disorders* at its website.
http://www.kidshealth.org/teen/bodymind/eat_disorder.html

American Medical Association. The AMA posts the fact sheet *Teen Talk: Eating Disorders Take Weight Loss to the Max* at its website.
http://www.ama-assn.org

American Psychiatric Association. The American Psychiatric Association posts the fact sheet *Let's Talk Facts About Eating Disorders* at its website.
http://www.psych.org/public_infotalk_facts.html

American Psychological Association. The American Psychological Association posts the fact sheet *How Therapy Helps Eating Disorders* at its website.
http://helping.apa.org/therapy/eating.html

National Association of Anorexia Nervosa and Associated Disorders (ANAD), P.O. Box 7, Highland Park, IL 60035.
Telephone 807-831-3438
http://anad.org

American Anorexia/Bulimia Association, 165 West 46 Street, Suite 1108, New York, NY 10036.
Telephone 212-575-6200
http://www.aabainc.org

Anorexia Nervosa and Related Eating Disorders (ANRED), P.O. Box 5102, Eugene, OR 97405.
Telephone 503-344-1144
http://www.anred.com

Overeaters Anonymous (OA), 6075 Zenith Court, N.E., Rio Rancho, NM 87124.
Telephone 505-891-2664
http://www.overeatersanonymous.org

See also
Anemia
Anxiety Disorders
Depressive Disorders
Dietary Deficiencies
Gum Disease
Heart Disease
Hypoglycemia
Menstrual Disorders
Metabolic Diseases
Obesity
Osteoporosis
Seizures
Substance Abuse
Thyroid Disease

Ebola Fever

Ebola (E-bo-la) fever is a serious disease caused by the Ebola virus, which is named for the Ebola River in the Congo (formerly Zaire).

KEY WORDS
for searching the Internet and other reference sources

Filovirus

Hemorrhagic fever

Marburg virus

The U.S. and the World

Ebola Confirmed

- In 1976, an Ebola outbreak occurred in the Sudan and in Zaire, which is now known as the Democratic Republic of the Congo. More than 600 people in those African nations were infected, and 397 died.
- The second worst Ebola outbreak occurred in 1995 in Zaire. There were 315 cases, and 244 deaths.
- According to the World Health Organization, since 1976 there have been nearly 1,100 confirmed cases of Ebola worldwide, with 793 deaths.

Ebola Suspected

- Researchers wonder whether Ebola was responsible for the death of a doctor in Zaire in 1972. He died after performing an autopsy. Was the cadaver he autopsied also an Ebola death?
- In 1961–1962, there was a yellow fever epidemic in Ethiopia, a country next to the Sudan. Was Ebola a factor in that epidemic?
- Researchers even ask: Was a plague in Athens more than 2,400 years ago due to Ebola?

Ebola Fever causes high fever, rash, and bleeding throughout the body. People with Ebola fever often die very quickly. Although scientists know that the disease results from a viral infection, they still have not solved the mystery of its origin and mode of transmission to humans.

The Ebola virus belongs to the group of viruses called filoviruses, as do the Marburg and Reston viruses. Scientists first identified the Marburg virus in 1967, when it caused a small outbreak among sick monkeys brought from Africa to a medical laboratory in Marburg, Germany. In 1976, a filovirus named for the Ebola River in Zaire (now the Congo) caused an epidemic in central Africa that killed hundreds of people. Smaller outbreaks have occurred in Africa since then. In 1989 and 1990, many monkeys shipped from Asia to a research laboratory in Reston, Virginia, died from a disease that was found to have been caused by a filovirus.

How Do People Catch Ebola Fever?

The Ebola virus is spread from person to person through contact with infected blood and body fluids. Doctors also believe that it passes through the air when an infected person coughs or sneezes. Hospital workers are at high risk for Ebola during outbreaks, because they come into contact with blood and body fluids when they care for infected patients. Infected patients often die very quickly, limiting the opportunity for the virus to be transmitted to many other people. This may be why Ebola outbreaks have not become widespread.

What Are the Symptoms?

About 5 to 10 days after infection, people with Ebola get a fever, headache, and body aches. Frequently there is nausea, vomiting, diarrhea, cough, chest pain, and sore throat. Often there is sensitivity to light, swollen lymph glands, rash, as well as other symptoms. Patients also begin excessive bleeding where injections are given. During the second week of infection, people with Ebola may get better, but often they develop severe bleeding from many parts of the body. If this occurs, then the patient will probably not survive.

How Is Ebola Treated?

Treatment of Ebola includes supportive measures, such as blood transfusions, but there is not yet a vaccine or medicine to prevent or cure Ebola virus infection. Isolating people with Ebola fever from other people and wearing masks, gloves, and gowns when taking care of infected patients in the hospital can reduce the chance of an outbreak.

Scientists do not yet know which species of animals harbor filoviruses or how to prevent new outbreaks. They are studying a theory that the virus spreads to people when monkeys from Africa or the Philippines are killed and eaten for food. For now, however, the causes and treatment of Ebola fever remain a medical mystery.

Resources

Close, William T. *Ebola: A Documentary Novel of Its First Explosion.* New York: Ivy Books/Ballantine, 1995.

Preston, Richard. *The Hot Zone.* New York: Random House, 1994. A suspenseful and factual account of Ebola outbreaks and research.

See also
Viral Infections

Eczema *See* Allergies; Skin Conditions

Elephantiasis

Elephantiasis (el-e-fan-TY-a-sis) is the result of a tropical worm infection called filariasis (fil-a-RY-a-sis). When infected mosquitoes transmit the parasitic worm* Wuchereria bancrofti *to people, the worm blocks the lymphatic system. The blockage causes swelling in the legs or other parts of the body, making these body parts appear large and puffy, or elephant-like. Elephantiasis is not "elephant man disease," which is an inherited condition with completely different causes and symptoms.

KEYWORDS
for searching the Internet and other reference sources

Filariasis

Infestation

Lymphatic system

Mosquitoes

Nematodes

Parasites

Tropical diseases

Wuchereria bancrofti

Elephantiasis was known to the early Greeks and Romans. It is a tropical or subtropical disease, occurring where many kinds of disease-carrying mosquitoes are found: South America, Cuba, Puerto Rico, West Indies, Africa, Spain, Turkey, Asia, Australia, and many South Pacific Islands. About 100 million people worldwide are affected.

The Mosquito Carrier

Insects that carry diseases are known as vectors*, and several species of mosquito are vectors of *Wuchereria bancrofti*, the nematode worm that causes elephantiasis. When a Culex (KYU-lex), Anopheles (a-NOF-e-LEEZ), Aedes (ay-EE-deez), or Mansonia (man-SO-ne-a) mosquito carrying the *Wuchereria bancrofti* organism bites a human, the mosquito may inject worm larvae* into the body. The tiny larvae then may make their way into the lymph glands and the lymphatic system.

* **vectors** are animals or insects that carry diseases and transfer them from one host to another.

* **larvae** are worms at an intermediate stage of the life cycle between egg and adult.

Lymphedema The lymphatic system is a complicated network of very fine tubes, about the diameter of a needle, which criss-cross body tissues to collect a fluid known as lymph. Lymph is a milk-like substance (containing white blood cells, proteins, and fats) that plays an important role in absorbing fats from the intestine, in fighting infections, and in the proper functioning of the immune system. Lymph is returned to the bloodstream via many vessels known as lymphatics. At various points, the lymphatics drain into masses of tissue known as lymph nodes or glands. If a blockage occurs, fluid may collect in the tissues, causing a

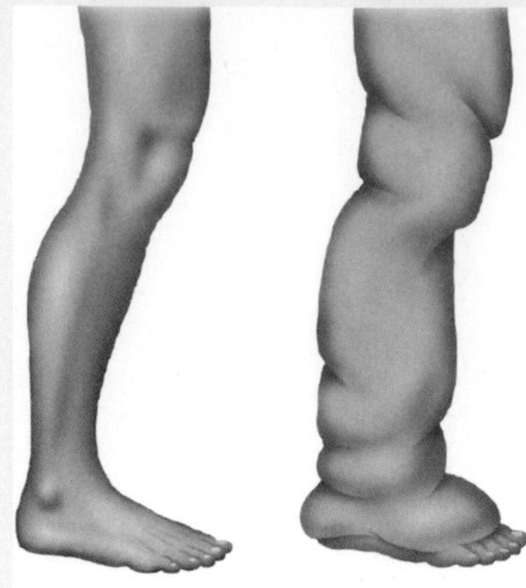

Parasitic worms transferred to people by infected mosquitoes can block the lymphatic system, causing the puffiness and swelling of lymphatic filariasis (elephantiasis).

type of swelling known as lymphedema (limf-e-DEE-ma). In the lymph system draining the legs, for example, few connections exist, and the legs often are a site of swelling when lymphedema occurs.

Lymphatic filiariasis Worm larvae that make their way into lymph vessels can mature into adult worms. Male worms are long and slender, about 4 to 5 cm long, and 0.1 mm in diameter. Female worms are much larger, 6 to 10 cm long, and about three times wider than the males. The adults make their home mostly near the lymph glands in the lower part of the body. The adult female releases eggs enclosed within an egg membrane (microfilariae), and the microfilariae (mi-kro-fi-LAR-ee-i) develop into larvae to continue the life cycle.

In most parts of the world, microfilariae are at their peak in the blood during the night. The worms restrict the normal flow of lymph, resulting in swelling, thickening of the skin, and discoloration. This is what can cause the appearance of an elephant's leg. However, the swelling of elephantiasis usually does not occur until a person has been bitten by the disease-carrying mosquitoes many times and has had years of exposure to infected mosquitoes.

What Happens to People with Elephantiasis?

Symptoms In addition to the characteristic swelling, people with this disorder sometimes have bouts of fever and headache. Sometimes their swollen limbs become infected.

Diagnosis Microfilariae sometimes can be seen in blood under a microscope. Often the doctor diagnoses the disorder based on the symptoms and a medical history, after ruling out other disorders with similar symptoms.

The Elephant Man

Joseph "John" Cary Merrick was known as the Elephant Man, but he did not have elephantiasis.

Born in 1862 in Leicester, England, Merrick became a human attraction in circus side shows. His appearance was normal at birth, but when he was about age 5, he developed extensive overgrowths of skin that affected his face, head, torso, arms, and legs. He was reported to have had a 12-inch wrist and a fin-like hand.

For many years, researchers believed that Merrick had neurofibromatosis (neur-o-fib-ro-ma-TO-sis), a genetic condition that causes large growths on the skin and in tissues. Recent research using x-ray studies, however, suggests that Merrick in fact had Proteus syndrome, a condition so rare that only 100 cases in history have been reported.

Treatment Medications are not very effective against adult worms. New microfilariae produced by the adult worms often continue to show up months after treatment.

Prevention Because elephantiasis is found mainly in poorer countries, money for research into the cure and prevention of the disease has been limited. Effective treatment and preventive efforts would include:

- spraying to kill mosquitoes
- giving antibiotics to prevent infection
- giving medications to kill microfilariae circulating in the blood
- applying pressure bandages to reduce swelling
- surgically removing infected tissue.

Resource

World Health Organization, Avenue Appia 20, 1211 Geneva 27, Switzerland. WHO posts a fact sheet about lymphatic filariasis at its website.
http://www.who.org/home/map_ht.html

▶ *See also*
Bites and Stings
Parasitic Diseases
Worms

Embolism

An embolism (EM-bo-liz-um) is a blockage in the bloodstream, caused by a blood clot, air bubble, fatty tissue, or other substance that plugs a blood vessel.

KEYWORDS
for searching the Internet and other reference sources

Circulatory system

Coagulation

The body's circulatory system is like a huge network of small roads and large interstate highways. It is important that blood continuously flow through the body to carry nutrients, oxygen, and other substances to cells and organs. But like a road, sometimes a part of the circulatory system can become blocked by an accident.

What Is an Embolism?

An embolism is a blockage that plugs up an artery in the body and slows or even stops blood flow to the area of the body supplied by the artery. Many substances can cause blockages. Usually, the embolus (EM-bo-lus) is something small that has broken free from another part of the body and has traveled through the bloodstream until it gets jammed in a blood vessel that is too narrow for it to pass freely.

Emboli (EM-bo-ly; plural of embolus) are dangerous. They may cause death if they block a major artery, such as the large pulmonary artery that

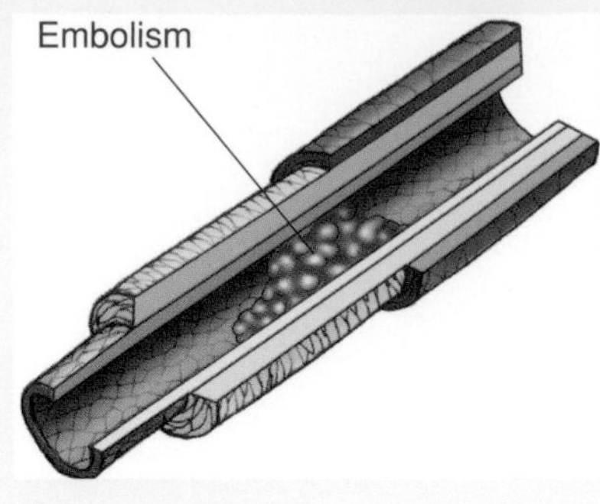

▲

An embolism in an artery. An embolism blocking blood flow through an artery may be a serious problem.

*clotting is a process in which blood changes into a jellylike mass that stops the flow of blood.

*thrombosis is the formation or development of a blood clot or thrombus.

*tumor usually refers to an abnormal growth of body tissue that has no physiologic purpose and is not an inflammation. Tumors may or may not be cancerous.

runs through the lungs. They also may cause tissue to die if they prevent blood flow to the area. Emboli are sometimes called "accidents waiting to happen."

How Do Emboli Happen?

The most common type of embolism results from the clotting* of blood. When blood clots form inside veins, which is a process called thrombosis*, they may break free and travel to the pulmonary artery. The pulmonary artery carries blood from the right side of the heart into the lungs. In the lungs, blood disposes of carbon dioxide and picks up more oxygen. When blood clots get stuck in the pulmonary artery, they prevent blood from picking up oxygen. This is a medical emergency that causes symptoms similar to a heart attack.

Other substances may cause embolism, for example:

- Bubbles. This sometimes occurs in underwater divers as they ascend, and as the compressed nitrogen bubbles out of solution. This is called "the bends." It also can happen during injections of fluids or medications into veins or arteries, which is one reason why doctors and nurses squeeze the air out of needles before injecting patients.
- Tumors*. These may grow and block blood flow, or a piece of a tumor may break off into the bloodstream and get caught in another part of the body.
- Fat. This occurs when fat breaks off in an area of the body. For example, after a serious injury occurs to a body part like the liver, fat may break off and travel through the bloodstream.
- Bone fragments. A bone chip from a broken arm or leg may become lodged in an artery.

The embolism may occur in any artery, but often occurs in the pulmonary arteries. This is because all the blood returning to the heart from the body is pumped through the pulmonary arterial system first.

What Are the Signs and Symptoms of Embolism?

Symptoms of a pulmonary embolism include chest pain that can feel worse when breathing deeply; shortness of breath; coughing, which sometimes results in blood coming up from the lungs; dizziness; anxiety*; sweating; and rapid breathing and heartbeat.

*anxiety may be experienced as a troubled feeling, a sense of dread, fear of the future, or distress over a possible threat to a person's physical or mental well-being.

These symptoms are similar to those of a heart attack, and some symptoms even resemble those of an anxiety attack. But sometimes embolism does not cause any symptoms at all.

How Do Doctors Diagnose and Treat Embolism?

Embolism is often difficult for doctors to diagnose. Doctors may use an x-ray, a CT scan*, or a lung scan to check for the embolism. Sometimes dye is injected into the person to make it easier to see the embolism on the x-ray or scan.

*CT scans or CAT scans are the short form for computerized axial tomography, which uses computers to view structures inside the body.

Pulmonary emboli develop in as many as 500,000 Americans each year, and up to 10 percent die within the first hour. With treatment, many are saved and lead normal lives. Doctors may use drugs that dissolve the embolism and prevent others from forming. Exercise, weight loss if needed, and a proper diet can help prevent emboli from forming.

Resource

The U.S. National Heart, Lung, and Blood Institute posts a fact sheet about pulmonary embolism at its website.
http://www.nhlbi.nih.gov/nhlbi/infcntr/topics/pulemb.htm

See also
Bends
Clotting
Phlebitis
Thrombosis

Emphysema

Emphysema (em-fe-ZEE-ma) is a lung disease in which the alveoli (al-VEE-o-ly), tiny air sacs in the lungs, lose elasticity, causing difficulty in breathing.

KEYWORDS
for searching the Internet and other reference sources

Alveoli

Chronic obstructive pulmonary disease

What Is Emphysema?

Air reaches the lungs through a series of ever-smaller tubes. First air passes through the trachea (TRAY-kee-a), which is the large windpipe from the throat down the neck. Then the trachea branches into smaller tubes called the bronchi (BRONG-ky), then into even smaller bronchi called bronchioles (BRONG-kee-olz) that branch still further deep into the lungs. The bronchioles end in tiny air sacs called alveoli. It is in the alveoli that the transfer of oxygen into the bloodstream and of carbon dioxide out of the bloodstream occurs.

In emphysema, the bronchi and bronchioles are inflamed and continually swollen and clogged. This causes the alveoli to swell. These fragile air sacs burst and merge together. This damage to the alveoli makes it more difficult for the transfer of oxygen and carbon dioxide to take place.

People with emphysema have difficulty breathing. It is usually caused by cigarette smoking, or a severe form of bronchitis called chronic obstructive bronchitis. Very often, a combination of these factors produces emphysema.

Because severe bronchitis, smoking, and emphysema are closely interrelated, physicians often refer to a combined disorder known as chronic obstructive lung disease (COLD), or chronic obstructive pulmonary (PULL-mo-nar-ee) disease (COPD).

Who Gets Emphysema?

Both emphysema and COPD are very rare in young people, but the incidence* steadily increases as people grow older, particularly during or

***incidence** means rate of occurrence.

300 Years Ago: No Smoking Please

Sir John Floyer (1649–1735), an English physician who had asthma, first described emphysema in the seventeenth century. Floyer was studying pulmonary (lung) disorders and described the characteristic prolonged expiration and progressive nature of emphysema.

Floyer warned his patients to avoid tobacco smoke, metallic fumes, and other potential irritants because he believed that they caused pulmonary disorders. He was right.

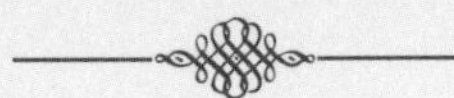

after middle age. This is believed to be due in large part to the cumulative effect of smoking on the lungs. One person cannot catch it from another. Emphysema is more common in men than it is in women, probably because more men smoke cigarettes than women. However, it is believed that this difference will become smaller because more teenage girls and young women are smoking cigarettes today than years ago. Heavier smoking among men over the past several decades is believed to account for the present imbalance in numbers.

In the United States, more than 2 million people have emphysema, making it a common disorder. More than 6 million people suffer from COPD. About 6 or 7 people per 100,000 die from emphysema each year, and COPD is the fourth most common cause of death in the United States. The incidence of emphysema is even higher in European countries.

Effects of Smoking and Other Causes The great majority of emphysema cases are associated with cigarette smoking. It has been found that people who are heavy smokers of cigarettes are 10 to 15 times more likely to develop emphysema than are nonsmokers.

Additional factors may contribute to emphysema or be directly responsible for it. For example, if someone develops emphysema early in adult life, usually it is due to a rare genetic deficiency of a chemical that helps to maintain elasticity* in the lungs. Environmental air pollution also may make a person more likely to develop chronic bronchitis and emphysema. With on-the-job exposure to mineral dusts, such as coal dust in a mine, emphysema may occur as part of a disease known as pneumoconiosis (noo-mo-ko-nee-O-sis).

* **elasticity** is the ability to be stretched and to return to original shape.

Emphysema also may accompany diseases such as asthma and tuberculosis that can obstruct the airways in the lungs. A less serious form of emphysema sometimes develops in elderly people whose lungs have lost elasticity only as a part of the aging process. Another usually mild form, called compensatory emphysema, results when a lung overexpands to occupy the space of another lung that has collapsed or has been removed surgically.

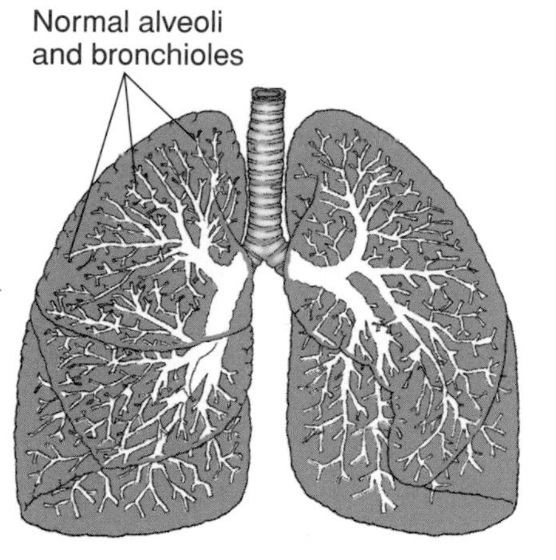

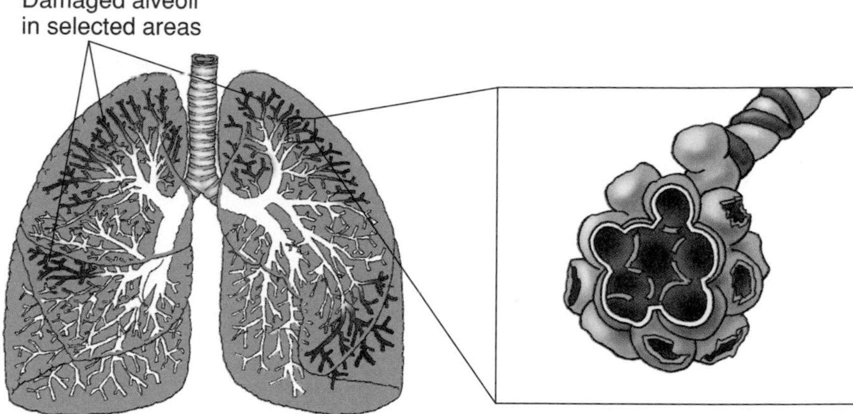

Healthy lungs (left). Lungs with emphysema showing damaged alveoli (center). Close-up of damaged alveoli.

A Close-Up Look at the Alveoli Understanding the alveoli, and the airways in the lungs that lead to them, is key to understanding emphysema. These tiny sacs or pockets are grouped in grapelike clusters and are so small that each lung contains 300 to 400 million of them. Because there are so many alveoli, their total surface area is about 50 times greater than the entire surface area of the skin on the body. This huge surface area is important because it allows oxygen from the air we inhale to be transferred to the bloodstream, and it allows carbon dioxide in the bloodstream to be transferred out.

Inhaled air reaches the alveoli through bronchial tubes and repeatedly branching smaller bronchioles in the lungs that resemble an upside-down tree. The walls of the alveoli contain tiny blood vessels called capillaries, which lead to larger vessels that return blood to the heart to be pumped throughout the body. It is in the delicate capillaries of the alveoli that the transfer of oxygen and carbon dioxide takes place.

What Changes Occur in the Lungs from Emphysema? In emphysema, tobacco smoke and other inhaled irritants damage the alveoli, causing them to lose elasticity. Moreover, smoking often causes chronic bronchitis, which tends to narrow and obstruct the bronchial airways with mucus, scarring, and muscle spasms in the walls of the bronchial tubes. As a result, air becomes trapped in the alveoli, stretching their walls and causing some to break down and form larger pockets by joining with other alveoli. As the lungs become less elastic, they tend to become distended, or overinflated.

What Are the Symptoms of Emphysema?

The main symptom of emphysema is shortness of breath. The decrease in lung elasticity, the trapping of air in the lungs, and the loss of alveolar surface area means that the person must breathe harder to force carbon dioxide out of the lungs and draw in oxygen. A common outward sign of emphysema is a barrel-shaped chest caused by overinflation of the lungs.

Why Do We Breathe?

All living things need energy for their life processes, such as growth and reproduction. Plants get energy from the sun, whereas animals get it from food (plants and other animals). Because humans are animals, we might think we could get energy just by eating food, but this only gets the food to our stomachs; it does not get it to all the cells of our bodies, where it is needed. For this purpose, our digestive systems break down the food into sugar, fats, and proteins, and our circulatory systems carry it to our cells as food energy in this form.

This is still not enough to help our cells, however. The cells need to have oxygen from the blood to be able to carry out chemical reactions to release the energy from the food we eat. We breathe in so that our lungs can transfer oxygen to the bloodstream for delivery to our cells. We breathe out to carry away carbon dioxide, a waste product of the chemical reactions in our cells, that is returned in the bloodstream.

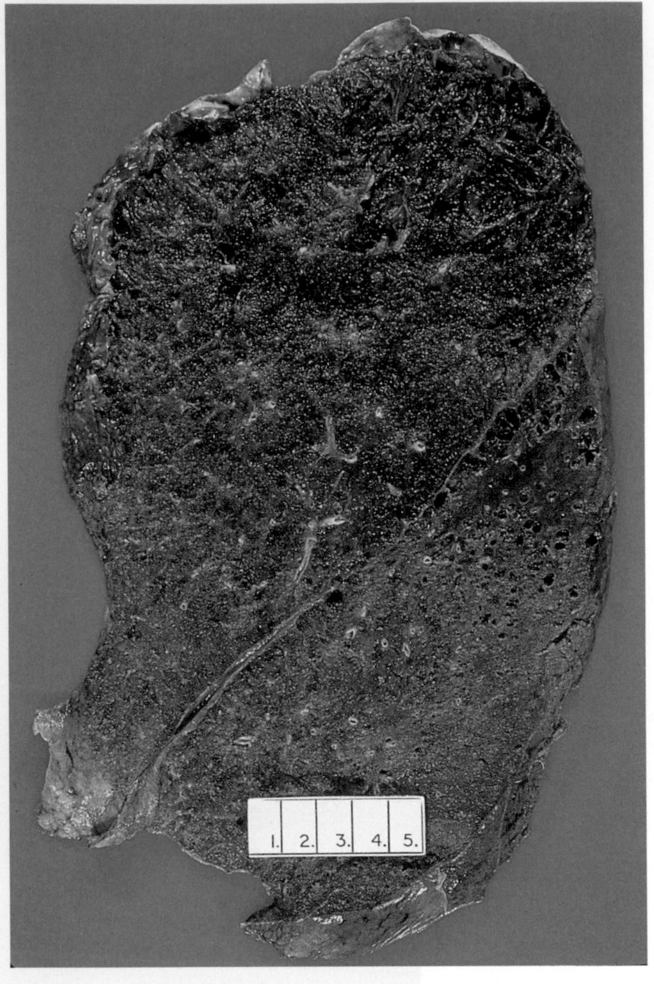

▲

A slice of human lung tissue with pulmonary emphysema. The affected lung area is the top portion, with severe lung damage in the blackened area. Normal lung tissue is shown on the bottom for comparison.
Dr. E. Walker/ Science Photo Library, Photo Researchers, Inc.

As emphysema progresses, some people compensate by breathing faster. Others develop a condition known as cor pulmonale (KOR pul-mo-NAL-ee), in which the right side of the heart becomes enlarged because of the difficulty it has pumping blood through the damaged lungs.

How Is Emphysema Diagnosed and Treated?

A doctor can diagnose emphysema from a physical exam, symptoms, and a chest x-ray, which may show such signs as overinflation of the lungs and other changes. A lung function test can detect reduced ability to exhale fully. Blood tests can measure the concentrations of oxygen and carbon dioxide in the blood. Blood levels of carbon dioxide tend to rise in patients with emphysema, and blood levels of oxygen tend to fall.

Currently no form of treatment can reverse emphysema, but measures can be taken to control the disease and its symptoms. The person must stop smoking permanently. Antibiotics may be used to treat and prevent respiratory infections. Other medicines can be taken to widen the airways and relax spasms in their walls. Special breathing exercises often are helpful, and breathing equipment that delivers extra oxygen and medications may be provided for home use.

How Can Emphysema Be Prevented?

Because the damage that emphysema does to the lungs cannot be undone, it is especially important to try to prevent this disease from developing in the first place. Adopting healthy habits early in life—especially not smoking—is very important. It can prevent health problems later on that include not only emphysema, but lung cancer, heart disease, and other disorders as well.

Resources

Haas, Francois, and Sheila Sperber Haas. *The Chronic Bronchitis and Emphysema Handbook.* New York: John Wiley and Sons, 1990. This is a well-written and well-illustrated source.

Adams, Francis V. *The Breathing Disorders Sourcebook.* Los Angeles: Lowell House, 1998. This book has more information on lung conditions, including a chapter on emphysema, and lists many helpful local and regional organizations.

The American Lung Association's national office is located at 1740 Broadway, New York, NY 10019. Call them at 212-315-8700 or

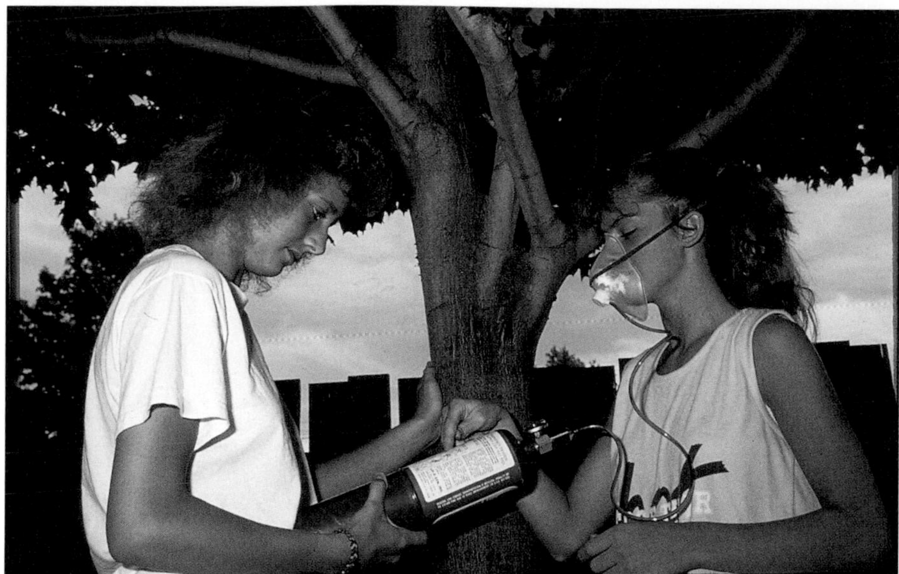

A young woman with emphysema shows her portable oxygen tank to a friend. © *1992 Amy Meister, Custom Medical Stock Photo.*

locate a local office by calling 1-800-LUNG-USA (586-4872). The Association's website includes valuable information about lung diseases and tobacco control. Material is available in English and in Spanish. http://www.lungusa.org.

See also
Bronchitis
Pneumoconiosis
Asthma
Tuberculosis

Encephalitis

Encephalitis is an inflammation of the brain that can range from mild to extremely serious. It is usually caused by one of many viruses. Often the inflammation also affects the meninges (the lining around the brain and spinal cord). Such cases are called meningoencephalitis.

KEYWORDS
for searching the Internet and other reference sources

Arboviral encephalitides
Immunization
Inflammation
Japanese encephalitis
Meningoencephalitis
St. Louis encephalitis
West Nile encephalitis

Viruses and other microbes rarely get into the brain, but when they do, they can cause an inflammatory condition* called encephalitis (en-sef-a-LY-tis). Most cases of encephalitis are so mild that they are never identified. A person, often a child, may have fever, headache, nausea, or sleepiness—symptoms much like the flu—that go away on their own. But in more severe cases, the viral infection destroys so many neurons (nerve cells) in the brain that it can cause seizures, breathing problems, personality changes, and coma*. When white blood cells arrive to fight the virus, they may cause brain tissues to swell, which also can destroy neurons or lead to bleeding within the brain. Permanent brain damage, or even death, can result.

About 20,000 cases of encephalitis a year are reported in the United States, but many more—mainly mild ones—are thought to occur. Serious encephalitis is particularly common in people with weakened immune systems, such as those with AIDS.

* **inflammation** is the body's reaction to irritation, infection, or injury that often involves swelling, pain, redness, and warmth.

* **coma** is an unconscious state, like a very deep sleep. A person in a coma cannot be awakened, and cannot move, see, speak, or hear.

Culex mosquitoes lay their eggs in water, and the eggs hatch into larvae as shown here. The larvae mature into adult Culex mosquitoes that carry the viruses that cause Japanese encephalitis, St. Louis encephalitis, and West Nile encephalitis. © *Kevin and Betty Collins/ Visuals Unlimited.* ▶

The U.S. and the World

Some kinds of encephalitis are caused by arboviruses, which are viruses that are spread from animals to humans by insects. In the United States these include:

- St. Louis encephalitis, a virus found in birds. The most common form of encephalitis, with about 200 cases reported in an average year, mostly in midwestern and eastern states. Of cases severe enough to diagnose, about 5 to 15 percent are fatal, with the elderly at greatest risk.
- LaCrosse encephalitis, found in chipmunks and squirrels. It averages 75 cases reported a year, mostly in midwestern states in children younger than age 16. It is rarely fatal.
- Eastern equine encephalitis, found in horses. The most severe, it can kill as many as one third of those who get it, but usually only a handful of cases occur each year, in southeastern states.
- Western equine encephalitis, also found in horses. Despite its name, it can occur in any part of the country, although there have been no recent reports. It is rarely fatal, but it sometimes causes permanent brain damage in babies.

In Asia, by contrast, Japanese encephalitis virus is common, with more than 45,000 cases reported each year in the region, usually in rural and agricultural areas. It is fatal in less than 10 percent of cases, but can be more dangerous in children. A vaccine to prevent it is widely used in Japan, China, India, Korea, and Thailand. The Japanese encephalitis virus is related to the St. Louis one and infects mostly pigs, ducks, and wading birds.

What Causes Encephalitis?

Many viruses and a few other microbes can cause encephalitis. These include herpes simplex viruses, HIV, rabies, mumps, polio, and cytomegalovirus; the bacterium that causes Lyme disease; and the parasite that causes toxoplasmosis. Herpes simplex is the most common identifiable cause of encephalitis, but often the cause cannot be found at all.

In addition, several arboviruses (meaning viruses spread by insects) cause encephalitis in horses or other animals and are sometimes spread to humans by mosquitoes. In the United States, this is rare, with a few hundred cases in an average year, but in Asia it is a bigger problem.

In some cases, encephalitis develops as a reaction five to ten days after a person has a viral illness like measles, chickenpox, or rubella (German measles). This condition is called postinfectious or parainfectious encephalitis.

What Happens When People Get Encephalitis?

Symptoms The symptoms usually start with sudden fever, headaches, nausea, vomiting, and sometimes muscle pain. If the meninges (me-NIN-jez) are involved, the neck and back often are stiff. Other symptoms can include muscle weakness and seizures.

In more serious cases, a person may grow lethargic, or become angry and irritable, and eventually fall into a coma. Such cases have a high death rate. Encephalitis can be particularly severe in elderly people and in babies, who are more likely to suffer permanent brain damage than adults.

Diagnosis The symptoms will suggest encephalitis to the doctor. He or she usually will check for signs of a viral infection with various blood tests and with a lumbar puncture (spinal tap), a procedure in which a sample of cerebrospinal fluid is taken from around the spinal cord for testing. The doctor also may get a CT scan (a computerized x-ray) or an

MRI (a magnetically produced image) of the brain to look for signs of bleeding or swelling in the brain. These test cannot make the diagnosis certain. Instead, the diagnosis is often made by ruling out other possible causes of the symptoms. In many cases, the microbe causing the encephalitis is never identified. In some instances, a doctor may get a brain biopsy, in which a small piece of brain is removed with a needle so it can be examined under a microscope.

Treatment If the cause is herpes simplex, the antiviral drug acyclovir is given. Antiviral drugs may be tried in some other cases, as well. Corticosteroids (anti-inflammatory medications) may be prescribed to lessen swelling in the brain, and anticonvulsant drugs may be given to stop seizures.

Supportive care is important. This means making sure people with encephalitis get proper fluids, providing machines to help with breathing, if needed, and caring for comatose patients to prevent bedsores or other infections.

After recovery from encephalitis, some people will have lasting problems with memory, speech, or muscle control. For them, physical, occupational, or speech therapy can help to varying degrees.

How Is Encephalitis Prevented?

To prevent the arboviral (insect-borne) forms of encephalitis, public health officials spray with insecticides and drain swamps to control the mosquito population. If an outbreak does occur, individuals can use insect repellents or mosquito netting. Rabies encephalitis can be prevented by vaccinating pets and by avoiding contact with wild mammals. Avoiding ticks can prevent Lyme disease encephalitis, as can a partially effective Lyme vaccine. Preventing HIV infection—by avoiding sexual contact and by never sharing needles—would eliminate many cases of encephalitis.

Resources

The World Health Organization posts a fact sheet about Japanese encephalitis and vaccinations at its website.
http://www.who.org/gpv-dvacc/research/Jap_.Ence.htm

U.S. Centers for Disease Control and Prevention (CDC), National Center for Infectious Diseases, Division of Vector-Borne Infectious Diseases, 1300 Rampart Road, Colorado State University Foothills Research Campus, P.O. Box 2087, Fort Collins, CO 80522. CDC posts fact sheets about Japanese encephalitis and about arboviral encephalitis at its website.
Telephone 970-221-6400
http://www.cdc.gov/ncidod/dvbid/jespot.htm (Japanese encephalitis)
http://www.cdc.gov/ncidod/dvbid/arbor/arboinfo.htm (arboviral encephalitis)

Other regional forms of encephalitis include:

- Venezuelan equine encephalitis. Causes occasional epidemics in Central and South America. Usually mild.
- Russian spring-summer encephalitis. Spread by ticks, with death rates as high as 25 percent in some outbreaks. A vaccine is available in Russia and Europe.
- West Nile encephalitis. A milder relation of Japanese and St. Louis encephalitis, it occurs in Africa, Asia, and Europe. A strain similar to the West Nile virus was first detected in the Western Hemisphere in New York City during the summer of 1999.
- Murray Valley encephalitis. Found in parts of Australia and New Guinea, it is also related to St. Louis and Japanese encephalitis. It is rarely fatal.

▶ *See also*
AIDS and HIV
Chickenpox
Cytomegalovirus
German Measles (Rubella)
Herpes
Lyme Disease
Measles
Mumps
Poliomyelitis
Rabies
Toxoplasmosis
Viral Infections
Zoonoses

Endocarditis

Endocarditis (en-do-car-DY-tis) refers to inflammation of the lining of the heart, usually caused by an infection in a heart valve or the heart lining, called the endocardium (en-do-CAR-de-um). People at increased risk for endocarditis are sometimes given antibiotics to prevent it.

KEYWORDS
for searching the Internet and other reference sources

Antibiotic therapy

Bacteremia

Cardiovascular system

Circulatory system

Inflammation

The heart contains four chambers, each of which has a special function as the heart pumps blood through the body. The inner walls of these chambers are called the "endocardium" and are lined with small blood vessels and smooth muscle. Valves, like swinging doors between the chambers, open and close as the heart beats and as the blood flows. They keep the blood going in one direction, with no back flow.

Who Is at Risk for Endocarditis?

About 1 percent of people have defects in the endocardium or heart valves that are present since birth. Other people may develop defects from heart disease, rheumatic fever*, or use of intravenous* drugs. The defects can include tiny folds in the endocardium or a valve that does not open and close properly. Bacteria in the bloodstream sometimes settle into these malformed areas and cause an infection that swells the endocardium. This dangerous and often deadly condition is called "endocarditis," which strikes about 4 of every 100,000 Americans each year.

* **rheumatic fever** is a disease that causes fever, joint pain, and inflammation affecting many parts of the body. It varies in severity and duration, and it may be followed by heart or kidney disease.

* **intravenous** (in-tra-VEEN-us) drugs are injected directly into the veins.

What Causes Endocarditis?

Bacteria cause endocarditis. Bacteria are present in normal amounts in different parts of the body, especially the mouth, throat, lungs, and intestines. They enter the body in many ways, such as by catching strep throat* or pneumonia*. Most times, the body's own defenses fight bacterial infections or doctors prescribe antibiotic medications to help rid the body of invading bacteria.

* **strep throat** is a contagious sore throat caused by a strain of bacteria known as *Streptococcus*.

* **pneumonia** is an inflammation of the lungs usually caused by bacteria, viruses, or chemical irritants.

People who have normal hearts are rarely at risk for endocarditis. But when bacteria find a malformed heart valve or endocardium, they may settle in to reproduce. That can cause the heart to lose its ability to pump properly, as swollen valves start to stick partly open and blood clots form. The body and brain may fail to get enough oxygen, and heart failure or stroke* may result. The bacteria that cause endocarditis usually enter the bloodstream from an infection in another part of the body. Sometimes, however, the normal bacteria present in the mouth or intestines may become dislodged and settle in a damaged or abnormal heart. Surgery or dental procedures may cause such bacteria to get loose into the bloodstream, where they may start an infection in the endocardium.

* **stroke** may occur when a blood vessel bringing oxygen and nutrients to the brain bursts or becomes clogged by a blood clot or other particle. As a result, nerve cells in the affected area of the brain, and the specific body parts they control, do not properly function.

What Happens to People with Endocarditis?

The symptoms of endocarditis can develop quickly. They may include:

- fever
- extreme weakness
- shortness of breath
- chills and excessive sweating
- swollen feet, ankles, and joints
- loss of appetite

It is very important for people at risk for endocarditis to see their doctors if they experience these symptoms.

Diagnosis It can be difficult for doctors to diagnose endocarditis, because its symptoms are similar to those of other conditions. But doctors may suspect that a person has endocarditis if they are aware of a recent infection or if they know a person has a history of heart abnormalities. Doctors also will listen for a heart murmur* and rapid heartbeat. They look at the skin, which may appear abnormally pale with small, red spots on the palms and soles of the feet. A sample of blood often can identify the organism causing the infection.

* **heart murmur** is an extra sound heard during a heartbeat that is caused by turbulence in blood flow through the heart.

Treatment Antibiotics are used to treat the bacterial infection. Bed rest usually is necessary to allow time for recovery. If the infection has damaged a heart valve severely, surgery might be necessary to replace the damaged valve with an artificial one.

How Is Endocarditis Prevented?

Avoiding intravenous drugs is important for many reasons, including the fact that drug use puts people at risk for endocarditis. People with abnormal heart valves often are given antibiotics before surgery or before certain dental procedures. Although a recent study did not find a strong link between dental work and endocarditis, the American Dental Association and the American Heart Association continue to recommend that doctors give antibiotics to people with known heart defects before surgery or dental work.

Resources

The U.S. National Heart, Lung, and Blood Institute posts a fact sheet about endocarditis at its website.
http://www.nhlbi.nih.gov/nhlbi/infcentr/topics/endocard.htm

American Heart Association National Center, 7272 Greenville Avenue, Dallas, TX 75231. The American Heart Association posts fact sheets about bacterial endocarditis and about dental care and heart disease at its website.
Telephone 1-800-AHA-USA1
http://www.amhrt.org/Heart_and_Stroke_A_Z_Guide/bend.html

See also
Bacterial Infections
Heart Disease
Heart Murmur
Rheumatic Fever
Substance Abuse

Endometriosis

Endometriosis (en-do-me-tree-O-sis) is a chronic condition in which pieces of the lining of the uterus (YOO-ter-us) become embedded in tissues outside the uterus.

KEYWORD
for searching the Internet and other reference sources

Gynecology

What Is Endometriosis?

Endometriosis is a condition in which endometrial tissue grows outside the uterus. The endometrium (en-do-ME-tree-um) is the lining of the uterus (womb), which is the muscular organ in which a fetus develops during pregnancy. During the monthly menstrual cycle, chemicals called hormones* cause the endometrium to grow thick in preparation for pregnancy. If the egg is not fertilized, the endometrium is shed as blood and tissue in the monthly menstrual period.

*__hormones__ are chemicals that are produced by different glands in the body. Hormones are like the body's ambassadors: they are created in one place but are sent through the body to have specific regulatory effects in different places.

In a woman with endometriosis, fragments of endometrial tissue are implanted outside the uterus. The origin of endometriosis is not known for sure, but scientists speculate that parts of the endometrium may not leave the body during menstruation. Instead, these stray fragments find their way into other parts of the pelvic cavity. These stray pieces of tissue can attach to other organs, stick organs together, or form scar tissue.

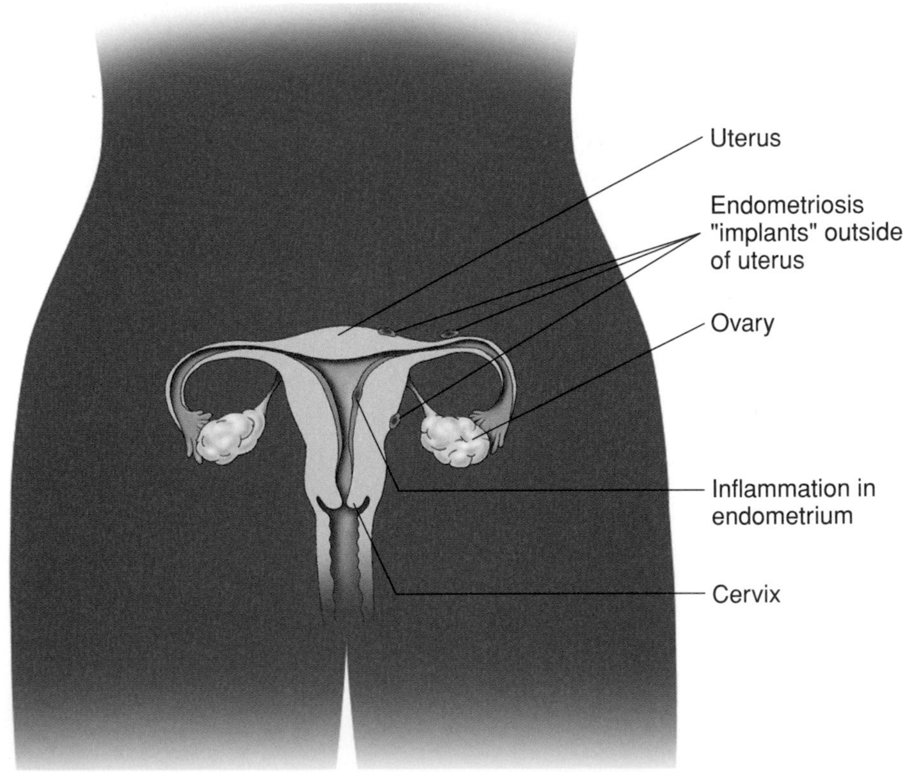

The endometrium is the lining of the uterus. In women with endometriosis, fragments of endometrial tissue become attached to other organs outside the uterus. The symptoms of endometriosis may include heavy bleeding, abdominal pain, lower back pain, and tenderness and pain in the pelvic area.

What Are the Symptoms and Effects of Endometriosis?

Endometrial implants outside the uterus respond to hormones in the same way as endometrial tissue inside the uterus: they grow, break down, and bleed. The blood released by implants is irritating to the internal tissues and causes pain. Although some women with endometriosis do not have any symptoms, for others the symptoms of endometriosis include heavy bleeding during menstruation, abdominal and lower back pain, tenderness and pain in the pelvic area, diarrhea, constipation, and bleeding from the rectum.

Endometriosis affects women mostly between the ages of 25 and 40. It is a major cause of infertility (the inability to conceive a child) in women, because endometrial implants may block the fallopian tubes or may prevent the eggs from leaving the ovaries, making it impossible for a women to get pregnant. About 30 to 40 percent of women who have endometriosis have difficulty becoming pregnant, and women with endometriosis represent about 10 to 15 percent of women who are infertile.

How Is Endometriosis Diagnosed?

A doctor may suspect that a woman has endometriosis based on her history of symptoms. To diagnose endometriosis, the doctor uses a procedure called laparoscopy (lap-a-ROS-ko-pee), in which a viewing instrument (a laparoscope) is inserted into the abdomen or pelvic cavity through a small incision. This allows the doctor to examine the abdominal or pelvic cavity for pieces of endometrium that may have become implanted on surfaces where they usually are not found.

How Is Endometriosis Treated?

Endometriosis is treatable, but there is no cure for the condition. In mild cases, treatment may not be necessary. When treatment does become necessary, it may be complicated. The age of the woman, her general health, how severe her condition is, and whether she wants to have children all must be considered.

Hormone medications have been developed that can suppress the development of endometrial tissue or cause the fragments to wither away, which may take as long as six months. Other medications may be prescribed to relieve pain. Sometimes surgery is involved to remove some of the abnormal tissue. Older women not planning to have more children may consider having a hysterectomy (his-ter-EK-to-mee) to solve the problem. This is surgery to remove the uterus and sometimes other reproductive organs.

Hormones and Endometriosis

The menstrual cycle is controlled by changing levels of hormones. Estrogen, progesterone, and prostaglandins regulate the buildup and the shedding of the endometrial lining of the uterus. Changes in these hormone levels, caused by pregnancy or by oral contraceptives, (birth control pills), can be helpful in relieving symptoms of endometriosis.

Most women with endometriosis are able to have children, and many are free of symptoms when they are pregnant. During pregnancy, the hormone balance that usually causes the monthly menstrual cycle changes. Instead of causing the endometrium to grow and then break down, different hormones work to take care of a developing fetus. Therefore, the implants may be free of the hormonal effects that cause the symptoms of endometriosis.

Oral contraceptives (birth control pills) are mixtures of reproductive hormones that, when taken every day, act to change the hormone balance in the body to prevent pregnancy. Side effects of oral contraceptives include less cramping and lighter menstrual periods. By altering the body's hormonal balance, they also can be effective in reducing the symptoms of endometriosis.

Resources

Book

Ballweg, Mary Lou. *The Endometriosis Sourcebook*. New York: Contemporary Books, 1995.

Organizations

The U.S. Food and Drug Administration posts a fact sheet called *On the Teen Scene: Endometriosis: Painful, but Treatable* at its website. http://www.fda.gov/opacom/catalog/ots_endo.html

Endometriosis Association International Headquarters, 8585 North 76th Place, Milwaukee, WI 53223-2600.
Telephone 800-992-3636

▶ *See also*
Infertility
Menstrual Disorders
Pregnancy, Complications of

Environmental Diseases

Environmental diseases are illnesses and conditions that result from manmade environmental problems.

KEYWORDS
for searching the Internet and other reference sources

Carcinogens

Herbicides

Hydrocarbons

Mercury

Pesticides

Pollution

Radiation

Silent Spring

Rachel Carson's 1962 book *Silent Spring* described an environment ravaged by pesticides:

> Over increasingly large areas of the United States, spring now comes unheralded by the return of birds, and early mornings are strangely silent where once they were filled with the beauty of bird song.

Carson questioned the use of pesticides, particularly DDT, and described how people were slowly destroying the world around them. Carson and her ideas were attacked from many sides, and one chemical company tried unsuccessfully to stop the book from being published.

Silent Spring marked the beginning of the environmental movement. The public listened to Carson, and ultimately, the government listened too. In 1972, the United States banned the use of DDT because it had been linked to cancer in laboratory studies with mice.

What Are Environmental Diseases?

Illnesses and conditions caused by factors in the environment are collectively called environmental diseases. Pesticides, chemicals, radiation, air pollution, and water pollution, are some of the manmade hazards that are believed to contribute to human illnesses. Potential illness-causing agents are everywhere: at home, at work, and at play. However, the likelihood of an individual developing a specific disease depends on the hazards present in their particular environment and their genetic susceptibility to a specific hazard. For example, x-ray technicians are at risk for radiation-induced illnesses, whereas coal miners are prone to lung diseases caused by inhalation of dust. Proper use of safeguards can prevent these and other environmental diseases.

What Happened at Love Canal?

From 1942 to 1953, the Hooker Chemicals and Plastics Corporation used the Love Canal in Niagara Falls, New York, as a dumpsite for its chemical wastes. When the site was full, it was covered with soil and later sold to the Niagara Falls School Board with a warning about the chemical wastes buried beneath the land.

The land that once had been a hazardous waste site became a neighborhood called Love Canal, complete with a school and hundreds of homes atop the waste site. Homeowners, however, were not warned about the hazards underneath their houses.

From the 1950s to the 1970s, residents of Love Canal smelled unusual odors and discovered strange substances in their yards. Some people developed unexplained health problems. At various times, the city investigated complaints, but nothing was done to remedy the problems until 1978.

In April of that year, the Love Canal area was declared a threat to human health, and by August the school was closed and many families were evacuated from the neighborhood. Ultimately, President Jimmy Carter declared the Love Canal neighborhood a disaster area, and federal funds were used to relocate the 239 families living closest to the dump site.

Love Canal became a symbol for citizens, scientists, activists, and politicians who became more aware of their environment. It resulted in the passage of federal laws designed to force the clean up of landfill sites.

Myth Versus Reality: Proving Cause and Effect

People like Rachel Carson have made Americans aware of the potential health consequences of many everyday processes and products. Because many things present in the environment have the potential to cause illness in some susceptible people, environmental diseases often are controversial. Unfortunately, when a large group of people begin claiming that something in the environment is making them sick, fear can grow into a myth without any proof. For example some people believe that exposure to high-voltage electric power lines causes cancer. So far, however, there is no conclusive evidence that this is true.

For scientists, showing that something in the environment is the cause of a disease is a difficult process that can take many years.

Reality: What Are Some of the Common Environmental Diseases?

Lung Diseases Any substance other than air that is breathed into the lungs has the potential to cause damage to these organs. For example, air

Gulf War Syndrome

Many United States veterans have complained about disabling symptoms that they attribute to their participation in the 1991 Persian Gulf War. Gulf War Syndrome encompasses symptoms such as chronic fatigue, aching muscles and joints, skin rashes, memory loss, miscarriages, and babies born with birth defects.

Gulf War Syndrome is a mysterious condition. While veterans are experiencing very real medical problems, physicians and scientists cannot agree on the source of these problems. Some people believe that the syndrome actually consists of multiple illnesses for which symptoms overlap. Veterans could be reacting to chemical weapons, biological weapons, pesticides, vaccines, oil fires, or infectious diseases that they were exposed to in the Gulf War. A presidential commission set up to study the controversy surrounding the Gulf War Syndrome proposed that stress was the major cause behind the symptoms the veterans were experiencing. A decade after it began, the controversy continues as conflicting reports emerge.

pollution, including smoke from other peoples' cigarettes (secondhand smoke), and workplace chemicals can lead to lung diseases. Examples of lung diseases include:

- Asthma (AZ-ma), a condition in which breathing is difficult, affects millions of Americans. Environmental triggers for asthma are everywhere and include naturally occurring triggers such as animal dander, plant pollen, dust, and mold, and manmade triggers such as chemicals. Not everyone is sensitive to these triggers, but many people are sensitive to some of them.
- Black lung disease is an illness in which coal miners' lungs become coated with coal dust, causing a chronic condition in which breathing becomes difficult and painful.
- Bronchitis (brong-KY-tis), an inflammation of the airways of the lungs, can be caused by breathing in certain chemicals or smoke. Welders and fire fighters are some of the people at risk for this condition. Smokers are also at increased risk for the development of bronchitis and lung cancer.
- Breathing asbestos (a natural mineral fiber) can lead to asbestosis (as-bes-TO-sis), a severe lung disorder, and lung cancer. Schools, homes, and businesses that have asbestos in them as a fire retardant put people at risk when the asbestos dust begins to leak into the air during repairs and renovations. These buildings used asbestos in the walls and ceilings as insulation before laws were passed to ban their use.
- Silicosis (sil-i-KO-sis) is a lung disease caused by exposure to the silica dust in clay. Pottery workers are at risk of developing this disease.

Cancers In addition to lung cancer, other cancers have been linked to environmental toxins (poisons). For example, pesticides, herbicides, and radioactive substances have the potential to cause cancer. There are almost 2,000 chemicals that are suspected of causing cancer. Of these, only several hundred have had their use restricted by law in the United States.

Asbestos, chromium, and coal tar have been linked to lung cancer. Construction workers, welders, and steelworkers may be repeatedly exposed to these compounds. People working in plastics manufacturing are at risk for liver or bladder cancer. People who work with radioactive substances are at increased risk for cancer caused by radiation. Fortunately, legal restrictions and careful oversight of hazardous materials can reduce risks.

Birth Defects Infertility*, miscarriage*, stillbirth (the baby is born dead), childhood cancer, and birth defects may have links to various environmental toxins. When a pregnant woman is exposed to lead, her child has a higher than usual risk of being born with behavior and nervous system problems. Exposure to radiation, chemical wastes, pesticides, solvents, paints, lead, and methyl mercury all can cause problems in a developing fetus*.

* **infertility** is when a man or woman is unable to conceive a child.

* **miscarriage** occurs when a pregnant woman loses the fetus in her uterus, causing the end of the pregnancy.

* **fetus** (FEE-tus), in humans, is the unborn offspring in the period from nine weeks after fertilization until birth. Before nine weeks it is called an embryo.

Chemical Poisonings Lead is a serious environmental hazard to children in many parts of the world, including the United States. It affects children's mental and physical development, and high doses can cause paralysis and death. People can be exposed to lead through lead paint, leaded gasoline, lead water pipes, and certain ceramics. Although lead is no longer used in most of these products in the United States, it can still be found in older homes and in some imported products.

The metals mercury and cadmium can cause nerve damage, cancer, and liver and skin diseases. Mercury has been used since the beginning of the nineteenth-century in many industrial processes. In earlier times, people who worked with mercury were often unknowingly poisoned. Mercury can accumulate in the food chain and present a health risk. For example, some fish in the Great Lakes are contaminated with mercury they acquired through eating plants and other fish. Eating a lot of these contaminated fish can transfer unhealthy levels of mercury to a person. The effects are cumulative, (build up), because the body cannot rid itself of mercury. Mercury can be found in fluorescent lights, latex paint, batteries, dental fillings, and mercury thermometers.

Other sources of environmental poisoning can arise from the manufacture of refrigerants, plastics, and other industrial products and from the manufacture and misuse of pesticides.

Can Environmental Diseases Be Prevented?

Regulations protecting people from environmental hazards vary widely from country to country. In the United States, Congress has enacted laws to protect workers from intentional and accidental exposure to environmental hazards. For example:

- The National Institute of Occupational Safety and Health (NIOSH) was established in 1971 to set standards for health and safety in the workplace.
- The Occupational Safety and Health Administration (OSHA) was also established in 1971 to enforce rules and regulations based on NIOSH's findings.
- In 1983, OSHA required industries to make full disclosure to their workers about the dangerous chemicals used in their facilities and to teach workers how to protect themselves from these hazardous substances.
- In 1987, the 1983 standards were extended to include more workers. Later, a regulation to set standards to prevent occupational exposure to infectious diseases such as AIDS and hepatitis B and C was added.

Resources

U.S. National Center for Environmental Health (NCEH), Centers for Disease Control and Prevention (CDC), Mail Stop F-29, 4770 Buford

Sick Building Syndrome

Sick Building Syndrome describes an elusive health problem in which people attribute a variety of symptoms to the buildings where they work. Common complaints include headaches, dizziness, nausea, tiredness, concentration problems, sensitivity to odors, dry itchy skin, a dry cough, and irritated eyes, nose, and throat. Generally, as soon as affected people leave the building, their symptoms vanish and they feel well again.

Sick Building Syndrome is elusive in that neither one specific illness nor a common cause has been identified. No specific set of symptoms is common to all people complaining of Sick Building Syndrome. While nothing has been proven, theories as to the causes of Sick Building Syndrome abound. Many factors may contribute to it, including humidity, poor ventilation, and poor temperature control. Pollution from outdoor sources, (for example car exhaust, pollen, or smoke) or chemicals from inside a building, (cleaning supplies, glues, upholstery, or copy machine chemicals), may affect people who are sensitive to them. Bacteria, viruses, and molds also can invade buildings and make people sick.

Chemical discharges from some industrial plants are an important cause of water pollution. © *Ray Pfortner/Peter Arnold, Inc.*

▶ *See also*
Asthma
Birth Defects
Cancer
Carbon Monoxide Poisoning
Cold Related Injuries
Heat Related Injuries
Lead Poisoning
Lung Cancer
Pneumoconiosis
Radiation Exposure Conditions

Highway, N.E., Atlanta, GA 30341-3724.
Telephone 888-232-6789
http://www.cdc.gov/nceh/

U.S. National Institute of Environmental Health Sciences, P.O. Box 12233, Research Triangle Park, NC 27709.
Telephone 919-541-3345
http://www.niehs.nih.gov/

World Health Organization (WHO), Avenue Appia 20, 1211 Geneva 27, Switzerland. WHO's website posts fact sheets about environmental health and related topics.
http://www.who.org/home/map_ht.html

Epilepsy

KEYWORDS
for searching the Internet and other reference sources

Brain function

Neurology

Seizures

Epilepsy (EP-i-lep-see) is a condition of the nervous system characterized by recurrent seizures that temporarily affect a person's awareness, movements, or sensations. Epileptic seizures occur when powerful, rapid bursts of electrical energy interrupt the normal electrical patterns of the brain. The cause of epilepsy is unknown in most cases, but it is known that some cases are hereditary, or run in families. Epilepsy is not contagious.

Erin's Story

It happened at her birthday party. Eleven-year-old Erin was ready to blow out the candles on her cake when she suddenly released a loud cry and dropped to the carpet. Her arms and legs thrashed and twitched. When her friends called to her she did not respond. Her mother knelt beside her, turned Erin gently onto her side, and loosened the top button on her shirt. In a few moments, Erin regained consciousness, exhausted and more than a little embarrassed that her friends had seen what had happened. She was not scared because it had occurred before. Her mother explained to her friends that Erin had had an epileptic seizure, and that as soon as she had time to rest, she would be fine.

What Is Epilepsy?

In a normal brain, millions of tiny electrical charges pass between nerve cells and to all parts of the body. Those cells "fire" in an orderly and controlled manner. In the brain of a person with epilepsy, overactive nerve cells send out powerful, rapid electrical charges that disrupt the brain's normal function. During a seizure such as the one experienced by Erin, brain cells can fire at up to four times their normal rate, temporarily affecting how a person behaves, moves, thinks, or feels.

Some people with epilepsy know what will trigger a seizure, but others do not. Many people with epilepsy can sense that they are about to have a seizure. The attack may be preceded by a feeling of unease, anxiety, or discomfort. They may sense or see flickering lights. Despite these warning signals, people with epilepsy still cannot stop the oncoming seizure.

What Causes Epilepsy?

Because epilepsy is not contagious, one person cannot catch epilepsy from another. In about 7 out of 10 cases, doctors describe the disease as idiopathic (id-ee-o-PATH-ik), which means the cause is unknown. Most people with idiopathic seizures are between ages 5 and 20 and have no brain injuries or abnormalities. Many do, however, have a family history of epilepsy or seizure disorders.

In other cases, the following have been identified as causes of epilepsy:

- Maternal injury, infection, or illness that affects a developing fetus during pregnancy.
- Brain injuries. Although brain injuries can occur at any age, the highest incidence is among young adults. These injuries often result from car collisions, sports accidents, and falls. Blows to the head and gunshot wounds, particularly those that injure brain membranes and tissues, can lead to epilepsy. In general, the more severe the injury, the greater the chance of developing the disease.
- Brain tumor or stroke. Either can lead to injury or irritation of brain tissue.
- Metabolic abnormalities. Complications from diabetes, kidney failure, lead poisoning, use of alcohol or drugs, or withdrawal from alcohol or drugs can cause seizures.

The U.S. and the World

- Epilepsy is a common neurologic disease in the United States, affecting more than 6 out of every 1,000 people.
- Epilepsy most frequently begins in early childhood, during adolescence, or after age 65.
- Among people with epilepsy, 20 percent develop the disorder before age 5, and 50 percent develop it before age 25.
- Worldwide, some form of epilepsy affects about 40 million people. About 32 million of those people have inadequate access to medical treatment.

The Road to Understanding

Ancient Greeks believed epileptic seizures were blessed visitations from the gods. During the Renaissance, a seizure was seen as a sign that a person was possessed by the devil.

In the early 1800s, epilepsy was still misunderstood. It was believed to be contagious, and people with the disease were often locked away in hospitals or "epileptics only" sanitariums.

By the mid-1800s, neurologists (doctors who treat disorders and diseases of the brain and spinal cord) began to investigate epilepsy and to make progress toward a better understanding of the disorder.

Fyodor Dostoyevsky

Fyodor Dostoyevsky (1821–1881) was a Russian writer who is considered one of the world's great novelists. With brilliant psychological and philosophical insight, Dostoyevsky examined the human soul in *Notes from the Underground, Crime and Punishment,* and his masterpiece in 1880, *The Brothers Karamazov*. Dostoyevsky had epilepsy, and his fiction includes characters with epilepsy.

- Degenerative disorders. Stroke, cardiovascular disease, and Alzheimer's disease are causes of epilepsy, particularly in people over 65.
- Infections. Epilepsy may develop after a major brain illness such as meningitis, encephalitis, brain abscess, or severe infections of any part of the body. Less frequently, mumps, measles, and diphtheria can lead to the disease.
- Complications of AIDS or other immune disorders, including systemic lupus erythematosus, also can cause epilepsy.

What Triggers a Seizure?

Anyone can have a seizure, but a person with epilepsy has many more seizures and experiences them over a longer period of time. For a person with epilepsy, many conditions that affect the brain can trigger a seizure. These triggers include: hormonal changes, such as those that occur during the menstrual cycle or pregnancy; hunger; exhaustion or sleep deprivation; rhythmic patterns of sound, touch, or light (particularly strobe lights). An epileptic seizure is not a medical emergency. However, if a person goes into status epilepticus (where a seizure lasts longer than 30 minutes or two seizures rapidly follow one another), the condition could be life threatening. Medical assistance should be summoned at once.

How Do Seizures Differ?

Because of the way they appear during or after an attack, people experiencing an epileptic seizure are sometimes mistakenly believed to be drunk, drugged, or mentally ill. Epileptic seizures have different symptoms or characteristics depending on where the seizure begins in the brain and how the electrical discharge spreads across the brain. Epileptic seizures can be divided into two categories: generalized seizures and partial seizures.

Generalized seizures Generalized seizures affect nerve cells throughout the cerebral cortex (the cauliflower-like outer portion of the brain), or all of the brain. The most common generalized seizures are:

- Generalized tonic-clonic seizure (formerly called grand mal). In the tonic phase of this seizure, people often lose consciousness, drop to the ground, and emit a loud cry as air is forced through their vocal cords. In the clonic phase, body muscles can contract at once or in a series of shorter rhythmic contractions, causing the thrashing motions experienced by Erin. Usually, this kind of seizure lasts for about one or two minutes, and is followed by a period of relaxation, sleepiness, and possibly a headache. Incontinence* often occurs during this type of seizure.
- Absence seizure (formerly called petit mal). Loss of consciousness in this seizure is often so brief that a person does not even change positions. The person may display a blank stare, rapid blinking, or chewing movements. Facial or eyelid muscles may jerk rhythmically. Absence seizures often are genetic and occur mostly in children.

* **incontinence** (in-KON-ti-nens) is loss of control of urination or bowel movement.

Partial seizures Partial seizures are contained within one region of the cerebral cortex. Types of partial seizures include:

- Simple partial. In this type of seizure, the seizure-related brain messages remain very localized, and the patient is awake and alert. Symptoms vary depending on what area of the brain is involved. They may include jerking movements in one part of the body, emotional symptoms such as unexplained fear, or an experience of abnormal smells or nausea.
- Complex partial. In this type of seizure, a person loses awareness of surroundings and is unresponsive or only partially responsive. There may be a blank stare, chewing movements, repeated swallowing, or other random activity. After the seizure, the patient has no memory of the experience. In some cases, the person who has had the seizure may suddenly become confused, begin to fumble, to wander, or to repeat inappropriate words or phrases.

How Is Epilepsy Diagnosed?

Because not every person who has a seizure necessarily has epilepsy, the doctor must determine the seizure's cause by a physical exam and medical history, including the seizures that have already occurred. Risk factors such as sleep deprivation and alcohol use need to be assessed, as well as any head injuries, childhood seizures, or family history of seizures.

Physicians also will be interested to know if the patient has experienced an aura* because that can help confirm that the seizure is a brain disorder and help establish its location. The doctor also will ask about the nature of the movements the person made during a seizure.

* **aura** is a warning sensation that precedes a seizure or other neurological event.

If it is established that the patient has experienced an epileptic seizure, the next step is to identify the type of seizure. The first tool doctors use is an electroencephalograph (e-lek-tro-en-SEF-a-lo-graf). Commonly known as an EEG, this machine records electric currents in the brain, and it can track abnormal electrical activity. If the EEG does

Epileptic seizures have different phases, as shown on these positron emission (PET) scans. The stage shown in the middle is the most severe. *NCI/Photo Researchers, Inc.*

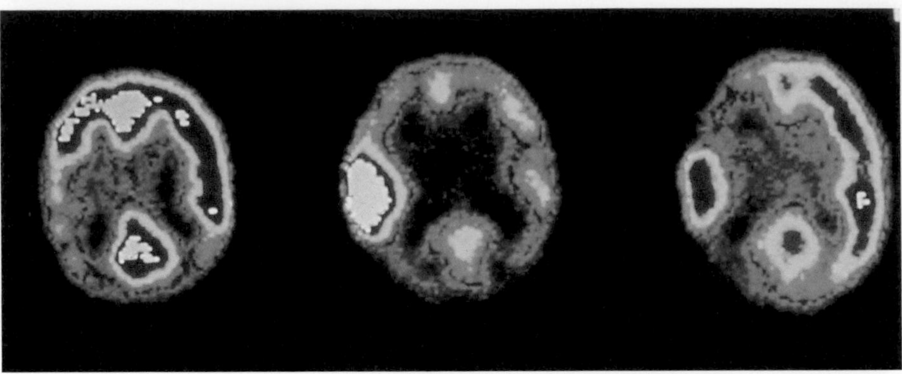

not show the seizure activity, or if there are certain other features in the patient's physical exam or medical history, then doctors may try other types of scans, including CT (computerized tomography) or MRI (magnetic resonance imaging).

How Is Epilepsy Treated?

Treating epilepsy involves three goals: to eliminate seizures or at least reduce their frequency, to avoid side effects of long-term medical treatments, and to assist in maintaining or restoring normal activities of daily living.

Medication Most cases of epilepsy can be fully or partially controlled with anticonvulsant medications, although some seizure disorders of infancy or early childhood may not respond well to medications. If a person is free of seizures for several years, doctors may reduce or even eliminate medication. In many cases, however, epilepsy remains a lifelong, chronic condition with no medical treatment guaranteeing remission* or a permanent cure.

* **remission** is an easing of a disease or its symptoms for a prolonged period.

Surgery If drug therapy does not work, a surgical procedure can remove the damaged cells that cause partial seizures. To qualify, however, the tissue must be located in one small area of the brain and the surgeon must be able to remove this tissue without harming a person's mental abilities or personality. Although adults have undergone the surgery successfully, the results are usually better when the surgery is performed on children and infants.

Diet A ketogenic diet (a doctor-monitored, high-fat, high-calorie diet) that was discontinued as a therapy when medicines became available, is being revived as a treatment. Some people believe the diet can stop seizures by creating ketosis (ke-TO-sis), a condition in which the body burns fat for energy instead of glucose. The ketogenic diet may be recommended for children who do not respond to standard treatment.

Biofeedback Biofeedback has been beneficial to some patients, when combined with other therapies. Biofeedback uses electronic instruments to monitor a person's brain waves, blood pressure, heart rate, and skin temperature. This information is then "fed back" to the patient, who has been taught techniques to alter these bodily functions to a lower, more relaxed level.

New treatments Epilepsy research is an active field. One promising technique now in development is called vagus nerve stimulation.

Can Epilepsy Be Prevented?

Because so many cases of epilepsy have no known cause, there are no prevention guidelines. However, anything that injures the brain can cause epilepsy. With that in mind, safety precautions and good health practices would include:

- In a car, always buckling seat belts and observing speed limits.
- Always wearing approved helmets and protective headgear while skating, bicycling, playing sports, or riding motorcycles.
- Using drugs only as prescribed.
- Immunizing children against infectious diseases.

Living with Epilepsy

Most people with epilepsy can lead normal and active lives, although they must follow a few safety restrictions. People with epilepsy must be free of seizures for a period of time specified by their home state before they are permitted to drive. People with uncontrolled seizures are prohibited from driving a car.

A person with a seizure disorder should avoid working in jobs that involve heights, dangerous machinery, or underwater environments. To avoid the risk of drowning during a seizure, showers are safer than baths, and swimming in a pool or lake with other people is safer than swimming alone.

People with epilepsy also are at risk for depression. In part, the depression may stem from loss of mobility, or from the effects of prejudice at school or at work on the part of those who fear or do not understand the condition. Parents may be overly protective of children with epilepsy, keeping them from normal childhood activities. It is common for depressed adolescents to refuse to comply with their medication schedules, running the risk of additional seizures. Alcohol also may increase the risk of seizures for some people, and mixing alcohol with anticonvulsant medications can be deadly.

Understanding the facts about epilepsy and providing a positive environment in which treatment becomes a part of everyday life can help people with epilepsy and their families.

Medic Alert Tags

People with epilepsy often wear medical alert identification tags or bracelets that provide vital information for caregivers during seizures.

Some companies offer tags with identification numbers so that medical personnel anywhere can retrieve a patient's medical history.

Resources

Book

Wilner, Andrew N. *Epilepsy: 199 Answers. A Doctor Responds to His Patients' Questions.* New York: Demos Vermande, 1996.

▶ *See also*
Brain Tumors
Diabetes
Encephalitis
Incontinence
Kidney Disease
Lead Poisoning
Lupus
Meningitis
Seizures
Stroke

Organization

The Epilepsy Foundation, 4351 Garden Drive, Landover, MD 20785. Formerly the Epilepsy Foundation of America, this national organization offers advocacy and resources. The website provides general information on diagnosis and treatment, plus web links and a chat room for teenagers.
Telephone 800-332-1000
http://www.epa.org

Epstein-Barr Virus *See* Mononucleosis, Infectious

F

Fainting (Syncope)

Fainting is a brief loss of consciousness caused by a temporary drop in blood flow to the brain.

KEYWORDS
for searching the Internet and other reference sources

Circulatory system

Blood pressure

The Attorney General Passes Out

One minute, U.S. Attorney General Janet Reno was sitting in church. The next minute, she was peering up at a circle of concerned faces. Sixty-year-old Reno had just had a fainting spell, her second in less than a year. The September 1998 incident made the news because of Reno's famous name, but fainting is common. The cause of Reno's spell was unknown, but doctors said it might have been due to her heavy work load or the tremendous job stress that comes with being the chief law officer of the United States.

What Is Fainting?

Fainting, also known as syncope (SING-ko-pee), is a brief loss of consciousness caused by a temporary drop in blood flow to the brain. Blood carries

Blacking Out in Blue Skies

In World War II, fighter pilots sometimes lost their lives because of fainting.

During high-speed flight, very rapid changes in speed create a force that is expressed as a unit of gravity (g). A force of 4 to 6 g makes blood become very heavy and pool in the lower part of the body, robbing the brain of its blood supply. Many high-speed moves create a force this great. For example, pulling out of a dive can produce a force up to 9 g. When this happened, pilots fainted and crashed.

It was up to scientist Wilbur R. Franks to find a solution to this problem. In 1942, Franks invented the first anti-gravity suit. This is a flight suit with special pants that apply pressure to the legs and belly, forcing blood back into the upper part of the body. Franks's invention gave Allied pilots a competitive edge during the war. The suits worn by jet pilots and astronauts today are still based on his design.

oxygen to the brain. Without enough oxygen, brain processes slow down, and the person may pass out briefly. There can be several reasons for the sudden drop in blood flow, including an irregular heart rate or rhythm, a dip in blood pressure, or the pooling of blood in the legs usually after a prolonged period of standing. Although fainting can be scary and embarrassing, it usually is not a cause for panic. Healthy people sometimes faint when they are extremely tired, get bad news, or see something upsetting. In other cases, however, fainting may be a sign of a more serious medical condition.

What Causes Fainting?

One in three people faints at some point in life. The problem occurs in people of all ages, although it is most common in people over age 65. There are many possible causes. These are some of the more frequent ones:

Heart disorders The most serious causes of fainting usually involve the heart or blood vessels. In some cases, the heart beats too fast or with an irregular rhythm, reducing the amount of blood it pumps. In other cases, there is a narrowing of the valve that lets blood out of the heart or a partial blockage of the blood vessels that carry blood to the head, limiting blood flow to the brain.

Emotional stress Stress, fright, or sudden pain can arouse the nervous system, which, in turn, can signal the heart to slow down or the blood vessels to widen. If such changes happen too quickly, a person's blood pressure can drop suddenly. This reduces blood flow to the brain, and the person may faint.

Heavy sweating Sweat contains sodium, a mineral that plays a key role in blood pressure control. Heavy sweating is another possible cause of a sudden dip in blood pressure. This often is a problem for people who take part in strenuous physical activities under hot, humid conditions.

Dancing Mania and Mass Fainting

The phenomenon of mass fainting was reported to have occurred in the Middle Ages as a result of what was known as dancing mania.

Dancing mania reportedly was induced by minstrels who played intoxicating music at medieval festivals. The music stimulated fits of wild dancing, leaping, hopping, and clapping that led to hyperventilation, heart palpitations, and other symptoms.

Dancing mania curiously parallels the fainting that sometimes occurs at present day rock concerts.

Standing up quickly When most people stand up, the nervous system triggers a reflex response that increases the heart rate and blood pressure. This insures that enough blood gets to the brain. In some people, particularly the elderly, these responses may not occur fast enough. Blood may pool in the legs. When too little blood reaches the brain, the person may faint.

What Happens When People Faint?

Symptoms Some people simply lose consciousness and slump down without warning. However, many people feel dizzy, lightheaded, or sick to their stomach just before they faint. They may become sweaty and pale, and they may have a graying out of vision. By definition, a faint does not last long. Falling down places the head at the same level as the heart. This helps restore blood flow to the brain. The person soon regains consciousness, usually within a minute or so.

Treatment A person feeling faint should lie down immediately and not try to stand or walk. If the person who faints dos not regain consciousness within a minute or two, it is important to get emergency medical help immediately. While awaiting emergency help, adult bystanders probably will elevate the legs of the person who has fainted; loosen belts, collars, or tight clothing; and check that the person's airway remains open, as people who faint may vomit as well. They will not move the person who has fainted until medical help arrives because a fall may have injured the person.

The person who has fainted probably will regain consciousness quickly, but may continue to feel a bit weak for a little while. To keep from fainting again, the person should stay lying quietly for a few minutes.

Even when people recover promptly, they should contact their doctors about a first fainting attack, about repeated fainting spells, or about other possible symptoms including irregular heartbeat, chest pain, shortness of breath, blurred vision, confusion, or trouble talking.

Resource

American Heart Association, 7272 Greenville Avenue, Dallas, TX 75231, (800) AHA-USA1. This group has information about syncope on its website.
http://www.americanheart.org

▶ *See also*
Altitude Sickness
Heart Disease
Hypertension
Stress-Related Illness

Farsightedness

Farsightedness is an eye disorder that causes objects that are close to a person to appear out of focus or blurry, while objects at a distance may seem clear.

KEYWORDS
for searching the Internet and other reference sources

Hyperopia
Ophthalmology
Optometry
Vision

To people with farsightedness, the words on this page would seem blurry, unless they were wearing prescription (pre-SKRIP-shun) eyeglasses or contact lenses designed to correct the problem. But if they looked up from the page to read a sign across the room, they probably could read it easily.

What Is Farsightedness?

In most cases, farsightedness occurs when the eyeball is shorter than normal. For an object to appear clear, the light passing through the eye must focus on the retina, a layer of photosensitive* cells on the back of the eye. The retina is something like the film in a camera. It is where the image passing through the eye is projected and then sent along the optic nerve* to the brain. In the brain, the image is "developed" into what we see. If the eyeball is too short, the image that is projected onto the retina by close objects is blurred, and the person is said to be farsighted.

* **photosensitive** means responsive to light.

* **optic nerve** is the nerve that sends messages, or conducts impulses, from the eye to the brain, making it possible to see. The optic nerve is also referred to as the second cranial nerve.

People with farsightedness usually have the disorder from birth. It is probably inherited from parents, although just because a parent is farsighted does not mean the child necessarily will develop the problem too. Babies and younger children often are able to adapt to the problem. Muscles around the eyeball can change its shape, which makes it longer and allows the image to be focused properly on the retina. But as a child gets older, the muscles cannot do as good a job changing the eyeball's shape, and images close up are out of focus.

How Do Doctors Diagnose and Treat Farsightedness?

It can take many years for the symptoms of farsightedness to become noticeable. Eventually, people with farsightedness notice problems while reading or seeing objects that are close, whereas things that are farther away remain clear. They also may start to get headaches after reading or doing other close work, and they may feel as if their eyes are tired.

Ophthalmologists* can diagnose farsightedness and correct it easily with prescription eyeglasses or contact lenses. These change the focus of the images passing into the eye so they are projected properly onto the retina. Surgery to correct the problem is available, but it is not as widely used as surgery to correct nearsightedness.

* **ophthalmologist** (off-thal-MOLL-o-jist) is a medical doctor who specializes in treating diseases of the eye.

Presbyopia Many people become more farsighted as they age. They develop a condition known as presbyopia (pres-be-O-pe-a), which is

Anatomy of the eye. If the eyeball is too short, an object held close to the eye appears to blur as its image is projected onto the retina.

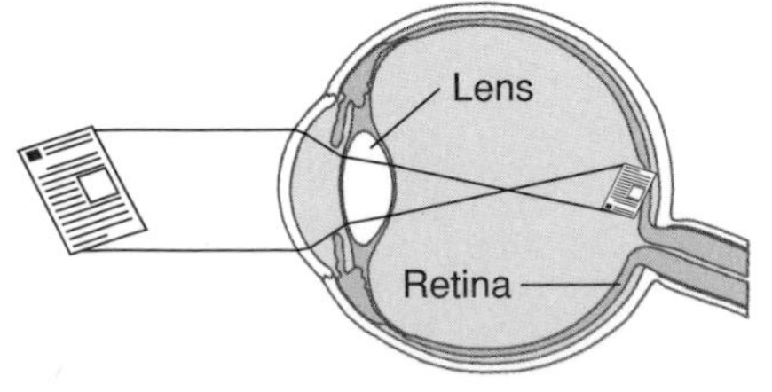

Normal vision: near object is focused on the retina

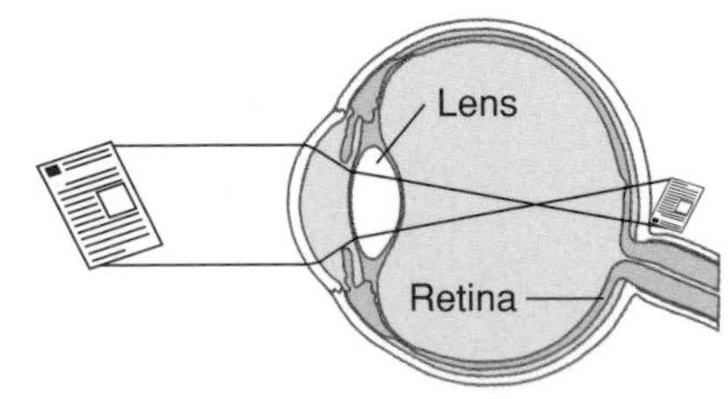

Farsightedness: near object is focused behind the retina

Latin for "old eyes," that causes close objects to appear out of focus. Presbyopia results because the lens at the front of the eyeball becomes thicker and less flexible as a person ages. This causes the eye to have trouble clearly focusing the images passing through the lens. The first sign of presbyopia may be noticed when adults pass age 40. They start to find they cannot read the newspaper as well. It is one reason one hears people joke that their arms are too short, because they try holding the paper or book farther away so they can see it clearly. People with farsightedness may need stronger prescription eyeglasses once they pass age 40. People with nearsightedness may need bifocal* or multifocal lenses.

* **bifocal** or multifocal (progressive) lenses are prescription eyeglasses that have lenses divided into two or more sections. The bottom section allows a person to see things clearly that are close, and the top section allows a person to see things clearly that are far away.

Resources

The U.S. National Eye Institute posts a resource list of eye health-related publications and organizations at its website.
http://www.nei.nih.gov/publications/sel-org.htm

American Academy of Ophthalmology, P.O. Box 67424, San Francisco, CA 94120-7424. The American Academy of Ophthalmology website includes a search engine that locates information about many disorders of the eye.
Telephone 415-561-8500
http://www.eyenet.org

▶ *See also*
Nearsightedness
Presbyopia

Fetal Alcohol Syndrome

Fetal alcohol syndrome is a set of physical, mental, and behavioral problems that may develop in a child whose mother drank alcohol during pregnancy. It is the most common known cause of mental retardation in the United States.

KEYWORDS
for searching the Internet or other reference sources
Alcoholism
Obstetrics
Pediatrics

Sarah, Child of Alcohol

Sarah was always very quiet and never caused any trouble in elementary school, but she had few friends and never did fit in. Although she got fair grades, the teachers never knew how difficult the lessons were for her. When Sarah got to high school, however, she stopped trying to learn the lessons that were difficult for her, and she just barely graduated. Sarah had "fetal alcohol effects," which were the result of her mother's drinking during pregnancy.

A person with fetal alcohol effects (FAE) has some of the symptoms of fetal alcohol syndrome (FAS), but not enough to be diagnosed with the full syndrome*. Many of Sarah's teenage friends outgrew their immaturity, forgetfulness, and learning problems, but Sarah did not. The

* **syndrome** means a group or pattern of symptoms and/or signs that occur together.

effects of her mother's drinking while she was pregnant with Sarah continue to follow Sarah throughout her life.

Not everyone with FAS or FAE has been identified, and researchers estimate that one in every 300 to 350 children born may have FAE or FAS. FAE and FAS are not contagious.

What Causes Fetal Alcohol Syndrome?

Alcohol use during pregnancy can cause fetal alcohol syndrome. When a woman drinks alcohol during pregnancy, it can cause a range of effects on the fetus*, from subtle symptoms, such as Sarah had, to full fetal alcohol syndrome. Fetal alcohol syndrome is a grouping of similar characteristics found in affected babies. These characteristics may include low birth weight, distinctive facial features, learning problems, and mental retardation.

* **fetus** (FEE-tus) is the term for an unborn human offspring during the period after it is an embryo, from 9 weeks after fertilization, until childbirth.

* **placenta** (pla-SEN-ta) in humans is the organ that unites the fetus to the mother's uterus.

Like most drugs, alcohol passes through the mother's placenta* directly into the fetal bloodstream. In the fetus, alcohol slows down the central nervous system and is broken down by the immature liver of the fetus, which cannot handle this poisonous substance effectively. Alcohol stays in the fetus for a long period of time—even after it has left the mother's body.

The more the mother-to-be drinks, the greater the danger to the unborn baby. Women who have three or more alcoholic drinks a day, and women who are binge drinkers (drinking heavily but not every day), are likelier to have children with fetal alcohol syndrome. All types of alcohol can cause damage. The same amount of alcohol is found in one beer, one glass of wine, and one shot of hard liquor like gin, whiskey, or vodka.

What Happens When Babies Have Fetal Alcohol Syndrome?

Facial characteristics Babies with fetal alcohol syndrome have a distinctive appearance. Characteristics may include:

- Small openings for the eyes, which appear widely spaced.
- Flat cheekbones.
- Ridges between the nose and upper lip tend to be flatter than usual.
- Bridge of the nose tends to be low and flat.
- Upper lip tends to be thinner than usual.
- Cleft palate*.
- Epicanthal (ep-i-KAN-thal) folds, which are folds of skin at the inner corner of the eye.
- Minor abnormalities in the shape and placement of ears.
- Nose is shorter than usual so the child has an elf-like appearance.

* **cleft palate** is a gap or split in the roof of the mouth (the palate). It occurs when the palate of a fetus does not develop properly during the first months of pregnancy.

Other characteristics The general characteristics associated with fetal alcohol syndrome include:

- Premature birth.
- Low birth weight. Babies with FAS are small at birth and may continue to grow slowly after birth as well.
- Possible heart defects.
- Possible skeletal problems or differences in the hands.
- Misaligned or misshapen teeth.
- Central nervous system problems, which may include microcephaly (my-kro-SEPH-a-lee) (an abnormally small head) and varying degrees of brain damage.
- Some children have mental retardation, ranging from mild to severe.
- Children may have problems concentrating and understanding concepts like time, money, and cause and effect.
- Children may have difficulty making friends and controlling their impulses. As a result, they may get into trouble at home and at school.

2,500 Years of Warnings About Alcohol and Pregnancy

In 1973, researchers at the University of Washington named the group of symptoms that can result from alcohol use during pregnancy "fetal alcohol syndrome." In 1987, the U.S. Surgeon General said that no known safe level of alcohol use during pregnancy exists. Among those who issued earlier warnings were:

- The Hebrew Bible and Talmud
- Plato (c. 428–348 B.C.E.), Greek philosopher
- Aristotle (384–322 B.C.E.), Greek philosopher
- Plutarch (c. 46–119), Greek biographer
- Francis Bacon (1561–1626), English philosopher
- Dr. William Sullivan, a U.S. doctor who conducted the first scientific study of the fetal effects of alcohol (1899)
- Taav Laitenen, a Finnish doctor who observed the low birth weight of babies born to mothers who drank alcohol during pregnancy (1910)
- Dr. Lemoine, a French doctor who described facial features, growth retardation, and central nervous system problems resulting from alcohol use during pregnancy (1968).

Fetal alcohol effects Children with fetal alcohol effects may not have the facial and physical characteristics of children with fetal alcohol syndrome, but they do have many of the same behavior and learning problems related to prenatal alcohol exposure.

How Can Fetal Alcohol Syndrome Be Prevented?

Fetal alcohol syndrome is 100 percent preventable. A pregnant woman should not drink at all. Since there is no amount of alcohol that has been proven safe to drink, the best choice for the mother-to-be is not to drink at all.

Resources

Books

Dorris, Michael. *The Broken Cord.* Demco Media, 1999. A true story about parents who adopt a boy with fetal alcohol syndrome.

Streissguth, Ann, Jonathan Kanter, and Mike Lowry, Eds. *The Challenge of Fetal Alcohol Syndrome: Overcoming Secondary Disabilities.* Seattle: University of Washington Press, 1997.

Organizations

U.S. National Institute on Alcohol Abuse and Alcoholism (NIAAA), 6000 Executive Boulevard, Suite 409, Bethesda, MD 20892. The NIAAA website posts the fact sheet "When You Are Pregnant, Drinking Can Hurt Your Baby" and provides referrals to other resources.
Telephone 301-443-3860
http://silk.nih.gov/silk/niaaal/publication/brochure.htm

The National Organization on Fetal Alcohol Syndrome, 418 C Street, N.E., Washington, D.C. 20002.
Telephone 800-66-NOFAS
http://www.nofas.org

March of Dimes Defects Foundation, Office of Government Affairs, 1901 L Street N.W., Suite 200, Washington, D.C. 20036.
Telephone 202-659-1800
http://www.modimes.org

Connecticut Clearinghouse, 334 Farmington Avenue, Plainville, CT 06062. Provides resources and referrals to groups dealing with fetal alcohol syndrome.
Telephone 800-232-4424
http://www.ctclearinghouse.org

► *See also*
Alcoholism
Birth Defects
Cleft Palate
Mental Retardation
Prematurity

Fever

Fever is an abnormally high body temperature that usually occurs during an infection, inflammation, or some other kind of illness. Fever is not a disease itself, but it is one of the most common signs of illness, especially among children.

How Is Body Temperature Controlled?

The body adjusts its temperature in much the same way that the thermostat in a house works. With a thermostat, people set the temperature they want, and the heating or cooling system clicks on until the inside of the house reaches the right temperature. After that, the heater or air conditioner clicks on and off automatically to keep the temperature in the house hovering around the desired temperature.

The body's thermostat is located in the hypothalamus (hy-po-THAL-a-mus), a small part of the brain that also helps control hunger, thirst, pleasure, and pain. The thermostat, called the thermoregulatory (ther-mo-REG-u-la-tor-ee) center, normally keeps the body's temperature hovering around 98.6 degrees Fahrenheit (F) (37 degrees Centigrade).

Like a house, the body has sensors that tell the thermostat if the temperature inside is rising or falling. In the body, these sensors are cells located in the skin and in the brain itself. If the sensors report that the body's temperature is rising, the body's cooling system clicks on, telling the cells to burn less fuel and produce less heat. The blood vessels expand to let heat escape from the skin, sweat pours out to cool the body as it evaporates, and the brain may get a bright idea: "Let's go into the shade and have a cold drink."

Fever With fever, the thermostat in the brain is reset to a higher temperature. Instead of keeping the body's temperature hovering around 98.6 degrees F, the body's heating and cooling systems may keep the temperature at 100 to 102 degrees F or even higher.

Normal temperature varies a bit from person to person and from morning to evening, making it hard to state precisely where normal ends and fever begins. Many doctors, however, say that a temperature of more than 99 or 100 degrees F (37.2 or 37.8 degrees C) should be considered a fever. A temperature of 104 degrees F or higher could be considered a high fever.

Hyperthermia Sometimes a person's temperature can rise for a different reason. Hyperthermia (hy-per-THER-me-a) occurs if the heat outside is too much for the body's cooling system to handle, making body temperature rise. The most severe cases of hyperthermia tend to occur in people who can not sweat as much as normal, such as elderly people or those taking certain medications.

KEYWORDS
for searching the Internet and other reference sources

Body temperature

Febrile convulsion

Hyperthermia

Infection

Inflammation

Pyrexia

Ups and Downs

A person's temperature normally varies each day by about 1 degree F (0.6 degrees C). It is lowest in the early morning and highest in the late afternoon. This daily variation is called the circadian (sir-KADE-ee-an) rhythm. When a person has a fever, it usually follows the same daily pattern.

Other factors also can affect what is normal. In women of childbearing age, for instance, the early morning temperature usually goes up each month just before ovulation (ov-u-LA-shun), the release of an egg from the ovary. It stays elevated briefly and then returns to the lower level.

Fever of Unknown Origin

Sometimes a person has a fever that lasts for two or three weeks, and the doctor cannot find a cause, despite performing the usual array of medical tests. This condition is referred to as fever of unknown origin.

In about 90 percent of cases, a cause eventually is found. The most common causes are infectious diseases. Fever of unknown origin is particularly common in people infected with HIV, the human immunodeficiency virus that causes AIDS.

How Does Illness Cause Fever?

Bacteria and viruses themselves, as well as toxins (poisonous waste products) produced by some bacteria, cause fever. In some cases, they work directly on the brain to raise the thermostat. More commonly, they cause the body's immune system* to produce proteins called cytokines (SY-to-kines). The cytokines help fight the infection, but they also reset the brain's thermostat, causing fever.

Any substance that causes fever is called a pyrogen (PY-ro-jen), from the Greek word for "fire-causer." If the substance comes from outside the body, such as a toxin from bacteria, it is called an exogenous (ek-SOJ-e-nus) pyrogen. The prefix "exo-" means "outside" in Greek. If the substance comes from inside the body, such as a cytokine, it is called an endogenous (en-DOJ-e-nus) pyrogen. The prefix "endo-" means "inside" in Greek.

Sometimes the immune system produces pyrogens even without an infection. For instance, this may happen if a person:

- has an autoimmune disease*, such as rheumatoid arthritis or lupus
- has inflammation* anywhere in the body
- has cancer, such as leukemia or lymphoma
- was a given a blood transfusion* that is not compatible with the person's own blood type
- has a reaction to a medication

People sometimes say that fever is a sign that the immune system is active, working to protect the body from illness. That may be true in some cases, but it is not always so. People often get fevers, for instance, if their immune system is weak or damaged. In reality, scientists are not sure exactly what, if anything, fever indicates about the state of the immune system.

* **immune system** (im-YOON SIS-tem) is the body system made up of organs and cells that defend the body against infection or disease.

* **autoimmune disease** (aw-to-i-MYOON disease) is a disease resulting from an immune system reaction against the body's own tissues or proteins.

* **inflammation** (in-fla-MAY-shun) is an immune system reaction to an injury, irritation, or infection. It often includes swelling, pain, warmth, and redness.

* **transfusion** (trans-FYOO-zhun) is the transfer of blood or blood products directly into a person's bloodstream.

Who Gets Fever?

Fever is caused by so many common illnesses, including colds and flu, that it happens to everyone many times in the course of a lifetime. Young children are particularly likely to get bacterial and viral infections that cause fever, such as strep throat and ear infections. Sometimes minor viral infections cause high fevers in children, while illnesses that are more serious cause milder fevers. People of all ages get fever.

Helpful fever There is some evidence that fever can make the immune system more effective and weaken certain bacteria. However, most of this evidence comes from animals or experiments on human cells in test tubes. Scientists really do not know whether fever helps people fight off infections in real life. It could turn out that fever helps in certain cases but not in others.

Fever often can help in another way, however. It can be an important sign that a person is sick. Its movements up and down can indicate whether a person is getting better or worse.

The Name Is Familiar

Many infectious diseases are named for the major symptom of fever. Most of those listed below lead to fevers of about 102 to 104 degrees F (39 to 40 degrees C). Dengue fever, Lassa fever, and yellow fever are caused by viruses. The others are caused by bacteria.

- Dengue (DENG-e) fever causes sudden high fever, headache, extreme tiredness, severe joint and muscle pain, swollen lymph nodes, and a rash. It is spread by mosquitoes.
- Lassa (LAH-sa) fever causes fever, headache, dry cough, back pain, vomiting, diarrhea, sore throat, and facial swelling. It is spread by rats and from person to person.
- Q fever causes sudden high fever, severe headache, and chills. It is spread by farm animals and insects.

Harmful fever Fever often makes an illness more unpleasant. In addition, a feverish body needs more oxygen, which means that the heart and lungs have to work harder as the fever rises. This can be a problem for people who already have heart or lung problems.

Fever can make mental problems worse for elderly people who have dementia (de-MEN-sha), which is a form of mental confusion and loss of memory that can develop gradually as people age. High fever also can cause temporary mental confusion, called delirium (de-LEER-e-um), even in healthy people.

Febrile convulsion Children under age 5 can have a different problem if their temperature rises quickly. They may experience a kind of seizure called a febrile convulsion (FEB-ryl kon-VUL-shun). Their muscles may twitch, and they may lose consciousness for several minutes. Usually, a febrile convulsion needs no treatment and may not recur. However, febrile convulsions can be very upsetting and frightening. They also can lead to injury; for example, if a child falls.

Extremely high temperatures of around 107 degrees F or higher can do permanent brain damage at any age if they last for a long time. Temperatures that high usually are caused by hyperthermia, not by fever from an illness.

How Is Fever Diagnosed?

People with a fever often feel hot, tired, achy, and generally sick. They sometimes have shaking chills as their temperature rises. Shaking helps raise the temperature to the feverish level set by the body's thermostat. They may sweat heavily when the fever "breaks" (starts to go away) or if it falls temporarily as part of an up-and-down pattern. Sweating helps lower the temperature to the new, lower point set by the thermostat.

Although the classic way of checking for fever at home is to touch the person's forehead to see how warm it feels, this often does not work. The only way to tell for sure if a person has a fever is by taking the temperature with a thermometer. Three kinds of thermometers can be used: digital, mercury, or tympanic.

Digital thermometers, usually used in medical offices and hospitals as well as at home, are electronic. They can take an oral temperature when placed under the tongue, a rectal temperature when placed into the rectum, or an axillary (AK-si-lar-y) temperature when placed in the armpit. In general, rectal temperatures are about 1 degree F higher than oral ones.

Mercury thermometers, which used to be the only kind available, are made out of glass and contain liquid mercury. They come in oral or rectal versions. Either kind can be used in the armpit as well. They are cheaper than digital thermometers, but they take longer to use.

Tympanic (tim-PAN-ik) thermometers are a special kind of digital thermometer that is placed into the ear. While the other thermometers take several minutes to give a reading, the tympanic thermometer takes only a few seconds. However, tympanic thermometers are more expensive and can be inaccurate if placed improperly in the ear.

- Rheumatic (roo-MAT-ik) fever causes painful, swollen joints, fever, and heart murmurs (abnormal heart sounds). It is caused by the same bacterium that causes strep throat.
- Rat-bite fever causes sudden chills, fever, headache, vomiting, back pain, a rash on the hands and feet, and temporary arthritis (joint inflammation). It is spread by rats and mice.
- Relapsing (re-LAPS-ing) fever causes sudden chills and high fever, fast heartbeat, severe headache, vomiting, muscle pain, and sometimes mental confusion. Symptoms can recur several times. It is spread by ticks and lice.
- Rocky Mountain spotted fever causes fever, headache, skin ulcers (open sores), and a rash. It is spread by ticks.
- Scarlet fever causes high fever, sore throat, flushed cheeks, and a rash, especially in children. It is caused by the same bacterium that causes strep throat.
- Typhoid (TY-foid) fever causes fever along with abdominal pain, headache, and extreme fatigue. It is spread by food and water that contain Salmonella bacteria.
- Yellow fever causes sudden fever, slow pulse, nausea, vomiting, constipation, muscle pains, liver failure, and severe fatigue. It is spread by mosquitoes.

Fiery Language

Many medical terms dealing with fever start with the prefix "pyro-" or "pyr-," from the Greek word for "fire." Fever itself is called pyrexia (pi-RECKS-ee-a). Substances that cause fever are called pyrogens, and medicines that reduce fever are called antipyretics.

The same Greek root has given rise to words outside medicine. A funeral pyre is a consuming blaze used to cremate (turn to ashes) a body. Pyromania is a compulsion to set fires. Pyrotechnics are fireworks. Pyrex is the trade name for a kind of glass used in baking pans because it can withstand high heat.

When Should a Doctor Be Consulted?

A doctor should be consulted if a fever is high, lasts longer than a few days, or is accompanied by other symptoms, such as a rash; pain in the joints, neck, or ears; unusual sleepiness; or a dazed or very sick feeling. For babies under about 3 months old, a doctor should be consulted about any fever.

The doctor will try to find and treat the underlying cause of the fever. Antibiotics can cure many bacterial infections, such as those that cause many earaches and sore throats. There are no medications to treat most viral infections.

How Is Fever Treated?

In a basically healthy adult or older child, there usually is no medical reason to treat the fever itself unless it is very high. In fact, lowering the fever with drugs can make it harder to tell if a person is actually getting better or if the drugs are just keeping the fever down. In younger children, though, doctors often treat fevers of 100 or 101 degrees F, in part to avoid febrile convulsions. Of course, if a person of any age is very uncomfortable or unable to sleep, even a low fever can be treated to provide relief.

Fever can be lowered by drugs called antipyretics (an-ti-py-RET-iks) that do not require prescriptions. The major ones are acetaminophen (a-seet-a-MIN-oh-fen), ibuprofen (i-byoo-PRO-fen), and aspirin. However, aspirin should not be given to children with a fever. If children have a viral illness, such as influenza or chickenpox, aspirin makes it likelier that they may get a rare but dangerous illness called Reye's syndrome*. This does not happen with acetaminophen or ibuprofen.

Antipyretic medicines are available in pills for adults, chewable tablets for children, and liquid drops for babies. Acetaminophen also comes in suppositories (su-POZ-i-tor-eez), waxy pellets that are inserted into the rectum. They are used for people who cannot take medicine by mouth for some reason.

A lukewarm bath also can help lower a high temperature. However, cold water or alcohol rubs can do more harm than good by causing the body to shiver, which just raises body temperature more. In addition to these treatments, it is important for a person with a fever to drink plenty of liquids to avoid dehydration*. In extreme cases, a person in the hospital with a very high fever may be wrapped in a special cooling blanket or immersed in ice water.

How Can Fever Be Prevented?

Many of the diseases that cause fever can be prevented by vaccination*. These include influenza, measles, mumps, rubella (German measles), chickenpox, diphtheria, and typhoid fever. A number of other diseases that cause widespread fever in poorer nations are prevented in the United States by good sanitation systems and access to clean water. Still other diseases, such as colds and strep infections, often can be prevented

* **Reye's syndrome** (RYZE SIN-drome) is a rare and sometimes fatal disease that causes vomiting, confusion, and coma. It occurs mainly in children, usually after a viral infection such as influenza or chickenpox.

* **dehydration** (de-hy-DRAY-shun) is a condition caused by the loss of fluids from the body faster than they can be replaced. Babies, small children, and the elderly may become dehydrated faster than older children and adults.

* **vaccination** (vak-si-NAY-shun) means giving a person a vaccine to protect against a particular disease. A vaccine is a preparation of a weakened or killed germ or of part of the germ's structure. It stimulates the immune system to fight the germ but does not cause infection itself.

by washing the hands properly before eating and, if possible, by avoiding contact with people who already have those infections.

Resource

American College of Emergency Physicians, P.O. Box 619911, Dallas, TX 75261-9911. An organization of physicians that provides information about fever on its website.
http://www.acep.org

Fever Blister *See* Herpes

Fibrocystic Breast Disorder

Fibrocystic (fy-bro-SIS-tik) breast disorder is the general term used to describe noncancerous changes in the breast, such as the formation of fluid-filled sacs called cysts.

When a Breast Lump Is Not Breast Cancer

It is estimated that more than half of all women will experience the breast changes that are known as fibrocystic breast disorder. The symptoms vary from person to person. Some women have no symptoms at all. Others notice a lump that feels like a smooth grape under the skin. These lumps, or cysts, are sometimes painful or tender to the touch.

What Causes Fibrocystic Breast Disorder?

The breast is made up of fatty tissue filled with pockets called lobes, each of which contains many smaller pockets called lobules. After a woman gives birth, these lobules produce milk if she chooses to breast-feed the baby. As a woman goes through her menstrual cycle, the body releases hormones that cause the pockets in the breast to enlarge and hold extra fluid. At the end of the cycle, this swelling disappears, but fluid can sometimes get trapped in these openings. Over time, cysts can form.

Fibrocystic breast disorder usually affects women between the ages of 30 and 50. The lumps often are especially noticeable before and during menstruation. When a woman reaches her 50s or 60s and stops menstruating, her symptoms usually disappear as well.

How Does the Doctor Know It Is Not Cancer?

A doctor will start with a physical examination and mammogram, or x-ray of the breast, because benign* breast lumps often look and feel different from cancerous ones. If the lump turns out to be a cyst, the doctor may use a small needle to drain the fluid. If the fluid is bloody or appears

▶ *See also*
Bacterial Infections
Chickenpox
Cold
Dengue Fever
Diphtheria
German Measles (Rubella)
Heat-Related Injuries
Infection
Influenza
Lassa Fever
Measles
Mumps
Reye's Syndrome
Rheumatic Fever
Rocky Mountain Spotted Fever
Scarlet Fever
Seizures
Strep Throat
Typhoid Fever
Yellow Fever
Viral Infections

KEYWORDS
for searching the Internet and other reference sources

Cysts

Mastalgia

***benign** (be-NINE) means a condition is not cancerous and will probably improve or go away.

unusual in any way, it may be sent to the laboratory for analysis. In most cases, no other treatment is needed.

If the lump is solid, a biopsy (BY-op-see) will be performed. During this procedure, some or all of the tissue is removed and examined under a microscope for the abnormal cell shapes and growth patterns that indicate cancer. Researchers are investigating whether there is a connection between fibrocystic breast disorder and a woman's risk for breast cancer.

Resource

U.S. National Cancer Institute, Building 31, Room 10A03, 31 Center Drive, Bethesda, MD 20892-2580. This U.S. government agency provides information about both noncancerous and cancerous breast changes. Telephone 800-4-CANCER
http://rex.nci.nih.gov

See also
Cyst
Breast Cancer
Tumor

Fibroids *See* Menstrual Disorders

Fibromyalgia

Fibromyalgia (fi-bro-my-AL-ja) is a chronic disorder that causes widespread aching, stiffness, and fatigue in the muscles and joints.*

KEYWORDS
for searching the Internet and other reference sources:

Musculoskeletal system

Rheumatic disorders

* **chronic** (KRON-ik) means long lasting.

* **joints** are places in the body where two bones fit together, usually in such a way as to allow motion.

What Is Fibromyalgia?

Fibromyalgia is a relatively new term for an old disorder. It means pain in the muscles and joints*. The term fibrositis (fi-bro-SY-tis) was once used to describe the same condition. Three to 6 million Americans are thought to be affected by fibromyalgia. It occurs mostly in women aged 50 and older. Fibromyalgia is found throughout the world, among all ethnic groups. It is only rarely seen in children.

What Causes Fibromyalgia?

No one knows what causes fibromyalgia, but there are several theories. One is that fibromyalgia is caused by injury to the central nervous system (the brain and spinal cord), which sends messages to the muscles. A second theory is that biochemical changes in muscle tissue cause fatigue and loss of strength. A third theory suggests that fibromyalgia may be caused by a virus. Some patients with fibromyalgia have psychological problems, but it is unclear whether there is any relationship between the two.

How Do People Know If They Have Fibromyalgia?

Fibromyalgia begins gradually. The main symptom is pain in the muscles and joints. The pain moves around but is most common in the neck, chest, arms, legs, hips, and back. In addition, patients may complain of headaches, tiredness, sleep disorders, digestive disturbances, anxiety, or depression.

Fibromyalgia can be frustrating to diagnose for both the doctor and the patient. The muscles hurt, but they look normal. Blood and x-ray tests are also normal. The symptoms can resemble those of a variety of illnesses, including infections, and the doctor needs to rule out such possibilities. Fibromyalgia also shares similarities with chronic fatigue syndrome. If no other explanation for a patient's symptoms is found, a doctor may diagnose fibromyalgia if the pain keeps coming back, occurs in many different muscles, and has lasted for more than 3 months.

How Is Fibromyalgia Treated?

A doctor who suspects fibromyalgia will reassure the patient that the condition will not harm the muscles. The most effective treatment is a combination of exercise, medication (sometimes including antidepressant medications), physical therapy, and relaxation. Other approaches, such as massage and acupuncture, do not seem to be particularly helpful. There is no known way to prevent the condition.

Living with Fibromyalgia

Fibromyalgia is a chronic disorder, which means that the symptoms may get better or worse but can last for months to years. Many communities have support groups for patients with fibromyalgia.

What Progress Is Being Made in Treating Fibromyalgia?

Because fibromyalgia is a source of serious disability for many people, organizations such as the National Institute of Arthritis and Musculoskeletal and Skin Diseases are sponsoring research to help diagnose, treat, and prevent it. For example, researchers are studying how structures of the brain are involved in the painful symptoms of fibromyalgia. They are also using sophisticated imaging technologies to study how the muscles perform.

Resources

Book

McIlwain, Harris H., and Debra Fulghum Bruce. *The Fibromyalgia Handbook*. New York: Owl Books, 1996.

Organizations

American College of Rheumatology, 1800 Century Place, Suite 250, Atlanta, GA 30345.
http://www.rheumatology.org

Arthritis Foundation, 1330 West Peachtree Street, Atlanta, GA 30309.
http://www.arthritis.org

▶ *See also*
Arthritis
Chronic Fatigue Syndrome

Flat Feet

Flat feet are feet whose inner arches are flat, and whose soles completely touch the ground when the person is standing.

KEYWORDS
for searching the Internet and other reference sources

Orthotics

Pes planus

Pes valgus

Podiatry

What Are Flat Feet?

Flat feet can happen at any age, and babies are born with them. Babies have fatty pads in the soles of the foot and in front of the heel, which fills the arch and gives feet their flat appearance. By age 3 years, when they are walking properly, their feet no longer have a flat look. From ages 3 to 6 years, the muscles of the foot become stronger, the fat disappears, and an arch develops. If the arches have not appeared by about age 5 or 6—as happens with approximately one in every 10 children—a child is likely to have flat feet through adulthood.

If the soles of a person's shoes are worn out on the inside edge, that person probably has flat feet. People may have flat feet but still have good muscle tone and no pain. If feet are extremely flat, a doctor may recommend orthotics (arch supports) in a firm shoe to enable the person to walk without foot strain.

What Makes Feet Flat?

For some people, flat feet are the result of congenital bone malformation, evident if the doctor takes x-rays. For others, flat feet develop later. Each day as people walk, they take 8,000 to 10,000 steps on pavement, floor, tile, and other surfaces. With each step a person takes, gravity-induced pressure puts three to four times the body's weight on each foot. Over the years, the imbalance on the muscles of the feet may cause a disorder in the natural arch. Excessive weight or pounding stress may cause the longitudinal (lonj-i-TOO-di-nal) arch (which runs the length of the foot) or the metatarsal (met-a-TAR-sal) arch (which runs perpendicular to the longitudinal arch, from one side of the foot to the other) to fall, or flatten.

Other causes of flat feet are shoes that do not fit well, obesity, rickets, and metabolic disorders that may cause the arch muscles to weaken. In older adults, decreased exercise and increased weight can cause mechanical disturbances in the foot.

What's Bad About Flat Feet?

Flat feet in themselves are not a problem. But running on flat feet is almost like running on gelatin. Flat feet turn inward (overpronation*), causing legs to turn inward, and contribute to such "overuse" injuries as shin splints and back problems. Flat feet also can produce heel spurs*. If pain develops as a result of any of these conditions, flat feet and the problems they cause need treatment.

* **pronation** is the rotation of the foot inward and downward so that, in walking, the foot comes down on its inner edge.

* **heel spur** is a bony growth under the heel that causes pain when a person walks.

Correcting Flat Feet

Reducing pronation can help to prevent further problems. Experts recommend:

- Buying shoes with arch support.
- Buying shoes that are motion controlled, or stability shoes with a medial post.
- Avoiding shoes with lots of cushioning and little support.
- Avoiding uneven running surfaces like golf courses and trails.

Surgery is rarely recommended for flat feet alone.

Resources

Book

Tremaine, M. David, M.D., and Elias M. Awad, Ph.D. *The Foot and Ankle Sourcebook: Everything You Need to Know*. Lowell House, 1998.

Organization

American Podiatric Medical Association, 2 Chevy Chase Circle NW, Washington, DC 20005. The APMA's website features information about bunions and other disorders affecting the feet.
http://www.apma.org

Flat-Footed Slang

In American slang, the term "flat-footed" is sometimes used to describe:

- A comment that is blunt and insensitive.
- Writing that is plodding and unimaginative.
- A police officer who "pounds the pavement" or "walks a beat."

During World War II, young men who had flat feet were disqualified from military service because it was believed they could never make it in the infantry.

▶ *See also*
Bunions

Flu *See* **Influenza**

Food Poisoning

Food poisoning results from eating foods that contain bacteria or their toxic byproducts. This can happen when foods have not been properly stored or prepared. Food poisoning also can result from eating poisonous plants or animals.

KEYWORDS
for searching the Internet and other reference sources

Bacterial infections

Botulism

Digestion

E. coli

Gastroenteritis

Salmonella

Staphylococcus

Robin's Story

Robin and her friends squeezed every pleasure they could into the early days of September, milking summer vacation for all it was worth. The make-your-own-sundae party at Robin's was the best time they had all summer. But within a day or two of the party, Robin and her friends all were suffering from diarrhea, fever, stomach cramps, and had vomited more times than they had ever imagined possible. Why? Robin and her friends were among the nearly quarter million Americans who became ill after eating ice cream that fall. The culprit? *Salmonella enteritidis* bacteria. Unseen, odorless, and tasteless, the microscopic creatures poisoned the ice cream ingredients on the truck ride to the ice cream factory. The reason? The truck had not been cleaned from its previous load: unpasteurized raw eggs, a prime breeding ground for Salmonella.

What Is Food Poisoning?

Food poisoning is caused by eating harmful bacteria or the poisons they produce. These bacteria live in soil, raw meat, raw milk products, pets, bugs, rodents, and on unwashed hands and food-related equipment. Food becomes contaminated when food handling, preparation, or equipment is unsanitary. The most common sources are unrefrigerated, perishable* food; raw or undercooked foods; or preserved foods that were not cooked at high enough temperatures.

* **perishable** means able to spoil or decay, as in perishable foods.

Although the food in the United States is among the most clean and safe in the world, outbreaks of food poisoning kill about 9,000 people a year and cause between 6.5 and 33 million illnesses each year. Food poisoning is not contagious like chickenpox, but an infected person can pass along the infection by hand-to-hand contact (for example, serving food).

How Does It Happen?

Food poisoning occurs when bacteria or their toxic products are present in the foods we eat. They usually cause inflammation in the intestines, and the body does everything it can to get rid of them.

How Do People Know If They Have Food Poisoning?

People with mild cases of food poisoning may have diarrhea, fever, vomiting, and stomach pains. The first signs of food poisoning can appear as

Avoiding Food Poisoning

- Bacteria need time to grow, so do not eat perishable foods that have been out of the refrigerator for more than 2 hours.
- Do not eat raw or undercooked eggs, poultry or meat.
- Meat and poultry should be well cooked, not pink in the middle.
- Do not eat raw or unpasteurized dairy products.
- Wash fruits and vegetables before eating.
- Wash all plates, cutting boards, counters, and utensils that have come into contact with raw meats or poultry thoroughly before using them for something else.
- Wash hands thoroughly between handling raw meat and other items.
- Wash hands thoroughly after using the bathroom.
- Wash hands thoroughly after having any contact with animals and reptiles (which sometimes carry bacteria on their skin).
- Make sure the refrigerator temperature is kept between 34 and 40 degrees Fahrenheit.

80 Years Ago: A Kansas Cannery

Poisoning that results from eating food contaminated by *Clostridium botulinum* bacteria is called "botulism." The word "botulism" is derived from the Latin word "botulus," which means sausage.

Originally, scientists believed that the botulinum toxin could only be produced in the presence of animal protein, as found in sausage. In 1919, however, a botulism outbreak was traced to canned vegetables from a commercial cannery in Kansas. That same year, another botulism scare involved canned olives. Both incidents prompted stricter regulatory control of food processing technology.

early as 1 hour after eating or up to 3 days later. These symptoms may occur in others who ate the same food.

Diagnosis

Doctors diagnose food poisoning by asking about symptoms; conducting laboratory "stool cultures," which test for the presence of specific bacteria; and having food samples analyzed. Outbreaks may be investigated by the local or state department of health.

How Is Food Poisoning Treated?

Food poisoning lasts for 1 to 7 days and usually does not require hospitalization. Hospitalization is necessary for serious cases of certain types of food poisoning or when the diarrhea or vomiting has caused dehydration*. To treat dehydration, the doctor may give a person fluids intravenously, that is, directly into the veins. People also might be hospitalized if the infection spreads from the intestines to the rest of body. In some cases, doctors will give them antibiotics to fight the infection.

▲

Federal, state, and local governments all enforce strict rules for food-related businesses. Food handlers, for example, are required to wear gloves to prevent food contamination. © *Jeff Greenberg/Photo Researchers, Inc.*

* **dehydration** (dee-hy-DRAY-shun) is loss of fluid from the body.

Prevention

Following three basic guidelines will help prevent food poisoning:

1. Do not eat perishable foods that have been at room temperature for more than 2 hours.
2. Wash hands and utensils before and after handling any food, after using the bathroom and after handling raw meat, poultry, or eggs.
3. Cook food thoroughly, and do not eat marinade from raw meat or poultry until it has been thoroughly boiled.

But even when individuals keep themselves and their food clean, contamination may have happened long before it comes into people's kitchens, as with Robin's ice cream. Food processors, growers, and distributors also need to take steps to keep food safe (for example, clean processing plants and safe and sanitary storage of food). The U.S. Department of Agriculture, the Food and Drug Administration, and local state and city Departments of Health have strict rules for these businesses that are carefully enforced.

Resource

The U.S. Food and Drug Administration publishes a *Bad Bug Book* with fact sheets about many different foodborne toxins. http://vm.cfan.fda.gov/~mow/intro.html

▶ *See also*
Bacterial Infections
Botulism

Frostbite *See* Cold-Related Injuries

Fungal Infections

Fungi are organisms that can grow in or on the body, causing infections of internal organs or of the skin, nails, and hair.

KEYWORD
for searching the Internet or other reference sources

Mycology

Bread mold and mushrooms are among the most familiar examples of fungi (FUN-ji), organisms that grow in an irregular mass without roots, stems, or leaves. Fungi feed on other organisms, living or dead, and play an important role in helping dead plants and animals decay. Of the thousands of species of fungi, a few can cause human disease.

These fungi cause a wide range of illnesses, from minor skin conditions to life-threatening diseases. They produce two kinds of infections: systemic and superficial. Systemic infections affect internal organs. They often start in the lungs, but in severe cases may spread to the blood, heart, brain, kidneys, liver, or other parts of the body. Superficial infections affect the surface of the body, the skin, the nails, and the hair. They most often occur in moist areas, such as between the toes, in the crotch, or in the mouth.

What Are Superficial Fungal Infections?

Superficial fungal infections attack tissues on the surface of the body, which include the skin, nails, or hair. Some common examples are ringworm, athlete's foot, jock itch, and yeast infections. Candida yeast* infections are usually found on the skin, in the mouth, in the vagina, on the head of the penis, or around the nails. Superficial fungal infections are somewhat contagious and pass from person to person through direct contact or, less commonly, through clothes or contact with surfaces of other objects in the environment.

* **yeast** (YEEST) is a type of fungus.

What Are the Signs and Symptoms of Superficial Fungal Infections?

Although the symptoms produced by infection with different types of fungi varies, these infections generally cause itching, reddened skin, and inflammation. Some superficial skin infections are mild and produce few or no symptoms. Others are more irritating. Superficial fungal infections are rarely life threatening, but they may cause considerable discomfort or embarrassment.

How Do Doctors Diagnose and Treat Superficial Fungal Infections?

Skin infections Superficial fungal infections are often diagnosed on the basis of their appearance and their location on the body. Most skin infections respond well to topical antifungal creams, some of which are available over the counter, which means they do not require a doctor's prescription. Other skin infections, however, do not respond to such treatment. They require a doctor's attention and systemic treatment with prescription antifungal medications.

Candidiasis Candida yeast infections are diagnosed by staining specimens of sputum or urine, or scrapings from the skin or the lining of the mouth or vagina, and by examining them under a microscope. People with vaginal yeast infections can be effectively treated with medications. Occasionally, repeated courses of treatment may be required.

How Do People Prevent Superficial Fungal Infections?

Preventing superficial fungal infections is difficult because people are continually exposed to fungi. Keeping the skin dry and clean is probably helpful.

What Are Systemic Fungal Infections?

Some fungi are normally present in the body, kept under control by the body's immune system. If the immune system is abnormally weak, however, the fungi can grow out of control and cause illnesses. These are termed opportunistic infections. Among the most common opportunistic fungal infections that affect people are:

- candidiasis
- aspergillosis
- phycomycosis
- cryptococcosis

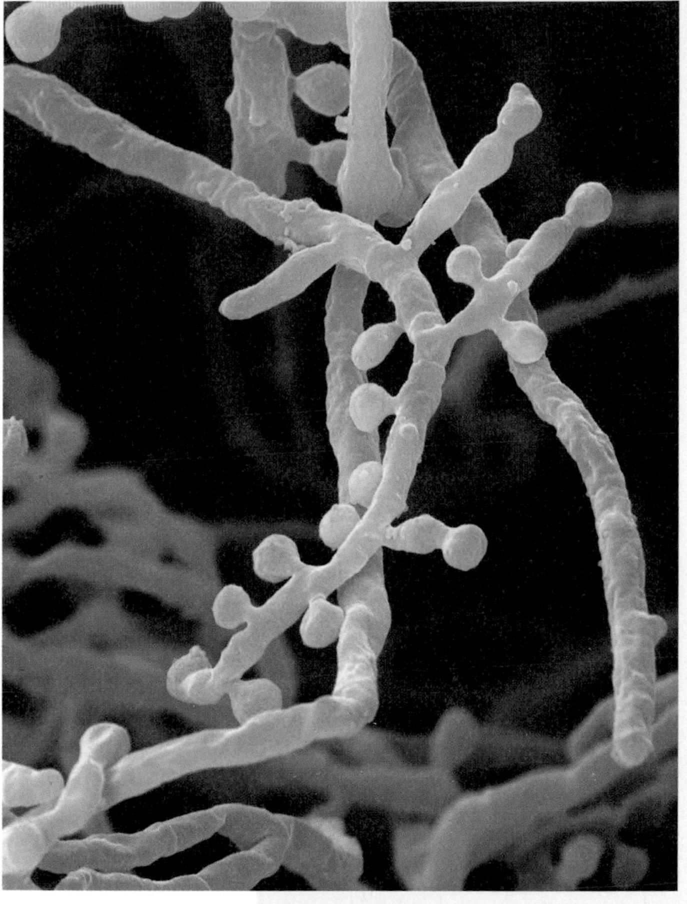

▲

The *Trichophyton* fungus, photographed under an electron microscope at more than 4,000 times its original size, causes ringworm of the scalp (tinea capitis). The fungus is reproducing by flowering. © *Oliver Meckes/Photo Researchers, Inc.*

People with AIDS (acquired immune deficiency syndrome), people with leukemia (cancer of the blood cells), and people with Hodgkin's disease or other kinds of lymphoma (cancer of the immune system) are at risk for opportunistic fungal infections because their immune systems have been weakened. Such infections may also occur in people who are receiving radiation therapy or chemotherapy, or who are taking corticosteroids* or immunosuppressants* drugs, such as the drugs a person takes after an organ transplant.

People who have received prolonged courses of antibiotics for treatment of serious bacterial infections are also at risk for fungal infections.

Other fungi cause illnesses even in otherwise healthy people with normal immune systems. In these cases, people inhale the spores (immature form) of fungi that normally live in the environment, especially the soil, in certain geographical areas. Examples include:

* **corticosteroid** (kor-ti-ko-STEER-oids) are medications that are prescribed to reduce inflammation and sometimes to suppress the body's immune responses.

* **immunosuppressants** (im-yoo-no-su-PRES-ants) are substances that weaken the body's immune system.

- Histoplasmosis (his-to-plaz-MO-sis) occurs in the United States in the east and midwest, in Mexico, and in Central America. The fungus that causes it often grows on chicken droppings and bat guano.
- Coccidioidomycosis (kok-sid-e-oi-do-my-KO-sis), or Valley fever, is found in the southwestern United States.
- North American blastomycosis (blas-to-my-KO-sis) is found throughout North America, and outbreaks recently have been reported in Africa as well.
- South American blastomycosis, which is caused by a different fungus, is seen in South and Central America.

What Are the Symptoms of Systemic Fungal Infections?

* **chronic** (KRON-ik) means continuing for a long period of time.

Systemic fungal infections often are chronic* and develop slowly, taking weeks or months to become a problem. Symptoms are sometimes similar to those of the common cold, but sometimes, especially in people with weakened immune systems, symptoms may be sudden and severe, requiring hospitalization. Symptoms may include cough, fever, chills, night sweats, anorexia (loss of appetite), weight loss, general fatigue, and depression.

If the infection spreads from the lungs to other organs, it may be particularly severe, especially if the patient has a weakened immune system. For example, cryptococcosis (krip-to-ko-KO-sis) may lead to meningitis (men-in-JY-tis), which causes inflammation and swelling of the lining around the brain and spinal cord.

How Do Doctors Diagnose and Treat Systemic Fungal Infections?

Diagnosis Diagnosing and treating systemic fungal infections can be a challenge for a doctor. Many of the symptoms are mild and vary greatly from person to person. Blood or skin tests exist for only a few of these infections and often are inconclusive or fail to find a fungus that really is there, a result called a false negative. Chest x-rays may show abnormalities in the lungs as fuzzy white spots on the black x-ray film, but the spots do not identify the specific cause.

A diagnosis of systemic fungal infection usually is confirmed when a fungus is cultured, or grown, in a laboratory dish from a sample of the patient's sputum, bone marrow, urine, blood, cerebrospinal (ser-e-bro-SPY-nel) fluid, or other tissue.

Treatment Treatment varies, depending on which fungus is causing the condition and how severe the symptoms are. Doctors usually prescribe antifungal medications, with drug therapy sometimes continuing for several weeks. In some cases, particularly if the immune system is weak, drug treatment may fail, or the doctor may recommend surgery to remove infected tissues.

Resources

The U.S. National Institutes of Health has a search engine at its website that locates information about fungal infections and mycology, which is the scientific study of fungi.
http://www.nih.gov

The U.S. National Eye Institute posts a fact sheet at its website about how the fungal infection histoplasmosis affects vision.
http://www.nei.nih.gov/TextSite/publications/histo.htm

See also
Athlete's Foot
Immunodeficiency
Ringworm
Yeast Infection, Vaginal

G

G

Gallstones

Gallstones are crystal-like particles that form in the gallbladder when certain substances separate out of bile. Gallstones can vary dramatically in size and the degree to which they cause problems.

KEYWORDS
for searching the Internet and other reference sources

Bile duct

Bilirubin

Cholesterol

Gallbladder

What Does the Gallbladder Do?

The gallbladder is a small pear-shaped organ that sits under the liver on the right side of the abdomen. The gallbladder concentrates and stores a greenish-brown liquid called bile that is made by the liver. When a person eats food, the gallbladder contracts and sends bile into the small intestine through tubes called bile ducts, where it helps break down fats in the food.

Bile has a number of ingredients, including water and bile salts. Bile salts act like detergent and help dissolve globules of fat. Bile also contains cholesterol, fats, and bilirubin (which is a waste product secreted by the liver, formed by the breakdown of red blood cells).

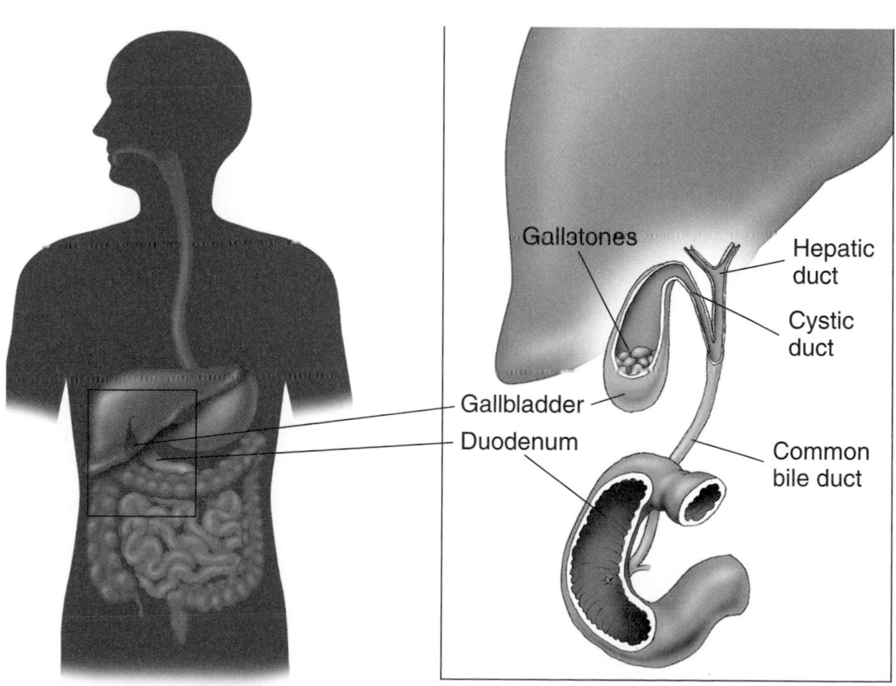

The gallbladder sits under the liver on the right side of the abdomen near the pancreas. When gallstones are formed, they can block the bile ducts, leading to pain and damage to the gallbladder, liver, and pancreas.

What Are Gallstones?

Gallstones are pieces of solidified bile. The components of bile usually remain dissolved, but when something goes wrong that upsets the normal chemical balance, gallstones can form. There are two main types of stones: cholesterol stones (which account for about 80 percent of gallstones in the United States) and pigment stones, which form from bilirubin and calcium.

Gallstones can form when bile contains more cholesterol (or bilirubin and calcium) than the bile salts can dissolve, when a chemical imbalance causes them to crystallize, and when the gallbladder does not contract enough to empty itself of bile on a regular basis. Gallstones can range in size from gravel-like particles to golf ball–sized spheres. Some people have single stones whereas others develop many stones.

Who Is at Risk for Gallstones?

One in every 10 people in the United States, or about 20 million people, have gallstones. Gallstones are rare in children and adolescents, although anyone can get them.

Cholesterol Diets high in cholesterol seem to be linked to gallstones, although some researchers believe that a high cholesterol diet must be accompanied by a genetic predisposition* toward gallstones. Anything that increases the cholesterol level in bile—including pregnancy, hormone therapy, and birth control pills—can increase a person's susceptibility to getting cholesterol stones.

* **genetic predisposition** is a tendency to get a certain disease that is inherited from a person's parents.

Obesity and other health conditions Obese people also have a higher risk of gallstones, as do people who are fasting or on fad diets, who may develop stones because lack of food means that the bile sits in the gallbladder for a long time. People with liver diseases, infections of the bile ducts, and blood cell disorders (such as sickle cell anemia) also are prone to developing pigment stones.

Other populations Other groups of people who seem to be at higher risk of developing gallstones include:

- women, especially those who have had several children, are two to three times more likely than men to develop gallstones
- people of Native American or Mexican ancestry
- people who are older than age 60.

What Happens When People Have Gallstones?

Most gallstones do not cause symptoms; only one in five people with gallstones experiences problems.

Symptoms Symptoms usually are felt after a meal, when the gallbladder contracts to secrete bile. If a stone is sent into the bile duct, a person will feel cramping pain in the abdomen that may also be felt in the shoulder and back. Some people experience nausea and vomiting, and some develop jaundice (yellow skin and eyes). Gallstones can block the bile ducts, and this can lead to damage of the gallbladder, liver, and pancreas*.

*pancreas (PAN-kree-us) is a large gland that secretes digestive enzymes and the hormones insulin and glucagon.

Diagnosis Gallstones usually are diagnosed only if they are causing problems. To look for gallstones, doctors may use x-rays and ultrasound, a painless procedure in which sound waves passing through the body create images on a computer screen.

Treatment The standard treatment for gallstones, and the only one guaranteed to cure gallstones permanently, is surgical removal of the gallbladder, usually through laparoscopic surgery (surgery performed through tubes that are inserted into the abdomen through small incisions). More than 500,000 of these operations are done every year in the United States. If a person cannot have laparoscopic surgery, the gallbladder can be removed through an open incision 5 to 8 inches long in the abdomen.

People who cannot have surgery, or do not want to have surgery, can take medication to help dissolve gallstones, or they may undergo lithotripsy (LITH-o-trip-see). In this procedure, shock waves are passed through the skin to shatter the stone into tiny particles that may be able to pass out of the gallbladder on their own.

Resource

U.S. National Digestive Diseases Information Clearinghouse, 2 Information Way, Bethesda, MD 20892-3570. The NDDIC publishes a brochure about gallstones and posts a fact sheet at its website.
http://www.niddk.nih.gov/health/digest/pubs/gallstns/gallstns.htm
http://www.healthtouch.com/level1/leaflets/nddic/nddic080.htm

See also
Eating Disorders
Jaundice
Obesity
Pancreatitis
Pregnancy, Complications of
Sickle Cell Anemia

Gangrene

Gangrene (gang-GREEN) is a condition that leads to the death of living tissue. It is caused by blocked blood flow or by bacterial infection.

KEYWORDS
for searching the Internet and other reference sources

Arteriosclerosis

Bacterial infections

Debridement

Frostbite

Hyperbaric chamber

What Is Gangrene?

Gangrene is a condition in which living tissue (skin, muscle, or bone) dies and decays. Gangrene most often affects the legs, feet, arms, and fingers, but it also can affect internal organs such as the intestine or gallbladder. Gangrene can occur when blood flow to an area of the body is blocked or when certain types of bacteria* invade a wound.

*bacteria are round, spiral, or rod-shaped single-celled microorganisms without a distinct nucleus that commonly multiply by cell division. Some types may cause disease in humans, animals, or plants.

Dry gangrene Dry gangrene can occur when blood flow to a part of the body is blocked. When tissues in the body are deprived of the nutrients and oxygen carried by blood, they begin to die. Dry gangrene

MILITARY MEDICINE

U.S. CIVIL WAR (1861–1865)

The biggest killer in the U.S. Civil War was not instant death by bullet or by cannonball: it was disease resulting from wounds. An estimated 388,500 men died from wounds and other illnesses, including gangrene. Doctors with dirty hands unknowingly infected wounds with gangrene-causing bacteria while trying to treat the injured soldiers.

During this war, doctors noticed that the wounds of some of the soldiers were infested with maggots, which are the larvae of houseflies or blowflies. Those maggot-infested wounds tended to heal faster than those without maggots, because the maggots were eating the dead or decaying tissue that resulted from gangrene infection. Thus, the maggots were cleaning out the dead and decaying tissue, allowing the remaining tissue to heal. They were doing the work that surgeons do today to treat gangrene through debridement of wounds.

WORLD WAR I (1914–1918)

During World War I, 15,000 miles of trenches stretched along the western front in Europe. Troops who spent many weeks in these cold, wet trenches often developed swollen limbs, damaged sensory nerves, and inflammation, a condition that they called "trench foot."

Trench foot often resulted in gangrene, loss of tissue, and sometimes in loss of limbs to amputations. Physicians and military officers responded to the problem by instituting strict standards of hygiene that became part of the military's ongoing preventive health regimen.

Amputation saws for treating gangrene infections were part of the military doctor's field equipment. © *John Watney/Photo Researchers, Inc.*

can result from injury or frostbite*, but it most commonly is a complication of diabetes. Diabetes can lead to hardening of the arteries (arteriosclerosis), which restricts blood flow. This is especially common in the legs and feet.

Dry gangrene usually starts in the toes. A person might first feel numbness or tingling in the feet. As gangrene progresses and tissue starts to die, the person will experience severe pain in the affected area. Eventually, the tissue turns black, marking where tissue has died. This type of gangrene needs to be treated promptly, but it is usually not life threatening.

* **frostbite** is damage to tissues as the result of exposure to low environmental temperatures. It is also called congelation (kon-je-LAY-shun).

Wet gangrene Wet gangrene occurs when certain types of bacteria invade an injured area of the body. It occurs most often after an injury in which a body part was crushed or when blood flow was obstructed by a blood clot or a tight bandage. The lack of blood flow causes some cells to die and leak fluid, which moistens the surrounding tissue. The moist environment allows bacteria, such as *Streptococci* (strep-to-KOK-sy) and *Staphylococci* (staf-i-lo-KOK-sy), to invade the wound and multiply. Wet gangrene causes swollen and blistered skin, and it has a foul odor. Once wet gangrene sets in, it spreads quickly to surrounding tissue. If left untreated, it can kill a person in a few days.

Gas gangrene Gas gangrene is a type of wet gangrene that usually is caused by the bacterium called *Clostridium* (klo-STRID-e-um). This type of bacteria requires very little oxygen to live, and it releases gases and toxins as waste products. Gas gangrene causes a high fever, brown pus*, and gas bubbles on the skin.

* **pus** is a thick, creamy fluid, usually yellow or greenish in color, that forms at the site of an infection.

How Is Gangrene Treated?

When a person has diabetes, frostbite, or an injury, preventing gangrene is a high priority. Taking medications, maintaining good blood circulation, avoiding foot injuries, and not smoking are essential for preventing dry gangrene in people with diabetes. Prompt cleaning of wounds to avoid bacterial infection can prevent wet gangrene.

If a person develops gangrene, dead tissue needs to be surgically removed before healing can begin (a process called debridement). Doctors try to improve circulation to the affected part of the body and surgeons remove dead tissue. Because bacterial forms of gangrene can spread quickly, part or all of the affected limb might require amputation.* People with wet gangrene also are treated with antibiotics.* Sometimes, people with gangrene are treated in a hyperbaric chamber. This procedure exposes the body to oxygen at high pressure, which promotes healing of the gangrenous tissue.

* **amputation** (am-pu-TAY-shun) is the removal of a limb or other appendage or outgrowth of the body.

* **antibiotics** (an-ti-bi-OT-iks) are drugs that kill or slow the growth of bacteria.

▶ *See also*
Bacterial Infections
Cold-related Injuries
Diabetes

Gastroenteritis

Gastroenteritis (gas-tro-en-ter-I-tis) is a disease in which the lining of the stomach and intestines becomes inflamed, resulting in what is sometimes referred to as an upset stomach or "stomach flu."

KEYWORDS
for searching the Internet and other reference sources

Gastrointestinal system

Food poisoning

Infection

Inflammation

What Is Gastroenteritis?

Gastroenteritis is a general term for inflammation* of the gastrointestinal (gas-tro-in-TES-ti-nal) tract, the part of the digestive system consisting of the stomach, small intestine, and large intestine. Loss of appetite, vomiting, cramps, nausea*, and diarrhea* are the most common symptoms of gastroenteritis. In the United States, gastroenteritis usually is a mild disease. In countries where water supplies are dirty, sewage treatment is poor, or medical facilities are scarce, it sometimes leads to death.

* **inflammation** (in-fla-MAY-shun) is the body's reaction to irritation, infection, or injury that often involves swelling, pain, redness, and warmth.

* **nausea** (NAW-zha) refers to a feeling of being sick to one's stomach or needing to vomit.

* **diarrhea** (di-ah-RE-a) refers to frequent, watery stools (bowel movements).

What Causes Gastroenteritis?

There are many different causes of gastroenteritis. Viral infections are the most common cause in the United States. Certain bacteria and parasites that can get into food or water supplies also can lead to the disease. In addition, gastroenteritis can result from food allergies or sensitivities, side effects of certain medications, and alcohol or toxic (poisonous) substances.

How Is Gastroenteritis Treated?

Mild gastroenteritis usually lasts just two or three days. Often, the only treatment needed is rest and drinking lots of clear fluids. However, gastroenteritis can be serious if vomiting and diarrhea cause dehydration (de-hy-DRAY-shun), a condition that results when a person loses fluid and body salts faster than they can be replaced by drinking. If a person becomes dehydrated, hospitalization may be needed to deliver intravenous (in-tra-VEE-nus) fluid replacement therapy. Intravenous (IV) therapy replaces lost fluid by dripping liquids and salts directly into the bloodstream through a small needle inserted into a vein.

How Can Gastroenteritis Be Prevented?

Washing the hands thoroughly after using the toilet, and before handling food, and before eating are important ways to prevent infectious gastroenteritis. Preparing and storing food properly also are important. For travelers who plan to visit developing countries, vaccines* are available against some of the diseases that cause gastroenteritis.

* **vaccines** (vak-SEENZ) are preparations of a weakened or killed germ or of part of the germ's structure. A vaccine stimulates the immune system to fight the germ but does not cause severe infection.

Resource

U.S. Centers for Disease Control and Prevention (CDC), 1600 Clifton Road, Atlanta, GA 30333. This U.S. government agency posts a fact sheet about viral gastroenteritis at its website.
Telephone 800-311-3435
http://www.cdc.gov

▶ *See also*
Diarrhea
Food Poisoning
Viral Infections

Genetic Diseases

Genetic diseases are disorders that are inherited by a person from his or her parents or are related to some type of spontaneous genetic change.

KEYWORDS
for searching the Internet and other reference sources

Birth defects

Gene therapy

Genetic counseling

Genetics

Hereditary diseases

Human genome

Prenatal diagnosis

What Is Heredity?

Every person develops under the influence of a mix of genes inherited from his or her mother and father. These genes, or small parts of chromosomes, determine the architecture and activity of the entire body. They determine visible characteristics, such as eye color, skin color, and height, as well as traits that cannot be seen, such as the likelihood of certain diseases, the chemicals made by the body, and the functioning of body systems.

Normally, each cell in the body contains two copies of each gene: one that originally came from the egg of the mother and one from the sperm of the father. In many instances, these two copies are slightly different from each other. The result is a child who has some characteristics from the mother and some from the father, but who is never identical to either parent.

Because there are two copies, a gene that works normally usually can make up for one that has a defect. For example, a gene with a defect that causes a particular disease may be passed through generations of a family without causing illness. That is because the normal gene in the pair may work well enough to mask the defect. However, if a child inherits two genes with the defect, the child will develop the illness. This explains how a child with the disease can be born to parents without it.

What Causes Genetic Diseases?

Genetic disorders can be inherited, in which case people are born with them, even if they are not noticeable at first. Some disorders, however, are not inherited but develop spontaneously when disease-causing mutations* occur during cell division*. These also are genetic disorders, because they involve changes in the genes.

Some inherited genetic disorders, such as cystic fibrosis* and phenylketonuria* (PKU), are caused simply by the inheritance of genes that do not work properly. In other disorders, however, genetic and environmental factors seem to work together to cause changes in otherwise normal genes. For example, some forms of radiation or chemicals can cause cancer in people who are prone to be affected because of their genetic makeup.

How Are Diseases Inherited?

The beginning of modern genetics Gregor Mendel (1822–1884) is considered the father of modern genetics*. Mendel was an Austrian monk. While growing peas in the monastery garden, Mendel noted that certain traits appeared in offspring in predictable patterns, and he began to understand the basic rules of inheritance. These rules are called Mendelian (men-DEL-ee-an) law.

* **mutations** (mu-TAY-shuns) are changes in a chromosome or a gene.

* **cell division** is the process by which a cell divides to form two daughter cells, each of which contains the same genetic material as the original cell.

* **cystic fibrosis** (SIS-tik fi-BRO-sis) is a genetic disorder of the body's mucus-producing glands. It mainly affects the respiratory and digestive systems of children and young adults.

* **phenylketonuria** (fen-ul-ke-ton-U-ree-a), or PKU for short, is a genetic disorder of body chemistry that, if left untreated, causes mental retardation.

* **genetics** is the branch of science that deals with heredity and the ways in which genes control the development and maintenance of organisms.

A Genetic Glossary

- **Cells:** The units that comprise living beings. The human body is made of about 60 trillion cells.
- **Nucleus:** A membrane-bound structure inside cells that contains DNA.
- **Chromosomes:** DNA is packaged into units called chromosomes. Humans have 23 pairs of chromosomes, for a total of 46.
- **DNA (deoxyribonucleic acid):** A double-stranded molecule, made of chemical bases called nucleotides, that contains the genetic code necessary to build a living being.
- **Genes:** Segments of DNA located on the chromosomes. Genes are the units of heredity. They help determine a person's characteristics, from eye color to how various chemicals work in the body.
- **Genome:** An animal's entire collection of genes. The human genome contains 50,000 to 100,000 genes.

Under Mendelian law, a dominant (DOM-i-nant) trait is one that appears even when the second copy of the gene for that trait is different. For example, for the seeds of Mendel's peas, "smooth" is dominant over "wrinkled." Thus, if a pea plant contains one gene for smooth and one for wrinkled, the seed will be smooth. Wrinkled is a recessive (re-SES-iv) trait, which is one that only appears when two copies of it are present.

Dominant and recessive genes Normally, each person has two copies of every gene, one from the mother and one from the father. A physical feature or a disorder carried by genes can be either a dominant (**G**) or a recessive (**g**) trait. If the affected gene is dominant, a person with one or two copies of the gene will have the disorder. Therefore, a person with the patterns (**GG**) or (**Gg**) will be affected, but (**gg**) will not be affected by the disorder. Two copies of a dominant gene produce a much more serious form of the disorder.

If the affected gene is recessive, only a person with two copies of the gene will have the disorder. Therefore, a person with the pattern (**gg**) will be affected, but (**GG**) and (**Gg**) will not be affected by the disorder.

Autosomal and sex-linked traits Of the 23 pairs of chromosomes in human cells, 22 are autosomes (AW-to-somes), or non-sex chromosomes. The other pair contains the two sex chromosomes, which determine a person's gender. Females have two X chromosomes (**XX**), and males have one X and one Y chromosome (**XY**). The reproductive cells, or eggs and sperm, each have only one set of 23 chromosomes. While an egg always carries an X chromosome, a sperm cell can carry either an X or a Y, so it is the sperm that determines gender.

Inherited genetic disorders that are carried on the sex chromosomes are referred to as sex-linked. Disorders carried on the other chromosomes are referred to as autosomal (aw-to-SOME-al). In general, autosomal disorders are likely to affect males and females equally, but sex-linked disorders usually affect males more often than females. This gender difference has to do with the fact that males have only one X chromosome. The X chromosome

DNA is a double-stranded molecule that is twisted in a spiral shape, known as a double helix. DNA is made of chemicals called nucleotides that occur in pairs: adenine (A) with thymine (T), and guanine (G) with cytosine (C). ▼

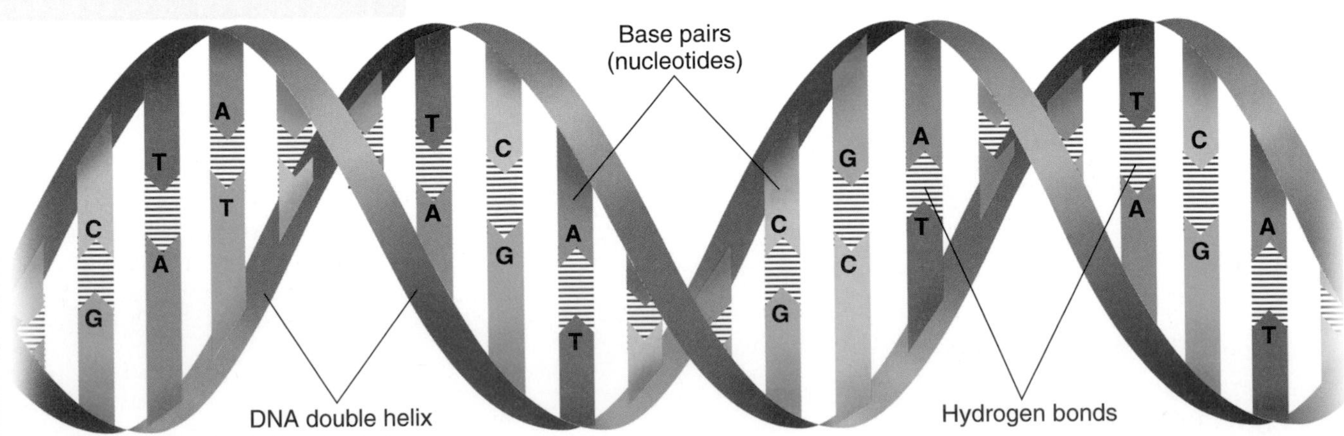

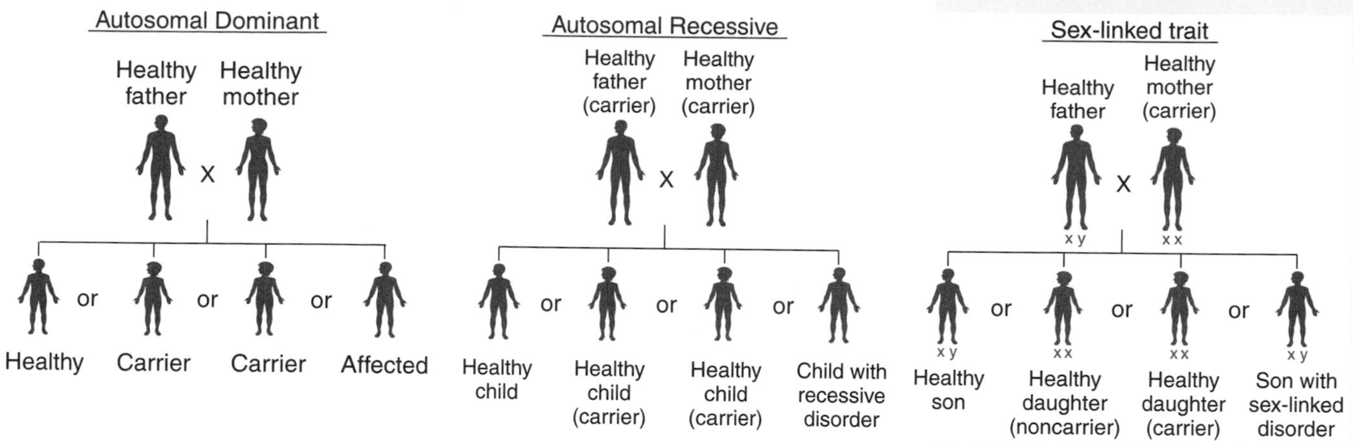

▲ Three common inheritance patterns.

carries genes for which there is no second copy on the Y. Therefore, a male has only one copy of these genes. If his copy is damaged or defective, he has no normal copy to override or mask the defective one. Depending on the problem with the gene, the result can be an X-linked disorder.

What Are the Common Inheritance Patterns of Genetic Diseases?

Single-gene autosomal diseases Most genetic disorders are caused by defective genes on the autosomes. If an autosomal genetic disorder is caused by a problem with a single gene, then the following rules of inheritance usually apply. There are exceptions to these rules, but they are useful guidelines for understanding inheritance. In an autosomal dominant disorder:

- It takes only one copy of the gene to cause the disorder. So if a child inherits the disease, at least one of the parents has the disease as well.
- It is possible for the gene to change by itself in the affected person. This change is called a mutation.
- Unaffected children of a parent with the disorder have unaffected children and grandchildren.

In an autosomal recessive disorder:

- If two people without the disorder have a child with the disorder, both parents carry one copy of the abnormal gene.
- If a person with the disorder and a carrier* have a child, there is a fifty-fifty chance that the child will have the disorder. Any child without the disorder will be a carrier.
- If a person with the disorder and a noncarrier have children, all of the children will be carriers but will not have the disorder.
- If two people with the disorder have children, all of the children will have the disorder.

* **carrier** is a person who has one copy of the defective gene for a recessive disorder. Carriers are not affected by the disorder, but they can pass on the defective gene to their children.

Single-gene sex-linked diseases More than 150 disease traits are carried on the X chromosome. X-linked dominant disorders are rare. In an X-linked recessive disorder:

- Nearly all people with sex-linked disorders are male. The disorder is transmitted through the female, because a son's X chromosome always comes from his mother. She is unaffected, however, because she has a second X chromosome which usually contains a normal gene for the trait.
- A male with the disorder never transmits it to his sons, because a father passes his X chromosome only to his daughters.
- A son born to a female carrier has a fifty-fifty chance of having the disorder.
- All daughters of an affected male will be carriers.

Multiple-gene diseases Many disorders are exceptions to the Mendelian laws of inheritance. Genetic disorders caused by a combination of many genes are called multifactorial (mul-tee-fak-TOR-e-al) disorders. In addition, some disorders show reduced penetrance (PEN-e-trance), which means that a gene is not wholly dominant or recessive. For example, a person who has one recessive gene for a disorder might show milder symptoms of the disorder, but someone with two copies will have the full-blown disorder.

Chromosome disorders Other genetic disorders are caused by extra or missing chromosomes. In Down syndrome*, a person has three copies of chromosome 21, rather than the usual two copies. In a disease called cri du chat*, a piece of chromosome 5 is missing. In Turner syndrome*, which affects only girls, all or part of an X chromosome is missing. In most cases, chromosome disorders are not inherited. Instead, the problems occur for unknown reasons when the egg and sperm meet to form the embryo.

* **Down syndrome** is a genetic disorder that can cause mental retardation, shortness, and distinctive facial characteristics, as well as many other features.

* **cri du chat** (kree-doo-SHA), French for "cat's cry," is a genetic disorder that can cause mental retardation, a small head, and a cat-like whine.

* **Turner syndrome** is a genetic disorder that can cause several physical abnormalities, including shortness, and lack of sexual development.

Spontaneous (new) genetic mutations Particularly in the case of dominantly-inherited disorders, a child may be born with a condition despite the fact that neither parent has the disorder as would be expected. When this happens, it is usually because a spontaneous (or new) mutation in a gene or genes has occurred. The mutation may occur in a parent's egg or sperm cell, or it may occur after the egg has been fertilized and begins to develop into an embryo. This is frequently the case in achondroplasia (a-kon-dro-PLAY-zha), a form of dwarfism in which 90 percent of children born with the condition have unaffected parents. When this child grows up, the child will pass the gene on to his or her children according to the autosomal dominant inheritance pattern described above.

The Past and Future of Genetic Diseases

Mendel figured out the basic concepts of inheritance in the 1800s, before people knew that genes are the units of inheritance. It was not until 1953 that the structure of DNA was described. From the 1980s to the present, scientists' understanding of genes and how they work has grown at an incredibly rapid pace. Many disease-causing genes now have been identified, opening the door to research on ways to fix genetic defects. This field of science is referred to as gene therapy.

Gene therapy Genetic disorders can be treated in a number of ways. In some disorders, special diets are used to prevent the buildup in the body of compounds that are toxic to patients. In other disorders, the treatment involves blocking or rerouting chemical pathways. A third kind of treatment is new and controversial. It involves actually replacing defective genetic material with normal genetic material inside the cells. Researchers currently are looking for ways to do this. A variety of methods are being considered, including the use of microscopic "bullets" coated with genetic material and viruses to deliver normal genes to cells.

Prenatal testing A fetus* can be tested for many genetic disorders before it is born. Tests for prenatal (before birth) diagnosis are done on samples taken from the tissue or fluid surrounding a fetus. The fetus's chromosomes then can be studied using a karyotype (KAR-e-o-type), which is a visual display of the chromosomes from cells viewed under a microscope. Newer techniques enable scientists and doctors to look directly at the DNA that makes up the genes contained in the chromosomes. Common prenatal tests include:

- Amniocentesis (am-nee-o-sen-TEE-sis): In amniocentesis, a needle is passed through the mother's belly into her uterus* to collect some of the fluid in which the fetus lives. This fluid, called amniotic fluid, contains cells from the fetus.
- Chorionic villus (kor-e-ON-ik VIL-us) sampling (CVS): CVS also involves collecting cells from the fetus with a needle. In this case, the cells are taken from the chorionic villi, which are structures in the uterus that are part of the placenta.
- Percutaneous umbilical (per-ku-TAY-ne-us um-BIL-i-kal) blood sampling (PUBS): In PUBS, fetal blood is taken from the umbilical cord*.

Genetic testing and counseling Geneticists believe that each person probably carries about 5 to 10 defective recessive genes. Thus,

* **fetus** (FEE-tus) in humans is the developing offspring from nine weeks after conception until birth.

* **uterus** (U-ter-us), also called the womb, is the organ in a woman's body in which a fertilized egg develops into a fetus.

* **umbilical cord** (um-BIL-i-kal cord) is the flexible cord that connects a fetus at the navel with the placenta, the organ that allows for the exchange of oxygen, nutrients, and other substances between mother and fetus.

Inheritance Patterns of Some Genetic Diseases

Autosomal dominant	Autosomal recessive	X-linked dominant	X-linked recessive	Multiple genes
Achondroplasia Huntington's disease Neurofibromatosis	Albinism Cystic fibrosis Phenylketonuria (PKU) Sickle-cell anemia Tay-Sachs disease	Diabetes insipidus (one form)	Color blindness Hemophilia Hunter's syndrome Muscular dystrophy (Duchenne type)	Alzheimer's disease Some cancers (breast, colon, lung) Gout Rheumatoid arthritis

Punnett Squares

Punnett squares often are used to visualize the chances of inheriting a particular gene. Using **G** for a healthy gene and **g** for an affected recessive gene, the Punnett Square shows which offspring are likely to inherit two healthy genes, which offspring are likely to be carriers of the gene, and which are likely to have the disorder caused by the defective gene.

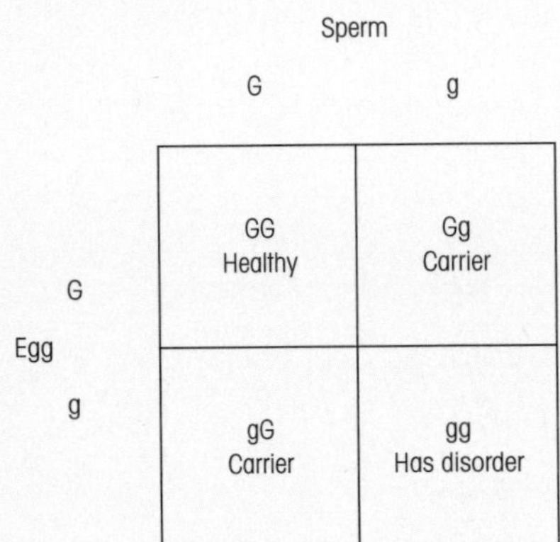

both potential parents may be worried about having a child with birth defects. If relatives have genetic disorders—or if ethnic or other background factors increase the risk of certain genetic diseases—parents-to-be may worry even more.

Many medical centers now offer genetic testing and genetic counseling. Parents and relatives can be tested to determine whether they carry genes for a variety of disorders. Using this information, a genetic counselor can help couples calculate genetic risks realistically, and inform them about the options they may have to increase the likelihood of having a healthy child.

Ethical concerns Increasingly, people will have the option to be tested to find out if they carry genes for genetic disorders. For example, women now can find out if their unborn children have certain genetic defects or if they themselves have genes that make them more likely to develop breast cancer. Already there is controversy about how this information should be used. Genetic testing can have far-reaching social, financial, and ethical effects. For example, a woman who thinks she will develop breast cancer might opt not to have children, or she might decide to have her breast tissue removed before cancer cells develop, or her insurance company might decide not to insure her because she is a high-risk client. With knowledge comes responsibility, and genetic testing surely will be at the forefront of debates about medical ethics in the twenty-first century.

Resources

Books

Baker, Catherine. *Your Genes, Your Choices.* Washington, DC: American Association for the Advancement of Science, 1997. A clear introduction to the ethical, legal, and social issues raised by genetic research. The full text of this book can be found on the association's website.
http://www.aaas.org

Jackson, John F. *Genetics and You.* Totowa, NJ: Humana Press, 1996. This book explains the basic principles of genetics, genetic counseling, and prenatal testing.

Organizations

Alliance of Genetic Support Groups, 4301 Connecticut Avenue Northwest, Number 404, Washington, DC 20008-2304. This national organization is an alliance of support groups for people who have or who are at risk for genetic disorders.
Telephone 800-336-GENE
http://www.geneticalliance.org

March of Dimes Birth Defects Foundation, 1275 Mamaroneck Avenue, White Plains, NY 10605. This large, national organization provides

information about genetic birth defects.
Telephone 888-MODIMES
http://www.modimes.org

U.S. National Human Genome Research Institute, 31 Center Drive, Building 31, Room 4B09, MSC 2152, Bethesda, MD 20892. This government institute is home to the Human Genome Project, an international research effort aimed at mapping the human genome.
http://www.nhgri.nih.gov

U.S. National Center for Biotechnology Information, National Library of Medicine, Building 38A, Room 8N805, Bethesda, MD 20894. This division of the U.S. National Library of Medicine provides detailed information about genes and genetic diseases.
http://www.ncbi.nlm.nih.gov

World Health Organization (WHO), Avenue Appia 20, 1211 Geneva 27, Switzerland. The World Health Organization posts an extensive list of publications from its *Human Genetics Programme* at its website.
http://www.who.int/ncd/hgn/hgn_pub.htm

▶ *See also*
Albinism
Alzheimer's Disease
Birth Defects
Breast Cancer
Color Blindness
Colorectal Cancer
Cystic Fibrosis
Down Syndrome
Dwarfism
Growth Disorders
Hemophilia
Huntington's Disease
Muscular Dystrophy
Neurofibromatosis
Phenylketonuria
Sickle-Cell Anemia
Tay-Sachs Disease
Turner Syndrome

Genital Warts

Genital warts are small fleshy growths of skin on or near the sexual organs that are caused by the human papillomavirus and are usually spread by sexual contact.

KEYWORDS
for searching the Internet and other reference sources

Condylomata acuminata

Human papillomavirus (HPV)

Sexually transmitted diseases

Venereal warts

What Are Genital Warts?

Genital warts may be dome shaped or nearly flat, but most commonly they grow on stalks in clumps that look like small heads of cauliflower. Warts of this shape are called condylomata acuminata (kon-dil-o-MAT-a a-koo-min-NAT-a). Genital warts usually cause no pain, but they can be very upsetting to have.

Human papillomavirus (HPV) The human papillomavirus (pap-i-LO-ma vi-rus) is common and has many subtypes. Genital warts usually are caused by HPV-6 or HPV-11. Many people may become infected with HPV at some point during their lives but not know it because they do not get visible warts. Among sexually active people in the United States, about 1 percent (1.4 million people) have genital warts and another 14 percent (19 million) have HPV infection without warts.

Cervical cancer Other kinds of HPV (mainly HPV-16 or HPV-18) can cause cancer of the cervix, part of the female reproductive tract. Even though visible genital warts usually do not contain cancer-causing forms of the virus, women who have warts should be sure to get the yearly test for cervical cancer, called the Pap test, that is recommended for all women.

Removing genital warts Genital warts can be removed in a number of ways—by surgery, laser* treatment, freezing (cryotherapy), or repeated treatment with chemicals that the doctor paints directly on the warts. They often recur after being removed. If untreated, they may grow, remain the same, or disappear on their own.

* **laser surgery** uses a very narrow and intense beam of light that can destroy body tissue.

Preventing genital warts The surest protection is sexual abstinence, that is, not having sex at all. Those who have sex with multiple partners have a higher chance of getting infected (though all it takes is having sex with one partner with an HPV infection to become infected). It is not known for certain whether using condoms protects against HPV, or whether getting rid of visible warts makes a person's infection less contagious.

Resources

The U.S. Centers for Disease Control and Prevention (CDC) has a National STD Hotline that is open from 8 AM to 11 PM EST.
Telephone 800-227-8922

The U.S. National Institute of Allergy and Infectious Diseases posts a fact sheet about human papillomavirus and genital warts at its website.
http://www.niaid.nih.gov/factsheets/stdhpv.htm

The American Social Health Association has an HPV Support Program and posts an *HPV Questions and Answers* fact sheet at its website. Its Sexually Transmitted Diseases Information and Referral Center has a hotline that takes calls from 9 AM to 7 PM EST.
Telephone 800-653-4325
http://www.ashastd.org/hpv/hpvref.html

The American Cancer Society posts a fact sheet about cervical cancer and human papillomavirus at its website.
http://www3.cancer.org/cancerinfo/main

▶ *See also*
Pregnancy, Complications of
Sexually Transmitted Diseases
Uterine/Cervical Cancer
Viral Infections
Warts

German Measles (Rubella)

Rubella (roo-BELL-a) is the medical name for German measles. Usually a mild viral infection that causes a rash, it can cause severe birth defects if a woman gets it while pregnant.

KEYWORDS
for searching the Internet and other reference sources

Immunization

Infection

What Is Rubella?

Rubella is not considered a serious illness, except when a pregnant woman gets the infection. It is spread through the air from an infected person to another person. The virus incubates for a period of 2 to 3 weeks in an infected person before symptoms appear.

A person who has contracted rubella can transmit the infection to another person from a period of a week before symptoms appear to about a week after they fade. Rubella infection occurs mainly in children between the ages of 6 and 12 if they have not been immunized.

What Are the Symptoms of Rubella?

The main symptom of rubella is a rash that appears first on the face. It then spreads to a person's arms, legs, and body. The rash generally lasts for 2 to 3 days. Some people with rubella also develop a slight fever. Sometimes the lymph nodes at the back of the neck become swollen.

There are cases of rubella where no symptoms appear at all. Among adolescents and adults who contract rubella, the symptoms can include headache and a high fever. Sometimes the joints of the body become inflamed from the virus, but this condition passes after a short time.

How Is Rubella Diagnosed and Treated?

The diagnosis of rubella is usually made by the patient's history and by physical exam of its typical rash. A throat swab isolating the rubella virus from the patient is used to confirm the diagnosis. Sometimes a blood test is used looking for antibodies to the virus in the patient's blood.

There is no specific treatment for rubella when a young person contracts the infection. Sometimes acetaminophen (a-set-a-MEE-no-fen) is used to help reduce fever if it is present.

Can Rubella Be Prevented?

Rubella can be prevented through immunization. At one time rubella was a common infection throughout the world. Today, there are few cases reported because of widespread vaccination programs. In the United States, all children must be vaccinated against the rubella virus before starting school. In 1993 only 200 cases of rubella were reported to the U.S. Department of Health and Human Services.

What Is Congenital Rubella?

Congenital rubella occurs when the rubella virus has been passed from the mother to the infant during pregnancy. The most dangerous period for a fetus is in the early months of pregnancy, when rubella can cause a miscarriage (spontaneous termination of the pregnancy) or birth defects.

Some of the birth defects congenital rubella can cause include:

- deafness
- heart disease
- mental retardation

- eye disorders
- cerebral palsy, a brain disorder that impairs movement
- purpura (PUR-pur-a), a bleeding disorder that appears as purple rashes

Doctors advise women who have not been vaccinated against rubella to do so before they become pregnant. The vaccination might also be harmful to a fetus and cannot be given to a woman who is already pregnant.

Resources

Book

Oldstone, Michael. *Viruses, Plagues, and History*. New York: Oxford University Press, 1998.

Organization

KidsHealth.org website from the Nemours Foundation contains information about a number of infections, including rubella. http://KidsHealth.org

▶ *See also*
Infection
Measles

Giardiasis

KEYWORDS
for searching the Internet or other reference sources
Gastrointestinal system
Waterborne diseases

Giardiasis is an infection of the small intestine by the Giardia lamblia ***parasite. It is spread from person to person or by contact with contaminated water or food. Its major symptom is diarrhea.***

What Is Giardiasis?

Giardiasis (je-ar-DY-a-sis) is a common infection caused by the *Giardia lamblia* (je-AR-de-a LAM-bli-a) protozoan, which is a one-celled organism that lives as a parasite*. *Giardia* contamination can occur in any water source, from clear mountain streams to poorly filtered city water supplies. The most common carriers of giardiasis are dogs, beavers, and humans. Giardiasis is easily passed from person to person through poor hygiene.

* **parasites** are creatures that live in and feed on the bodies of other organisms. The animal or plant harboring the parasite is called its host.

Giardiasis is found worldwide in both developed and developing countries and in both temperate and tropical climates. In developing nations, infection rates from 20 to 50 percent may occur. In the United States, it is estimated to affect up to 20 percent of the population, with toddlers in diapers at busy day care centers at particular risk.

What Are the Signs and Symptoms of Giardiasis?

It is estimated that more than 50 percent of people with giardiasis have no symptoms or only mild symptoms. When symptoms of giardiasis do occur, they may start gradually or suddenly, usually within one to three weeks after exposure to the parasite. The illness usually begins with frequent watery diarrhea without blood or mucus. Because giardiasis affects the body's ability to absorb fats and carbohydrates from ingested foods (malabsorption), giardiasis often produces foul-smelling, oily stools that float. Symptoms also may include abdominal cramps, a swollen or large abdomen, excessive gas, nausea and vomiting, loss of appetite, and sometimes a low-grade fever. Persistent symptoms can lead to weight loss and dehydration.

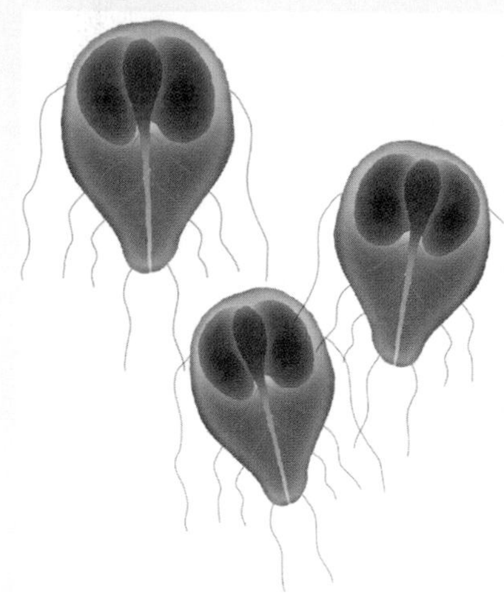

▲ *Giardia lamblia* protozoa.

How Do Doctors Diagnose Giardiasis?

Giardiasis is diagnosed by examination of stool samples under a microscope. Doctors look for evidence of trophozoites (tro-fo-ZO-ites), which are active *Giardia* protozoa inside the body, or for evidence of cysts, which are *Giardia* surrounded by a protective wall, the form of the protozoan during the resting stage of its life cycle. Detecting *Giardia* is difficult, so doctors often need to repeat the stool sample tests several times before they can confirm or rule out *Giardia* infection. Diagnostic tests may sometimes take as long as four or five weeks.

How Do Doctors Treat Giardiasis?

Several drugs are available for treatment of giardiasis, and some of them work well in a single dose. Sometimes a second round of drug treatment is required. There is some controversy among doctors about whether to treat people who carry the parasite but who do not have symptoms of giardiasis. Treatment is sometimes considered because these individuals may transmit the infection to others and may eventually show symptoms themselves.

How Do People Prevent Giardiasis?

There is no vaccine or prophylactic (disease-preventing) drug for giardiasis. Preventing giardiasis depends on maintenance of safe supplies of drinking water, the sanitary disposal of human and animal waste, washing of fruits and vegetables before eating or cooking, and proper hygiene, which includes thorough washing of hands after going to the bathroom and before eating.

The *Giardia* protozoan can be filtered from water but is otherwise difficult to destroy. It can survive in cold water for as long as two months, and it is resistant to chlorine levels used to purify municipal water supplies. When municipal water supplies have been approved by local health departments, the water may be considered safe to drink. But when camping or traveling, it is important to make sure that drinking water, cooking water, and ice come only from safe sources. Clear cold mountain streams may look safe and inviting but they may also carry the *Giardia* parasite.

Resource

The U.S. National Institute of Allergy and Infectious Diseases posts a fact sheet about giardiasis at its website.
http://www.niaid.nih.gov/factsheets/GIARDIA.htm

▶ *See also*
Diarrhea
Gastroenteritis

Gigantism *See* Growth Disorders

Gingivitis *See* Gum Disease

Glaucoma

Glaucoma (glaw-KO-ma) is a group of disorders that cause fluid pressure to rise inside the eye, which may result in vision loss.

KEYWORDS
for searching the Internet and other reference sources

Ophthalmology

Vision

If a balloon is slowly filled with water, eventually it will burst. But if the same balloon has several pin-sized holes at one end, then it becomes possible to continue adding water to the balloon to maintain its round shape, without breaking the balloon, as long as the amount of water being added is equal to the amount escaping through the pinholes.

The eye has a similar system of liquid that continuously flows in and out of a small chamber at the front of the eyeball. The problem for people with glaucoma is that the drainage out of the eye is blocked or not working properly. It is similar to the balloon that is filling with water. Without a way to make room for more liquid, pressure builds up. Although a pressure buildup will not cause the eye to burst, it may damage nerves at the rear of the eyeball that carry images to the brain.

Glaucoma is one of the leading causes of blindness in the United States. It affects more than 3 million people, especially the elderly and people of African ancestry. The disease also is one of the sneakiest eye disorders. Pressure can grow in the eye for years before the effects on vision are noticed. By then, often the damage has been done.

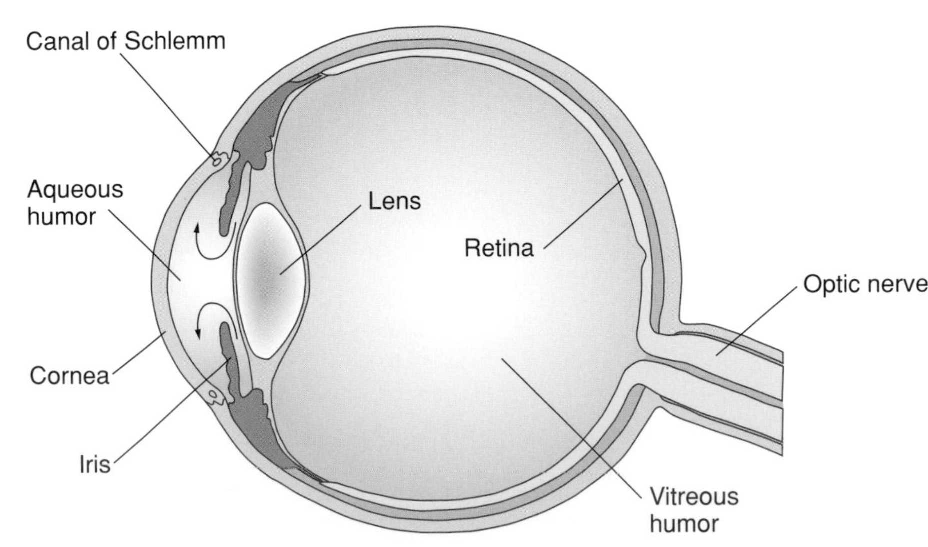

Anatomy of the eye. The arrows show the flow of aqueous humor from behind the iris, through the pupil, to the front of the eye, where it drains through the canal of Schlemm.

How Does Glaucoma Affect the Eye?

The eye is about the same size as a ping-pong ball and is divided into two compartments. The larger compartment at the rear of the eye contains a gel-like substance called vitreous (VIT-re-us) humor, which helps to maintain the eyeball's shape and to transmit light. The front compartment, or anterior chamber, is smaller and is filled with a watery liquid called aqueous (AY-kwee-us) humor. This clear liquid brings in nutrients vital to the eye's health and carries out waste that can damage it.

The aqueous humor flows from behind the front colored portion of the eye, which is called the iris. It moves through the pupil, the opening in the center of the iris, into the front chamber of the eye. The liquid flows through the chamber and out a tiny drainage canal that has a fine, mesh-like covering. The small hole on the canal rests at an angle where the colored iris meets the cornea, the clear cup-shaped disc at the front of the eyeball.

About 90 to 95 percent of people with glaucoma have a problem with this drainage system. The cause is unknown, as there is no visible blockage. It appears that the cells in the mesh covering the drainage canal do not do their job properly, or lose their ability to allow proper drainage over time. Glaucoma develops gradually, but there is a rarer acute* form of glaucoma that develops suddenly when the iris closes off the drainage canal. This causes a painful medical emergency that requires immediate treatment.

*__acute__ means sudden, short, and severe.

The cause of most cases of glaucoma is not understood, although people of African ancestry, people who have diabetes or other family members with glaucoma, or those who have suffered eye injuries are at greater risk. Aging is another risk factor for glaucoma.

How Is Glaucoma Diagnosed?

Except for the rare cases of acute glaucoma that develop suddenly, most people do not realize they have glaucoma. As pressure is building in the eye, many of the millions of nerve cells at the rear of the eye are destroyed. The nerves that die first affect peripheral (pe-RIF-er-al) vision, or how well people see out of the sides of the eyes. When the loss of vision becomes severe enough for a person to notice, the damage is so great that little can be done.

The best way to diagnose glaucoma is through an eye exam that uses an instrument called a tonometer (to-NOM-e-ter) to measure the pressure in the eye. One type of tonometer registers eye pressure by lightly touching the eye's surface. Eyedrops are used to make this procedure painless. Another tonometer uses a puff of air to measure eye pressure. The doctor or eye specialist (ophthalmologist or optometrist) also may use a scope that shines light in the eye to look for damage to the optic nerve. Peripheral vision can be checked as part of the eye exam.

Why Are Early Diagnosis and Treatment Important?

Diagnosis Early diagnosis of glaucoma is the key to preventing vision loss. If glaucoma is discovered before the increased eye pressure has

No Mountain Too High

Glaucoma rarely occurs in young people, but Erik Weilenmayer was born with an eye disease that caused glaucoma. By age 13, he was totally blind. Erik did not let glaucoma prevent him from becoming a teacher and a mountain climber. He has scaled some of the toughest peaks, including Alaska's Mt. McKinley, the highest in the United States.

"When I first went blind, I wondered what I could do," Weilenmayer said in 1998. "It's really a kick to do extreme activities and do them well—and no more dangerously than anyone else."

Erik's accomplishments are a reminder that physical challenges and differences do not have to prevent people from participating in life's most difficult and demanding activities.

See also
Blindness
Cataracts

KEYWORDS
for searching the Internet and other reference sources

Antibiotics

Antibiotic resistance

Infection

Sexually transmitted diseases

Venereal diseases

destroyed many nerves, vision can be saved in many cases. Routine eye exams, including tests for glaucoma, are important, especially as adults pass age 35. Such eye exams are especially important for people at greatest risk for glaucoma, including people of African ancestry, people with relatives who have glaucoma, people with diabetes, and people with previous eye injuries.

Treatment The most common treatment involves eyedrops that reduce pressure. Sometimes surgery is necessary either to open the drainage canal or to create a new one.

Resources

Glaucoma Research Foundation, 200 Pine Street, Suite 200, San Francisco, CA 94104. The Glaucoma Research Foundation offers helpful publications about glaucoma, including *Childhood Glaucoma: A Reference Guide for Families.*
Telephone 800-826-6693
http://www.glaucoma.org

The U.S. National Eye Institute posts a fact sheet about glaucoma at its website.
http://www.nei.nih.gov/publications/glaucoma.htm

Goiter *See* Thyroid Disease

Gonorrhea

Gonorrhea is a bacterial infection that usually spreads from person to person during sexual contact, making it a sexually transmitted disease (STD). It also can be transmitted from an infected mother to a baby during childbirth. If untreated, gonorrhea may result in infertility in women, among other problems.

Gonorrhea is an infection caused by *Neisseria gonorrhoeae* (ni-SEE-ree-a gon-o-REE-i) bacteria, which grow rapidly in the warm, moist tissues of the body's genital areas. Gonorrhea infection may cause pain during urination and a pus-like discharge from the genitals. Sometimes women have such mild symptoms that they ignore them. If left untreated, however, gonorrhea may lead to pelvic inflammatory disease (PID), infection of babies during childbirth, or infertility.

Who Is at Risk for Gonorrhea?

Anyone who has sexual relations with an infected person is at risk. The risk increases when people do not use condoms, or when people have multiple sexual partners. Gonorrhea may be spread by genital, anal, or

History: Ancient and Modern

Gonorrhea has been known since ancient times. Its name is from the Greek words for "flow of seed," apparently a reference to the genital discharge that is a major symptom.

It was not until the nineteenth century, however, that researchers understood the difference between syphilis, caused by *Treponema pallidum*, and gonorrhea. The gonorrhea bacterium *Neisseria gonorrhoeae* was identified in 1879 by the German biologist Albert Neisser, for whom it was named.

During the 1930s and 1940s, antibiotics were found to treat syphilis and gonorrhea effectively. With treatment, fewer people spread the diseases, and the number of cases fell sharply in the United States. But then the numbers began to rise again. Some researchers believe that a change in attitude toward sex during the 1960s and 1970s contributed to this increase, as people became sexually active earlier and with more partners than before.

When AIDS became a problem during the 1980s, people began to practice what has come to be known as "safer sex." That meant, among other things, using condoms and trying harder to have monogamous relationships, in which two people have sex only with each other. Greater efforts also were made to teach people about the health and social benefits of abstaining from sex and of not becoming sexually active at a young age. Since the early 1980s, rates of gonorrhea and syphilis in the United States mostly have fallen.

oral-genital sex. In the United States, the highest rates of gonorrhea infection occur among teenagers and adults in their twenties. People who have chlamydial (kla-MID-e-al) infections, or other sexually transmitted diseases, are more likely to have gonorrhea as well. Public health officials recommend that all sexually active young women and young men be tested regularly for both gonorrhea and chlamydia.

What Are the Symptoms of Gonorrhea?

Many women, and some men, have no symptoms or have such mild symptoms that they go unnoticed. Some women, however, have especially severe symptoms. For both men and women, symptoms may include:

- a burning sensation when urinating
- frequent urination
- pus-like discharge from the vagina or penis
- tenderness or pain in the genital area or abdomen
- for women, bleeding between menstrual cycles

How Do Antibiotics Work?

There are two ways antibiotics attack bacteria. Some medications (like penicillins) destroy the bacterium's wall, causing it to disintegrate. Other antibiotics block the production of proteins inside the bacterium, which prevents it from reproducing.

If a rectal infection occurs, there may be rectal pain and discharge. If a throat infection occurs (from oral-genital sex), there may be a sore throat as well. If the *Neisseria gonorrhoeae* bacteria get into the bloodstream, they may travel throughout the body and cause a mild fever, joint pains, and a rash, particularly on the palms of the hands. This condition is called disseminated gonococcal infection. Or one or two joints may be swollen, tender, and extremely painful, a condition known as gonococcal arthritis.

How Is Gonorrhea Diagnosed and Treated?

Diagnosis Three tests are available to diagnose gonorrhea:

- **Gram stain test:** A smear from the genital discharge is stained with a dye and examined under a microscope to see if *Neisseria gonorrhoeae* bacteria are present. This test, which gives immediate results, is reliable mostly for men.
- **Bacterial gene detection**: This test uses high-tech means to look for evidence of bacterial DNA (genetic material) in a sample of urine or in a smear of fluid from the cervix (the bottom of the uterus or womb). It is reliable for both sexes and gives instant results, but not all laboratories perform it.
- **Culture:** A sample of discharge is placed in a dish of culture medium, which is a jelly-like material containing nutrients that support the growth of the bacteria. If *Neisseria gonorrhoeae* bacteria are present, they will multiply in one or two days and can then be identified. This test is also very reliable for both sexes, but it does not give instant results.

Treatment Gonorrhea can be treated with one or more antibiotics. Doctors usually prescribe an antibiotic that can be taken by mouth or by injection, which may cure the disease within a week or two. When people with gonorrhea have chlamydial infections, the doctor may prescribe a combination of antibiotics that treats both infections at the same time.

How Is Gonorrhea Prevented?

Because it is almost impossible to know if a sexual partner has gonorrhea, not having sexual relations (abstinence) provides the best protection. Using latex condoms can lead to safer sex when they are used correctly, and when worn every single time a person has sexual relations. Having fewer sexual partners or only one partner may reduce the risk, but some risk remains unless a person is certain that his or her partner is uninfected. This is very difficult, since many people with gonorrhea infection have no symptoms and don't know they are infected.

What Is the Future of Gonorrhea Treatment?

Bacterial resistance Penicillin once was routinely prescribed to cure gonorrhea, but bacteria grew resistant to it, and some could survive treatment. At first, larger doses of penicillin worked, but by the 1980s those treatments began to fail. Doctors then switched to newer and more expensive antibiotics, but some strains of gonorrhea bacteria already show signs of becoming resistant to the most commonly used of the newer drugs (ceftriaxone). Although many other antibiotics exist, public health officials around the world are now monitoring bacterial resistance.

Vaccination In another approach, the U.S. National Institute of Allergy and Infectious Diseases is sponsoring research to investigate the possibility of developing a vaccine to prevent gonorrhea infection.

Resources

Brodman, Michael, M.D., John Thacker, and Rachel Kranz. *Straight Talk about Sexually Transmitted Diseases*. New York: Facts on File, 1998.

The U.S. Centers for Disease Control and Prevention (CDC), located in Atlanta, Georgia, posts information about gonorrhea at its website. http://cdc.gov/ncidod/dastlr/gcdir/gono.htm

▶ *See also*
Chlamydial Infections
Infertility
Pelvic Inflammatory Disease
Pregnancy, Complications of
Sexually Transmitted Diseases
Syphilis

Gout

Gout (pronounced GOWT) is a painful, inflammatory disease of the joints caused by crystals of uric acid.

KEYWORDS
for searching the Internet and other reference sources
Hyperuricemia
Inflammation

What Is Gout?

Uric (YUR-ik) acid is a waste product made by normal chemical processes in the body, as well as by the breakdown of certain foods, and it is usually eliminated in urine. Sometimes uric acid builds up and forms crystals, like sugar crystals, that collect in joints such as those of the big toe. When that happens, it can cause a painful inflammatory condition known as gout.

Gout is not life-threatening, but it is extremely painful. An attack of gout begins with pain and inflammation (swelling, tenderness, and redness) in a joint. If the condition becomes chronic, that is, if it comes back many times over a long period, it can cause kidney stones and deformities of the joints.

Ninety percent of patients with gout are men over 40. The condition is not contagious. Doctors once believed that gout was caused by eating rich foods and by drinking too much alcohol. But today, factors such as age, a family history of gout, and obesity, among others, are believed to play more important roles.

How Is Gout Diagnosed and Treated?

There are several ways to diagnose gout, including blood tests, testing fluid in the joints for crystals of uric acid, and taking x-rays.

Rich Men and Rich Food

Members of the privileged classes throughout European history often were diagnosed with gout. Researchers once believed this was due to their frequent consumption of meat, starch, and fortified wine. Current research attributes the susceptibility to age (men over age 40), family history, obesity, and other factors.

Among the more notable names from history who qualify under both theories are:

- Ambroise Paré (1510–1590), chief surgeon to three kings of France
- Philip II (1527–1598), king of Spain
- Thomas Sydenham (1624–1689), English physician, sometimes called the "English Hippocrates"
- Benjamin Franklin (1706–1790), American philosopher, diplomat, and statesman
- Samuel Johnson (1709–1784), English lexicographer and writer.

Treatment often includes weight loss, a lower-protein diet, pain relievers, and medications to reduce the level of uric acid in the blood. Drinking plenty of fluids will help to flush uric acid from the body.

Resources

Book

Porter, Roy, and G. S. Rousseau. *The Patrician Malady*. New Haven: Yale University Press, 1998.

Organization

Arthritis Foundation, 1330 West Peachtree Street, Atlanta, GA 30309. The Arthritis Foundation provides information on gout. http://www.arthritis.org

See also
Arthritis

Graves' Disease *See* Thyroid Disease

Growth Disorders

Growth disorders are conditions of abnormal growth in children. The disorders may be caused by poor nutrition, abnormal levels of certain hormones involved in growth, genetic disorders of bone growth, and other diseases.

KEYWORDS
for searching the Internet and other reference sources

Endocrinology

Genetics

Human growth disorders

Human growth hormone

Puberty

Jeremy's Story

When Jeremy turned eight, he looked like he was trapped inside the body of a four-year-old. "My friends teased me and called me 'Shorty,'" he said. "I felt terrible being so much shorter than my brother who was three years younger."

His parents took him to see a pediatric endocrinologist*. The doctor took his medical history, blood tests, x-rays, and measurements. Jeremy's parents were told that his body was not making enough growth hormone. Daily shots of human growth hormone have helped Jeremy, and he is now taller than his brother.

*** endocrinologist** (en-do-krin-OL-o-jist) is a doctor who specializes in treating patients with hormone-related disorders.

What Is Normal Growth?

Everyone has a different size and shape, and there is a very wide range of what doctors consider "normal growth." In order to monitor growth, doctors use an established range of normal heights and weights for different age groups. From the time a child first goes to the doctor, measurements of height and weight are taken. The doctor uses a growth chart to compare a child's height and growth rate with those of others the same age. As a newborn, everyone starts out at about the same size. Yet, some end up short and some tall.

When developing a standard growth chart, researchers take a large number of children of different ages and make a graph of their heights and weights. The height at the 50th percentile means the height at which half of the children of that age are taller and half are shorter. The 25th percentile means that three quarters (75 percent) of the children are taller at that age, and one quarter (25 percent) are shorter. The 75th percentile means that three quarters of the children (75 percent) will be shorter and one quarter (25 percent) taller.

People vary greatly, and if children are between the 3rd and 97th percentile, and if they growing at a normal rate, they usually are regarded as normal. If children are outside these ranges (over 97th percentile or under 3rd percentile), the doctor may look for some explanation. Most often, these children simply have inherited "short" or "tall" genes from their parents, and they will continue to grow at a normal pace.

Growth and Puberty

At the time of adolescence, a growth spurt normally occurs. Generally, growth spurts for girls start about two years earlier than growth spurts for boys. Rates of growth and change during puberty vary with the individual. Parents' growth and puberty patterns often are passed on through their genes to their children: If one or both parents had a late puberty, then their children are more likely to reach puberty later and to experience a later growth spurt. The medical term for this "late bloomer" pattern is constitutional growth delay.

Sex hormones The increase in growth rate that occurs during puberty is driven by the body's increase in production of sex hormones: estrogen from the ovaries in girls, and testosterone from the testicles in boys. These hormones cause the skeleton to grow and to mature more rapidly. Hormones produced by the adrenal glands at puberty contribute to the development of pubic hair (near the genitals) and underarm hair, but have little effect on bone growth. It follows, then, that disorders of pubertal development can affect a child's growth pattern and ultimate height. Pubertal disorders usually are grouped into two categories: precocious or premature puberty (which starts earlier than expected), and delayed or late puberty.

Precocious puberty In general, puberty is considered precocious (early) if changes in sexual development occur before age eight for girls and before age ten for boys. Most cases of precocious puberty result from the premature "switching on" of the puberty control center in the brain, located in the part of the brain called the hypothalamus (hy-po-THAL-a-mus). Hormones from the hypothalamus trigger the release of hormones from the pituitary gland (located at the base of the brain), which in turn stimulate the ovaries in girls and the testicles in boys to produce the higher levels of sex hormones needed to bring about the bodily changes of puberty.

Children with precocious puberty experience early growth spurts because of the abnormally early rise in sex hormone levels in their bodies. Although initially this causes these children to grow taller than others their age, their skeletons mature more rapidly, often causing them to stop growing at an early age. Therefore, if precocious puberty is left untreated, it may lead to a decrease in a child's ultimate height.

There are many possible causes for precocious puberty, including brain tumors and other disorders of the central nervous system; and tumors or other conditions that cause the gonads or adrenal glands to overproduce sex hormones. In girls, however, the majority of cases of precocious puberty are idiopathic (id-ee-o-PATH-ik), which means the precise cause is unknown.

Precocious puberty often can be treated effectively or controlled with medications that decrease the overproduction of sex hormones or that block their effects on the body. In many cases, this type of treatment can prevent or decrease the shortening of the child's ultimate height that would otherwise occur.

Delayed puberty Delayed puberty occurs when the hormonal changes of puberty occur later than normal, or not at all. Puberty is considered late if it has not begun by age 13 in girls or by age 15 in boys. Most children who experience delayed puberty are following the normal pattern called constitutional growth delay discussed previously.

Several medical conditions (such as disorders of the hypothalamus, pituitary, ovaries, and testicles) can result in delayed puberty by interfering with the pubertal rise in sex hormones. Many chronic disorders of other body organs and systems (such as the intestines and lungs), as well as long-term treatments with certain medications (such as cortisone) also may cause delayed puberty.

As would be expected, children with delayed puberty do not experience growth spurts at the usual age, so they lag behind in height as their peers grow rapidly and mature sexually. When puberty finally occurs for these children, on its own or as a result of treatment, they "catch up": They may continue to grow into their late teens and may even exceed the final adult heights of some of their peers.

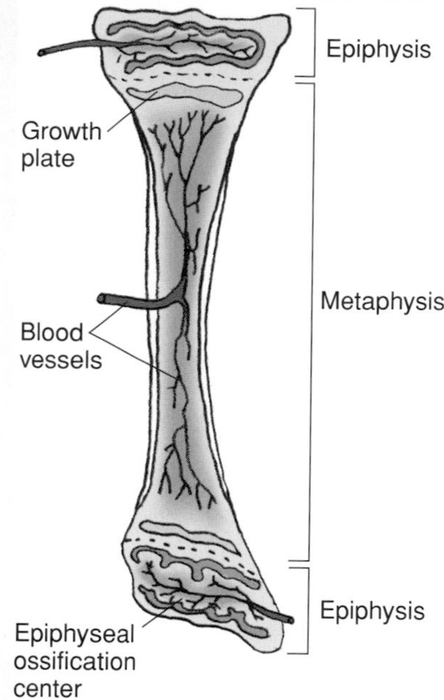

Anatomy of bones. When all of the cartilage in the growth plate turns to bone, growth stops.

How Does Growth Take Place?

Growth occurs when bones of the arms, legs, and back increase in size. The long bones of the limbs have a growth plate at the end. The growth plate is made of cartilage, which is a tough, elastic tissue. Cartilage cells in the growth plate multiply and move down the bone to produce a matrix, or tissue from which new bone is formed. These cartilage cells then die, leaving spaces. Special cells called osteoblasts (OS-tee-o-blasts), meaning bone beginners, then produce bone (by laying down the minerals calcium and phosphorus) to fill the spaces and replace the matrix. Once all the cartilage in the growth plate has been turned to bone, growth stops. This usually occurs before ages 16 to 18. An x-ray of the hand or knee can show the doctor the bone age (maturity of the bone) and how much potential growth remains.

Why Do Some Children Not Grow Normally?

Nutrition Children with poor nutrition may have poor growth. A balanced diet and adequate protein are essential for normal growth. Some parts of the world have serious problems with malnutrition, and the growth of children may be affected in these areas.

Chronic diseases Chronic diseases that may impair growth include diabetes, congenital heart disorders, sickle cell disease, chronic kidney failure, cystic fibrosis, and rheumatoid arthritis.

Bone Disorders One form of extreme short stature (height) is caused by abnormal formation and growth of cartilage and bone. Children with skeletal dysplasia* or chondrodystrophies* are short and have abnormal body proportions. Their intelligence levels usually are normal. Most of these conditions are inherited or occur due to genetic mutations (changes).

* **dysplasia** (dis-PLAY-zha) means abnormal growth or development.

* **chrondrodystrophy** (kon-dro-DIS-trof-ee) means abnormal growth at the ends of the bones.

Intrauterine growth retardation (IUGR) If growth in the uterus is interrupted while a fetus is forming or developing, the condition is called intrauterine (meaning within the uterus) growth retardation or IUGR. IUGR is not the same as when a baby is born prematurely. The small size of a premature infant usually is normal according to the gestational (jes-TAY-shun-al) age (or the age from conception).

Failure to grow normally in the uterus may result from a problem with the placenta (the organ that supplies nutrients and oxygen to the baby). Growth of the fetus can be affected if the mother smokes cigarettes or drinks alcohol during the pregnancy. Infections, such as German measles, may cause the problem, and sometimes the cause cannot be determined.

Failure to thrive (FTT) Failure to thrive (FTT), or inadequate weight gain anytime after birth, occurs frequently in infants. There are many possible causes, and the doctor must examine the child carefully. Often, the baby or child simply is not getting enough to eat. Sometimes there are other illnesses interfering with weight gain that must be treated.

Genetic conditions Several genetic conditions may involve problems with growth. One such condition is Turner syndrome. Girls with Turner syndrome have only one X chromosome or a second X chromosome that may be abnormal or incomplete. Affected girls are short and have underdeveloped ovaries.

Marfan syndrome is a hereditary condition affecting connective tissue and is associated with tall stature. People with Marfan syndrome have very long arms and legs, eye problems, and differences in facial features. Other physical problems, such as heart abnormalities, also may be present. It is commonly believed that Abraham Lincoln had Marfan syndrome.

Hormones and Growth Disorders

Growth is controlled by hormones (chemical messengers) from various glands. One of the most important, growth hormone, is secreted by the pituitary gland. The gland looks like a peanut sitting at the base of the brain. Other hormones also are essential for growth. The thyroid gland in the neck secretes thyroxine, a hormone required for normal bone growth. Sex hormones from the ovaries (estrogen) and testicles (testosterone) are essential for the growth spurt and other body changes that occur at puberty.

Pituitary hormones The pituitary gland is attached by a stalk to the hypothalamus, an area of the brain that controls the function of the pituitary. The anterior or front part of the pituitary gland secretes the following hormones that can affect growth:

- Growth hormone to regulate bone growth
- Thyroid-stimulating hormone to control the production and secretion of thyroid hormones
- Gonad-stimulating hormones for development of the sex glands (gonads) and secretion of sex hormones
- Adrenal-stimulating hormone to regulate the secretion of adrenal gland hormones.

Too little growth hormone (hypopituitarism) Sometimes the pituitary gland does not make enough growth hormone. Usually, this will slow a child's growth rate to less than 2 inches a year. The deficiency may appear at any time during infancy or childhood. When doctors have ruled out other causes of growth failure, they may recommend special tests for growth hormone (GH) deficiency. Children with growth hormone deficiency are treated with daily injections of the hormone, often for a period of years. With early diagnosis and treatment, these children usually increase their rate of growth, and may catch up to achieve average or near-average height as adults.

In pituitary dwarfism, caused by low amounts of growth hormone, the person is short but has normal body proportions. This is different from other forms of dwarfism due to genetic skeletal dysplasias. In these cases, the person with dwarfism is short, and the growth of the arms, legs, torso, and head often is out of proportion. For example, the person's arms and legs may appear relatively smaller than the head or torso.

Too much growth hormone (hyperpituitarism) Two conditions arise from excessive amounts of growth hormone in the body: acromegaly (ak-ro-MEG-a-lee) and gigantism. The cause usually is a benign* pituitary tumor.

* **benign** means not cancerous or spreading and contained in one area.

Acromegaly, a condition caused by increased secretion of growth hormone after normal growth has been completed, occurs in adults. The condition is rare, occurring in 6 out of 100,000 people. Because the adult cannot grow taller, the excess growth hormone in acromegaly causes adult bones to thicken and other structures and organs to grow larger. Usually, it does not appear until middle age, when the person notes a tightening of a ring on the finger, or an increase in shoe size. Tests at that time may reveal a pituitary tumor.

Gigantism occurs when excessive secretion of growth hormone occurs in children before normal growth has stopped. This results in the overgrowth of long bones. The vertical growth in height is accompanied by growth in muscle and organs. The result is a person who is very tall, with a large jaw, large face, large skull, and very large hands and feet. Many health problems may be associated with gigantism, including heart disease and vision problems. Delayed puberty also may occur in this condition. Surgery or radiation can correct the problem. Hormone replacement may be necessary if there is pituitary damage from this treatment.

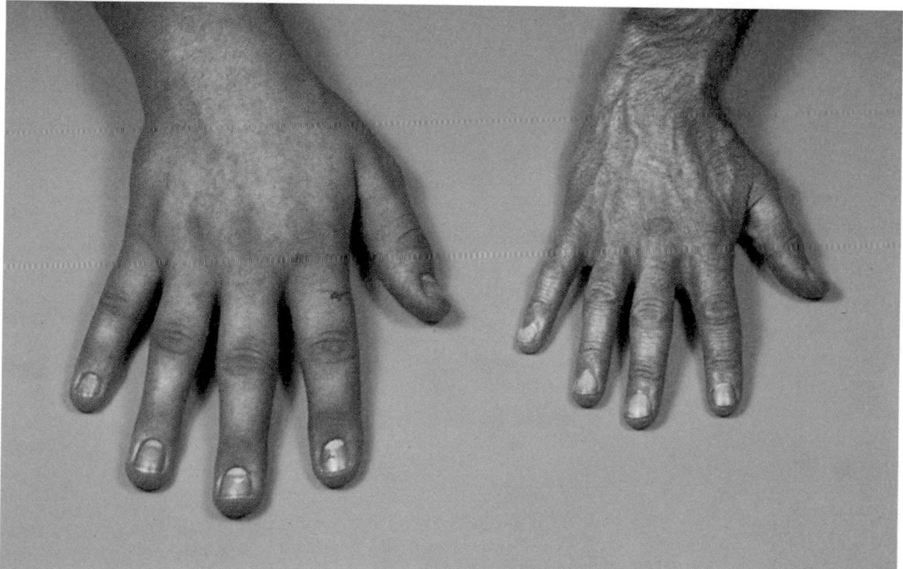

◀ Acromegaly results from excessive secretion of growth hormone and causes enlargement of many parts of the body, including the hands (left), fingers, toes, ears, nose, and jaw. © *1990 MMSB/ Custom Medical Stock Photo.*

Too little thyroid hormone (hypothyroidism) The thyroid gland looks like a big butterfly at the base of the neck. One wing is on one side of the windpipe or trachea, and the other on the other side. The wings are joined by a thin strip of thyroid tissue. The thyroid gland makes the hormone thyroxine (thy-ROX-een).

The thyroid is controlled by the pituitary gland, which makes thyroid-stimulating hormone. The hormone thyroxine controls the rate of chemical reactions (or metabolism) in the body. Too much thyroxine, or hyperthyroidism, speeds up metabolism.

Hypothyroidism is the opposite. Hypothyroidism is caused by the body's underproduction of thyroid hormone, and this affects many different body processes.

A child with thyroid hormone deficiency has slow growth and is physically and mentally sluggish. The lack of this hormone may be present at birth, if the thyroid gland did not develop properly in the fetus. Or the problem may develop during childhood or later in life as a result of certain diseases of the thyroid.

In most states, babies are tested for hypothyroidism at birth. Blood tests can detect the problem, and treatment usually is a daily pill that replaces the missing thyroid hormone. Early diagnosis and continuing treatment help these children grow and develop normally.

Too much cortisol (Cushing's syndrome) The adrenal glands, which are located on top of the kidneys in the abdomen, secrete the hormone cortisol. If too much cortisol is made by the child's adrenals, or if large doses of the hormone are given to the child to treat certain diseases, Cushing's syndrome may develop. Children with this syndrome grow slowly, gain weight excessively, and may experience delayed puberty due to the effects of the abnormally large amounts of cortisol in the body.

A Complex Problem

There are many causes for growth problems. In order to detect these disorders early, it is important for doctors to track growth carefully in infants and children. Many of these conditions can be treated effectively, resulting in more normal adult heights for children with growth disorders.

Resources

U.S. National Institute of Child Health and Human Development, and other institutes at the National Institutes of Health (NIH), offer many fact sheets and online resources about growth disorders. The NIH search engine is user friendly and provides many useful hypertext links.
http://www.nih.gov

March of Dimes Birth Defects Foundation, 1275 Mamaroneck Avenue, White Plains, NY 10605. This large, national organization provides

information about achondroplasia, other growth disorders, and many birth defects.
Telephone 888-MODIMES
http://www.modimes.org

KidsHealth.org from the Nemours Foundation posts a fact sheet that answers frequently asked questions about visiting an endocrinologist.
http://kidshealth.org

► *See also*
Birth Defects
Cushing's Syndrome
Dietary Deficiencies
Dwarfism
Genetic Diseases
Marfan Syndrome
Metabolic Diseases
Thyroid Diseases
Turner Syndrome

Guillain-Barré Syndrome *See* Paralysis

Gum Disease

Gum disease is an infection caused by bacteria that affect the tissues surrounding and supporting the teeth.

KEYWORDS
for searching the Internet and other reference sources

Dentistry

Gingivitis

Periodontal disease

Periodontitis

What Is Gum Disease?

Like getting gray hair and wrinkles, losing teeth once seemed to be an inevitable part of growing old. The number one cause of tooth loss in adults is still gum disease, also known as periodontal (per-ee-o-DON-tel) disease. This is an infection caused by bacteria that affect the tissues surrounding and supporting the teeth. About three out of four adults over age 35 have some type of gum disease. However, tooth loss does not occur until the disease is advanced. It often can be prevented by taking good care of the teeth and gums and seeing a dentist regularly.

The mildest form of gum disease is known as gingivitis (gin-gi-VY-tus). It causes the gums to become red and swollen and bleed easily. At this stage, gum disease is still easily treatable. If gingivitis is left untreated, though, it can turn into periodontitis (per-ee-o-don-TY-tis), a more serious gum disease. In advanced periodontitis, the gums and the

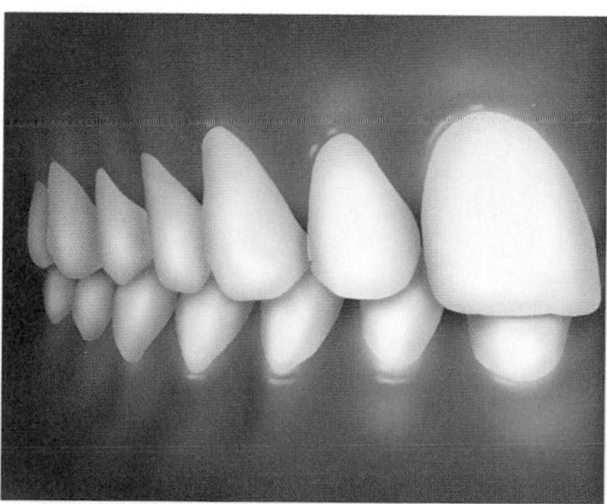

Healthy gums

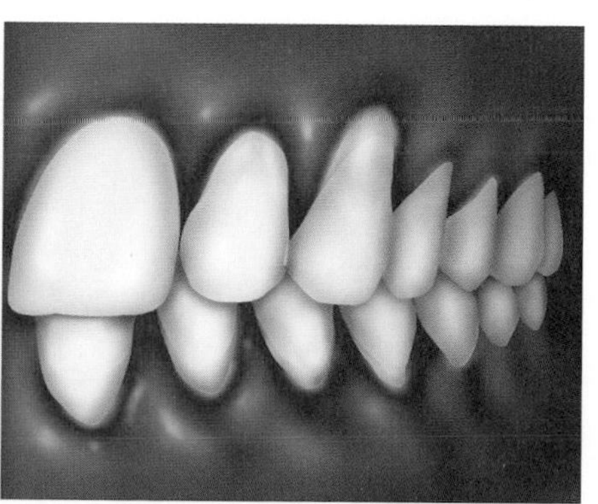

Inflamed, receding gums

◄ Gum disease causes the gums to become red, swollen, and inflamed. Compare the healthy gums on the left to the diseased gums on the right.

Long-term gum disease causes the gums to pull away from the teeth. *Biophoto Associates/Science Source, Photo Researchers, Inc.*

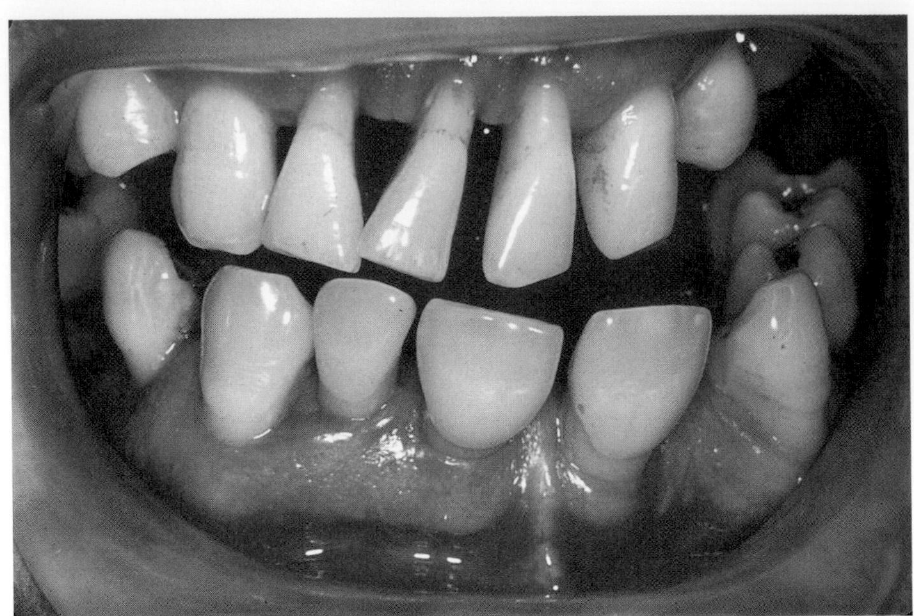

bone that supports the teeth can be badly damaged. The teeth may become loose and fall out, or they may have to be pulled by a dentist.

What Causes Gum Disease?

Gum disease is caused by plaque, a sticky film on the teeth made by bacteria that live in the mouth. If plaque is not removed each day by brushing and flossing, it hardens into a rough substance called calculus, also known as tartar. The bacteria in plaque produce chemicals that irritate the gums and cause infection. If left in place, these chemicals cause the gums to pull away from the teeth and create little pockets of space between the teeth and the gums. As the infection gets worse, the pockets get deeper. The result may be the destruction of the bones in the jaw that hold the teeth in place.

Most adults over age 35 have some degree of gum disease. People who smoke or use chewing tobacco, have uncontrolled diabetes, eat poorly, or have too much stress are all at greater risk for developing gum disease. Female hormones can play a part as well; girls who are going through puberty and pregnant women also are at risk.

What Happens When People Have Gum Disease?

Symptoms Gum disease is usually painless in the early stage. A person might not feel it until it has reached an advanced stage. However, these are some signs that a person may have gum disease:

- gums that bleed easily during tooth brushing or flossing
- red, swollen, or tender gums
- gums that have pulled away from the teeth
- bad breath that does not go away

- pus between the teeth and gums
- loose teeth
- a change in the way the teeth fit together when the person bites
- a change in the fit of a partial set of false teeth

Diagnosis A dentist can check the gums for signs of disease. In addition to looking at them, the dentist can use a probe with a special rounded tip. This probe is moved gently around the gum line to search for pockets in the gums.

Treatment Treatment depends on the type of gum disease and how far along it is. Cleaning the tooth surface and the root below the gum line helps the gum tissue heal and reattach to the tooth surfaces. Antibiotics can help control the growth of bacteria.

If the pockets are too deep to clean inside, the dentist may need to perform surgery to shrink the pockets. If part of the bone supporting the teeth has been destroyed, further surgery may be needed. Such surgery can reshape or rebuild the bone that has been lost.

How Can Gum Disease Be Prevented?

Brushing and flossing the teeth helps remove plaque. In the early stage of gum disease, brushing twice a day and flossing every day usually will cure the problem. Guidelines include:

- Using a soft-bristled toothbrush.
- Picking a brush that feels comfortable and will reach all the teeth, even those in back.
- Replacing the brush when the bristles show signs of wear.
- Brushing with a short, gentle, back-and-forth motion.
- Remembering to brush the inside surfaces, the back teeth, and the tongue.
- Flossing to reach plaque between the teeth and under the gum line, where a brush cannot go.

It also is important to see a dentist regularly for checkups and professional cleanings.

Resources

American Dental Association, 211 East Chicago Avenue, Chicago, IL 60611. The leading national organization for dentists has information about gum disease and dental care on its website.
Telephone 312-440-2500
http://www.ada.org

U.S. National Institute of Dental and Craniofacial Research, 31 Center Drive, MSC 2290, Bethesda, MD 20892-2290. Part of the U.S. National Institutes of Health (NIH), this agency publishes brochures and posts fact sheets at its website about gum disease and mouth care.
Telephone 301-496-4261
http://www.nidcr.nih.gov

► *See also*
Abscess
Bacterial Infections
Canker Sores
Cavities
Diabetes
Halitosis

H

Hair Loss

Hair loss refers to the partial or total loss of hair from part of the body where normally it grows.

KEYWORDS
for searching the Internet and other reference sources

Alopecia

Chemotherapy

Keratin

Trichotillomania

Hair Today, Gone Tomorrow

Hair is said to be a person's crowning glory. Most of the hair on a person's head is growing constantly. Scalp hair grows about half an inch per month, although this growth rate slows as people age. The growth stage lasts for 2 to 6 years. It is followed by a resting stage, lasting for 2 to 3 months, during which the hair still is attached but no longer grows. After the resting stage, the hair falls out, and a new hair starts to form in the same spot. The average person loses about 50 to 100 hairs a day as part of this normal cycle. Hair loss occurs when people lose more hairs than normal each day or when new hairs do not grow to replace the lost ones.

How Does Hair Grow?

To understand hair loss, it helps to know something about how hair is formed. Hair is made of keratin (KER-a-tin), the same protein that makes up nails and the outer layer of skin. The part of a hair that shows is called the hair shaft. Below the skin is the hair root, which is enclosed in the follicle (FOL-i-kul), a tiny, bulb-shaped structure. The root is alive, but the shaft is composed of dead tissue made by the follicle.

What Is Hair Loss?

Hair loss refers to the partial or total loss of hair from part of the body where normally it grows, especially the scalp. Alopecia (AL-o-PEE-sha) is the medical term for baldness, which is the loss of all or a significant part of the scalp hair. Unlike other parts of the body, hair is mostly decorative. Losing hair is not a medical problem in itself, although, in some cases, it can be a sign of illness. Many people are perfectly comfortable being bald. However, others feel that hair loss makes them less attractive.

What Causes Hair Loss?

More than 40 million men and 20 million women in the United States have some hair loss. It is quite normal for both men and women to see some thinning of their scalp hair as they get older. However, hair loss can occur for a number of other reasons as well. Following are some forms of hair loss and their causes.

Common baldness Loss of scalp hair due to aging affects most people of both sexes sooner or later. At least 95 percent of hair loss is of this kind. The condition is caused by a combination of age, genetics, and certain hormones* called androgens (AN-dro-jenz). These last two factors give the condition its medical name: androgenetic (AN-dro-je-NET-ik) alopecia. In men, the condition usually starts with a hairline that keeps moving higher, followed by a thin or bald spot that appears on top of the head. Eventually, all that may be left is a horseshoe-shaped fringe of hair around the sides and back of the head. This is known as male-pattern baldness. In women, the condition usually leads to thinning of the hair over the whole head. This is especially common after menopause*. It is known as female-pattern baldness.

*** hormones** are chemicals that are produced by different glands in the body. Hormones are like the body's ambassadors: they are created in one place but are sent through the body to have specific regulatory effects in different places.

*** menopause** (MEN-oh-pawz) is the time in a woman's life when she stops having periods and can no longer become pregnant.

Alopecia areata Alopecia areata (ar-ee-AY-ta) can strike people of any age, including children and young adults. This condition leads to sudden hair loss, often in round patches on the scalp about the size of a coin or larger. In severe cases, the hair may fall out from the whole head, including the eyebrows and beard, or the whole body. Alopecia areata may be caused by a problem with the immune system* in which immune cells attack the body's own follicles, for reasons that are not clear. The hair usually grows back on its own within 6 to 24 months.

*** immune system** is the body system that fights disease.

Medical problems Several medical conditions and treatments can cause hair loss in people of all ages and both sexes. Sometimes, people notice a lot of hair falling out within 1 to 3 months after having a high fever, a severe infection, or a major operation. Some women also lose a large amount of hair within a few months after giving birth. In addition, an overactive or underactive thyroid gland* can cause hair loss, as can ringworm (a fungus* infection) of the scalp. People with cancer often lose their hair during chemotherapy*. Other medications may cause hair loss as well, including blood thinners, birth control pills, and medicines for depression* and high blood pressure. Fortunately, this kind of hair loss usually is temporary. Typically, the hair grows back once the body adjusts, the disease is treated, or the medicine is stopped.

*** thyroid gland** (THY-roid GLAND) is located in the lower part of the front of the neck. The thyroid produces hormones that regulate the body's metabolism (me-TAB-o-LIZ-um), the processes the body uses to produce energy, to grow, and to maintain body tissues.

*** fungus** (FUN-gus) is any organism belonging to the kingdom Fungi (FUN-ji), which includes mushrooms, yeasts, and molds.

*** chemotherapy** (KEE-mo-THER-a-pee) is the treatment of cancer with powerful drugs that kill cancer cells.

*** depression** (de-PRESH-un) is a mental state characterized by feelings of sadness, despair, and discouragement.

Trichotillomania Trichotillomania (trik-o-til-o-MAY-nee-a) is a psychological* disorder in which people pull out their own hair, leading to noticeable hair loss. The most commonly affected spots are the scalp, eyebrows, and eyelashes. This nervous habit may be a reaction to emotional stress or anxiety. It often begins in childhood, although it occurs in adults, too. The hair grows back once the hair pulling is stopped.

*** psychological** (SI-ko-LOJ-i-kal) refers to mental processes, including thoughts, feelings, and emotions.

Poor diet When people do not get enough protein from their diet, the body may try to save protein by shifting hairs from the growing stage to the resting stage. As a result, a large number of hairs may fall out 2 to 3 months later, when the resting stage ends. Lack of iron also can lead to hair loss. Eating a healthy diet or taking iron pills can prevent or reverse this problem.

Improper hair care Chemicals, such as dyes, bleaches, straighteners, and permanents, can damage the hair if used too often or left on too long. Even shampooing, brushing, and combing can harm the hair if done too roughly. Hairstyles that pull the hair, such as tight ponytails and braids, also put a lot of stress on it. Mistreating the hair in any of these ways can lead to temporary hair loss.

How Is the Cause of Hair Loss Identified?

People who experience sudden, fast, or unusual hair loss should see a physician, who can identify the cause. In some cases, doctors may decide that the baldness is simply due to aging. In other cases, doctors may check the scalp and take samples from it to look for signs of disease. In addition, doctors may pluck several hairs from one spot on the head. These hairs then are examined under a microscope to see whether they are in the growing or resting stage. The percentage of hairs in each stage can provide another clue to the cause of the hair loss.

How Is Baldness Treated?

Hair loss due to alopecia areata usually clears up on its own with time. In the meantime, the condition sometimes is treated with corticosteroid* medicines that are rubbed onto the skin or taken by mouth or in a shot.

Common baldness due to aging does not need treatment for medical reasons. However, some people seek help, because they are concerned about the way they look. There are several major treatment options.

Hairstyles, wigs, and hair additions Simply getting the right haircut and styling the hair in a flattering way can make a big difference with thinning hair or scattered hair loss. For more widespread hair loss, wigs are an easy solution. Several kinds of partial wigs, known as hair additions, are available as well. They can be attached to the remaining hair or anchored to the scalp with special glues or fasteners.

Medication Two medications are now approved in the United States for regrowing lost hair or preventing further hair loss: minoxidil (mi-NOK-si-dil) and finasteride (fi-NAS-ter-ide). Minoxidil (Rogaine) can be bought without a prescription. It is a liquid that is rubbed onto the scalp. Only about a quarter of men and a fifth of women who use regular-strength minoxidil regrow a significant amount of hair, and it may take several months before these results are noticeable. Any new hair that grows often is thinner and lighter in color than the original hair. Also, any hair growth that occurs will cease once the treatment is stopped.

Finasteride (Propecia) is a second drug, which is sold by prescription. It is taken in pill form. This drug is marketed only for men, because it has not been shown to work in women, and it can cause birth defects if used by pregnant women. More than four out of five men who use finasteride have a slowing of their hair loss, and more than three out of five may have some hair regrowth. As with minoxidil, though, it can take months to see these effects.

Surgery Hair transplantation (trans-plan-TAY-shun) surgery is a lasting but expensive solution to hair loss. People who might benefit

Hair-Raising Facts

- Natural blondes have about 140,000 hairs on their head, on average. Brunettes have about 105,000 hairs, and redheads have about 90,000 hairs.
- At any given time, about 90 percent of the hairs on a person's head are growing. About 10 percent of the hairs are resting, getting ready to fall out.

* **corticosteroid** (KOR-ti-ko-STER-oid) is one of several medications that are prescribed to reduce inflammation and sometimes to suppress the body's immune response.

A Hairy Situation

Some people worry about having too little hair. Others worry about having too much. Hirsutism (HIR-soot-iz-uhm) is the medical term for excessive hair growth on the body and face, especially in women. Many women, particularly those of southern European and Middle Eastern descent, develop quite a bit of body and facial hair when they reach puberty. This is perfectly normal. In both women and men, the amount of body and facial hair often increases slowly with age. There is nothing abnormal or unhealthy about this, either.

If a person does not like the way the hair looks, it can be bleached or removed in a variety of ways. However, sometimes there is an increase in the growth of coarse, dark facial and body hair over a period of weeks or months. This can be a sign of a medical problem in which the level of androgens in the blood is abnormally high, as in certain disorders of the ovaries and adrenal glands.

Some medicines, such as steroids and certain blood pressure drugs, also may cause the growth of body and facial hair. In addition, anorexia nervosa (AN-o-REK-se-a ner-VO-sa), an eating disorder that involves self-starvation and often occurs in teenage girls, may cause an increase in fine body hair.

▶

See also

Cancer

Dietary Deficiencies

Fungal Infections

Ringworm

from this kind of surgery include men and some women with common baldness. The surgery also may help people who have lost some hair as a result of burns to or scars on the scalp, eyebrows, or eyelashes. The operation involves cutting tiny plugs of hair-bearing scalp from parts of the head where hair still grows, and then reattaching the plugs to bald parts of the head. No new hair is added. Existing hair simply is moved from one spot to another. Since hundreds or even thousands of the tiny plugs must be moved to get good results, the procedure usually is done in several surgery sessions that are months apart. Sometimes, a larger flap of skin is moved instead of many tiny plugs.

Scalp reduction surgery is another procedure, which may be combined with hair transplantation. It involves removing a bald area of scalp from the top of the head, and then pulling the hair-bearing scalp forward to cover the area.

Coping with Hair Loss

Hair loss can be upsetting, even when it is temporary. Hairstyles, wigs, hair additions, hats, and bandannas can help hide hair loss if it makes a person uncomfortable. For many people, hair loss simply does not matter. Others wear their baldness with pride. Many even shave any remaining hair if the hair loss is patchy. Often, it is just a matter of style.

Resources

American Hair Loss Council, 401 N. Michigan Avenue, Chicago, IL 60611. This nonprofit group provides information about hair loss on its website.
Telephone 312-321-5128
http://www.ahlc.org

American Society of Plastic and Reconstructive Surgeons, 444 E. Algonquin Road, Arlington Heights, IL 60005-4664. This organization for surgeons provides information about hair replacement surgery on its website.
Telephone 847-228-9900
http://www.plasticsurgery.org

National Alopecia Areata Foundation, P.O. Box 150760, San Rafael, CA 94915-0760. This nonprofit group provides information about alopecia areata.
Telephone 415-456-4644
http://www.alopeciaareata.com

Halitosis

Halitosis is bad breath.

Halitosis is the medical name for bad breath. Often people with halitosis do not know that they have it. Halitosis can be caused by many things:

- Eating certain spicy foods, such as garlic and onion, which have odors that are expelled through the lungs after being absorbed into the bloodstream
- Poor oral hygiene, which leaves food particles in the mouth to collect odor-causing bacteria
- Tooth decay
- Gum disease
- Smoking
- Sinus or respiratory infections
- Xerostomia (ze-ro-STO-me-a) of the mouth (unusual dryness)
- Medical disorders, such as liver disease, kidney disease, or diabetes
- Medications
- Dieting and ketone* build-up in the body.

KEYWORDS
for searching the Internet and other reference sources

Bad breath

Dentistry

Xerostomia

* **ketones** (KEE-tones) are the chemicals produced when the body breaks down fat for energy.

How Is Halitosis Treated and Prevented?

Treatment for halitosis depends on its cause. Dentists can identify oral causes, which account for most cases of halitosis, and develop an appropriate treatment plan. For halitosis due to gum disease, dentists may refer people to specialists in treating the gums called periodontists. Dentists may refer people with healthy mouths who have halitosis to doctors for diagnosis and treatment.

Good dental hygiene is very important in preventing halitosis. This includes:

- Brushing teeth at least twice a day
- Brushing the tongue
- Removing pieces of food caught between teeth with dental floss every day
- Having regular dental check-ups and dental cleanings

It also is important for people who wear dentures to take them out each night and to clean them well before putting them in again.

Resources

Book

Smith, Rebecca. *The Columbia University School of Dental and Oral Surgery's Guide to Family Dental Care.* New York: Norton, 1997.

Organization

American Dental Association, 211 East Chicago Avenue, Chicago, IL 60611.
Telephone 312-440-2500
http://www.ada.org

See also
Bacterial Infections
Gum Disease

Hantavirus

Hantavirus pulmonary syndrome is a lung disease caused by a virus carried by rodents, especially deer mice.

KEYWORDS
for searching the Internet and other reference sources

Hemorrhagic fevers

Infection

Pulmonary system

Renal system

What Is Hantavirus Pulmonary Syndrome?

Hantavirus pulmonary syndrome (HAN-ta-vi-rus PUL-mo-nar-ee SIN-drome), or HPS for short, is an uncommon but deadly lung disease. It is caused by a type of virus known as hantavirus, which is carried by rodents*, especially deer mice.

* **rodents** are small, gnawing mammals with large, chisel-shaped front teeth. They include rats, mice, and squirrels. Rodents carry a number of infectious diseases that affect humans.

The disease was first identified in 1993, when an outbreak occurred in the geographic area shared by New Mexico, Arizona, Colorado, and Utah, known as the Four Corners. Several healthy young adults there suddenly came down with serious breathing problems. About half soon died. Scientists traced the mystery illness to the Sin Nombre virus, a type of hantavirus carried by deer mice. It turns out that there were large numbers of deer mice in the Four Corners area that year due to heavy spring rains.

Since 1993, HPS has been found in more than half of states in the United States, especially in the west. Over 200 cases of HPS had been reported in the United States by mid-1999.

The U.S. and the World

- There are at least 14 kinds of hantavirus. This family of viruses is named for the Hantaan River in Korea.
- In North and South America, certain types of hantavirus cause hantavirus pulmonary syndrome (HPS).
- In Asia and Europe, other types cause a disease known as hemorrhagic (hem-mo-RAJ-ik) fever with renal (REE-nal) syndrome (HFRS).

How Do People Catch HPS?

Certain rodents shed hantavirus in their urine, droppings, and saliva. These rodents include deer mice, cotton rats, rice rats, and white-footed mice, but not common house mice. When the rodent urine, droppings, or nesting materials are stirred up, tiny droplets of virus can get into the air, where people can breathe them.

Anyone of any age or sex can catch HPS. Activities that put people at risk include opening cabins and sheds that have been closed for the winter, cleaning homes and barns, using trail shelters when hiking and camping, and working in crawl spaces under buildings.

What Happens When People Get HPS?

Symptoms The first symptoms of HPS show up one to five weeks after a person comes into contact with hantavirus. They include tiredness, fever, and muscle aches. People may have headache, dizziness, chills, nausea, vomiting, diarrhea, or stomach pain. Four to 10 days later, they start coughing and become short of breath as the lungs fill with fluid.

Diagnosis A blood test can quickly show if someone is infected with hantavirus. However, similar symptoms also occur with more common diseases. For this reason, doctors might not suspect HPS unless they know of an outbreak in the area.

Treatment People with HPS need intensive medical care. The sooner they get help, the better. In the hospital, people receive oxygen therapy to help them breathe more easily. The hospital staff also keeps a close watch for problems that may arise with fluid levels and blood pressure, so that such problems can be treated promptly.

Preventing HPS

The best way to prevent HPS is to make sure that homes, workplaces, and campsites are not attractive to rodents. Guidelines include:

- Keeping a clean home where food is not easy for rodents to find.
- Putting a tight-fitting lid on the garbage can.
- Throwing away uneaten pet food at the end of each day.
- Sealing any entry holes in the walls.
- Clearing brush and junk from around the base of the house to get rid of nesting materials.
- Avoiding contact with rodents when camping or hiking.
- Not disturbing or camping near rodent burrows.

Resource

U.S. Centers for Disease Control and Prevention, 1600 Clifton Road N.E., Atlanta, GA 30333. The website for this U.S. government agency has a section titled "All About Hantavirus."
Telephone 800-311-3435
http://www.cdc.gov/ncidod/diseases/hanta/hps

Hare Lip *See* Birth Defects; Cleft Palate

Hay Fever *See* Allergies

- About 150,000 to 200,000 people are hospitalized with HFRS each year worldwide.
- More than half of all cases of HFRS occur in China.
- Russia and Korea also have hundreds to thousands of cases each year.
- In addition, hundreds of cases each year are found in Japan, Sweden, Finland, Bulgaria, Greece, Hungary, France, and the Balkan countries formerly making up Yugoslavia.

Hemorrhagic Fever with Renal Syndrome (HFRS)

Hemorrhagic (hem-mo-RAJ-ik) fever with renal (REE-nal) syndrome (HFRS) is similar to hantavirus pulmonary syndrome (HPS) but occurs more often in Asia and Europe.

HFRS symptoms range from mild to severe. The severe form starts with a sudden, intense headache, backache, fever, and chills. Within days, people may develop tiny purple spots on their skin and bloodshot eyes, both signs of tiny leaks in their blood vessels. As the bleeding inside the body gets worse, the person may have a sudden, dangerous drop in blood pressure. This can lead to physical collapse and even death.

Approximately 5 to 10 percent of severe cases of HFRS will be fatal. As the blood pressure returns to normal, the person may develop life-threatening kidney problems. Complete recovery from severe HFRS can take weeks or months.

See also
Pneumonia
Viral Infections

Headache

KEYWORDS
for searching the Internet and other reference sources

Cephalagia

Inflammation

Migraine

Neurology

Headache is a pain or discomfort of the head. It is not a disease but a symptom of some other problem in the body, and there are many possible causes. When someone gets a headache it usually is temporary, and only very rarely is it a sign of serious illness.

What Are Headaches?

Headaches are so common that it is hard to imagine someone who has not had a headache, unless perhaps it is a newborn baby. Although there are dozens of causes of headaches, most headaches are due to tension or stress. About 20 percent of people in the United States at some point in their lives may have a recurrent, often severe type of headache known as migraine.

Up to 50 million people in America seek medical help for migraine and other severe headaches each year. It has been estimated that more than 180 million workdays are lost due to headache annually, and that more than a billion dollars are spent for over-the-counter remedies to relieve headaches.

Chronic headaches may accompany emotional disturbances such as depression. Many times, headaches are just one of a number of symptoms, such as fever or dizziness, that are brought on by various diseases or injuries. Migraine headaches frequently are accompanied by nausea and other symptoms that are characteristic of it.

Causes and Types of Headaches

The pain of headache may be mild, extremely severe, or anywhere in between. It may involve the entire head, one side only, the forehead, the base of the skull, or it may seem to move around. The pain may be sharp, a dull ache, or throbbing. A headache may last a few minutes or hours. It may recur from time to time, or may become chronic, coming back many times over an extended period.

How Did Migraine Get Its Name?

Aretaeus of Cappadocia, a medical writer in Greece in the second century A.D., is believed to have been the first to recognize migraine as a one-sided headache with stomach and visual disturbances. Galen, a contemporary of Aretaeus, gave this affliction the name *hemikrania,* meaning "half of the head," referring to the way it typically affects people. In Old English, the term became *megrim,* and finally evolved to "migraine."

An Ancient, and Drastic, Treatment

Prehistoric peoples are known to have surgically cut holes in the skulls of living persons, presumably to relieve some ailment. The purpose of this operation is not known with certainty. Perhaps it was carried out to relieve the pressure of a blood clot under the skull caused by a blow to the head. However, it is believed that in some instances it may have been done in an attempt to cure headaches by releasing evil spirits. Stone Age patients who underwent this surgery apparently often survived, because many of the skulls found by scientists showed new growth of bone around the holes.

Many people believe that the brain itself is involved in headaches, but neither the brain nor the skull has nerves that register pain. The sources of head pain are the nerve endings in the blood vessels and muscles in and around the head. Pain may be felt when these tissues become stretched, inflamed, or damaged. Headaches can arise in blood vessels within the brain, as well as in the meninges (me-NIN-jeez), which are the sensitive membranes that cover the brain.

Mild headaches may arise from such things as a change in the weather or hunger. Common causes of mild to severe headache pain include disorders of the eyes, ears, and sinuses. For example, eyestrain and diseases such as glaucoma can produce pain in the front of the head and around the eye. Mastoiditis, an inflammation of bone behind the ear, can cause severe pain on the affected side of the head. Sinusitis can cause sharp headaches in the front of the head (often called sinus headaches). A jaw or bite that does not close properly also can cause headache.

Many types of infection with fever, such as influenza (flu), cause headache. Other causes include drinking too much alcohol, heavy smoking, withdrawal from caffeine, or inhaling a noxious gas, such as carbon monoxide. Contrary to popular belief, high blood pressure rarely is a direct cause of headache.

Headache is one of the symptoms of concussion, and sometimes becomes chronic following this injury.

Rarely, headaches may be caused by brain abscesses, brain tumors, bleeding into the brain, and meningitis (an inflammation of the membranes covering the brain).

Physicians often classify headaches as those caused by disease or injury (described above); tension headaches; and vascular* headaches. Vascular headaches include migraine and a type called cluster headaches. Tension and migraine headaches are very common.

***vascular** refers to veins and arteries (the blood vessels).

Tension Headaches

Headaches that are associated with emotional stress or muscular tension are called tension headaches. The muscular tension may be in the neck, face, or scalp. It may be the result of poor posture or of constantly bending over one's work. These headaches are extremely common, and almost everyone has them at one time or another. A person may have one after working on the computer too long or bending over while doing homework.

Pressures from school, friends, or family may play a role. Adults may develop tension headaches because of stress at work. Tension headaches may be mild to moderate and occur in various parts of the head. The feeling has been described as a steady ache or as a tight sensation.

The pain of tension headaches can be chronic or recurrent, sometimes coming on every day. Muscles near the site of the pain, such as at the back of the neck, or on the sides of the head, are often tense and tender. Sometimes chronic tension headache is a symptom of depression.

Migraine

Migraine is a moderate to severe headache that can interfere with a person's life. The pain is typically, although not always, in one side of the head, at least at the beginning, and may last from hours to days. Migraine headaches occur every so often, usually beginning in adolescence or early adult life. They tend to become less frequent with age, and tend to be rare or absent after the age of 40 to 50.

Migraine is one of the most common types of headaches, affecting about 20 million people in the United States alone. Women are four times more likely to experience migraine than men. People in all walks of life have been afflicted, including Sigmund Freud, Thomas Jefferson, Charles Darwin, and Lewis Carroll, the author of *Alice in Wonderland.* Contemporary sufferers have included the late Princess Diana of Great Britain and the basketball player, Kareem Abdul-Jabbar.

The cause or causes of migraine headaches are not known with certainty. They are classified as vascular headaches because blood vessels in the head dilate, or expand, during an attack. It is believed that certain chemical substances in the nerve cells surrounding the vessels are involved in the attack. The precise mechanism is not fully understood, however.

Migraine headaches tend to run in families. However, one does not catch this headache from someone else.

Most migraine attacks begin without warning. Typically, the pain is throbbing, often growing in intensity. It usually is accompanied by nausea and sometimes vomiting. The slightest noise or movement can make it worse. Ordinary light coming through a window may seem unbearable.

The Aura In about 15 percent of people who get migraines, the headaches are preceded by a distinctive type of warning called an aura (OR-uh). An aura can be a blank spot in the vision bordered by zigzag and flashing lights or numbness or weakness in parts of the body. After several minutes, the aura goes away and the pain of the headache begins. Migraine preceded by an aura has been called a classic migraine, or migraine with aura.

Triggers In a number of individuals, certain factors, or triggers, can bring on a migraine attack. Common examples include red wine and foods such as cheese, nuts, chocolate, and citrus fruit. Nitrites, which are used as meat preservatives in products such as bacon or cold cuts, are another recognized trigger. Other triggers include excessive sleep, relaxation after exercise, fatigue, and stress. Still others are related to hormonal changes, such as those that occur at the onset of menstruation. Sometimes the trigger is not known.

Cluster Headaches

Intensely painful headaches that occur one or more times daily are called cluster headaches. These headaches may keep recurring for weeks or months, then not return for years. The pain is centered on one side of the head around the eye. Besides pain, the symptoms include a watery eye and a runny nose on the affected side.

Cluster headaches occur in men more often than in women, and usually first appear about age 40. Their cause is unknown.

Should I See a Doctor?

Most headaches, although unpleasant, are not signs of serious health problems. A person should see a doctor if the headaches are unusually persistent or severe, if there are any changes in vision or speech, or if there is weakness or numbness in any body part.

How Are Headaches Treated?

Over-the-counter pain-relieving drugs, such as acetaminophen, may ease mild headaches. Relief also may come from such simple measures as getting some fresh air, taking a hot bath, getting a muscle massage, or just lying down for a while. Tension headaches can be dealt with by addressing the cause of the emotional or physical stress.

For severe headaches, such as migraine, the best approach is prevention, that is, avoiding the factors that the individual knows are most likely to trigger an attack. Once an attack begins, pain-relieving drugs may help to ease symptoms. The doctor also can prescribe medicines that will narrow the blood vessels in the brain that have dilated during an attack. If migraine attacks occur frequently, the doctor can prescribe medications to prevent the migraine. Biofeedback, a relaxation technique, has proven helpful in relieving and avoiding some headaches.

Cluster headache attacks may be over before pain-relieving drugs can take effect. However, some prescription medicines may be useful in prevention.

Many common headaches can, of course, be prevented by maintaining a healthy lifestyle, including regular eating and sleeping habits, and avoidance of excess alcohol and caffeine intake.

▶ *See also*
Concussion
Ear infection
Glaucoma
Sinusitis
Temporomandibular joint syndrome

Hearing Loss *See* Deafness and Hearing Loss

Heart Attack *See* Heart Disease

Heart Disease

Heart disease is a broad term covering many conditions that prevent the heart from working properly to pump blood throughout the body.

KEYWORDS
for searching the Internet and other reference sources

Arteriosclerosis

Atherosclerosis

Cardiovascular system

Coronary artery disease

Heart failure

Myocardial infarction

Rheumatic fever

Max's Story

Max, who had just turned 14, and his grandfather Harry often shared a Saturday morning ritual: breakfast at their favorite diner, followed by a brisk game of tennis. On this occasion, they both ordered the special: two fried eggs, four strips of bacon, hotcakes, and a side of hash browns. Plates cleared, they hit the tennis courts, but only ten minutes into their game, Harry, breathing hard and sweating heavily, stopped and complained of a squeezing pain in his chest. Although his grandfather protested that it was most likely indigestion, Max went for help. At the emergency room, his grandfather was given aspirin and put on a heart monitor that showed

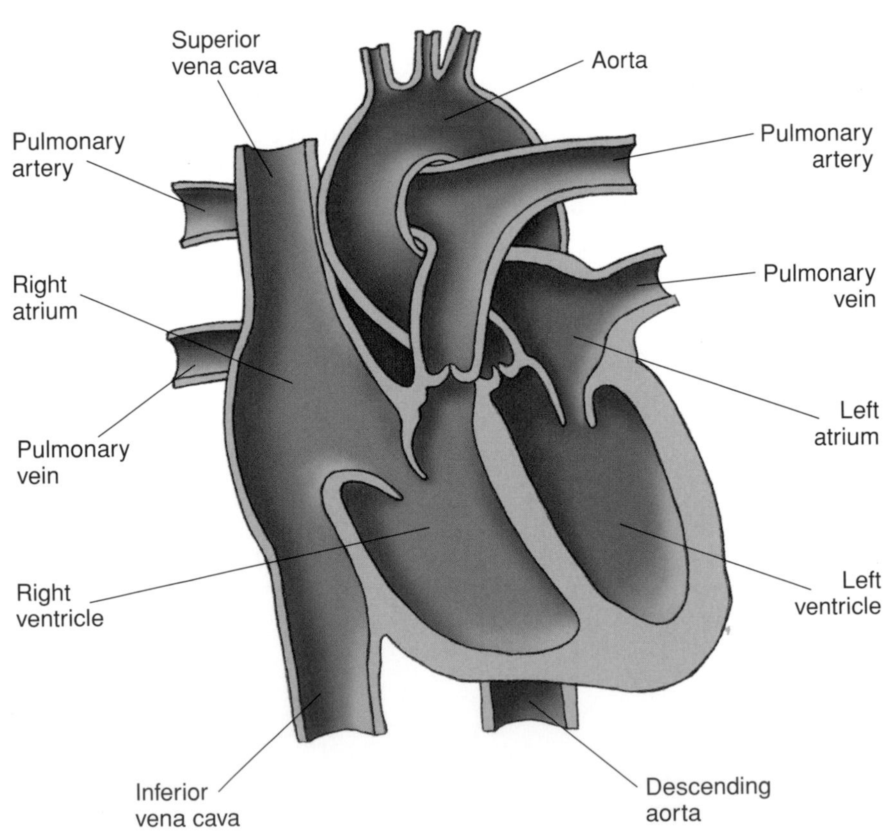

Anatomy of the heart.

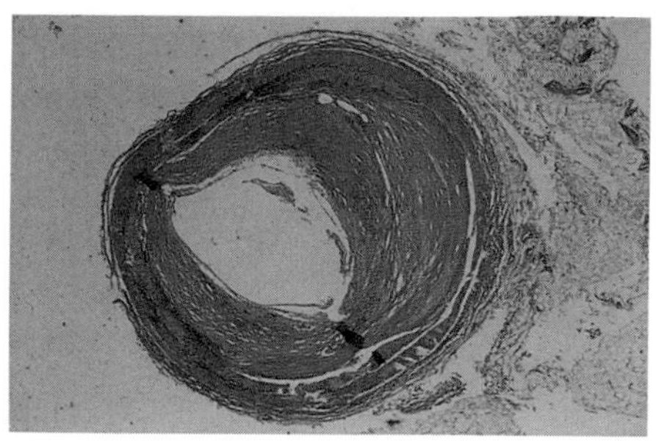
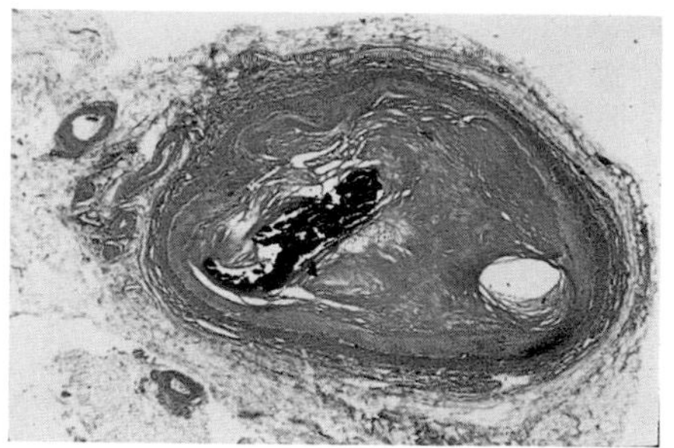

A coronary artery showing (*left*) moderate atherosclerosis and (*right*) severe atherosclerosis. © *W. Ober, Visuals Unlimited*

that he had experienced a mild heart attack. A nurse told Max that his quick action might have saved his grandfather's life.

What Is Heart Disease?

Heart disease is a group of diseases that prevent the heart from working as well as it should.

Only a little larger than a fist, a normal, healthy heart is at the center of the body's cardiovascular system*. Each day the average heart beats, or expands and contracts, about 100,000 times. In a 70-year lifetime, an average human heart beats more than 2.5 billion times.

The circulatory system* is responsible for providing nourishment to the body's cells and removing wastes from them. The arteries take oxygenated blood from the heart to the cells; the veins take blood from the cells to the lungs for reoxygenation and recirculation by the heart.

The coronary arteries encircle the heart from above and below like strands of ivy. With their strong, flexible walls and smooth linings, healthy coronary arteries supply blood to the heart itself, in much the same way as a hose transports water to a garden.

At birth, these coronary arteries are completely open and clear, permitting a maximum flow of blood to the heart, but as people age, these vessels can become clogged with a thick combination of lipids (fats), cholesterol, calcium, and other substances. As these layers accumulate inside the arteries, they can lead to arteriosclerosis (ar-teer-e-o-skle-RO-sis), a condition also known as "hardening of the arteries," since this buildup eventually stiffens the inner artery walls. Atherosclerosis (ath-er-o-skle-RO-sis), a buildup of plaque* on the innermost portion of the vessel, is the most common form of arteriosclerosis. Over time, plaque continues to accumulate in the blood vessels, much like grease that clogs a kitchen drainpipe. The result is a narrowing of the inside diameter of the vessel.

* **cardiovascular system** (kar-dee-o-VAS-ku-lur) is comprised of the heart and blood vessels.

* **circulatory system** (SIR-ku-la-tor-ee) is made up of the heart, arteries, veins, capillaries, and circulating blood.

* **plaque** (PLAK) is a raised patch or swelling on a body surface. Arterial plaque occurs on the inner surface of an artery and is produced by fatty deposits.

What Are the Different Types of Heart Disease?

Coronary arteries affected by atherosclerosis will eventually develop coronary artery disease, a condition in which the vessels are so narrow that they can no longer provide adequate nutrients or oxygen to nourish the heart. Blood flow is blocked either partially or totally.

Heart attacks are injuries to the heart muscle that occur when blood flow through a coronary artery is interrupted, cutting off the vital supply of oxygen to the heart. Blood can be kept from the heart by narrowing

During a heart attack, the flow of blood to the heart is blocked by atherosclerotic plaque or clots, causing tissue death in the areas deprived of oxygen.

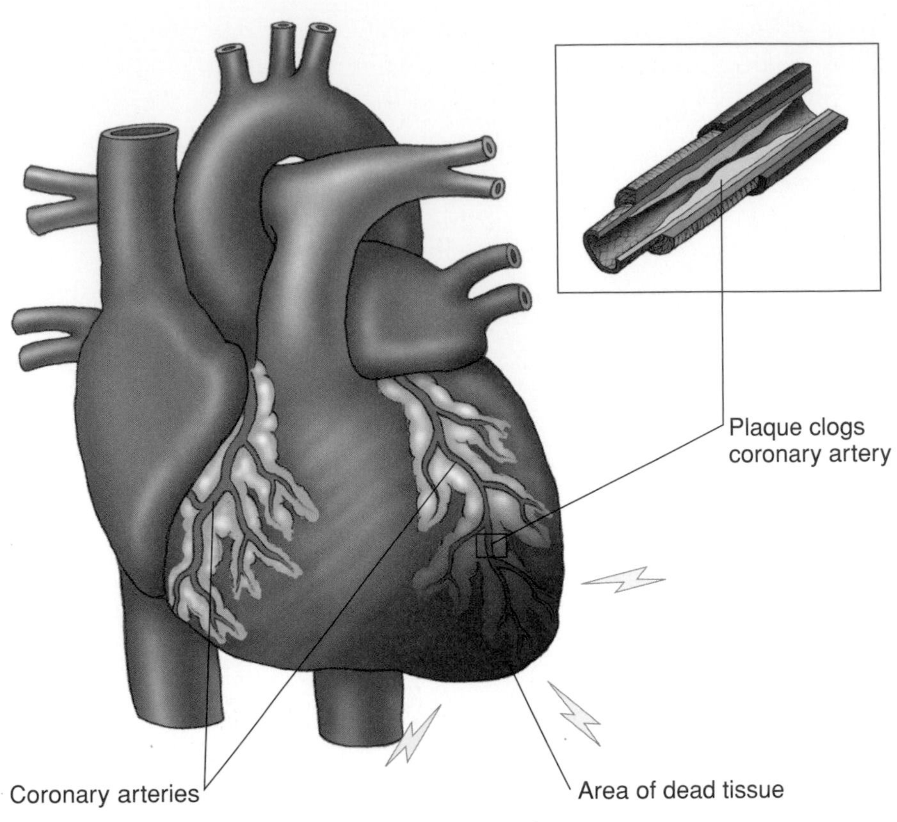

of the arteries by atherosclerotic plaque, by a blood clot blocking the narrowed vessel, or by a contraction (spasm) of the artery in response to a lack of oxygen or blood. The part of the heart muscle affected by the blockage is usually slowly starved of oxygen. The longer the heart muscle goes without nourishment, the more muscle tissue deteriorates or dies. Quick action, like that taken by Max, is essential.

Blocked arteries are not the only cause of heart attacks. Hypertension, or high blood pressure, can be a contributing factor. Pumping blood against high pressures in the blood vessels (as occur in people with uncontrolled hypertension) can put too much strain on the heart. Abuse of alcohol, viral infections, tuberculosis, parasites, or other vascular (blood vessel) diseases can also lead to heart disease.

Diseased valves can also put abnormal strain on the heart. The four valves, located between the atria (upper chambers) and ventricles (lower chambers) of the heart, open and close like tiny camera shutters to make sure that blood flows in the right amount and in the right direction. If a valve is scarred and cannot open completely, the heart has to work harder to pump enough blood through the obstruction. A valve that does not close completely can allow blood to go backward through the heart chambers, making the heart work harder by having to pump the same blood twice.

Bacterial endocarditis, or inflammation of the endocardium (the inner surface of the heart), is an infection that can cause the heart valves to malfunction. Such an infection may rarely follow oral surgery or dental work, when normally harmless bacteria are released into the bloodstream. This generally affects valves that were previously damaged from rheumatic heart disease or other conditions.

Various forms of heart disease can also cause dysrhythmias (dis-RITH-me-as), or disturbances in the normal heartbeat pattern. Although many of these are harmless, some are quite serious. For example, ventricular fibrillation (ven-TRIK-yoo-lar fib-rill-AY-shun), a type of heart rhythm in which pumping is uncoordinated and ineffective, can cause sudden death.

What Causes Heart Disease?

Risk factors Heart disease is not contagious and, to a large extent, can be prevented, controlled, and, in some cases, even reversed. When looking at what causes heart disease, researchers divide the risk factors* into those that people can control and those that they cannot. Among the factors that cannot be changed are:

- **Age.** As people age, their cholesterol levels usually increase and hardening of the arteries appears and progresses in most people.
- **Gender.** Men have higher cholesterol levels than women until around age 45. Women catch up after menopause*.
- **Family histories.** People with a family history of heart disease are at increased risk.

The good news is that some risk factors can be controlled. These include:

- **Smoking.** Smokers' risk of heart attack is almost twice that of nonsmokers, and their risk of sudden cardiac death is two to four times that of nonsmokers. Quitting (or never starting!) is a definite heart-healthy move.
- **High blood pressure.** Hypertension puts extra stress on the heart. Taking medication to lower high blood pressure, maintaining healthy body weight, avoiding salt, and increasing exercise can help people reduce blood pressure.
- **Blood lipids.** Lowering fats in the blood, such as cholesterol, can reduce the risk of heart disease. Individuals who come from a family with heart disease; who have other risk factors such as smoking, diabetes, hypertension, obesity, or physical inactivity; or who have a parent with a high cholesterol level should have their lipid levels monitored by a doctor.
- **Diabetes.** Many people with diabetes have high blood pressure or are obese. Diabetes can also increase lipid levels and accelerate the development of atherosclerosis, heart attack, and stroke.
- **Obesity.** Obesity is generally defined as having an adult body mass index greater than 27 (see sidebar). About one third of American adults are obese, even though maintaining a healthy weight throughout life seems to be one of the best ways of living longer and healthier.

* **risk factors** are things about people, such as their age, weight, or diet, that increase their chances of getting a certain disease.

* **menopause** (MEN-o-pawz) is the time of life when women stop menstruating (having their monthly period) and can no longer become pregnant.

Body Mass Index

The body mass index (BMI) has been used since the early 1980s as a medical standard for obesity measurement. To calculate BMI:

1. Multiply weight in pounds by 700
2. Divide that number by height in inches
3. Divide that number by height in inches again

The recommended BMI is 20 to 26. The overweight range is 26 to 27.3 for women and 26 to 27.8 for men. Most "experts" say that obesity begins with a BMI greater than 27.3 for women and 27.87 for men. All agree that anyone with a BMI over 30 is obese.

In a famous 30-year study of 5,127 adults in Framingham, Massachusetts, between 1948 and 1978, those who maintained their weight from age 25 on had a lower risk of heart disease. Those who lowered their weight over this time reduced their risk even further.

- **Physical activity.** Exercisers have a lower rate of cardiovascular disease; those who are inactive have a higher rate. Aerobic exercise* lowers the heart rate, lipid levels, and blood pressure and decreases body fat. Such activities include brisk walking, running, swimming, rowing, and jumping rope for at least ten to fifteen minutes. It is estimated that 60 percent of American adults get no aerobic exercise.

* **aerobic exercise** (air-O-bik) is exercise designed to increase oxygen consumption by the body; it helps keep the heart and lungs in shape.

Other risk factors that can be controlled include drinking too much alcohol and having too much stress.

The fat connection Cholesterol (ko-LES-ter-ol) is a soft, waxy substance that circulates in the blood and is found in every cell of the body. It is an important building material for cells and nerves and is used for the production of certain hormones. Cholesterol is used by the liver to make bile acids, which help digest food. Triglycerides (try-GLIS-er-ides) are fats in the blood that, like cholesterol, can come from either the diet or can be produced by the liver. Triglycerides are different from cholesterol, but like cholesterol, they are normally present in the blood. Elevated triglycerides may be associated with certain illnesses.

The body makes all the cholesterol it needs, but people also get cholesterol from their diets, particularly when they eat foods made from animal and dairy products. High blood cholesterol levels can have many causes, including genes (heredity) and lifestyle choices (diet). Too much cholesterol can lead to coronary heart disease. Hyperlipid disorders, in which there is too much cholesterol or too much triglyceride in the blood, are some of the most common inherited conditions in humans, affecting one in every 500 people. In persons with such disorders, risk factors such as obesity, cigarette smoking, and high blood pressure can increase the chance of coronary heart disease even further.

The U.S. and the World

The American Heart Association says cardiovascular disease has been the leading cause of death in the United States every year since 1900, except the year 1918. According to the AHA's *1999 Heart and Stroke Statistical Update:*

- Almost 60 million Americans have some form of cardiovascular disease. The most common condition is high blood pressure, which affects 50 million Americans.
- Heart disease killed 944,148 people in the United States in 1997, making it the leading cause of death. It accounts for about 40 percent of all deaths each year in America.
- About 84 percent of heart disease deaths occur in people who are 65 and older.

Heart disease also is a leading cause of death worldwide. The World Health Organization reports that in 1998, for example, 32 percent of all deaths (16.7 million) resulted from heart disease. It was the number 1 cause of death in all regions of the world, except Africa (where it was ninth) and the western Pacific (where it was third).

WHO predicts that worldwide heart disease death rates will climb during the next two decades if developing nations continue their trend toward increased smoking and more westernized diets.

How Do People Know They Have Heart Disease?

Heart disease is the number one killer in developed countries, and heart attacks are recognized as the most obvious sign of heart disease. Each year, 1.5 million Americans have heart attacks. But one problem with heart disease is that in 20 to 40 percent of people (like Max's grandfather), a heart attack is the first symptom of the disease. By then, plaque may have narrowed one or more arteries, limiting their ability to supply an area of the heart muscle with the oxygen and nutrients it needs.

Because a heart attack can cause severe damage by robbing the heart of oxygen, a quick reaction to the earliest signs of a heart attack is essential. Angina pectoris (an-JY-na PEK-to-ris), a squeezing, tightness, or heaviness in the chest that can extend to the left arm, neck, jaw, or shoulder blade, is often the first sign that someone with atherosclerosis is at risk for a heart attack. Physical exercise, a heavy meal, strong emotions, or extreme temperatures can bring it on. If angina occurs when a person is at rest, this means that the heart is starving for oxygen even when it is not working hard. Besides chest pain, weakness, fainting, profuse sweating, nausea, and vomiting can accompany a heart attack, although a heart attack that arrives without angina—a "silent" heart attack—may not be revealed until a patient shows up in the physician's office for an unrelated condition.

Valve disease can cause related symptoms of dizziness, fatigue, weakness, shortness of breath, and chest pain when exercising. These same signs, along with edema (e-DEE-ma), an accumulation of fluid that occurs when the heart cannot keep the circulation moving properly, can indicate heart failure*. Gravity often pulls the fluid downward, causing swelling in the feet, ankles, and legs.

* **heart failure** is a medical term used to describe a condition in which a damaged heart cannot pump enough blood to meet the oxygen and nutrient demands of the body. People with heart failure may find it hard to exercise due to the insufficient blood flow, but many people live a long time with heart failure.

Diagnosis

Depending on the type of heart disease, a physician can use a number of different tests to help pinpoint heart problems. They are divided into invasive tests done internally and noninvasive tests that can be performed externally.

Noninvasive procedures include:

- **Electrocardiogram** (ECG or EKG). A recording of the heart's electrical activity to help a doctor diagnose and monitor irregular heart rhythms, heart attacks, or other abnormalities. A portable ECG machine worn by a patient called a Holter monitor can also test the effectiveness of drug therapy for dysrhythmias and monitor pacemaker* functions for 12, 24, or 48 hours.
- **Stress test.** An ECG performed during exercise to determine the cause of chest pain and other symptoms related to physical activity.
- **Echocardiogram.** Ultrasonic waves, or high-frequency inaudible sound waves, are bounced off the surfaces of the heart and converted into an image that can be displayed on a monitor to diagnose congenital* heart disease, valve disease, congestive* heart failure, and other conditions.
- **Ultra-fast computed tomography.** Scanning that employs electron beams to detect calcium deposits in the coronary arteries.

* **pacemaker,** a device whose function is to send electrical signals that control the heartbeat. The heart's natural pacemaker is the sinoatrial node, a special group of cells. Sometimes it is necessary to implant a battery-powered pacemaker that sends small electrical charges through an electrode placed next to the wall of the heart.

* **congenital** (kon-JEN-i-tul) means existing at birth.

* **congestive** (kon-JES-tiv) means characterized by accumulation of too much fluid.

Invasive procedures include cardiac catheterization, which is used to evaluate coronary artery disease, causes of angina, complications following a heart attack, heart defects, and other internal disorders. A catheter, or long, thin tube, is inserted into the cardiovascular system, usually through

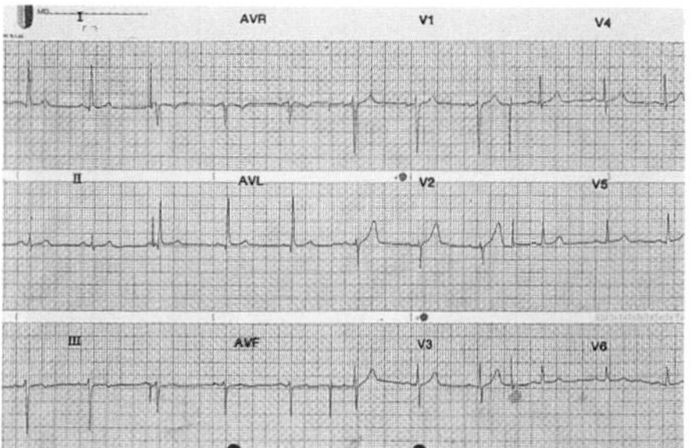

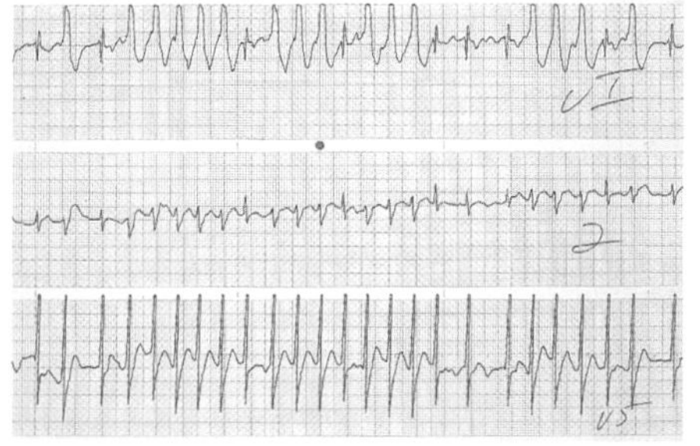

Doctors use electrocardiograms to monitor heart rhythms. Compare the healthy heart rhythm (left) to heart rhythm during a heart attack (right). *© 1984 Martin M. Rotker/Photo Researchers, Inc.*

Arteries in the circulatory system.

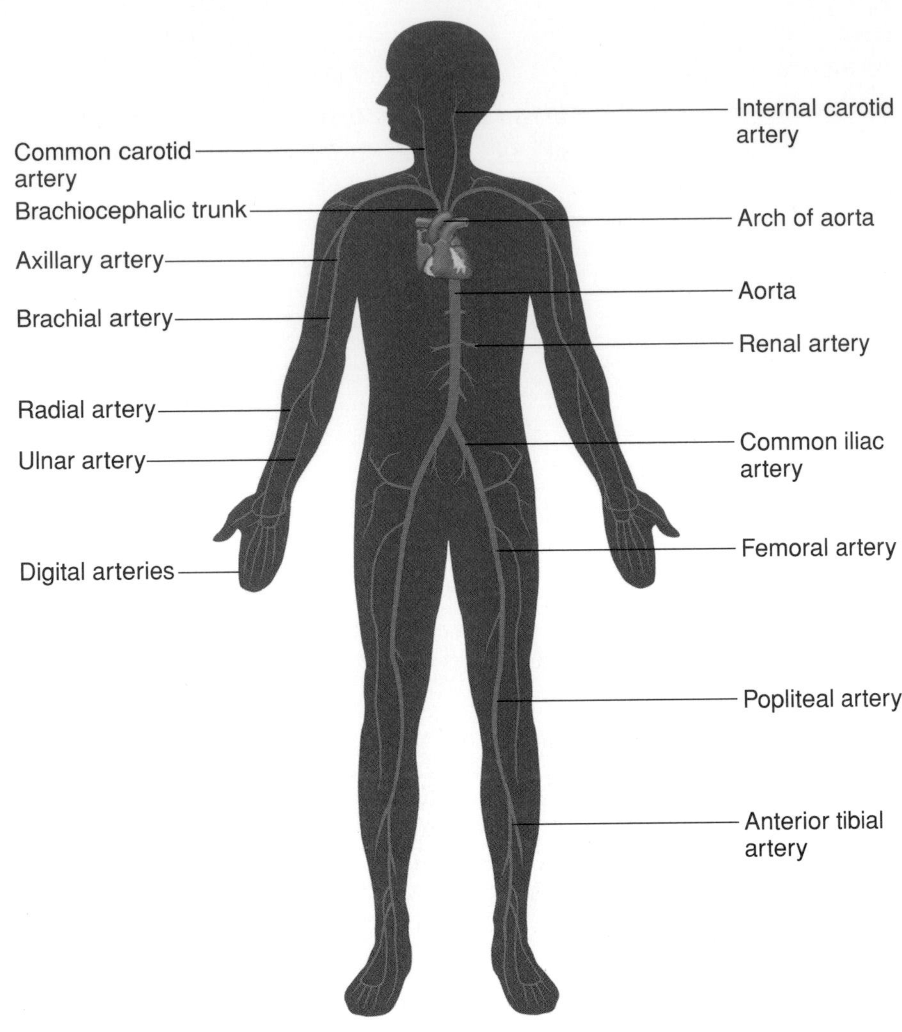

an arm or leg artery. A contrast solution (a dye that will show up on film) is then injected to visualize the blood vessels on film (angiography). Depending on where the catheter is positioned, it can diagnose the extent of coronary artery plaque buildup or abnormalities of the aorta* and valves.

* **aorta** (ay-OR-ta) is the major large artery that carries blood from the heart to the rest of the the body.

How Is Heart Disease Treated?

Although many heart conditions cannot be cured, they can be controlled with lifestyle changes, medication, or surgery, or a combination of these strategies.

Medications Irregular heartbeats, heart failure, and angina are often treated with a combination of healthy lifestyle changes and medications. One of the most common medications used is nitroglycerine (ny-tro-GLIS-er-in), in the form of a tiny pill dissolved under the tongue, which acts to open the heart's blood vessels and permit more oxygen to flow to the heart muscle. Beta-blockers decrease the heart's demand for oxygen by slowing down the heart rate. Aspirin, which helps keep the blood from clotting easily, is given to people who have heart disease or a high risk of heart disease to decrease the likelihood of blood clots and thereby lowers the risk of heart attack and premature death. At the time of a heart attack, patients may be given special clot-dissolving medications intravenously (injected into a vein) to help unclog the diseased coronary arteries. Medications are also used to control high blood pressure.

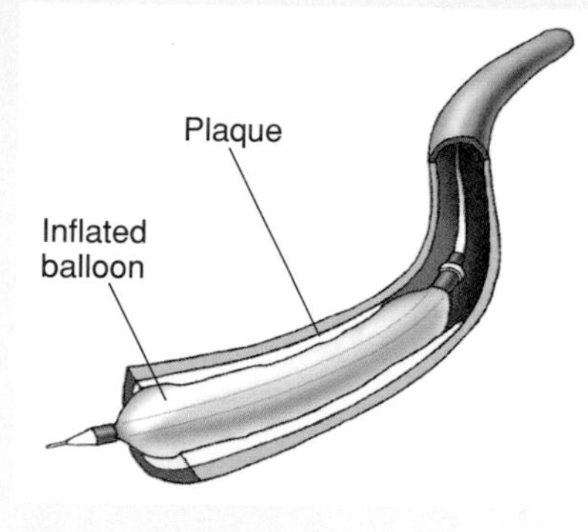

Balloon angioplasty.

Surgical procedures Angioplasty (AN-je-o-plas-tee), also called balloon angioplasty, opens up vessels blocked by plaque buildup. A specially designed balloon is threaded through an artery. Once positioned, the balloon is set at the narrowest portion of the blocked artery and inflated, pumping up and widening the channel. After the artery is opened, the balloon is withdrawn.

One problem is that coronary arteries opened by angioplasty often close within three to six months. To prevent this, surgeons often place a stent, a 1-inch tube of wirelike stainless steel shaped like a tiny coiled spring, into the vessel, where it is expanded. The stent props the vessel open like scaffolding supports a tunnel. Stents can also be lifesaving for

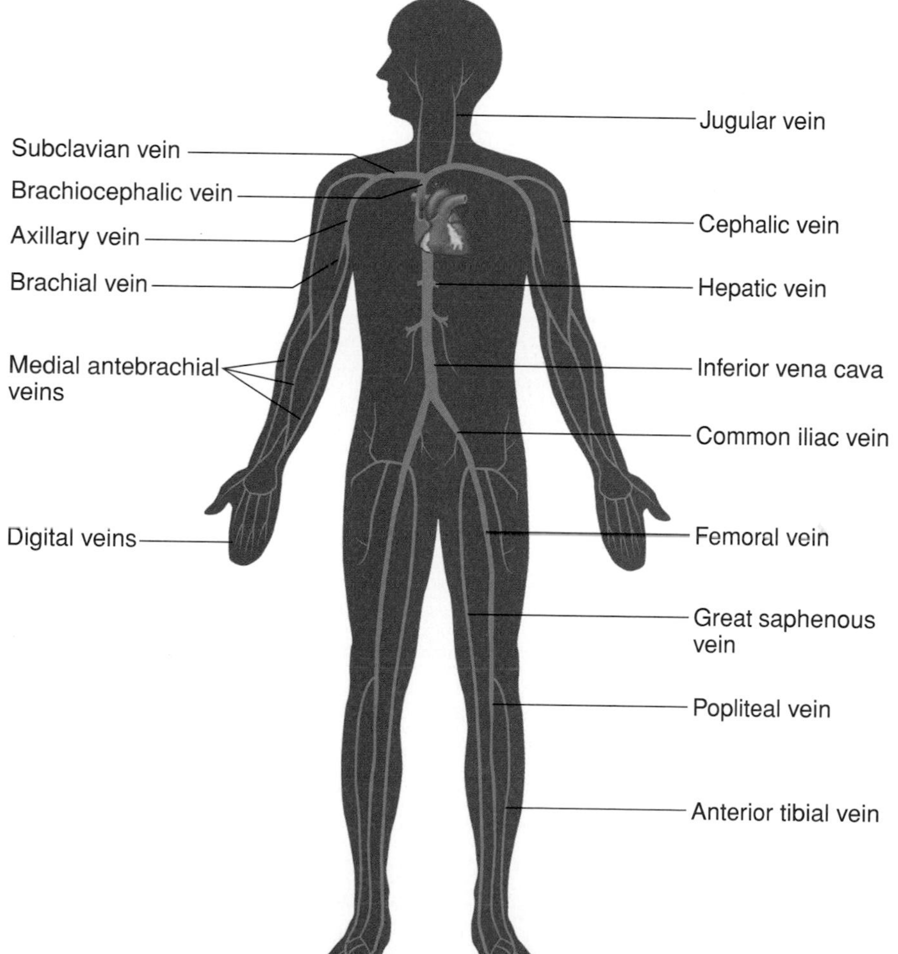

Veins in the circulatory system.

Did You Know?

- Coronary heart disease is the largest killer of American men and women. Every 29 seconds someone suffers a coronary problem; every minute someone dies from one.
- Managing heart failure costs Americans between $10 and $15 billion annually.
- Almost 15,000 heart transplants have been done since the 1980s, according to the United Network of Organ Sharing. About 2,500 are performed each year, with many other patients waiting in line.

Microwave Ovens

Convenience stores, cafeterias, and snack bars used to post warnings near their microwave ovens for people with pacemakers. Electromagnetic radiation emitted from the microwave ovens sometimes caused current variations in the pacemakers. Pacemakers today are shielded from stray electromagnetic forces and have a backup mode in case of disruption of the main circuit's programming.

Frogs' Legs and Galvanometers

Today's sophisticated electrocardiograph (ECG or EKG) began with the study of frogs' legs.

During the 1700s, scientists Luigi Galvani (1737–1798) and Alessandro Volta (1745–1827) used frogs to study muscle action. Their work led to development of the galvanometer (gal-va-NOM-e-ter), which measures current by electromagnetic action.

In 1903, William Einthoven (1860–1927) introduced the string galvanometer. Einthoven's galvanometer evolved into today's EKG machine, one of the fundamental tools that cardiologists use to monitor the heart's rhythms.

patients whose arteries suddenly collapse or spasm (contract) and close during angioplasty, setting off a heart attack.

Atherectomy (ath-er-EK-to-mee) is the excision (cutting out) and physical removal of plaque from arteries. It is used in place of or along with balloon angioplasty. Once the balloon is inflated, a miniature cutter whirs forward to scrape deposits from the wall of the vessel like a tiny rotor clearing a clogged drain. Debris is pushed to a special collection chamber, and when the device is withdrawn, the debris comes with it.

Pacemakers can be inserted to restore a regular heartbeat. Advanced devices can sense and respond to changes in body movement, temperature, and breathing rate.

Bypass surgery is a procedure in which a segment of vein taken from the leg or an artery from the chest is grafted to an opening in the side of the normal coronary artery above the obstructed (blocked) segment and then to the normal portion of the artery below the obstruction. Blood then "bypasses" the obstructed segment, much like taking a road detour around a construction site.

Damaged valves can be replaced with mechanical valves made of plastic or Dacron or a biological valve taken from a pig, cow, or human donor.

Cardiac transplantation is the most dramatic means of treating patients with severe heart failure. Although still filled with challenges, the procedure is well accepted around the world and is being performed more often. However, not enough human hearts are available from organ donors.

Living with Heart Disease

Heart disease often represents a turning point in a person's life. People who formerly led unhealthy, mainly inactive lives may be inspired to change the way they live by eating more healthily, exercising regularly, and quitting smoking.

In the case of a heart attack, full recovery generally takes about four to six weeks, depending on the extent of the injury, the patient's overall health, and the condition of the rest of the heart. Most people are able to resume regular activities within a few weeks or months. Like all patients with heart disease or damage, those who have had heart attacks need to adopt a healthier lifestyle, including eating a low-fat diet. Most go on to recover and enjoy many more productive years of life.

Chewing the Fat

Experts suggest that it is a good idea for all healthy Americans above the age of two to modify their diets. Among specific suggestions are:

- Reduce total dietary fat to no more than 30 percent of total daily calories.
- Reduce dietary saturated fat and cholesterol: switch from whole to skim milk, reduce the number of egg yolks eaten, avoid solid cooking fats like lard, give up foods containing certain vegetable oils such as palm or coconut oils, and substitute frozen yogurt, sherbet, or ice milk for ice cream.

Resources

Book

Arnold, Caroline. *Heart Disease.* Danbury, CT: Franklin Watts, 1992. Describes the heart and circulatory system and both genetic and acquired diseases that can affect the functioning of the heart.

Organizations

American Heart Association, 7272 Greenville Ave, Dallas, TX 75231.
http://www.amhrt.org

The National Institutes of Health posts information about heart disease on its website at:
http://www.nhlbi.nih.gov/health/public/heart/other/chdfacts.htm

See also
Diabetes
Dysrhythmia
Endocarditis
Heart Murmur
Hypertension
Obesity
Stroke

Heart Murmur

A heart murmur is an extra sound heard during a heartbeat that is caused by turbulence in blood flow through the heart. Most heart murmurs are innocent, which means they do not cause health problems and may disappear with age. But some heart murmurs require medical treatment because they are a sign of a problem in the heart's walls, lining, or valves, or are indications of other diseases or conditions.

KEYWORDS
for searching the Internet and other reference sources

Cardiovascular system

Circulatory system

Jill's baby wiggled as the doctor placed a stethoscope on his chest to listen to the heartbeat. Jill smiled, because she knew how cold the device could feel on bare skin. But Jill became concerned when the doctor reported hearing a heart murmur. The sounds of the heartbeat usually are described as a "lub" followed by a brief pause and then a "dub." Jill's doctor, however, heard another sound, like a faint rush of water in a pipe.

Is a Heart Murmur Always a Problem?

The sound of a heart murmur may occur as the heart is filling with blood or as it is contracting to send blood to other parts of the body. Sometimes the murmur means there is a defect in the heart or in one of its valves. But many times doctors also find "innocent" heart murmurs, which do not require any special treatment. Innocent murmurs are common in babies and children. The murmurs often disappear as a child gets older, and they are not a sign of heart disease. Fortunately, Jill's baby had an innocent heart murmur. The heart is healthy, but there is a faint murmur during heartbeats.

Heart murmurs, however, also can be caused when one or more of the heart's four valves is operating abnormally. Sometimes the valves do not close completely, which may allow blood to leak back from one chamber to another when it should not. Valves also might not open completely, which causes blood to rush through a smaller opening than normal. The murmur also can result from a hole, usually in the wall between the left and right sides of the heart.

Some people are born with valve defects or with holes that cause heart murmurs. Others develop a heart murmur after bouts with endocarditis* or rheumatic fever*. Both of these infections may damage heart valves. Anemia and other medical conditions may result in murmurs, even when the valves are perfectly normal.

* **endocarditis** (en-do-kar-DY-tis) refers to inflammation of the lining of the heart, or endocardium (en-do-KAR-de-um), usually after an infection settles in a heart valve or in the heart lining.

* **rheumatic fever** is a disease that causes fever, joint pain, and inflammation affecting many parts of the body. It varies in severity and duration, and it may be followed by heart or kidney disease.

What Does the Doctor Hear and Do?

Diagnosis A doctor listens to a patient's heart as part of the physical exam. That is how murmurs usually are detected. Certain defects cause

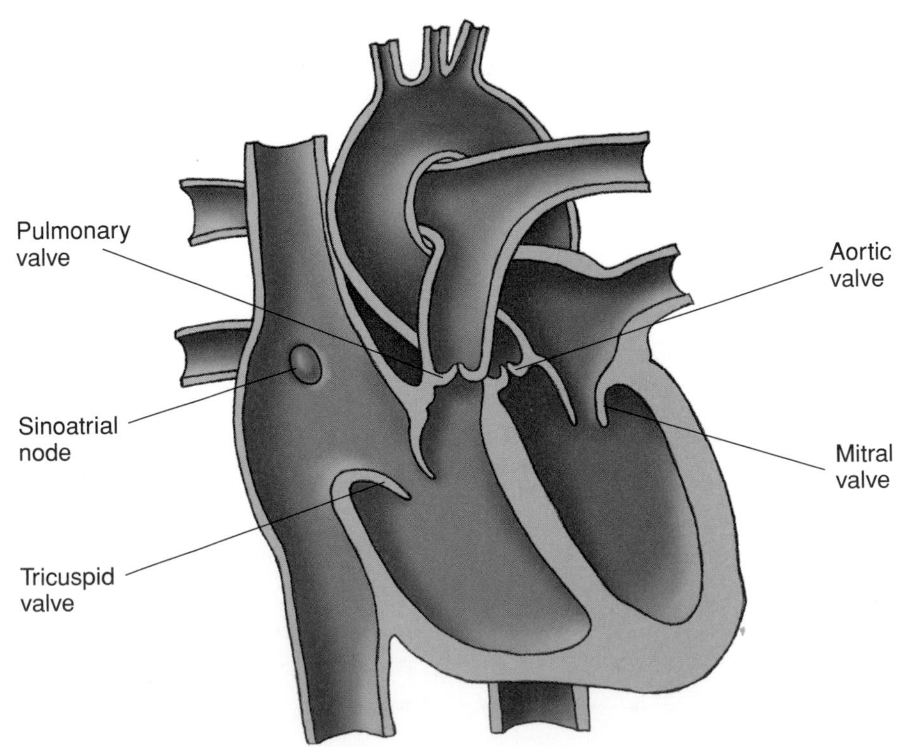

Anatomy of the heart showing heart valves and sinus node.

particular sounds, which help doctors make their diagnosis. For example, if a valve fails to close properly between the upper and lower chambers on the heart's left side, doctors may hear a distinctive murmur that will aid in diagnosing the problem.

Doctors also can use an echocardiogram to examine the heart and determine a murmur's cause. This test is done with a device that uses sound waves to create an image of the heart. It is similar to the ultrasound machine that creates images of unborn babies inside pregnant women.

Treatment If the murmur is innocent, nothing special needs to be done. People with innocent heart murmurs can play sports, eat the same foods, and do all the same things as their schoolmates.

Murmurs that indicate valve disease may need to be treated with medication or surgery. Such surgery may involve either replacing the valves or closing the hole. Although it is important to find and treat those murmurs caused by valve abnormalities or other medical conditions, most murmurs detected during childhood or adolescence are innocent.

"Lub-a-Dub-Dub"

These sounds come from the heart's valves "shutting" on the blood inside the heart. The "lub" happens when the blood reaches the mitral and tricuspid valves. The "dub" happens when the blood hits the aortic and pulmonary valves.

Resources

The U.S. National Heart, Lung, and Blood Institute posts a fact sheet about heart murmurs at its website.
http://www.nhlbi.nih.gov/nhlbi/infcentr/topics/hrtmurm.htm

American Heart Association National Center, 7272 Greenville Avenue, Dallas, TX 75231. The American Heart Association posts fact sheets about heart murmurs and about how the heart works at its website. Telephone 1-800-AHA-USA1
http://www.amhrt.org/Heart_and_Stroke_A_Z_Guide/hmur.html
http://www.amhrt.org/Heart_and_Stroke_A_Z_Guide/imurm.html

▶ *See also*
Endocarditis
Heart Disease
Rheumatic Fever

Heartburn (Dyspepsia)

Heartburn and dyspepsia (dis-PEP-see-a) are two terms used interchangeably to describe a burning feeling in the chest and other symptoms caused by problems digesting food.

KEYWORDS
for searching the Internet and other reference sources

Digestive system

Gastroenterology

Does the Heart Burn When Someone Has Heartburn?

Sarah's grandfather always comes to her house for Sunday dinner. For several weeks in a row, he seemed uncomfortable after eating and did not lie down for his usual nap. Sarah heard him talking to her father about heartburn. This scared Sarah, who thought that her grandfather was having heart problems.

When Sarah asked her grandfather what was wrong with his heart, he explained that people with heartburn, also called acid indigestion, often complain of a burning feeling in the chest, close to where the heart is located. But heartburn usually does not have anything to do with the heart. The discomfort in the chest and throat occurs when the contents of the stomach, which includes acid and digestive enzymes*, moves backward and up into the esophagus, or food pipe. This stomach juice escapes when the muscular valve between the stomach and esophagus relaxes. The acidic juice irritates the lining of the esophagus and results in a burning feeling and a bitter, sour taste in the throat and mouth. Heartburn usually occurs after a meal and can last for several hours. It is often worse when lying down.

* **enzymes** are proteins produced by cells to cause biological reactions, such as breaking down food into smaller parts.

What Is Heartburn?

Some people use the word "dyspepsia" to describe the symptoms experienced by Sarah's grandfather. Dyspepsia comes from the Greek words for bad digestion, and it covers a wide range of stomach ailments, including stomachache, heartburn, nausea, gas, pain, belching, loss of appetite, changes in bowel habits, and indigestion in general.

More than 60 million adults in the United States experience these stomach problems at least once a month, and pregnant women and elderly people especially are prone to them. Children usually do not have heartburn. They might feel indigestion, though, after eating too many hot dogs. Stomach ailments are some of the most common reasons why people visit their doctors.

By themselves, dyspepsia and heartburn are not really diseases. They are just uncomfortable symptoms people get, usually because they ate too much or are feeling stressed, anxious, or depressed. However, people who keep getting the symptoms, or who get them often, should see their doctors promptly, because heartburn and dyspepsia may be signs of other disorders, including:

- **Appendicitis** is inflammation of the appendix, a small tube connected to the large intestine.
- **Peptic ulcer** is a sore in the lining of the stomach or small intestine.
- **Hiatal hernia** occurs when part of the stomach pushes up into the chest through an opening in the diaphragm, the muscle between the chest and the abdomen.
- **Lactose intolerance** is a problem in digesting lactose, a sugar found in milk and other dairy products.
- **Gallbladder disease** is inflammation or blockage in the gallbladder, a small organ of the digestive system.
- **Gastroesophageal (gas-tro-e-sof-a-JEE-al) reflux disease (GERD)** is a digestive condition in which the muscular valve (lower esophageal sphincter) between the esophagus

Heartburn occurs when the contents of the stomach move backward through the muscular valve called the lower esophageal sphincter and up into the esophagus. The stomach's acid and digestive enzymes irritate the lining of the esophagus, causing a burning feeling in the chest and a bitter, sour taste in the throat and mouth.

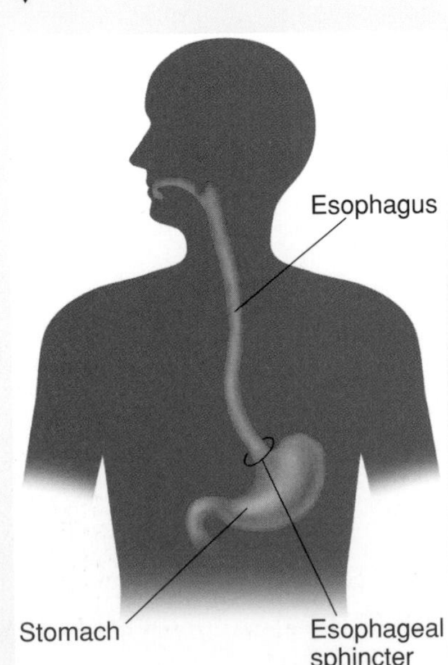

and stomach does not work properly, allowing stomach acid to flow backward into the esophagus.

- **True heart pain,** which is also called angina pectoris (an-JY-na PEK-tor-is).

How Is Heartburn Diagnosed, Treated, and Prevented?

Doctors use several different tests to diagnose heartburn. If they can rule out other diseases, as was true for Sarah's grandfather, then over-the-counter antacid medications, dietary changes, and lifestyle changes can help most people feel better.

Guidelines for preventing heartburn include:

- avoiding chocolate, coffee, and alcohol
- avoiding greasy or spicy foods
- quitting smoking
- losing weight
- not eating right before bed
- finding ways to deal with stress.

Before or After?

Two types of medication for heartburn are sold without a doctor's prescription (over the counter).

Acid blockers interfere with histamines that signal stomach cells to produce acid. Acid blockers need about 30 minutes to take effect, but usually last for up to eight hours. To work correctly, acid blockers need to be taken before a meal.

Antacids are taken after a meal to neutralize acids already present in the stomach. People usually feel better right away, but relief lasts only a few hours.

Resources

U.S. National Digestive Diseases Information Clearinghouse, 2 Information Way, Bethesda, MD 20892-3570. The NDDIC publishes information about digestive diseases for the public and for health care professionals.

The U.S. National Institute of Diabetes and Digestive and Kidney Diseases (NIDDK) posts a fact sheet about heartburn and gastroesophageal reflux at its website.
http://www.niddk.nih.gov/health/digest/pubs/heartbrn/heartbrn.htm

The American College of Gastroenterology has a toll-free telephone number that provides information about heartburn and other stomach problems.
Telephone 800-HRT-BURN

See also
Appendicitis
Gallstones
Hernia
Lactose Intolerance
Pancreatitis
Peptic Ulcer

Heat Stroke/Exhaustion *See* Heat-Related Injuries

Heat-Related Injuries

Heat-related injuries, including heat cramps, heat exhaustion, and heat stroke, are problems that occur when the body's cooling system is overloaded.

KEYWORD
for seaching the Internet and other reference sources

Hyperthermia

Too Hot to Handle

Texas was in the grip of a severe heat wave in August just as students were heading back to school after summer break. The extreme heat forced schools around the state to take action. In Plano, for example, children were kept inside for recess on very hot days. In Irving, the football coach cut short afternoon practices and had the players take extra water breaks. In Arlington, some football scrimmages were canceled, and others were scheduled after 7:00 p.m.

School officials were trying to prevent heat-related injuries. These are health problems that occur when the body's cooling system is overloaded. The body normally cools itself by sweating. Under some conditions, though, this system can start to fail. In such cases, a person's body temperature may rise quickly. Very high body temperatures can damage the brain and other vital organs.

What Are Heat-Related Injuries?

There three types of heat-related injuries:

- **Heat cramps.** These are painful muscle cramps, usually in the stomach, arms, or legs, that may occur during heavy activity. Heat cramps are the least serious type of heat-related injury. It can be dangerous to ignore them, however, since they are an early warning sign that the body is having trouble with heat.
- **Heat exhaustion.** This is the body's response to losing too much water and salt in sweat. It often occurs in people who exercise heavily or work in a hot, humid place, which makes them sweat a lot. Elderly people and those with high blood pressure are also prone to heat exhaustion. As the body overheats, blood flow to the skin increases, which decreases blood flow to other organs and causes weakness, confusion, and can cause collapse. If heat exhaustion is not treated, the person may suffer heat stroke.
- **Heat stroke.** This is the most serious type of heat-related injury. Heat stroke, also known as sun stroke, occurs when the body becomes unable to cool itself down. The body's temperature may rise to 106 degrees Farenheit or higher within minutes. If heat stroke is not treated quickly, it can lead to brain damage or death.

Who Is At Risk?

Several things affect the body's ability to cool itself during very hot weather. One of the main ways the body cools itself is by sweating. The evaporation of sweat from the skin cools the body. When humidity (the amount of moisture in the air) is high, the sweat does not evaporate from the skin. Other things that can limit the body's ability to control its temperature include old or very young age, being overweight, fever, heart disease, sunburn, alcohol or drug use, and dehydration (dee-hy-DRAY-shun), which is excessive loss of water from the body due to illness or not drinking enough liquids.

Some people have a high risk of heat-related injuries:

- **Babies and children under age four.** Babies and young children are very sensitive to the effects of high temperatures. They become dehydrated very quickly because of their small size. They are also unable to help themselves if they start to get overheated.
- **People over age 65.** An older person's body may not control its own temperature as well as a younger person's. Older people are also less likely to notice and respond to changes in temperature.
- **People who are overweight.** An overweight person's body may tend to hold onto more body heat than a normal-weight person's does.
- **People who are ill or taking certain medicines.** Any illness or medicine that leads to dehydration raises the risk of heat-related injuries.

What Are the Symptoms?

Heat Cramps

- Painful muscle cramps, usually in the stomach, arms, or legs
- Heavy sweating

Heat Exhaustion

- Heavy sweating
- Cold, clammy skin
- Paleness
- Tiredness
- Weakness
- Dizziness
- Headache
- Fainting
- Muscle cramps
- Nausea
- Vomiting
- Fast, weak pulse
- Fast, shallow breathing

Heat Stroke

- Very high body temperature (above 103 degrees Farenheit by mouth)
- No sweating
- Red, hot, dry skin

Having a Heat Wave!

A heat wave is a long period of very high heat and humidity. The National Weather Service has come up with a heat index (HI) to warn the public about such conditions. The HI, given in degrees Fahrenheit, is a measure of how hot it really feels when the actual air temperature is combined with the relative humidity (which is a measure of the amount of moisture in the air compared to the greatest amount of moisture the air could hold at the same temperature). For example, if the air temperature is 95 degrees Farenheit and the relative humidity is 55 percent, the HI, or how hot it really feels, is 110 degrees F. The National Weather Service issues alerts when the HI is expected to be greater than 105 to 110 degrees Farenheit for at least two days in a row.

- Dizziness
- Headache
- Confusion
- Nausea
- Vomiting
- Fast, strong pulse
- Unconsciousness

What Is the Treatment?

Heat Cramps Heat cramps usually occur during heavy activity. It is best for the person to stop being active and sit quietly in a cool place and drink sips of water, clear juice, or a sports drink. To relieve the muscle cramps, firm pressure is placed on the muscles or the muscles are massaged gently. It is important for the person not to return to heavy exercise for a few hours after the cramps go away, because this might lead to heat exhaustion or heat stroke. A doctor should be called if the cramps do not go away within an hour.

Heat Exhaustion Medical help should be called immediately if the symptoms are severe, or if the person has heart disease or high blood pressure. Otherwise, it is important for the person to cool off by being taken to a shaded area and fanned or, if possible, moved into an air-conditioned room; it is best for him or her to lie down and remove heavy clothing. Sips of water and applying cool, wet cloths on the skin are helpful. A cool shower or bath may also help.

Heat Stroke Heat stroke is a serious medical emergency. Medical help should be sought right away. While waiting for help, the person can be cooled off by getting out of the sun, being fanned, or being moved into an air-conditioned room. It is important for the person to lie down and remove clothing. Applying cool, wet cloths, or putting the person in a cool bath or shower will help. If the humidity is low, another solution is to wrap the person in a cool, wet sheet. If the person is outside, spraying him or her with a garden hose can be effective. Taking the person's temperature regularly, and keeping up the cooling efforts until it drops to 101 to 102 degrees Farenheit is important. Sometimes the person's muscles may start to twitch wildly as a result of heat stroke. If this happens, the person should be kept from getting hurt. It is important not to put anything in the person's mouth, and do not give him or her anything to drink. If vomiting occurs, the airway is kept open by turning the person onto his or her side.

How Can Heat Injury Be Prevented?

To prevent heat-related injuries, keep cool and use common sense. The following tips may help on hot, summer days:

- It is important to consume plenty of fluids, regardless of thirst. During heavy exercise in hot weather, it is important to drink at least two to four glasses of cool fluid each hour. Water is always a good drink choice. Very cold drinks can cause stomach cramps. Avoiding drinks containing caffeine, such as iced teas and colas, is important because they just cause the body to lose more fluid. Salt tablets should be avoided.
- Slowing down the pace is important also. It is important to cut back on heavy exercise, or to move it to the coolest time of day, usually very early in the morning.
- Staying indoors if possible also can help. The best way to beat the heat is to stay in an air-conditioned room. An electric fan can make things more comfortable, too, but a fan alone may not be enough during a severe heat wave. If it is very hot at home, spending a few hours at an air-conditioned mall or public library can help.
- Lightweight, loose-fitting clothing also helps. Light-colored fabrics are the best, because they reflect away some of the sun's energy.
- It is helpful to eat smaller, more frequent meals, to avoid generating the extra body heat associated with digesting large meals.

Resources

American Red Cross. "Are You Ready for a Heat Wave?" To order, contact the American Red Cross, 1621 N. Kent Street, 11th Floor, Arlington, VA 22209, (703) 248-4222.
http://www.redcross.org

U.S. National Center for Environmental Health. "Extreme Heat: A Prevention Guide to Promote Your Personal Health and Safety." To order, contact the National Center for Environmental Health, Mail Stop F-29, 4770 Buford Highway N.E., Atlanta, GA 30341-3724.
Telephone 888-232-6789
http://www.cdc.gov/nceh/ncehhome.htm

U.S. Federal Emergency Management Agency (FEMA), 500 C Street S.W., Washington, DC 20472. A government agency that provides information about extreme heat.
Telephone 800-525-0321
http://www.fema.gov

U.S. National Weather Service, 1325 East-West Highway, Silver Spring, MD 20910. The government agency that issues alerts based on the heat index.
Telephone 301-713-4000
http://www.nws.noaa.gov

See also
Cold-Related Injuries
Fever

Hemophilia

Hemophilia (he-mo-FIL-e-a) is a hereditary disorder in which the blood does not clot normally and excessive bleeding results.

KEYWORDS
for searching the Internet and other reference sources

Bleeding disorders

Blood transfusion

Clotting factors

Coagulation disorders

Fibrin

Hematology

Most people take certain bodily functions for granted: breathing, digestion, healing. We do not have to think about them; they just happen. Blood clotting is one of these things—at least it usually is. But for the approximately 20,000 people in the United States with hemophilia A or B, a simple thing like losing a tooth or falling off a bicycle can cause life-threatening complications. This is because their blood does not clot, or coagulate, normally. And without clotting, any injury will just continue to bleed.

What Is Hemophilia?

Hemophilia is an inherited deficiency of a blood-clotting factor that results in excessive bleeding. When a healthy person is injured, a sequence of events occurs to cause the blood to turn from liquid to solid (a clot) and to stop flowing. First, platelets (tiny capsule-shaped cells in the blood) begin to stick together and form a small plug at the point of bleeding. Platelets contain an enzyme, or protein, that causes fibrinogen (fy-BRIN-o-jen), a substance in the blood, to change to fibrin (FY-brin), a hard substance that does not dissolve. Like firemen racing to a burning building, fibrin rushes to the area of blood vessel injury and piles up, helping the platelets to block the opening and stop the blood flow.

Fibrin can perform this task only by using substances in the blood manufactured by the body called clotting factors. The clotting factors are numbered I through XIII. In hemophilia A, clotting factor VIII is deficient. Factors I through VII function properly, but then the clotting

The gene for hemophilia is unintentionally passed from mothers (XX) to sons (XY) via the X chromosome. A son who inherits a defective X chromosome from his mother does not have a healthy X chromosome to rely on the way daughters (XX) do. ▶

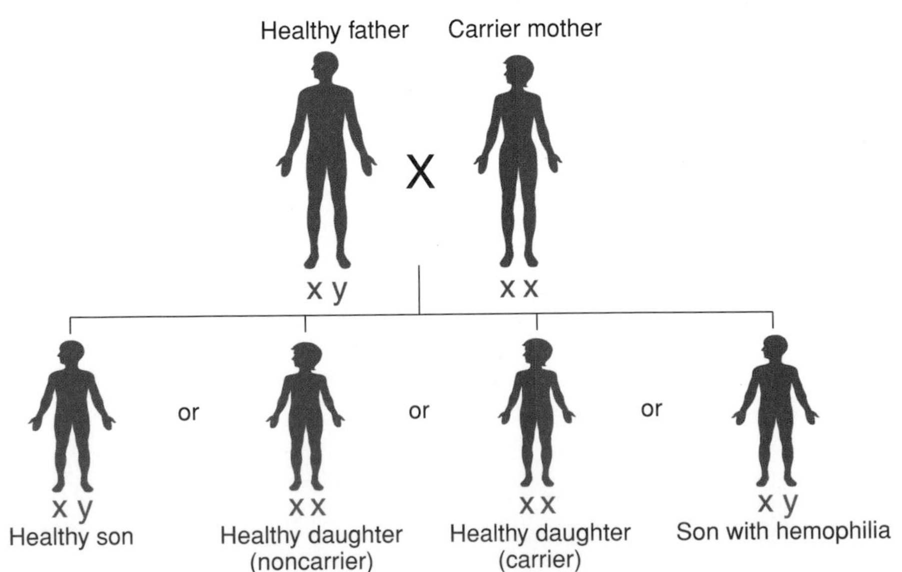

process is interrupted and blood from a wound continues to flow. Hemophilia B, which occurs less frequently, is caused by a deficiency of factor IX. Sending fibrin to clot blood without these factors is like sending firemen to a fire without enough water to put it out.

Hemophilia varies in severity. Most healthy people have 100 percent levels of clotting factor VIII or IX in their blood. In contrast, people with the most severe forms of hemophilia have less than 1 percent of the normal amount. Unable to clot blood at all, they can begin to hemorrhage, or bleed internally, even without external injuries.

Those with moderate hemophilia have factor VIII or IX levels between 1 and 5 percent. Excessive bleeding follows minor injury as well as dental extractions and surgeries. Mild hemophilia is seen in those with factor VIII or IX levels between 6 and 50 percent. For this group, excessive bleeding is usually associated only with major injuries, surgical procedures, or tooth extractions. People with mild cases may not be diagnosed as having hemophilia until adulthood, when unexplained and excessive bleeding accompanies an operation or a visit to the dentist.

What Causes Hemophilia?

Hemophilia is not contagious like a cold or flu. It is usually inherited, which means that it often runs in families. Hemophilia almost exclusively affects boys. It is caused by a defective gene that is unintentionally passed from mothers to sons via the X chromosome.

Usually, female "carriers" have normal levels of clotting factors themselves. If a man with hemophilia marries a woman who is a carrier, there is a possibility of having a daughter with hemophilia, but this is rare. Up to one third of the people with hemophilia have no family members who have the condition or who are carriers. In these cases, a mutation (a change in a gene) has produced a new hemophilia gene, which may be passed on to following generations.

How Do People Know They Have Hemophilia?

Although hemophilia is present at birth, babies who are not circumcised (a surgical procedure to remove the foreskin of the penis) seldom experience problems until they begin to crawl. Once they start to bump into hard surfaces or fall, they begin to bleed into muscles or joints, places where two bones meet. Such internal bleeding can cause joints to bruise and swell painfully.

Joint bleeding is serious, because it can lead to arthritis (inflammation of the joints), deformity, and disability. Prompt treatment is necessary to prevent severe pain and swelling. As boys with hemophilia grow older, they often learn to recognize joint bleeding before the pain or swelling appears as a "funny," tingling feeling.

Bleeding into a muscle, most often the calf, thigh, or forearm, commonly occurs after injury; sometimes this occurs spontaneously. The resulting swelling, which may develop over several days, may create pressure inside the muscles and damage nerves and blood vessels. Symptoms include muscle

What Are Chromosomes and Genes?

A chromosome is a paired, thread-like structure found in the nucleus or central, controlling part of the body's cells that determines the development of characteristics for each individual person. The one obvious characteristic to be determined is whether a person is male or female. A female has two X chromosomes, and a male has one X and one Y.

Chromosomes are composed of genes, units that determine everything from the color of eyes to how a body functions. The X chromosome carries genes that control the production of clotting factors VIII and IX. In people with hemophilia, these genes cause the body to produce too little VIII or IX. But even if a woman (XX) has one X chromosome with the hemophilia gene, the other X chromosome is probably normal, and her body will produce enough factor VIII or IX to ensure that the blood will clot. The Y chromosome, however, has no part in the production of blood-clotting factors. Boys (XY) who inherit a defective X chromosome from their mothers have no other X chromosome to fall back on to prevent them from having hemophilia.

HIV and Hemophilia

One of the greatest risks faced by those with hemophilia in the late 1970s and early 1980s was the possibility of contracting HIV, the AIDS virus. This happened when people got transfusions of clotting factors drawn from infected blood. It is estimated that 55 percent of people with hemophilia were infected with HIV in this way between 1979 and 1985.

In those days, blood donations were not tested for HIV. And people with hemophilia were especially likely to get infected for two reasons: They got many transfusions and each transfusion contained pooled clotting factors drawn from the blood of many, many donors in order to get enough clotting factors to be effective. If any one of those donors was infected with HIV, the person with hemophilia was at risk.

Today, however, the blood supply is much safer. Potential blood donors are screened to eliminate those who might have been exposed to HIV, and all blood is tested for the virus. These measures apply to all blood transfusions. In addition, clotting factors drawn from blood are treated with heat and other virus-killing techniques, although these methods are not used for other kinds of transfusions because they can damage other blood products.

The safety measures produced dramatic results. From 1986 to 1999, according to the National Hemophilia Foundation, no one with hemophilia contracted HIV from a transfusion in the United States. Now new technology allows clotting factors to be genetically engineered without the use of blood donations.

European Royalty and Hemophilia

History's most famous carrier of the gene for hemophilia was Victoria (1819–1901), Queen of England and grandmother to most of the royalty in Europe. In 1853, Queen Victoria gave birth to her eighth child, Leopold, Duke of Albany, who had hemophilia and died at the age of 31 from internal bleeding after a fall.

Two of Queen Victoria's four daughters, Alice (b. 1843) and Beatrice (b. 1857), also carried the gene for hemophilia and subsequently transmitted the disease to three of Victoria's grandsons and to six of her great-grandsons.

Alice's daughter Alexandra also was a carrier of hemophilia, and she transmitted the disease to her son Alexis (b. 1904), whose father was Czar Nicholas II (1868–1918) of Russia. Alexis is perhaps the most famous of the European royals with hemophilia. Alexis was the heir to his father's throne and his medical condition caused much anxiety in the royal household. Historians are still discussing the role Alexis's condition played in the Russian revolution of 1918.

Czar Nicholas II of Russia and his family, photographed c. 1916, showing his wife Alexandra (who was a carrier of hemophilia), his four daughters, and (in the foreground) his son Alexis, perhaps the most famous European royal with hemophilia. *Corbis.*

tightness, pain, skin temperature change, and tingling or numbness. Early treatment is needed to prevent paralysis or permanent immobility.

Any type of neck or head injury can be extremely dangerous for anyone with hemophilia. Neck and throat hemorrhages can obstruct breathing. Head injury, even a minor fall or bump on the head, can cause bleeding into the brain; the symptoms include irritability, headache, confusion, nausea, vomiting, and double vision.

People with hemophilia bruise very easily, but skin bruises are rarely serious. Bleeding from small cuts and scrapes can usually be stopped by applying firm pressure to the area for several minutes. Deep cuts, on the other hand, can bleed profusely and require treatment.

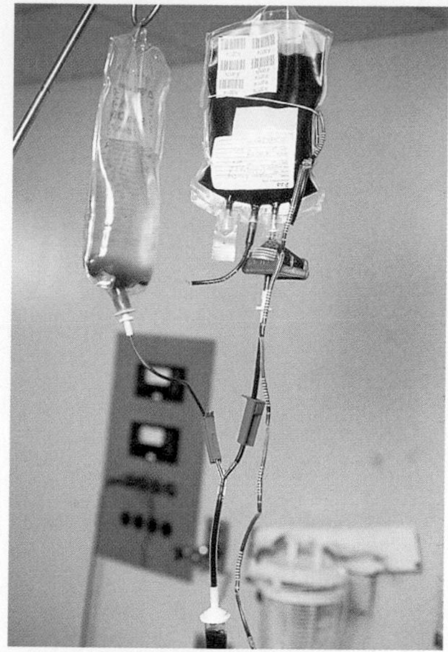

▲

Clotting factors are transfused through the vein, often at a hospital or doctor's office. With proper training, people with hemophilia or their parents can perform transfusions at home. © *SIU/Visuals Unlimited.*

Diagnosis

Using DNA testing (direct analysis of the genes), it is possible to determine whether a woman is a "carrier" of the hemophilia gene. Blood tests can measure the level of clotting factors in the blood. Tests can be performed on fetuses to see if they have inherited hemophilia.

Treatment

People with hemophilia often need to be given the blood-clotting factors they lack. These factors may be drawn from the blood donations of many people and purified. Or, since the mid-1990s, they may be produced by genetic engineering, which does not require blood donations. The clotting factors are transfused through the person's vein, often at a hospital or doctor's office. With proper training, a person can perform transfusions at home, or parents can do it for their children.

One medication that should not be used by those with hemophilia is aspirin, a pain reliever, since it interferes with normal blood clotting and increases people's tendency to bleed.

How often transfusions are needed depends on how severe the illness is and how often the person gets injured. In cases of major injury or surgery, a person may need transfusions two or three times a day for days or weeks. Even without being injured, some people with severe hemophilia may get transfusions on a regular basis to prevent problems. People with mild cases of hemophilia may rarely or never need transfusions.

A medication called DDAVP (desmopressin), which is not a blood product, can sometimes help to release any extra factor VIII stores in people with mild or moderate hemophilia A. This temporary treatment may help a person avoid a transfusion after a minor injury, for instance.

Prevention of Bleeding Episodes

As soon as a child is diagnosed with hemophilia, parents should try to prevent or reduce the occurrence of bleeding. Doctors recommend choosing soft toys without sharp corners and padded clothing—particularly at the elbows and knees—while a child is learning to walk. Children should be immunized, but the injections should be given under the skin rather than into the muscles to prevent hemorrhages. Children should also be taught to clean their teeth regularly and to visit the dentist to prevent tooth decay and gum disease.

Living with Hemophilia

Hemophilia is usually not a fatal disorder, and people with hemophilia often live long and active lives. Activities such as swimming, walking,

Did You Know?

- Hemophilia A occurs in about one out of every 5,000 male births; hemophilia B in about one out of every 30,000.
- The average person with hemophilia infuses 80,000 to 100,000 units of blood-clotting factor a year.
- Care for a typical severe hemophilia patient costs $100,000 to $150,000 per year.
- Severe hemophilia accounts for 60 percent of all those with the disease.

and bicycling can help build up muscles that support the joints. Contact sports such as football or wrestling, however, are prohibited because of the high risk of head or neck injury.

Explaining hemophilia to friends and family can help boys feel less self-conscious about their condition and educate others about the importance of prompt treatment.

The Future

At present, there is no cure for hemophilia, but trials with gene therapy are under way. Many of them are concentrating on replacing the gene that causes hemophilia with a normal one that will raise the level of deficient clotting factors to promote coagulation.

Other researchers have produced genetically engineered animal cells into which they have inserted the genetic sequence to produce human factor VIII.

Resources

Books and Magazines

White, Ryan, and Anne Marie Cunningham. *Ryan White: My Own Story*. Signet, 1992.

Hemalog. A quarterly magazine for people with bleeding disorders.

Organizations

National Hemophilia Foundation
http://www.infonhf.org/

World Foundation of Hemophilia
http://www.wfh.org/

See also
AIDS and HIV
Clotting
Genetic Diseases
Hemorrhage

Hemorrhage

Hemorrhage (HEM-or-ij) is bleeding or the escape of blood from the blood vessels. The term hemorrhage usually refers to significant bleeding.

KEYWORDS
for searching the Internet and other reference sources

Bleeding disorders

Hematology

What Causes Hemorrhage?

Hemorrhage is any profuse internal or external bleeding from the blood vessels. The most obvious cause of hemorrhage is trauma or injury to a blood vessel. Hemorrhage can also be caused by aneurysms or weak spots in the artery wall that are often present at birth. Over time, the blood vessel walls at the site of an aneurysm tend to become thinner and bulge out like water balloons as blood passes through them, making them more likely to leak and rupture.

Hypertension, or high blood pressure, is often a contributing factor in brain hemorrhage, which can cause a stroke. Other times, vessels simply wear out with age. Uncontrolled diabetes can also weaken blood vessels, especially in the eyes; this is called retinopathy (ret-i-NOP-a-thee). Use of medications that affect blood clotting, including aspirin, can make hemorrhage more likely to occur.

Bleeding disorders can also spark hemorrhages. Among them are hemophilia (he-mo-FIL-e-a), an inherited disorder that prevents the blood from clotting.

How Can You Spot a Hemorrhage?

Visible blood is the most obvious sign, but sometimes the only way to know a hemorrhage has occurred inside the body is when it causes symptoms or an illness, such as a stroke. In the case of a brain hemorrhage, depending on where the bleeding is occurring, symptoms can include headache; loss of function on one side of the body; vision changes; numbness or weakness; difficulty speaking, swallowing, reading, or writing; balance problems; decreased alertness; vomiting; stiff neck; and confusion, drowsiness, or coma.

People with hemophilia often experience a tingling feeling that alerts them to a hemorrhage.

How Is a Hemorrhage Diagnosed?

When bleeding is visible, the causes of most hemorrhages are obvious. Blood tests and spinal fluid tests can show evidence of brain hemorrhage. Computed tomography (CT or CAT) scanning is an important imaging test used to evaluate the brain and other tissues to see if bleeding has occurred.

How Is a Hemorrhage Treated?

The first goal in treating a hemorrhage is to stop the bleeding. Hemorrhage caused by trauma or the tearing of blood vessels can be treated by clamping or surgically repairing the tears. Hemorrhage resulting from vessel leakage due to high blood pressure can be treated with medicines to reduce blood pressure, prevent vessel spasm, and reduce pain. Surgery may be needed to reduce the pressure of collected blood in the brain. Blood factors to help the blood clot may be administered to those with bleeding disorders.

How Can Hemorrhage Be Prevented?

A healthy diet, regular exercise, cutting down on excess sodium intake, maintaining a normal weight, and taking prescribed medication properly can often control high blood pressure. Avoiding drug use can also help prevent brain hemorrhage. Cocaine, amphetamines, and alcohol are increasingly associated with brain hemorrhages, particularly in young people. Wearing helmets when bicycling, skateboarding, and rollerblading and always wearing seatbelts in motor vehicles can help prevent serious head injuries. Retinopathy can be prevented or lessened by good control of diabetes, that is, keeping blood sugars at near-normal levels.

See also
Anemia
Clotting
Hemophilia
Hypertension
Nosebleeds
Stroke

Hemorrhoids

Hemorrhoids (HEM-o-roids), sometimes called "piles," are enlarged veins in the rectum, which is the lower portion of the digestive tract. They are similar to varicose veins of the legs. Hemorrhoids may bleed and cause pain.

KEYWORDS
for searching the Internet and other reference sources

Anorectal disorders

Digestive tract

Vascular system

Where Do People Get Hemorrhoids?

Hemorrhoids occur in two places. When they are located in the upper part of the rectum, the hemorrhoids are called internal hemorrhoids. In the lower part of the rectum, they are called external hemorrhoids. Hemorrhoids are said to be prolapsed if they have slipped down from their usual position and extend outside of the anal opening.

What Causes Hemorrhoids?

Hemorrhoids have a number of different causes. They occur often in women who are pregnant or who have just given birth to babies. People with chronic constipation are at risk for hemorrhoids because of added pressure to the anorectal area when they pass stools (solid waste matter) that are hard and dry.

What Are the Symptoms of Hemorrhoids?

Pain during bowel movements and blood in the stool are the usual symptoms that accompany hemorrhoids. Sometimes there is a discharge of mucus, and there may also be itching, burning, or pain in the area. The enlarged vein in the rectum sometimes develops a clot, which can be very painful. People with hemorrhoids sometimes develop iron deficiency anemia* from the bleeding that occurs.

* **anemia** results when people have too few red blood cells and hemoglobin to carry oxygen in the blood.

How Are Hemorrhoids Diagnosed and Treated?

The doctor first examines the anal area through a viewing tube called an anoscope to rule out other conditions that cause similar symptoms. For mild cases of hemorrhoids, doctors may recommend:

- a diet with adequate amounts of fiber (whole grains, vegetables, and fruit) to prevent constipation
- drinking lots of liquids to prevent constipation
- sitz baths, which are shallow baths of warm water

- medicines that soften stools and make them easy to pass
- creams that can be applied to the hemorrhoids to reduce pain, swelling, and itching.

When the hemorrhoids are internal, they can be removed in the doctor's office by a simple procedure. Tiny rubber bands are wrapped tightly around the hemorrhoids. Following this procedure, the hemorrhoids wither away and drop off without causing pain.

Internal hemorrhoids that stay prolapsed outside the body, or external hemorrhoids that have clotted, are often removed surgically. This method of removal is usually done on an outpatient* basis with local anesthesia*.

*__outpatients__ are people who go to a doctor's office or hospital for treatment but do not stay overnight in a hospital bed.

*__local anesthesia__ (an-es-THEE-zha) means using medicine to block or numb pain in one part of the body while patients remain awake. General anesthesia blocks pain over the entire body while patients sleep.

Resource

U.S. National Digestive Diseases Information Clearinghouse, 2 Information Way, Bethesda, MD 20892-3570. This division of the U.S. National Institute of Diabetes and Digestive and Kidney Diseases (NIDDK) posts information about hemorrhoids at its website.
http://www.niddk.nih.gov/health/digest/pubs/hems/hemords.htm

▶ *See also*
Constipation
Varicose Veins

Hepatitis

Hepatitis (hep-a-TY-tis) is inflammation* of the liver, an abnormal condition that harms liver cells. It usually is caused by the hepatitis A, B, or C virus and may be acute* or chronic*, mild or extremely serious. Hepatitis also can be caused by other germs, by toxic chemicals, or by certain medications.

KEYWORDS
for searching the Internet and other reference sources

Cirrhosis

Hepatic necrosis

Inflammation

Jaundice

Liver transplant

What Is Hepatitis?

The liver, a red-brown, wedge-shaped organ in the upper abdomen, is the largest internal organ in the body and performs the widest range of jobs. It gets rid of harmful substances in food, disposes of old blood cells, helps digest fat, produces chemicals to make the blood clot, and makes sure the blood carries the right balance of fat, sugar, and amino (a-ME-no) acids (the building blocks of proteins) to all the cells of the body.

Complex as it is, the liver is also open to a wide range of problems. Many of these fall under the heading "hepatitis," a general term that means the liver is experiencing inflammation.

Hepatitis can be caused by many things: excessive drinking of alcohol, overdoses or side effects of medication, inhaling of toxic chemicals, or problems with a person's immune system*. It can also result from infection with a range of microbes.

*__inflammation__ (in-fla-MAY-shun) is the body's reaction to infection or irritation.

*__acute__ means sudden, short, and severe.

*__chronic__ (KRON-ik) means continuing for a long period of time.

*__immune system__ is the body system that fights disease.

* **virus** (VY-rus) is a tiny infectious agent that lacks an independent metabolism (muh-TAB-o-liz-um) and can only reproduce within the cells it infects.

* **fulminant** (FUL-mi-nant) means occurring suddenly and with great severity.

* **cancer** is an uncontrolled growth of cells or tissue, the natural (untreated) course of which can be fatal.

* **transplants** (TRANS-plantz) are organs or tissues from another body used to replace a poorly functioning organ or tissue.

Most hepatitis is caused by infection with a hepatitis virus*, usually the hepatitis A, B, or C virus. Each one can cause acute viral hepatitis, an inflammation of the liver that usually lasts 4 to 6 weeks. Typically, people who have acute viral hepatitis feel exhausted, and their skin and the whites of their eyes take on a yellowish tint, a condition called jaundice (JAWN-dis). In rare cases, acute viral hepatitis can develop into a life-threatening illness called fulminant* hepatitis. But usually it is milder, and the person recovers without needing special care. Often, viral hepatitis causes no symptoms at all.

Hepatitis B and C, however, can do long-term damage as well. About 75 to 85 percent of people infected with hepatitis C (and 5 to 10 percent of those infected with hepatitis B) cannot fight off the virus. They become infected chronically, meaning the virus remains active in their body for more than 6 months. In most cases, the infection lasts for decades.

Because the liver is large and resilient, it usually keeps working well despite the virus. In fact, most people with chronic hepatitis live a normal life span and do not even realize that they have the infection. But after 10, 20, 30, or more years, some people with chronic infections eventually will have serious liver damage, such as cirrhosis (si-RO-sis), or scarring of the liver. These unlucky people also have a much greater than normal risk of developing a kind of liver cancer* called hepatocellular carcinoma (hep-a-to-SEL-yoo-lar kar-si-NO-ma). Cirrhosis and liver cancer are both serious, often fatal illnesses.

In the United States, hepatitis C is second only to alcohol abuse as a cause of liver damage and is the leading reason people get liver transplants*. Hepatitis C is less likely to cause a noticeable acute illness than hepatitis B, so that most people do not know they have it, but it is more likely to lead to a chronic infection.

Worldwide, hepatitis C is believed to infect 170 million people, and health officials fear it will cause major public health problems in the future. Yet HCV, as it is called, is not as well-known as many rarer diseases. The virus was not identified until 1988, and much remains to be learned about how it behaves. One of its apparent effects is to make alcohol more toxic to the liver: many people with liver damage from alcohol turn out to have hepatitis C as well.

In addition to hepatitis A, B, and C, scientists have identified three less-common hepatitis viruses:

- Hepatitis D acts as hepatitis B's sidekick. It is found only in people who already have hepatitis B, and it makes their illness worse.
- Hepatitis E occurs only in the developing world. It resembles hepatitis A in that it causes only a short-term illness, but it can be more dangerous, especially to pregnant women. It is usually spread through water that has been contaminated by sewage, often after flooding.
- Hepatitis G virus was identified in 1996, but it is not clear that it causes any illness.
- There is some evidence for a hepatitis F virus as well, but scientists are not sure.

Hepatitis A: How Does It Spread?

Every now and then, local news reports will tell of an outbreak of hepatitis. Often, the announcers will say that people who ate in a certain restaurant or attended a certain nursery school in the last few weeks should consult their doctor to see about preventing infection.

Hepatitis A is the virus that causes that kind of outbreak. Sometimes called infectious hepatitis, it is highly contagious*, but it almost never does permanent damage. In the United States, hepatitis A most commonly is spread in day care centers to young children and their parents. It spreads by what doctors call the "fecal-oral route." Virus in the feces (stool) of an infected person somehow gets into the mouth of someone else. This can happen if people fail to wash their hands after changing a diaper or using the toilet and then go on to prepare or serve food. Or one toddler may handle another's cup or pacifier. In addition, sewage that is not treated properly can contaminate water supplies. Shellfish from contaminated waters can spread the virus if eaten raw or undercooked.

* **contagious** (kon-TAY-jes) means able to be transmitted from one person to another.

Once people have recovered from hepatitis A, it is over. They are not "carriers" of the virus and cannot infect anyone else.

Hepatitis A: How Is It Prevented?

Good hygiene, including washing hands after using the toilet and before handling food, can prevent hepatitis A.

Vaccination* against hepatitis A also is available. It is recommended for children and adults traveling to developing countries, for children in communities with high rates of hepatitis A, such as among people of Native American ancestry, and for children who live in states with above-average levels of the disease.

* **vaccination** (vak-si-NAY-shun) is taking into the body a killed or weakened germ, or a protein made from such a microbe, in order to prevent, lessen, or treat a disease.

Once people have been exposed to the virus, infection often can be prevented by an injection of immune globulin (GLOB-yoo-lin), a substance that helps the immune system. But the globulin must be given within two weeks of exposure to the virus.

Hepatitis B and C: How Do They Spread?

Hepatitis B and C are spread chiefly by contact with an infected person's blood. People with chronic hepatitis B and C are "carriers," meaning their blood can transmit the virus to others even if they have no symptoms of illness.

In the United States, these viruses spread most commonly when intravenous (in-tra-VEE-nus) drug users share needles. About 90 percent of people who inject illegal drugs are believed to be infected with hepatitis C, for instance.

Accidental needle sticks, a risk to health care workers, can also spread these viruses. So can organ transplants, tattooing, body piercing, and sharing razors, toothbrushes, or other objects that may have small amounts of blood on them.

Transfusions (trans-FEW-zhunz) of infected blood used to be the biggest source of infection. People with hemophilia (he-mo-FIL-e-a), a blood-clotting problem, were especially likely to be infected when they got blood products drawn from large numbers of donors. Today, however, donors and blood in the United States are screened for both hepatitis B and C, and the risk of getting them from a transfusion is extremely low. But anyone who got a transfusion before July 1992 should be tested for hepatitis C.

Hepatitis B is more contagious than hepatitis C. It is also more contagious than HIV, the virus that causes AIDS*. Hepatitis B spreads readily through sexual contact. Women and men, especially homosexual men, who have sex with many partners are at increased risk.

* **AIDS** is short for acquired immunodeficiency (im-yoo-no-de-FISH-un-see) syndrome, the disease caused by the human immunodeficiency virus (HIV). In severe cases, it is characterized by the profound weakening of the body's immune system.

Hepatitis C is less likely to spread through sexual contact, although it is not clear exactly how easily it spreads this way. In several studies of marriages where one partner is infected with hepatitis C, the other partner does not seem to have an increased risk of getting it. But people who have sex with many partners seem to run a greater risk of infection. Women appear more likely to get hepatitis C from men than vice versa.

Hepatitis B, and more rarely hepatitis C, can also spread from infected mothers to newborns.

Finally, in more than 10 percent of hepatitis C cases, there is no obvious source of infection. It is possible that some means of transmission has yet to be identified.

Neither hepatitis B nor C, however, are known to spread through air, water, or food. A person cannot catch them by being near infected people or by hugging, working, going to school, or swimming with infected people.

How Is Hepatitis B Prevented?

A vaccine can prevent hepatitis B. Since 1991, U.S. health officials have recommended that all newborns receive the necessary three injections. All children ages 11 or 12 should be vaccinated if they did not get the shots as babies. This, officials hope, may virtually eliminate the disease in the youngest generation of Americans.

The vaccine is also recommended for everyone at high risk, including health care workers, people who have had sex with multiple partners, and anyone who lives with, has sex with, or takes care of a person who has hepatitis B.

Once a person has been exposed to hepatitis B, speedy treatment with hepatitis B immune globulin (HBIG), coupled with vaccination, sometimes can prevent infection in adults. When mothers have hepatitis B, immediate treatment of their newborns can prevent the babies from developing chronic hepatitis.

For people who have not been vaccinated, hepatitis B can be prevented by not having unprotected sex, using condoms, and not using intravenous drugs.

In addition, people should avoid contact with blood. They should not share razors, toothbrushes, or any items that have even the slightest amount of blood on them. Infected people should cover any wounds they may have and should dispose of or wash any tissues, clothes, or sanitary napkins that may contain their blood.

The U.S. and the World

In the United States, 4 million people (or 1.8 percent of the population) are estimated to have chronic hepatitis C, and 8,000 to 10,000 people a year die of it. An estimated 1 million to 1.5 million people have chronic hepatitis B, and 5,000 to 6,000 people a year die of it.

Worldwide, hepatitis B is more common, with 400 million people infected. In Southeast Asia and sub-Saharan Africa, where chronic hepatitis B is most common, 10 to 25 percent of all people may carry the virus. Hepatocellular carcinoma, the liver cancer linked to chronic hepatitis, is also most common in these areas. Worldwide, an estimated 170 million people have chronic hepatitis C.

In the United States, hepatitis B is most common in young adults (intravenous drug users, health care workers, prison inmates, and people, especially homosexual men, who have sex with many partners).

In developing countries, hepatitis B is most common in infants and young children, who get it from their mothers or within the family. When hepatitis B infects a child, it is much more likely to become chronic. That is why chronic B is more common in Asia and Africa than in the United States.

Hepatitis C: How Is It Prevented?

There is no vaccine for hepatitis C, and there is no reliable treatment after a person is exposed. Prevention consists of not sharing needles, avoiding contact with blood, limiting sexual contact, and using condoms, as with hepatitis B.

What Are the Symptoms of Hepatitis?

Acute hepatitis can cause loss of appetite, nausea, vomiting, fatigue, fever, jaundice, darkening of the urine, abdominal pain, arthritis (ar-THRY-tis; joint pain), and skin rash. Often symptoms are absent or so mild they go unnoticed.

The incubation* period is 15 to 45 days for hepatitis A, 15 to 150 days for hepatitis C, and 50 to 180 days for hepatitis B.

Chronic hepatitis can cause loss of appetite, tiredness, low-grade fever, and a general sense of "not feeling well" that doctors call malaise (ma-LAZE). Again, there are often no symptoms.

If the illness causes liver damage, additional symptoms can include weakness, weight loss, itching of the skin, enlargement of the spleen*, fluid in the abdomen, and a pattern of red blood vessels showing through the skin.

In severe cases, massive bleeding can occur in the stomach and the esophagus*, which requires emergency treatment. If the liver is no longer able to remove toxins from food, the brain can be affected, causing drowsiness, confusion, and even coma*.

* **incubation** (in-ku-BAY-shun) means the period of time between infection and first symptoms.

* **spleen** is a large organ in the upper left part of the abdomen that stores and filters blood and also plays a role in making and breaking down blood cells.

* **esophagus** (e-SOF-a-gus) is the tube connecting the stomach and the throat.

* **coma** (KO-ma) is an unconscious state, like a very deep sleep. A person in a coma cannot be awakened and cannot move, see, speak, or hear.

How Is Hepatitis Diagnosed?

Viral hepatitis is diagnosed on the basis of symptoms and several kinds of blood tests. Liver enzyme tests indicate whether the liver is inflamed. If it is, other blood tests can look for specific evidence of hepatitis B or C and can help doctors distinguish between acute and chronic cases.

In chronic cases, doctors may look for liver damage by doing a biopsy (BY-op-see), in which a sample of the liver is removed by a needle through the skin and examined under a microscope.

In many cases, the first hint of hepatitis comes when a routine blood test done for a physical shows signs of abnormalities in the liver. In other cases, a person may try to donate blood and be rejected after his or her blood is tested.

How Is Hepatitis Treated?

For acute hepatitis, there is no specific treatment. In severe cases, people may be hospitalized to get proper fluids, fever control, and nursing care.

For chronic viral hepatitis, the main treatment for years has been interferon alpha (in-ter-FEER-on AL-fa), a naturally occurring substance that interferes with the viruses' ability to reproduce themselves. Treatment requires injections three times a week for at least 6 months and often causes flulike symptoms or more serious side effects. People often relapse after treatment, which does not eliminate the virus completely.

Hepatitis A Vaccine

The vaccine for hepatitis A is thought to provide protection for at least 20 years, although the protection may last for life. The vaccine is administered in two or three doses during a 6-month interval.

The vaccine was tested in Thailand on children living in an area with a high rate of infection. More than 40,000 children aged 1 to 6 were given the vaccine in two or three doses. The children who received two doses achieved 94 percent protection, and those receiving three doses had almost 100 percent protection. In the cases that did occur, the symptoms were milder and lasted a shorter time.

People who are planning to travel to areas known to have hepatitis A should discuss vaccination with their doctors. Among those who may be candidates for the vaccine are:

- Military personnel
- Employees of day care centers
- Institutional care workers
- Laboratory workers who handle live hepatitis A virus
- Handlers of primates that may harbor the hepatitis A virus
- People living in, or relocating to, areas with a high rate of infection
- Residents of communities experiencing a hepatitis A outbreak
- People who engage in high-risk sexual activity
- Users of injectable street drugs

* **sonograms** (SON-o-gramz) are images or records made on a computer using sound waves passing through the body.

* **depression** (de-PRESH-un) is a mental state characterized by feelings of sadness, despair, and discouragement.

Hepatitis at a Glance

	Hepatitis A	Hepatitis B	Hepatitis C	Hepatitis D	Hepatitis E
How is it spread?	Fecal-oral	Blood	Blood	Blood	Fecal-oral
Is there a vaccine to prevent it?	Yes	Yes	No	No	No
Can it become chronic, causing permananent damage?	No	Yes	Yes	Yes	No
Does it spread through food or water?	Yes	No	No	No	Yes
Does it spread through air?	No	No	No	No	No

In recent years, though, research has been yielding some promising new treatments. A drug called lamivudine, which was developed to treat HIV, also appears to be effective in treating chronic hepatitis B. For chronic hepatitis C, a combination of interferon alpha and a drug called ribavirin (ry-ba-VY-rin) seems to be more effective than interferon alone. Several other treatments are being studied.

People with chronic hepatitis need to be monitored closely by doctors, who may want to see them at least once or twice a year. Doctors will do liver enzyme tests to see how well the liver is functioning and may get blood tests, sonograms*, or even liver biopsies to check for cancer.

In cases of liver cancer or cirrhosis, sometimes the only treatment is a liver transplant, in which a person's damaged liver is replaced with a healthy organ taken from a deceased person. If the person can get a new liver in time, which is not always possible, such transplants usually are successful, although the virus eventually may damage the new liver as well.

Living with Chronic Hepatitis

Most people with chronic hepatitis do fine. They can go to school, play sports, work, have children, and live a life like anyone else's.

They need to make sure, however, that they do not put any extra stress on their liver. In the view of most experts, that means that they should never drink alcoholic beverages. They should not take any medicines, even common over-the-counter or herbal remedies, unless they specifically are approved by their doctor. They should not use illegal drugs. In most cases, they should be vaccinated against hepatitis A and against hepatitis B, unless they already have it.

As with other chronic illnesses, people with hepatitis often struggle with feelings of grief, worry, and isolation. Some feel a stigma because their illness often is associated with drug abuse, even though there are many other ways of getting it. Because most people know little about hepatitis, friends and even family may have unrealistic fears about catching it and may avoid the infected person. Counseling for the entire family sometimes can help.

The illness and sometimes the treatment can also cause fatigue and depression*. Infected people may need to get help from family and friends, seek treatment for depression, or modify their schedules to take it easier. Many groups now offer advice, support, and solidarity for people with chronic hepatitis.

Resources

Books

Everson, Gregory T., and Hedy Weinberg. *Living with Hepatitis C: A Survivor's Guide*, revised edition. New York: Hatherleigh Press, 1999. A clear, detailed, and encouraging book from a doctor who has treated hundreds of hepatitis C patients and a writer who has hepatitis C herself.

Turkington, Carol. *Hepatitis C: The Silent Killer*. Chicago: Contemporary Books, 1998.

Organizations

U.S. Centers for Disease Control and Prevention (CDC), 1600 Clifton Road N.E., Atlanta, GA 30333. The U.S. government authority for information about infectious and other diseases, the CDC's Hepatitis Branch has a hotline and posts information about hepatitis at its website. Telephone 888-443-7232
http://www.cdc.gov/ncidod/diseases/hepatitis/index.htm

The World Health Organization (WHO), Avenue Appia 20, 1211 Geneva 27, Switzerland. This group's website posts a fact sheet about hepatitis.
http://www.who.int/emc/diseases/hepatiti/index.html

The Hepatitis Information Network offers a large amount of well-presented information on its website.
http://www.hepnet.com

Hepatitis without a Virus

Not all hepatitis is caused by a virus. It can also be caused by toxic chemicals such as carbon tetrachloride, a solvent used in some dry-cleaning fluids, or by some medications.

Many common medications, such as Dilantin (dy-LAN-tin) for epilepsy (EP-i-LEP-see) and isoniazid (i-so-NY-a-zid) for tuberculosis (too-ber-ku-LO-sis), cause hepatitis in a small fraction of the people who take them. But once the drug is stopped, the liver recovers. Life-threatening hepatitis can result, however, if a person accidentally or intentionally takes an overdose of many medicines, including the common over-the-counter pain reliever acetaminophen (a-set-a-MEE-no-fen).

Finally, some people experience a chronic condition called autoimmune hepatitis. In such people, it appears, the body's immune system attacks its own liver cells. Although treatment with corticosteroids* can improve the condition, it is often fatal unless a liver transplant is performed.

* **corticosteroids** (kor-ti-ko-STEER-oids) are medications that are prescribed to reduce inflammation and sometimes to suppress the body's immune response.

See also
AIDS and HIV
Alcoholism
Cirrhosis of the Liver
Infection
Jaundice
Viral Infections

Hernia

A hernia is the protrusion of an organ through an abnormal opening in the tissue that normally encloses it.

KEYWORDS
for searching the Internet and other reference sources
Digestive system
Gastrointestinal tract

Hernia Means Rupture

The word hernia, in Latin, means rupture. A hernia refers to an opening, or separation, in the muscle, tissue, or membrane that normally holds an organ in place. This opening allows the organ to poke through the hole. Hernias may be caused by muscular weakness, heavy lifting, straining, illness, obesity, or pregnancy.

Hernias commonly occur in the groin, where they are called inguinal (ING-gwi-nal) hernias; in the belly button (umbilical hernias); in the chest, where they are called hiatal (hi-AY-tal) hernias; and in the abdomen (abdominal hernias).

Inguinal hernias The wall of the abdomen is made of thick muscle, but holes exist normally in certain places, such as the groin, through which structures such as blood vessels pass. Hernias usually occur when the intestines push out against these built-in weaknesses. Hernias may be dangerous if the protruding piece of intestine gets trapped and twisted, thus obstructing the flow of food and fluid through the intestine, and sometimes stopping blood supply to that part of the intestine.

Inguinal hernias are the most common type and are often visible as large lumps. Some people with inguinal hernias do not feel anything,

Hernias may develop at different locations in the body, although an individual is unlikely to develop all four kinds of hernia shown here. A hiatal hernia occurs when the stomach pokes above the diaphragm into the chest. An umbilical hernia occurs at the belly button (umbilicus) and is most commonly seen in infants. An inguinal hernia occurs in the groin, where the thigh meets the torso, and happens more often to men than to women. A femoral hernia occurs between the abdomen and the legs, and happens more often to women than to men.

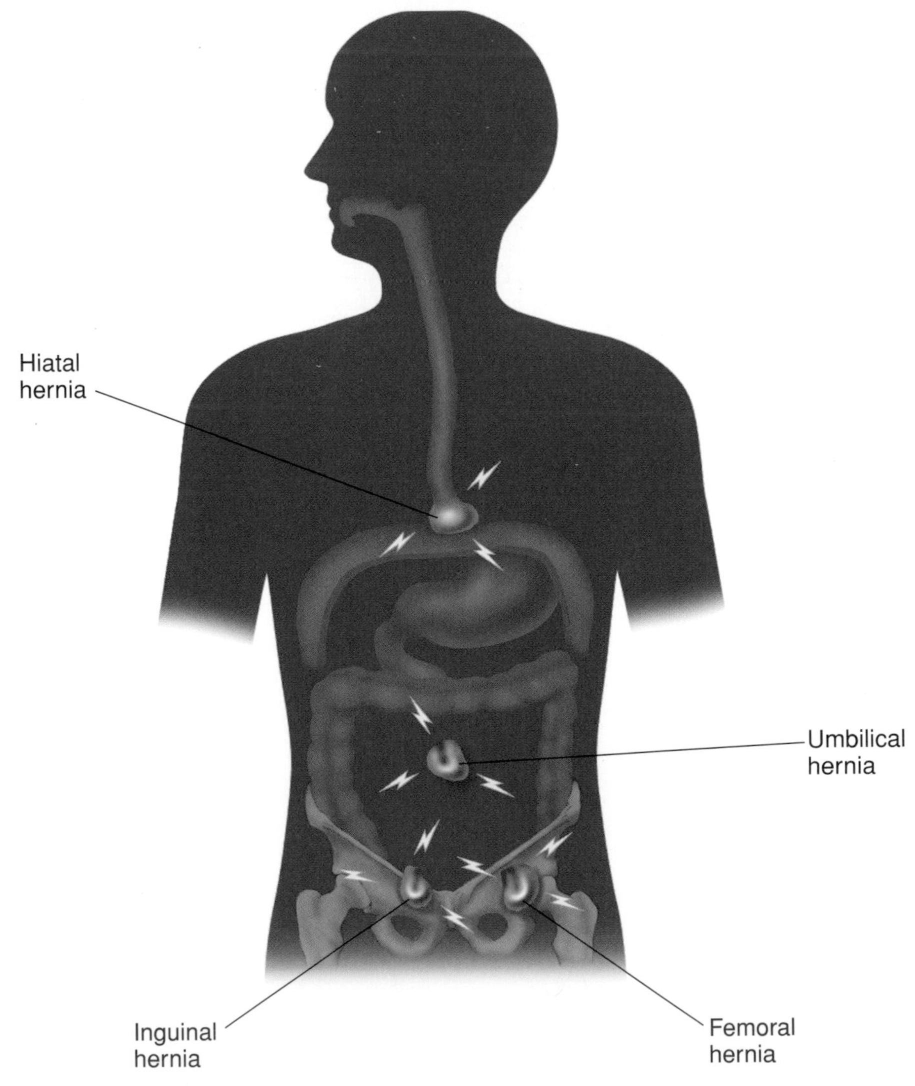

whereas others feel severe pain. The only way to fix this type of hernia is to repair it surgically, using stitches or mesh to close up the hole. Without surgery, an inguinal hernia will usually just keep getting bigger over time.

Hiatal hernias Another common type of hernia is a hiatal hernia. The esophagus, or food pipe, passes to the stomach through a gap in the diaphragm* called the hiatus (hi-AY-tus). A hiatal hernia occurs when the stomach pokes above the diaphragm into the chest. There are no visible bulges, but people have symptoms such as heartburn. Hiatal hernias do not necessarily require surgery. Often, lifestyle changes such as losing weight and avoiding smoking, drinking alcohol, and eating hot, spicy foods can make the symptoms go away.

* **diaphragm** (DY-a-fram) is the muscle that separates the chest and abdominal cavities. It is the chief muscle used in breathing.

Umbilical hernias Umbilical hernias are common in children. One out of five babies has one, but this type usually heals by itself.

Abdominal hernias Abdominal, or intra-abdominal, hernias occur more rarely, when an organ in the abdomen pokes through membranes that normally hold it in place.

Do Children Get Hernias?

Karen loved taking care of her baby brother. One day when she was changing his diaper, she noticed he had a plum-sized bump along the inside of his thigh where it met his torso (his groin). When he cried, it got bigger, like a small balloon being blown up. It looked pretty strange, but he did not seem to be in any pain. Karen's parents took him to the doctor, who said the baby had an inguinal hernia.

The doctor explained that up to 5 percent of healthy babies are born with inguinal hernias, and 80 to 90 percent of children with this type of hernia are boys. These hernias occur because certain openings do not close after birth the way they should, allowing the intestine to bulge out of the hole. The doctor scheduled an operation so that he could surgically repair the baby's hernia, but he assured Karen's parents that the surgery was a safe and common procedure.

Babies also sometimes have umbilical hernias, but these usually heal on their own without surgery.

Resource

The U.S. National Institute of Diabetes and Digestive and Kidney Diseases (NIDDK) posts fact sheets about inguinal hernia and hiatal hernia at its website.

Fact sheet about inguinal hernia may be found at URL http://www.niddk.nih.gov/health/digest/summary/inhernia/inhernia.htm

Fact sheet about hiatal hernia and its relation to gastroesophageal reflux may be found at URL http://www.niddk.nih.gov/health/digest/pubs/heartbrn/heartbrn.htm

▶ *See also*
Heartburn

Herpes

KEYWORDS
for searching the Internet and other reference sources

Herpes simplex

Herpesvirus

Herpetic infections

Herpes is an infection caused by a virus that sometimes produces painful, recurring skin blisters around the mouth or in the genital area.

Cold sores or fever blisters—those annoying purplish-reddish-whitish blisters that tend to pop up around people's mouths—are the most familiar sign of herpes, one of the world's commonest viral infections. Its full name is herpes simplex infection, and it occurs around the globe, even among remote Indian tribes in Brazil.

Herpes simplex is best known for causing cold sores or genital blisters that go away on their own, only to break out again weeks or months or even years later. While these can be painful and upsetting, they usually are not serious, and outbreaks get milder as time goes on. When herpes causes genital sores, it is considered a sexually transmitted disease.

In rare cases, herpes simplex can infect the eyes or internal organs, including the brain, where it may cause an infection called viral encephalitis (en-sef-a-LY-tis). If the virus spreads to newborn babies, or to people with weakened immune systems, it can be serious, even fatal. Most often, however, herpes causes no symptoms at all or symptoms so mild that people do not realize they are infected with the virus.

What Is Herpes?

There are two types of herpes simplex virus. Both types can infect the mouth or the genitals. Usually, however, mouth blisters are caused by herpes simplex virus 1 (HSV-1), and genital blisters are caused by herpes simplex virus 2 (HSV-2).

HSV-1 HSV-1 is common in children, and more than 90 percent of Americans become infected with it. It is spread by direct contact with an infected area—kissing a person with a cold sore, for instance—or by saliva. Although it does not usually spread on objects, some experts advise washing an infected person's eating utensils and towels before others use them.

HSV-2 HSV-2 usually is spread by sexual contact with an infected person. About 22 percent of adult Americans, or 1 in 5, have it. That number has risen sharply since 1980, with the fastest increase occurring among teenagers. HSV-2 spreads most easily when blisters are visible, or just before they appear. But it can be contagious* even when there are no symptoms, and infected people often pass it on without knowing they have it. For this reason, genital herpes is sometimes called a silent epidemic.

*** contagious** means transmittable from one person to another.

If a woman becomes newly infected with genital herpes during pregnancy, the infection can spread to the baby, who may be born prematurely, become very sick, or even die.

People can avoid infection by not engaging in sexual activity. For sexually active people, having few sexual partners and using latex condoms can reduce the chances of infection. Difficult as it may be, people with genital herpes should tell any potential sexual partner that they are infected. They should not have sex during an outbreak or if they feel an outbreak coming on.

What Happens During the First Herpes Outbreak?

In herpes of the mouth or of the genitals, the first signs are usually itching, fever, and aches. Within hours or days, the skin breaks out in clusters of small blisters filled with fluid. In a week or two, the blisters begin to heal, drying into a yellowish crust. After three weeks, they usually are gone. The first time symptoms occur, they usually are more severe, especially in young children, who may have many painful mouth sores, swollen gums, fever, and aching muscles. When the symptoms recur, they usually are milder. Although the first outbreak usually starts within 10 days of infection, sometimes people do not notice blisters until years after they were infected.

Why Does Herpes Keep Coming Back?

When the blisters fade away, the virus hides out in nerve cells in a latent*, or inactive, condition. Weeks, months, or years later, it becomes active again and begins replicating (making copies of itself) in the skin. During these active periods, the virus is contagious, whether or not blisters are visible. What triggers the active periods? Too much sunlight, infection with a cold or flu, stress at home, school, or at work—all these may help set it off.

A doctor who suspects that a person has herpes, based on the symptoms, can use a swab to take cells from a blister and examine them under a microscope. The doctor also can send the sample to a laboratory to make sure of the diagnosis.

Cold sores usually need no treatment, although ice or cold drinks can help relieve the pain. Steroid (cortisone) creams should be avoided, because they can make the blisters last longer.

To shorten outbreaks of genital herpes, a doctor may prescribe an antiviral drug such as acyclovir to be applied as a cream or taken as pills. Although there is no cure for herpes simplex, it usually can be controlled such that it causes a person little trouble.

Did You Know?

- More than 90 percent of American adults have been infected with herpes simplex virus 1, which can cause cold sores.
- An estimated 22 percent of American adults have been infected with herpes simplex virus 2, which can cause genital blisters.
- Among Americans thought to have genital herpes, probably only 10 percent know they have it.
- Besides herpes simplex, other kinds of herpes viruses cause different illnesses, such as chickenpox, shingles, and cytomegalovirus.

* **latent** infections are dormant illnesses that may or may not show the signs and symptoms of active diseases.

Resources

The National Herpes Hotline is open Monday-Friday, 9 AM to 7 PM EST. Run by the American Social Health Association, it offers written material on genital herpes and a chance to talk to a counselor, although there may be a wait. The American Social Health Association also has a *Herpes Resource Center* at its website.
Telephone 919-361-8488
http://www.ashastd.org/main/main.html

The U.S. Centers for Disease Control and Prevention (CDC) has a National Sexually Transmitted Diseases Hotline that is open Monday-

Friday, 8 AM to 11 PM EST. It has counselors who can answer many questions about genital herpes.
Telephone 800-227-8922
The CDC also posts information about herpes at its website.
http://cdc.gov/nchstp/dstd/Genital_Herpes_facts.htm

Cafe Herpe is a website, run by a drug company, that offers clear and easy-to-follow information about genital herpes.
http://www.cafeherpe.com

KidsHealth.org, the website created by the Nemours Foundation, has much information about herpes and other infections.
http://KidsHealth.org

See also
Canker Sores
Chickenpox
Cytomegalovirus
Encephalitis
Genital Warts
Pregnancy, Complications of
Sexually Transmitted Diseases
Shingles
Viral Infections
Warts

Hiccups

Hiccups occur when the diaphragm* suddenly contracts during breathing. The vocal cords quickly close, and an odd sound comes from the throat. Hiccups are involuntary. Their cause is not known, and hiccups do not seem to serve any useful purpose.

KEYWORDS
for searching the Internet and other reference sources

Pulmonary system

Respiratory system

Singultus

Are Hiccups Dangerous?

Most hiccups are not harmful. The frequency of most hiccups is usually from 4 to 60 hiccups a minute. Hiccups usually occur in people (even

Hiccups occur when the diaphragm and lungs suddenly contract during breathing.

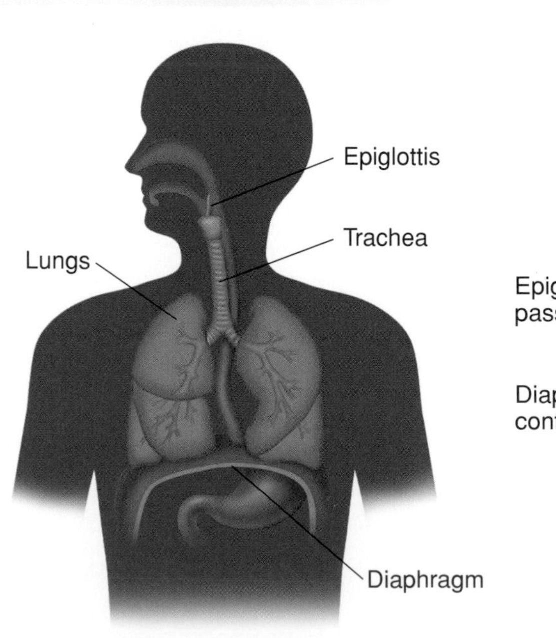

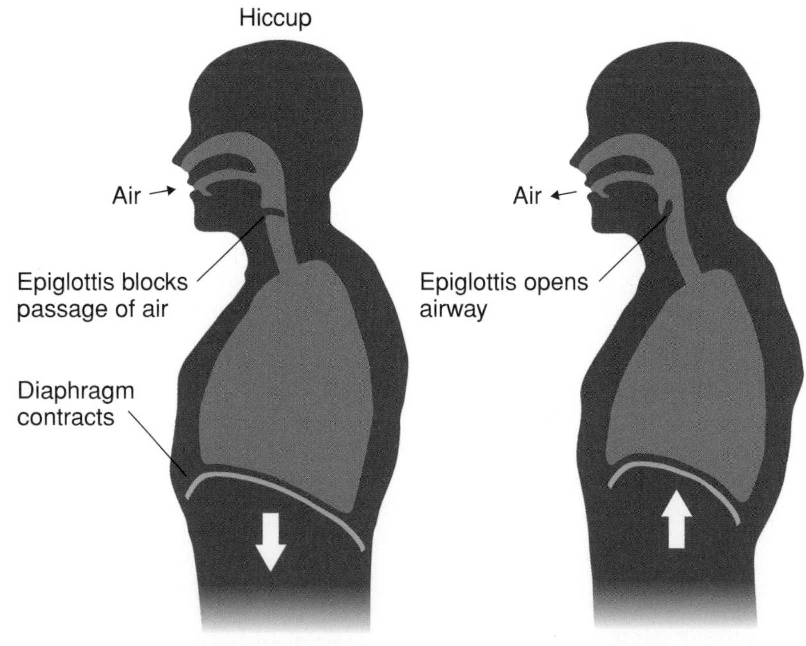

babies and fetuses) for a minute or two and then pass. There are, however, cases of prolonged hiccuping that can be dangerous, especially for people who are ill from other causes and who may become exhausted if they do not seek medical treatment.

What Are the Different Types of Hiccups?

Hiccups are classified into several categories. A "hiccup bout" can last from several seconds to several days. A "persistent hiccup" is one that lasts for several days or weeks. Hiccups lasting more than a month are called "intractable." In rare cases, intractable hiccups may continue for years.

What Is the Treatment for Hiccups?

Everyone seems to have a favorite cure for hiccups, but usually they just go away by themselves. In severe cases of hiccups, doctors may try to block the hiccup process (also called the "hiccup arc" or "pathway") by stimulating parts of the respiratory (breathing) system or by prescribing medications to relax the muscles involved. When all else fails, surgery is done to block the nerve signals from the phrenic (FREN-ik) nerve to the diaphragm. The purpose of this procedure is to paralyze part of the diaphragm.

* **diaphragm** (DY-a-fram) is the muscle that separates the chest and abdominal cavities. It is the chief muscle used in breathing.

What Is Your Home Cure for Hiccups?

Everyone seems to have a special way to stop hiccups even though none of these remedies has been proved to work consistently. Here are some of the most common home cures:

- Holding one's breath and then exhaling very slowly
- Holding the nose
- Breathing into a paper bag
- Sucking on ice cubes
- Sucking on hard candy
- Drinking water from the far side of a glass
- Gargling
- Pulling on the tongue
- Biting on a lemon
- Swallowing granulated sugar
- Swallowing hard crusts of bread
- Sneezing
- Peeling onions
- Bending over so that the head is lower than the chest
- Surprising or frightening the person with hiccups
- Slapping the person with hiccups on the back

High Blood Pressure *See* Hypertension

HIV *See* AIDS and HIV

Hives

Hives are itchy wheals (welts) that erupt on the skin, usually caused by an allergic reaction.

What Are Hives?

Hives, also known as urticaria (ur-ti-KARE-e-a), develop as a reaction to various stimuli. Certain foods, food additives or dyes, drugs, alcohol, or viral infections can cause hives in susceptible people. Foods that commonly cause hives include milk, eggs, shellfish, strawberries, other fruits, and nuts.

Penicillin and aspirin cause hives in some people. Some viral infections that are known to cause hives are hepatitis (inflammation of the liver), infectious mononucleosis, and rubella (German measles).

Some people develop hives after vigorous exercise that causes them to sweat. Sometimes the sun or cold air can cause hives to appear on people's skin. In some people, diving into cold water can result in severe hives—in a condition known as cold urticaria.

KEYWORD
for searching the Internet and other reference sources

Allergy

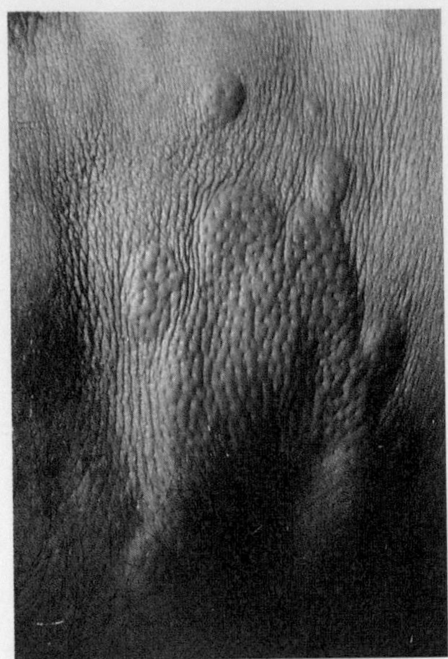

Close-up of hives. ©*1994 Caliendo, Custom Medical Stock Photo*

Signs and Symptoms

The first symptom of hives is itching, after which the wheals appear. Wheals usually are small, white welts with red, inflamed areas surrounding them; in some cases, however, they can be quite large. They usually erupt on the arms, legs, and trunk. Sometimes they develop into a ring, with the center clearing before the outer ring improves. Hives tend to come and go on different areas of the skin, and individual welts can last several hours.

What Is Angioedema?

A more severe form of hives, called angioedema (an-jee-o-e-DEE-ma), can cause swelling of the hands, feet, eyelids, lips, genital area, and airway passages, making breathing difficult. In some cases, angioedema is a hereditary disorder, and a family history usually is present. In these cases, it is a chronic condition, which means that it recurs from time to time.

Treatment for Hives

Most cases of hives clear up by themselves in 1 to 7 days. Some cases respond to medications such as antihistamines (an-tee-HISS-ta-meens) or corticosteroids (kor-ti-ko-STER-oids). Antihistamines are used to combat the allergic reaction, and corticosteroids are used to fight the inflammation.

Can Hives Be Prevented?

The only way to prevent hives is to avoid a known trigger (the substance that sets off the reaction). Many people who develop hives outgrow them over time without treatment.

See also
Allergies
Skin Conditions

Hodgkin's Disease *See* Cancer; Lymphoma

Hookworm

Hookworm is a parasitic roundworm that burrows through the skin, moves through the bloodstream to the lungs, and finally moves into the intestinal tract.

KEYWORDS
for searching the Internet and other reference sources

Infestations

Necator americanus

Nematodes

Parasitic infections

What Is Hookworm?

Hookworm is a type of parasitic* roundworm, known as a nematode (NEM-a-tode), that has hooked mouthparts. The worm uses these mouthparts to fasten itself onto the intestinal walls of various hosts*, including humans. Hookworm larvae (the stage between egg and adult) often enter the body through the skin between the toes in people who go barefoot. Hookworm affects about a quarter of the world's population, most often in warm, moist areas and in places with poor sanitation.

* **parasitic** (par-a-SIT-ik) refers to creatures that live in and feed on the bodies of other organisms.

* **hosts** are the animals or plants that harbor a parasite.

"The Germ of Laziness"

Charles Stiles started the National Hookworm Eradication Program in the early 1900s. At the time, hookworm was a serious problem in the southern United States because of the warm, moist climate and poor sanitation conditions, combined with the habit of going barefoot. Hookworm was called the "germ of laziness."

In 1914, oil magnate John D. Rockefeller gave Stiles a $1 million grant to target sanitation in the public schools. Stiles's program became a model used in hookworm eradication programs worldwide.

How Do Hookworms Grow?

Adult hookworms live inside the small intestine of humans and other animals, where they attach to the intestinal wall and feed on the host's blood. Eggs are passed in the host's stools. The eggs hatch into larvae in 1 to 2 days under warm, moist conditions out of direct sunlight. The larvae grow in the stools and/or soil for 5 to 10 days until they become filariform (fi-LARE-i-form), or threadlike. It is during this stage that hookworm can cause infection.

Filariform larvae can survive for up to 3 or 4 weeks. When they make contact with the bare skin of a human or another animal, they burrow into the skin and enter the host's bloodstream. They then are carried through the bloodstream to the lungs, where they burrow through the thin walls. Once inside the lungs, they move up the airways

◀ The parasitic hookworm *Necator americanus* uses its hooked mouthpart to attach to the intestinal wall. © *A. M. Siegelman/ Visuals Unlimited.*

The U.S. and the World

- Approximately 3.5 billion people worldwide have some form of infection from intestinal parasites, with about 450 million people in rich and poor countries alike experiencing symptoms of illness.
- Hookworms, roundworms, and pinworms are among the most common intestinal parasites and are a major public health problem.
- Children living in poor regions with tropical climates are especially at risk for hookworm and roundworm infections.
- Hookworm and roundworm infections also occur in countries like the United States, especially from contact with infected pets or their waste or from poor personal hygiene.
- Hookworms are responsible for 60,000 deaths annually. The large roundworm *Ascaris lumbricoides* (which causes ascariasis) is responsible for another 65,000 deaths worldwide each year.

to the throat, where they are swallowed. They then pass down the digestive tract to the small intestine. Inside the small intestine, they attach to the intestinal wall, and the cycle begins again.

How Is Hookworm Diagnosed and Treated?

The most common symptom of hookworm is anemia* caused by a loss of iron due to blood loss. Other symptoms include lack of appetite, weight loss, diarrhea*, and vague abdominal pain. When the larvae are in the lungs, there may be a dry cough and a mild fever. When the larvae burrow into the skin, there may be mild itching and a rash. It is not uncommon, however, for mild infections to show no symptoms at all.

An infection is confirmed in the laboratory by observing eggs in stool samples under a microscope. Medications can be prescribed to treat the infection. Anemia is treated with iron supplements.

* **anemia** (a-NEE-mee-a) results when people have too few red blood cells and hemoglobin to carry oxygen in the blood.

* **diarrhea** (di-a-REE-a) refers to large, frequent, watery stools (bowel movements).

Can Hookworm Be Prevented?

The most effective method of prevention is limiting direct contact between infected soil and skin. In areas where hookworm is common, people should avoid walking barefoot or touching soil with their bare hands.

Resources

U.S. Centers for Disease Control and Prevention (CDC), 1600 Clifton Road, Atlanta, GA 30333. CDC has a Division of Parasitic Diseases that posts a fact sheet about hookworm infection at its website.
Telephone 800-311-3435
http://www.cdc.gov/ncidod/dpd/hookworm.htm

U.S. National Institute of Allergy and Infectious Diseases (NIAID). NIAID posts a fact sheet about hookworm and other parasitic roundworm diseases at its website.
http://www.niaid.nih.gov/factsheets/roundwor.htm

▶ *See also*
Anemia
Ascariasis
Diarrhea
Parasitic Diseases
Pinworm (Enterobiasis)
Worms

Huntington's Disease

Huntington's disease, formerly called Huntington's chorea (kor-EE-a), is a rare disease that causes part of the brain to deteriorate. A person with the disease has involuntary and strange movements. It is a genetic disorder that is passed from parent to child.

KEYWORDS
for searching the Internet and other reference sources

Genetics

Neurology

Who Is at Risk for Huntington's Disease?

In the United States, only about 5 out of 100,000 people develop Huntington's disease. Because it is transmitted from parent to child, only children of a parent who has the abnormal gene are at risk, and they have a 50 percent chance of developing the disease.

What Is Huntington's Disease?

Huntington's affects the basal ganglia (GANG-lee-a, nerve cell bodies in part of the white matter of the brain). This part of the brain acts as an important pathway for the central nervous system*. Huntington's disease causes erratic movements, usually first affecting the face and speech. Memory, reasoning, and speech become affected. Eventually, the abilities to walk, swallow, and take care of oneself are lost. Males and females are equally affected. A person with Huntington's disease usually first has symptoms between the ages of 35 and 50. A person with the disease may live for a period of 10 to 20 years more, but the condition becomes worse over time.

*__central nervous system__ consists of the brain and the spinal cord. It controls and coordinates the activities of the entire nervous system.

What Are the Symptoms of Huntington's Disease?

A person with Huntington's disease may first make unusual or strange facial grimaces and become clumsy. Also, the person may become irritable or forgetful. The person may appear to be drunk even without having consumed any alcohol. The awkwardness that comes from the disease may put the person in danger, for example, by losing his balance while crossing the street.

What Is the Treatment for Huntington's Disease?

There is no cure for Huntington's disease, but there is medicine to control the erratic movements caused by the disease. This medicine blocks the production of dopamine* in the brain.

Children of someone with Huntington's disease are advised to seek genetic counseling before deciding whether or not to have children of their own, as they also could get the disease. A particular blood test can determine whether or not a person has the gene for Huntington's disease.

*__dopamine__ is a neurotransmitter (a chemical messenger) in the brain that helps to transmit messages between nerve cells in the brain.

GEORGE HUNTINGTON

The word "chorea" comes from the Greek language, by way of Latin, and means "dance." During the Renaissance, the Swiss physician Paracelsus (1493–1541) wrote about the uncontrollable rhythmic movements characteristic of several different movement disorders.

In 1872, the American physician George Huntington (1850–1916) described an inherited choreatic disorder that began late in life. Because of that research the disorder was named "Huntington's Chorea," now known as Huntington's disease.

Who Was Woody Guthrie?

Woody Guthrie was a folk singer who was well known during the 1930s and 1940s for his songs about the life of migrant workers and poor city people. Among his best known songs are "This Land Is Your Land" and "So Long, It's Been Good to Know You." Woody Guthrie died of Huntington's disease. When he first exhibited symptoms of the disease, people thought he was drunk. Only later was his behavior understood. His son Arlo Guthrie is also a famous singer. Arlo will not develop Huntington's disease because he did not inherit the gene from his father.

▶ *See also*
Genetic Diseases

Is There a Cure for Huntington's Disease?

There is no cure for Huntington's disease, but knowing if a person has the gene can influence a family as to whether to have children who might develop this disease later in their lives. The test will show whether or not the person has the gene that causes the disease. Sometimes people who are at risk may not want to know if they have the gene, and they take the chance of having children before the onset of the disease is noticed. They feel that knowing they have the gene will make it impossible for them to live a normal life.

Resources

Caring for People with Huntington's Disease, on line at http://www.edu/hospital/huntingtons/

Guthrie, Woody. *Bound for Glory,* 1943. An autobiography by the famous folk singer.

Huntington's Disease Society of America (HDSA), 140 West 22nd Street, 6th Floor, New York, NY 10011-2420. Telephone (212) 242-1968 or (800) 345-4372; e-mail: curehd@hdsa.ttisms.com; website: http://hdsa.mgh.harvard.edu

Hydrocephalus

Hydrocephalus (hy-dro-SEF-a-lus) is a condition that occurs when there is too much fluid inside the skull. The excess fluid inside the skull often creates pressure on the brain and may result in mental and physical handicaps.

KEYWORDS
for searching the Internet and other reference sources

Cerebrospinal fluid

Neurology

Ventricular system

Why Is the Baby's Head So Big?

When Liz saw her baby brother in the hospital nursery, she was upset by his appearance. His head seemed huge. The doctor explained that John had hydrocephalus, or too much fluid within his skull. Because he was a newborn, the bones in his head had not yet grown together, allowing his head to expand with the pressure caused by the extra fluid. The doctor warned Liz's family that John's brain might have been squeezed and damaged by the excess fluid, but that it was too soon to tell for sure.

What Is Hydrocephalus?

Hydrocephalus refers to fluid buildup in and around the brain. The term comes from two Greek words: "hydro" meaning "water," and "cephalie" meaning "brain." Hydrocephalus often is called "water on the brain," but the brain and spinal cord are actually bathed in cerebrospinal fluid (CSF). CSF is a mixture of water, protein, sugar, and minerals that is made by the tissues lining the inside of the brain to cushion and protect it.

The brain contains four cavities, or spaces, called ventricles (VEN-tri-kuls). CSF normally flows through the ventricles, through tiny openings at the base of the brain, over the brain's surface, and around the spinal cord. Normally, the pressure exerted on the brain by CSF is kept fairly constant because excess CSF is reabsorbed into the bloodstream.

People develop hydrocephalus when the flow of CSF is blocked (obstructive hydrocephalus) or when it cannot be reabsorbed (communicating hydrocephalus). In both cases, CSF accumulates and the extra pressure squeezes the brain and disrupts blood flow to the brain. Without the oxygen and sugar that blood carries, the brain cannot function properly. Over time, blood vessels and nerve cells are damaged, resulting in problems with learning, thinking, and moving. The severity of hydrocephalus varies from person to person.

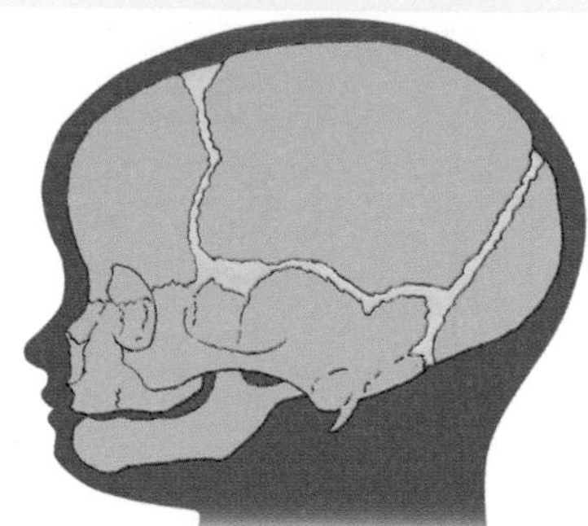

Healthy infant

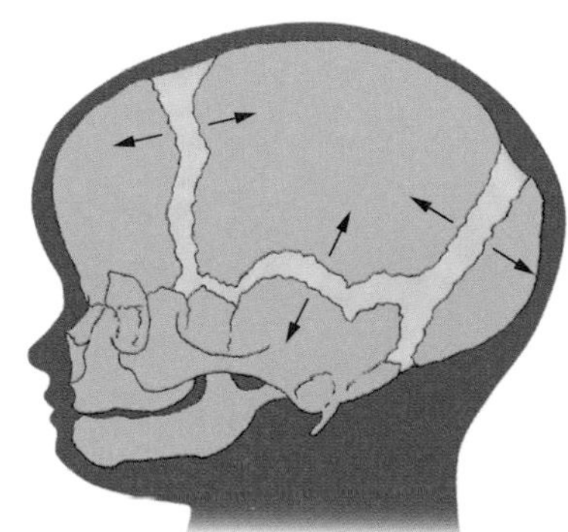

Hydrocephalus

When babies are born with hydrocephalus, excess fluid and pressure inside the skull cause the skull bones to pull apart and the head to enlarge.

What Causes Hydrocephalus?

The cause of hydrocephalus often is unknown, but in many cases a cause can be found. Congenital hydrocephalus means that a person is born with the condition, and it affects about 1 in 1,000 babies. It may occur because the brain did not develop properly or because the fetus developed a viral or protozoan infection, such as rubella (German measles), herpes, cytomegalovirus, or toxoplasmosis. Spina bifida is a congenital disorder in which there is an opening in the spinal cord and spinal column, and at least 80 percent of babies with spina bifida also develop some degree of hydrocephalus.

In infants, children, and adults, brain tumors can cause hydrocephalus by blocking the flow of CSF. Hydrocephalus also can be caused by meningitis, an infection of the linings of the brain and spinal cord, and by bleeding in the brain because of a stroke* or a head injury. Infants born very prematurely frequently experience bleeding in the ventricles of the brain, which often leads to hydrocephalus. Hydrocephalus is less common in adults.

*__stroke__ may occur when a blood vessel bringing oxygen and nutrients to the brain bursts or becomes clogged by a blood clot or other particle. As a result, nerve cells in the affected area and the specific body parts they control do not properly function.

How Is Hydrocephalus Treated?

Babies suspected of having hydrocephalus are watched closely. John's head kept getting bigger and ultimately his doctor used a CT scan* and an MRI* to examine his brain.

*__CT scans__ or CAT scans are the short names for computerized axial tomography, which uses computers and x-rays to view cross sections inside the body.

*__MRI__ means magnetic resonance imaging, which uses magnets to view inside the body.

Some forms of hydrocephalus require no treatment, but most, like John's, require surgery. The surgeon placed a device called a shunt in John's brain to drain the excess CSF. Shunts are thin flexible tubes that are placed through the skull and drain some of the excess CSF into the bloodstream or the abdomen to be reabsorbed by the body. This procedure relieves pressure on the brain, but it does not cure the brain damage that has occurred already.

Most babies born with hydrocephalus live if they receive treatment, but 60 percent of those babies have mental and physical handicaps. Liz's baby brother John was lucky. He was among the 40 percent of children born with hydrocephalus whose mental and physical abilities are unaffected.

Resources

Book

Toporek, Chuck, and Kellie Robinson. *Hydrocephalus: A Guide for Parents, Families, and Friends*. O'Reilly and Associates, 1999.

Organizations

The U.S. National Institute of Neurological Disorders and Stroke posts a fact sheet about childhood hydrocephalus at its website.
http://www.ninds.nih.gov/patients/Disorder/hydrochd/HYDROCHD.HTM

Hydrocephalus Association, 870 Market Street, Suite 955, San Francisco, CA 94102.
Telephone 415-732-7040
http://neurosurgery.mgh.harvard.edu/ha/default.html

Association for Spina Bifida and Hydrocephalus, 42 Park Road, Peterborough, PE1 2UQ, England.
Telephone 01733-555988
http://www.asbah.demon.co.uk

► *See also*
Brain Tumor
Cytomegalovirus
German Measles (Rubella)
Herpes
Meningitis
Spina Bifida
Stroke
Toxoplasmosis

Hyperactivity *See* Attention Deficit Hyperactivity Disorder

Hypertension

Hypertension, or high blood pressure, is a condition in which the pressure of the blood in the arteries is above normal.

KEYWORD
for searching the Internet and other reference sources
Heart disease

What Is Hypertension?

Hypertension is the medical term for high blood pressure. Arteries are the blood vessels that carry the blood from the heart through the entire body. High blood pressure results either when the output of the blood pumped by the heart increases, or when there is an increased resistance to the flow of blood through the arteries, or both. In terms of numbers, a resting blood pressure of 140/90 or greater in an adult is usually considered to be high. Normal blood pressure levels are lower in children and rise with age.

Everyone's blood pressure goes up in moments of excitement or stress, and that is considered to be normal. High blood pressure is considered a medical condition only when it continues over an extended period of time. This condition can then become a serious threat to health; the higher the pressure and the longer it is untreated, the greater the risk.

People who have hypertension are more likely to suffer a stroke, heart attack, or failure of the kidneys or heart. For this reason, and because there usually are no symptoms, hypertension has been termed "the silent killer."

Who Has High Blood Pressure?

Hypertension definitely is not the kind of condition one person can catch from another. Its causes are varied and complex: hereditary (genetic) factors, medical conditions, or medications can play roles. In most cases, no single cause for a person's hypertension can be found.

Certain generalizations can be made about its prevalance* in the overall population, however. It has been estimated that 60 million people in the United States have high blood pressure. This amounts to about 20 percent of the population, or one in every five persons. This prevalance is believed to be about the same in most industrialized Western countries; but the prevalance of high blood pressure is relatively low in developing (poor) or Third World countries.

* **prevalance** of a disease or condition means how common it is in a population of people.

It is further estimated that about one-third to one-half of people with high blood pressure are unaware of their condition. Many people first find out when they go for a routine medical check-up.

The prevalance of hypertension is slightly higher in women than in men. Men and women of African descent are both more likely than others to develop the disorder. Hypertension usually begins after ages 20 to 30, and is uncommon in children and teenagers. Besides age, gender, and race, factors that have been linked to high blood pressure include obesity, smoking, a diet high in sodium (such as that found in table salt), excessive use of alcohol, and a family history of the disorder.

What the Numbers Mean

Blood pressure is measured in units called millimeters of mercury (mm Hg). It is written as two numbers, one over the other. The number on top is the systolic pressure (when the heart contracts). The bottom number is the diastolic pressure (when the heart relaxes between beats).

BLOOD PRESSURE IN ADULTS

Normal Pressure	Systolic (mm Hg)		Diastolic (mm Hg)
Ideal	less than 120	and	less than 80
Normal	less than 130	and	less than 85
High normal	130–139	or	85–89
Hypertension			
STAGE 1 (Mild)	140–159	or	90–99
STAGE 2 (Moderate)	160–179	or	100–109
STAGE 3 (Severe)	180 or higher	or	110 or higher

Did You Know?

- People almost never can tell whether or not they have high blood pressure by how they feel.
- About one-third to one-half of the people who have high blood pressure do not even know it.
- Hypertension is called "the silent killer" because it can cause heart attack and stroke without warning symptoms.
- Many people with mild hypertension can be treated without the use of drugs.
- The guidelines for preventing high blood pressure are the same as the guidelines for leading a healthy life.

How Does the Body Control Blood Pressure?

As the heart forces blood into the arteries, the blood is kept under constant pressure. Many times a day, blood pressure rises briefly when the heart beats faster to supply blood to the parts of the body that need it. For example, a person's legs will need more blood when he or she is running a race. After the effort has ended, the blood pressure returns to its usual level.

Over time, when a person is at rest, the body controls blood pressure in two basic ways. One way is by constricting, or narrowing, the arterioles (ar-TEE-re-olz), blood vessels that branch off larger arteries. The other way is by regulating the fluid volume of the blood.

The kidneys have a key role in both of these functions. By secreting the hormone renin, they cause the arterioles to constrict, thereby raising the blood pressure. In addition, the kidneys control the fluid volume of the blood either by retaining sodium or by excreting it into the urine. Blood volume and blood pressure increase when sodium is retained in the body.

What Causes Hypertension?

Hypertension results when the body systems, which keep the width of the arterioles and the fluid volume of the blood in a normal relationship, become unbalanced. This disruption may occur because of disease or some other influence. Disease, such as disorders of the kidneys, certain tumors, or artery conditions, account for only about 10 percent of hypertension cases. In the great majority of patients, the precise cause remains unknown. In these instances, the disorder is referred to as "primary hypertension" or "essential hypertension."

Certain factors are known to be influential in producing hypertension. Factors that may contribute to the development of hypertension include a fatty diet and lack of exercise (which can lead to obesity) and too much salt in the diet. Hypertension also occasionally occurs in women who are taking birth control pills. Other factors include diabetes, smoking, and excessive alcohol consumption.

How Does Hypertension Affect the Body?

Hypertension rarely causes symptoms by itself. When it does, the blood pressure usually is extremely high. Symptoms may then include headache, nosebleeds, dizziness, confusion, and seizures. A florid (reddish) complexion is not, as is often believed, a sign of hypertension.

Hypertension leads to or speeds up the process of atherosclerosis (ath-er-o-skle-RO-sis), or hardening of the arteries. In this process, cholesterol and other materials carried in the blood can build up in places along the artery walls damaged by years of high pressure. If a blockage should occur in the coronary arteries, which supply blood to the heart muscle, a heart attack ensues. If artery blockage occurs in the brain, the result is a stroke. Damage to arterioles can lead to brain hemorrhage (another kind of stroke), kidney failure, or blindness. Over a period of years, hypertension can bring about heart failure by overworking the heart.

The course of hypertension if left untreated varies in different people. In most, the blood pressure tends to increase gradually over the years.

Hypertension During Pregnancy A serious condition called preeclampsia (pree-ee-KLAMP-see-a) develops during the second half of pregnancy in about 7 percent of women. This disorder is characterized by a sudden rise in blood pressure, along with severe headaches, visual disturbances, and retention of fluids in the body. The condition is most common in first pregnancies and in women younger than 25 or older than 35. If left untreated, preeclampsia can lead to eclampsia, which is characterized by seizures and extremely high blood pressure that may be fatal to the mother or baby.

Hypertension Is Defined by Numbers

Blood pressure is expressed as two numbers: the systolic (sis-TOL-ik) pressure and the diastolic (dy-a-STOL-ik) pressure. The higher number is the systolic pressure, which occurs during systole (SIS-to-lee), when the heart contracts. The lower number is the diastolic pressure, which occurs during diastole (dy-AS-to-lee), when the heart relaxes between beats.

These numbers are read from a special instrument, called a sphygmomanometer (sfig-mo-ma-NOM-e-ter). Written down, the two numbers are separated by a slash. Normal pressure taken at rest in adults is about 120/80, expressed as "120 over 80." Healthy young adults typically will have a pressure of about 110/75, however, and normal blood pressures are even lower in young children. As previously mentioned, a pressure of 140/90 or more in adults means hypertension.

How Is Hypertension Diagnosed?

When diagnosing hypertension, the physician may take more than one reading, especially if the first reading is high. This is so because blood

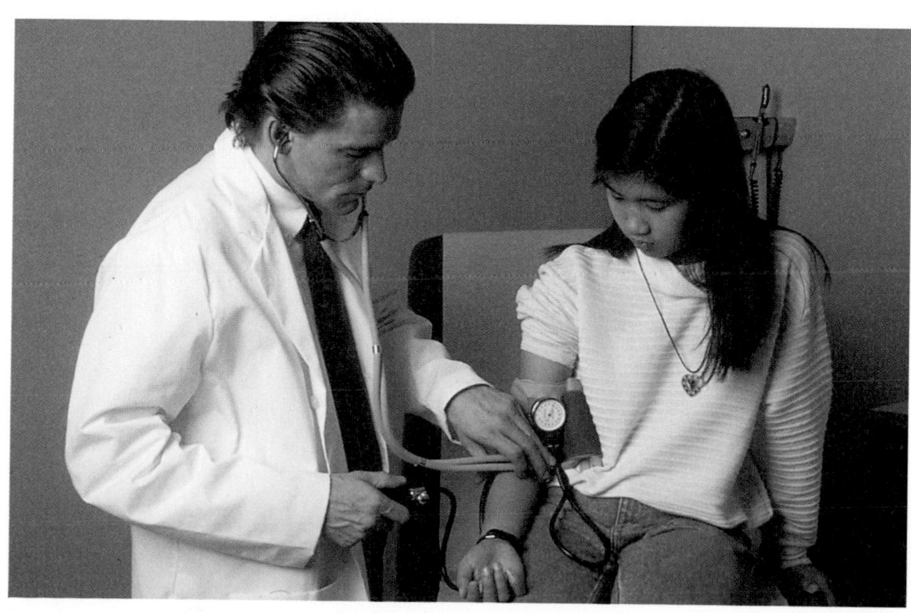

◀ A doctor uses a sphygmomanometer to measure blood pressure. *©1995 Custom Medical Stock Photo.*

pressure varies over time. Moreover, some patients have what is called "white coat hypertension." This means that their blood pressure tends to go up when they are in a doctor's office, because being in the presence of a physician makes them feel anxious. To get an accurate reading, doctors will try to have their patients feel as relaxed as possible. If the patient has never had his or her blood pressure taken before, it is important for the doctor to explain that the process is painless.

Diagnosing high blood pressure has to do with more than just numbers, however. The doctor will have to try to determine the cause. The patient may be asked about eating and exercise habits. If someone else in the family has a history of high blood pressure, that may be important. The doctor also may want to know about the patient's salt intake, consumption of alcohol, smoking habits, use of medications such as birth control pills, and use of street drugs. Urine and blood samples may be taken to check on kidney function and blood cholesterol levels.

It is commonly observed that blood pressure tends to go up with age. Although true statistically, this does not mean that it is acceptable from a health standpoint. Blood pressure of more than 140/90 usually is considered a cause of concern at any age.

How Is Hypertension Treated?

For the small percentage of patients whose hypertension is caused by particular disorders of the kidneys or certain tumors or artery conditions, surgery may be the chosen treatment and provide a cure. For the great majority, however, the choice of treatment will likely be lifestyle changes or medication in addition to lifestyle changes.

Good Health Habits Many people who have mild hypertension (not much more than 140/90) can lower their blood pressure by adopting certain modifications in their lifestyle and diet, without the use of drugs. These changes may involve losing weight, getting more exercise, or modifying the diet in certain ways.

Excess weight, especially obesity, can be a factor in raising blood pressure. In losing weight, usually it is best to take a gradual approach and to emphasize reduction of fat in the diet. Any weight loss program also should include regular exercise such as walking briskly or jogging (with a doctor's approval in adult patients). Many experts believe that it is almost impossible to lose weight permanently through diet alone.

Most people with hypertension can help to lower their blood pressure by going on a low-sodium, or low-salt, diet. Studies have shown that people can get all the salt they need in the foods they eat without adding any. Good rules to follow are to add less salt at the table and in cooking, and to shop for foods low in sodium. Labels on cans or packages of processed food will indicate how much sodium is contained in each portion.

Another factor that may be implicated in high blood pressure is stress. Although some stress is unavoidable in daily life, frequent unrelieved

What Is a Sphygmomanometer?

A sphygmomanometer (sfig-mo-ma-NOM-e-ter) is the instrument that measures blood pressure. It consists of an inflatable cuff, or wide band, that is wrapped around the upper arm, a rubber bulb to inflate the cuff, and a device that gives the pressure reading.

In measuring the pressure, the cuff is inflated until it briefly stops the flow of blood in the arm (a painless process). The air pressure is then gradually released while a stethoscope (STETH-o-skope), a listening device, is placed on the artery of the arm just below the cuff. The pressure when the sound of the pulse is heard as the blood first begins to flow again is called the systolic pressure (the higher number). As more pressure is released, the sound of the pulse becomes muffled and disappears. The pressure at that point is called the diastolic pressure (the lower number).

The pressure is read on a gauge, which can be a glass column filled with mercury (the earliest type), a dial, or a digital readout. In some instruments, the blood pressure may be read directly, without the use of a stethoscope. The actual numbers in blood pressure readings represent millimeters of mercury (mm Hg), based upon the original glass column filled with mercury.

The word "sphygmomanometer" comes from the Greek *sphygmos,* meaning pulse, plus *manometer,* a pressure gauge.

Closeup view of sphygmomanometer dial used to measure blood pressure. © *1994 Custom Medical Stock Photo*

stress can be harmful. It is worthwhile to find ways, such as relaxation techniques, to lower stress levels. Physical exercise is an effective way to decrease stress and blood pressure in many people.

Common-sense rules about avoiding harmful substances apply to people with normal as well as high blood pressure. It is inadvisable to smoke at any age or for adults to have more than one or two alcoholic drinks per day. The nicotine from cigarettes speeds up the heart and constricts blood vessels. Alcohol abuse has been associated with increased risk of developing hypertension, as well as many other health problems. Street drugs such as cocaine can have a direct adverse effect on the heart and increase blood pressure.

Medication If hypertension is moderate or severe, or if mild hypertension does not respond to diet, exercise, and other lifestyle changes, medicines may be prescribed. Doctors today have several different types to choose from, depending upon their patients' particular needs.

Diuretic drugs are among the more commonly used. They act to increase the flow of urine and decrease the blood volume. Another group, called beta-blockers, alters the way the nervous system functions in the control of blood pressure. A third group of drugs, called vasodilators (va-zo-DY-layt-orz), act to relax the blood vessels, thereby decreasing the resistance to blood flow. Other types may be prescribed as well.

Prescription drugs for hypertension may have various side effects, depending upon the drug and the person taking it. All antihypertensive drugs may cause dizziness and fainting, however, if the blood pressure is lowered too much. It is extremely important not to stop taking medication once begun without consulting the doctor.

Doctors treating hypertension may wish to have their patients keep track of their blood pressure by taking readings at regular intervals. Devices for home use are available for this purpose.

Can Hypertension Be Prevented?

For teenagers and young adults, who are unlikely to have the condition early in life, hypertension may seem only a remote consideration. However, establishing a healthy lifestyle by keeping fit and trim through exercise and good eating habits, and not smoking, can help prevent health problems such as hypertension from developing later on in life. This is particularly important for people who have a family history of hypertension.

Lastly, it is important for everyone to get their blood pressure checked regularly. Although doing so will not actually prevent hypertension, it can get someone who has the condition into treatment earlier, thereby keeping it under control and lessening the risk of developing such serious health problems as heart attack and stroke.

▶ *See also*
Atherosclerosis
Diabetes
Heart Disease
Stroke

Hyperthyroidism *See* Thyroid Disease

Hypochondria

Hypochondria (hy-po-KON-dre-a) is a mental disorder in which people believe that they are sick, but their symptoms are not related to any physical illness.

KEYWORDS
for searching the Internet and other reference sources

Factitious disorder

Hypochondriasis

Munchausen syndrome

Psychology

Somatoform disorders

What Is Hypochondria?

Researchers say that between 4 and 9 percent of visits to physicians involve people with hypochondria. These people say that they feel sick and often have detailed explanations for their beliefs. They might complain about chest pains or headaches. However, when the physician examines them for a specific disease or condition, nothing physical is found that explains the symptoms or their concern. Hypochondria is more than the occasional fear of illness that healthy people may have. It is an ongoing belief that something is medically wrong and is causing problems in everyday life.

What Causes Hypochondria?

Hypochondria often is related to other mental disorders, such as depression* or anxiety*. Sometimes children who see their parents exhibit hypochondria show similar signs when they become adults. Some people who have survived a serious illness go on to battle hypochondria, because they fear the return of their disease.

* **depression** (de-PRESH-un) is a mental disorder that causes long periods of excessive sadness and impairs a person's feelings, thoughts, and behavior.

* **anxiety** (ang-ZY-e-tee) is a mental disorder characterized by extreme, unpleasant, and unwanted feelings of apprehension or fear, sometimes accompanied by physical symptoms.

How Is Hypochondria Diagnosed and Treated?

Hypochondria leads to physical complaints that are not found to be caused by a medical disease or condition during a physician's exam. At the time of the exam, people with hypochondria may say that they understand that nothing is physically wrong. Later, however, their symptoms may return. Then they may visit a different physician, seeking one who will treat them for the illness they believe that they have. People with hypochondria often become passionate about their health. They may worry excessively about exercising and watching their diet. Treatment involves convincing the person that nothing is physically wrong or treating the related disorder, such as depression or anxiety.

Munchausen Syndrome

Munchausen (MOON-chou-zenz) syndrome is another mental disorder that is similar to hypochondria. It involves pretending to be sick in order to get attention.

One form, called Munchausen syndrome by proxy, involves a parent who makes false claims of illness in a child. In its extreme form, the parent might harm the child to cause a physical condition that requires medical care.

Both Munchausen syndrome and hypochondria result in physical complaints that are not caused by a true medical condition. In hypochondria, however, the symptoms are not intentionally faked.

Resource

Cantor, Carla, and Brian A. Fallon. *Phantom Illness: Shattering the Myths of Hypochondria*. Boston: Houghton Mifflin, 1996. An adult book that offers hope to those suffering from hypochondria.

▶ *See also*
Anxiety Disorders
Depressive Disorders
Mental Disorders

Hypoglycemia

Hypoglycemia (hy-po-gly-SEE-mee-a) is a condition that occurs when the amount of sugar in the blood gets too low.

KEYWORDS
for searching the Internet and other reference sources

Carbohydrate metabolism

Glycogen

Insulinoma

Melinda's Story

Melinda was at the mall with friends, when she started to feel weak and uncoordinated. She developed a pounding headache, began to shake and sweat, and could not see very well. Because Melinda had diabetes, her doctor had warned her about these symptoms, and she knew they meant that her blood sugar had gotten too low. She carried candy in her backpack at all times for just such an occasion. Melinda told her friends that she should not have skipped lunch because a sensible diet and regular meals help prevent hypoglycemia in people being treated for diabetes. Melinda told them that hypoglycemia can cause coma* if not treated. After eating her candy bar, Melinda felt better within minutes.

*__coma__ (KO-ma) is an unconscious state, like a very deep sleep. A person in a coma cannot be woken up, and cannot move, see, speak, or hear.

*__anorexia nervosa__ (an-o-REK-se-a ner-VO-sa) is an emotional disorder characterized by dread of gaining weight, leading to self-starvation and dangerous loss of weight and malnutrition.

*__tumor__ (TOO-mor) usually refers to an abnormal growth of body tissue that has no known cause or physiologic purpose.

What Is Hypoglycemia?

Hypoglycemia means low ("hypo") blood sugar ("glycemia"). Hypoglycemia is not a disease; it a symptom of a problem the body has with regulating blood sugar. Its opposite, hyperglycemia (hy-per-gly-SEE-mee-a), means too much sugar in the blood, which is one of the features of diabetes.

Many people being treated for diabetes experience hypoglycemia. Diabetes is a disorder characterized by high levels of sugar in the blood due to the body's inability to make enough of the hormone insulin or to respond to insulin normally. People being treated with insulin for diabetes sometimes take too much insulin or may not eat enough, as happened to Melinda at the mall. In fact, 90 percent of people with insulin-dependent diabetes have occasional periods of hypoglycemia.

Severe hypoglycemia sometimes is called "insulin shock," because symptoms occur if people take too much insulin or if their body makes too much insulin. It is rare for people without diabetes to have hypoglycemia. The two main categories of hypoglycemia are reactive hypoglycemia and fasting hypoglycemia.

Dried fruit for snacks: apple, apricot, prune, pear. *Adrienne Hart-Davis/Science Photo Library, Photo Researchers, Inc.*

Reactive hypoglycemia Reactive hypoglycemia occurs after eating, especially after a meal containing lots of sugary or starchy foods. The sugar from the meal causes the body to make a great deal of insulin rapidly in order to keep blood sugar from rising too high. But the body makes so much insulin that the blood sugar level drops too low instead.

Fasting hypoglycemia Fasting hypoglycemia occurs several hours after the person's last meal. It can happen to people with diabetes or as a result of several other conditions, including anorexia nervosa*, starvation, a tumor* of the pancreas (the gland that secretes insulin), cancer, and certain hormonal and metabolic diseases.

How Is Hypoglycemia Diagnosed?

To find out if a person has hypoglycemia, doctors ask about symptoms and whether they go away when the person eats sugar. The doctor also will examine the patient and take a medical history to look for the specific features of disorders known to be associated with hypoglycemia. Blood tests performed when the person is having symptoms of hypoglycemia can confirm low levels of sugar in the blood, if present, and can measure the levels of insulin and other hormones and substances involved in the control of blood sugar.

▶ *See also*
Cancer
Diabetes
Eating Disorders
Metabolic Diseases
Pancreatic Cancer

Hypothermia *See* Cold-Related Injuries

Hypothyroidism *See* Thyroid Disease

I–J

Immunodeficiency

Immunodeficiency is a condition in which the body's immune system is not able to fight off infections or tumors as well as a normal immune system would. As a result, the person tends to get sick frequently, with unusually severe and repeated infections and sometimes cancers or other chronic (long-lasting) diseases.

KEYWORDS
for searching the Internet and other reference sources

Antibodies

Antigens

Autoimmunity

Immunology

The immune system, which protects the body from disease, works through a complicated web of cells and chemicals. It has many intertwined parts. A defect in any one of these parts can damage the body's ability to fight off disease. Such a defect is called an immunodeficiency disease.

Immunodeficiency diseases fall into two broad categories: primary and secondary. Most cases of primary immunodeficiency occur in infants or children as a result of genetic abnormalities. Because many have a sex-linked* genetic cause, most affected newborns are male. Secondary immunodeficiency is far more common because many different medical conditions can cause it.

* **sex-linked** genetic traits involve the chromosomes that determine whether a person is male or female. They usually affect boys, who have only one X chromosome.

What Are Primary Immunodeficiency Diseases?

Many immunodeficiency diseases already are present when a person is born, although sometimes they show up later. The reason for the problem may not be known, but often the cause is a defect in one of the genes*. Depending on which gene is affected, specific chemicals or cells in the immune system may be missing, may be in short supply, or may not work properly. From birth onward, a person with an immunodeficiency is likely to get frequent infections. Skin, bone, and nerve problems sometimes occur as well, and the person later may develop autoimmune diseases*, such as rheumatoid arthritis, or cancers of the immune system, such as lymphoma (lim-FO-ma) or leukemia (loo-KEY-mee-a).

The disorder can range from mild to so severe that the person dies of an infection in childhood. Whether mild or severe, this kind of illness is called a primary immunodeficiency disease, meaning that it is not caused by another condition.

* **genes** are chemicals in the body that help determine a person's characteristics, such as hair or eye color. They are inherited from a person's parents and are contained in the chromosomes found in the cells of the body.

* **autoimmune disease** is a disease where the immune system attacks and destroys normal cells in the body.

Severe combined immunodeficiency disease (SCID) The most complete form of this condition is a rare illness called severe combined immunodeficiency disease, or SCID. A person who has SCID is born with an immune system that does not work at all. The most famous case was that of a Texas boy named David, who lived in a germ-free plastic bubble to protect him from infection. Known as "the bubble boy," David died in 1985 at age 12.

IgA deficiency At the opposite end of the continuum is a condition like IgA deficiency, which is the absence of just one protein, called an immunoglobulin. This condition is common, occurring in as many as 1 out of every 400 Americans. Although people with IgA deficiency tend to have allergies and to get colds or bronchitis, many have no symptoms at all.

What Are Secondary Immunodeficiency Diseases?

Sometimes people are born with healthy immune systems that later become damaged. The damage may be the result of malnutrition, burns, excessive exposure to x-rays, or certain immune-suppressing medications such as corticosteroids (cor-ti-ko-STER-oids).

Some diseases can cause immune system damage. These include diabetes, kidney failure, sickle-cell anemia, leukemia, lymphoma, and cirrhosis* of the liver. Many people with diabetes, for instance, get infections of the skin and urinary tract.

* **cirrhosis** (si-RO-sis) of the liver is scarring often caused by alcoholism or chronic active hepatitis (a long-lasting liver infection).

This kind of immune system disorder is called secondary immunodeficiency because it is secondary to (caused by) other medical problems. If the underlying problem is treated, often the immune system will recover partially or completely.

How Is AIDS Different?

The most common and best known immunodeficiency disease is AIDS (acquired immunodeficiency syndrome). Untreated, AIDS can affect the immune system as severely as SCID. AIDS is a secondary immunodeficiency disease, because most people who get AIDS were born with normal immune systems that later were damaged.

AIDS is said to be "acquired," or contracted, rather than genetic or inborn. With AIDS, the cause of the damage to the immune system is a virus called HIV (the human immunodeficiency virus). Unlike the causes of other immunodeficiency diseases, the virus can spread from person to person through contact with blood or through sexual activity. As a result, AIDS has quickly become common around the world, killing millions of people since the disease was first reported in 1981.

How Does the Immune System Work?

To understand immunodeficiency diseases, it helps to know a little about how the immune system works.

Lymphatic system Elements of the immune system circulate through the body via the lymphatic system. In this system, a clear fluid called lymph helps carry white blood cells, especially lymphocytes (LIMF-o-sites) around the body. The word "lymph" comes from a Greek word meaning a clear stream. The organs and tissues of the lymphatic system include the thymus (a gland in the chest), the spleen (an organ in the abdomen), the tonsils (tissue in the throat), and bone marrow (tissue inside the bones).

Humoral immunity and B cell lymphocytes B cell lymphocytes are white blood cells named for bone marrow, because that is where they grow to maturity. B cells produce antibodies, proteins that circulate in the lymph system and bloodstream. The antibodies attach to antigens, distinctive proteins on germs or other foreign* cells. The antibodies mark the germs or foreign cells so that other immune system cells can destroy them. The B cells produce antibodies to a germ only after they have learned to recognize the germ, in other words, after a person has been infected at least once with the germ. The immune response that involves B cells and antibodies is called humoral (HEW-mor-al) immunity. It is the reason that healthy people get measles only once. After that, they are immune to the disease.

*__foreign__ means coming from outside a person's body.

Cell-mediated immunity and T cell lymphocytes T cell lymphocytes grow to maturity in the thymus gland. They have several different roles. Helper T cells (also called CD4 cells) signal B cells to start making antibodies. They also can activate macrophages. Macrophages are immune system cells that engulf foreign cells and process them so they can be destroyed by other cells, such as killer T cells and natural killer cells (other kinds of immune system cells). The immune response that involves T cells is called cell-mediated immunity. Many other kinds of cells and internal chemicals are involved in this branch of the immune system.

How Serious Are Immunodeficiency Diseases?

Primary immunodeficiency Primary immunodeficiency diseases are grouped according to which part of the immune system is defective. B cell, or antibody, deficiencies are the most common, and include IgA deficiency, mentioned earlier. These tend to be the mildest and most treatable diseases, with people living normal life spans in many cases.

With T cell deficiencies, disease severity and chance of survival vary widely. One of the better known disorders in this group is DiGeorge syndrome, in which infants are born without a thymus, and with facial and heart abnormalities.

Disorders that affect both B and T cells are particularly dangerous. These include SCID, mentioned earlier, and Wiskott-Aldrich syndrome, a sex-linked genetic defect seen in boys.

Opportunistic infections People with primary and secondary immunodeficiency tend to have frequent infections, particularly infections caused by organisms that seldom cause illness in healthy people. Such infections are called opportunistic infections, because they take advantage of a person's weakened immune system. Opportunistic infections include thrush (an infection of the mouth with *Candida albicans*, often

A Gene Therapy Pioneer

On September 14, 1990, a four-year-old girl from Ohio sat playing quietly in her hospital bed while a solution containing white blood cells equipped with new genes dripped slowly through a needle into her vein. The girl, Ashanthi DeSilva, had been born with a serious immunodeficiency disease known as adenosine deaminase deficiency (or ADA deficiency). Because of a defective gene, she lacked an enzyme her immune system needed to work. Her treatment at the U.S. National Institutes of Health marked the first authorized test of gene therapy on a person in the United States.

In the nine years that followed, some 3,000 people received experimental gene therapy for various diseases, including several more children with ADA deficiency. As a result of this therapy, Ashanthi, who also received an enzyme treatment called PEG-ADA, was able to go to school like other children instead of staying isolated from others to prevent infection. She was reported to have grown into a thriving preteen.

Doctors credited both the gene therapy and the enzyme treatment with having helped her, but they said neither could be considered a cure. Her father said the enzyme treatment, which started first, saved her life, but the gene therapy "gave her life," meaning she had the vigor to enjoy living like any other child her age.

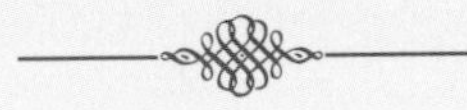

seen in children) and viral infections, such as cytomegalovirus, herpes simplex, and Epstein-Barr virus.

How Is Immunodeficiency Diagnosed and Treated?

Symptoms In addition to having opportunistic infections, people with immunodeficiency often seem unhealthy, with general weakness. They may be malnourished, and they may have skin rashes, hair loss, persistent diarrhea, or coughing.

Diagnosis Doctors may be able to diagnose immunodeficiency from symptoms and a medical history, but usually laboratory tests are needed to confirm the diagnosis. Pinpointing the nature of the deficiency can require sophisticated tests that only a few advanced laboratories can perform.

Treatment Antibody deficiency can be treated with monthly doses of the immunoglobulins (immune system proteins) that are lacking. Severe combined immunodeficiency disease often can be treated by giving the person a transplant of healthy bone marrow, which then can grow and help produce healthy immune system cells. Such transplants, however, can be risky. For T cell deficiencies like DiGeorge syndrome, transplants of thymus tissue sometimes work. For AIDS, combinations of drugs are given to fight the underlying virus.

In general, people with immunodeficiency need to be protected from infection. Antibiotics sometimes are given continuously to prevent bacterial infection. If infection does occur, it needs to be treated promptly, with medication, if possible. For many viral infections, however, no treatment currently exists.

Resources

U.S. National Institute of Allergy and Infectious Diseases (NIAID), Office of Communications, Building 31, Room 7A50, 31 Center Drive, MSC 2520, Bethesda, MD 20892-2520. NIAID publishes brochures and posts fact sheets at its website, including *Understanding the Immune System*, *Understanding Autoimmune Diseases*, and *Primary Immunodeficiency Disease*.
http://www.niaid.nih.gov/publications/

American Autoimmune Related Diseases Association, 15475 Gratiot Avenue, Detroit, MI 48205.
Telephone 800-598-4668
http://www.aarda.org

The Immune Deficiency Foundation, 25 West Chesapeake Avenue, Townson, MD 21204. This organization provides information about primary immune deficiency diseases.
Telephone 800-296-4433
http://www.primaryimmune.org

The National Jewish Center for Immunology and Respiratory Medicine, 1400 Jackson Street, Denver, CO 80206. This organization provides information on immune system diseases and research.
Telephone 303-388-4466
http://www.njc.org

See also
AIDS and HIV
Allergies
Arthritis
Cirrhosis of the Liver
Cytomegalovirus
Diabetes
Genetic Diseases
Infections
Inflammatory Bowel Disease
Leukemia
Lupus
Lymphoma
Multiple Sclerosis
Pneumonia
Psoriasis
Thrush
Vitiligo

Impetigo *See* Skin Conditions

Incontinence

Incontinence is a person's inability to control when he or she passes urine or feces.

KEYWORDS
for searching the Internet and other reference sources

Defecation

Urination

What Is Incontinence?

Older men and women, as well as some young children, find they cannot wait when they have to go to the bathroom. Usually, incontinence (in-KON-ti-nens) involves urinating at the wrong time, or it can mean having a bowel movement before reaching a bathroom. Although incontinence

Anatomy of the kidneys and urinary tract.

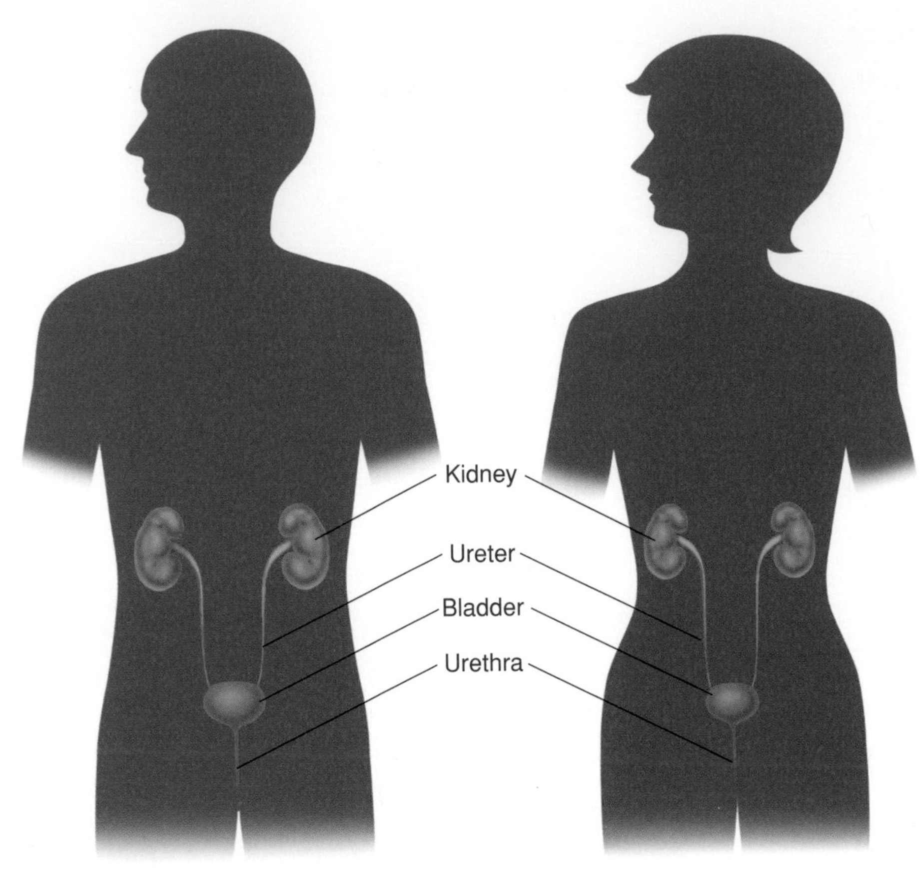

occurs mostly in older men and women and younger children, it can occur in people of all ages.

Sometimes it is simply a small amount of urine that is released when a person strains, such as with coughing or laughing too hard. For others, it occurs only when the bladder is too full.

What Causes Incontinence?

There are many causes for incontinence. Urinary tract infections, cancer, diabetes, stroke, Parkinson's disease, and Alzheimer's disease are some of the illnesses that can cause incontinence. Several problems in the brain or spinal cord can lead to urine and bowel incontinence. Surprisingly, severe constipation can cause bowel incontinence. Withholding stool can cause a hardened plug of stool to block the rectum. This plug irritates the lining of the rectum and causes watery stool to leak out from around the hardened plug.

Urinary incontinence affects more older women than men. One reason is that changes in a woman's hormone levels later in life can weaken muscles that control urination. Woman who have had children also may experience more incontinence because the muscles that are stretched during pregnancy and childbirth may become weakened.

Some over-the-counter cold medicines as well as some prescription drugs for conditions such as high-blood pressure can cause incontinence.

How Is Incontinence Treated?

Treatments for urinary incontinence involve avoiding liquids and caffeinated drinks such as coffee near bedtime and going to the bathroom at regular intervals. Also, a woman can do certain exercises to strengthen weakened muscles and help her control her urine. Some adults wear pads to absorb small amounts of urine that leak. Medications and surgery are helpful for some people.

The treatment for bowel incontinence depends on the cause. If the cause is chronic constipation, treatment involves adding fiber to the diet and correcting the constipation. Other causes may require surgery.

▶ *See also*
Bedwetting

Infection

Infection is a process in which bacteria, viruses, fungi or other organisms enter the body, attach to cells, and multiply. To do this, they must evade or overcome the body's natural defenses at each step. Infections have the potential to cause illness, but in many cases the infected person does not get sick.

KEYWORDS
for searching the Internet and other reference sources

Antibiotics

Immunization

Infection

Inflammation

How Does Infection Occur?

Organisms that can cause illness are all around us: in air, water, soil, and food, as well as in the bodies of animals and other people. Infection occurs when some of them get past a series of natural defenses. Those defenses include:

- **Skin:** The skin physically blocks germs, but may let them in if it is cut or scraped.
- **Coughing deeply:** This expels germs from the lungs and breathing passages but may be less effective for weak, sick, or injured people.
- **Bacteria:** Called "resident flora," harmless bacteria normally are present in some parts of the body. They compete with harmful germs and crowd them out. But they can be weakened or killed by medications, allowing harmful germs to thrive and cause illness.
- **Inflammatory response:** This is produced by the body's immune system. Certain kinds of white blood cells—including macrophages and neutrophils—surround and destroy or otherwise attack any kind of germs, often causing fever, redness, and swelling.
- **Antibodies:** These are proteins produced by the immune system. Some are targeted to attack specific microbes. This response is also called humoral immunity. Usually these antibodies are produced after a person is infected by or exposed to the microbe.

The immune system's responses may fail if the germs are too numerous, or if they are too virulent. "Virulent," from the Latin for "poisonous," describes germs that are particularly good at countering the body's defenses. For instance, some microbes can prevent antibodies from forming against them. Another important factor is the functioning of the immune system. If it is damaged—weakened, for instance, by age or illness—infection is more likely. Babies tend to get more infections because their immune systems have not yet learned to recognize and attack some microbes.

Where Does Infection Occur?

Localized infections Localized infections remain in one part of the body. Examples include a cut on the hand that gets infected with bacteria, but does not cause problems anywhere else. Localized infections can be very serious if they are internal, such as in the appendix (appendicitis) or in the heart (endocarditis).

Systemic infections Most serious infections, however, occur when the microorganisms spread throughout the body, usually in the bloodstream. These are called systemic infections, and they include flu, malaria, AIDS, tuberculosis, plague, and most of the infectious diseases whose names are familiar.

How Do Infections Lead to Illness?

The major causes of infection are viruses, bacteria, fungi, and parasites, including protozoa (one-celled organisms), worms, and insects such as mites (which cause scabies) and lice.

Bacteria can release toxins, or poisons. Viruses can take over cells and prevent them from doing their normal work. Bacteria and fungi—and larger infective agents like worms or other parasites—can multiply so rapidly that they physically interfere with the functioning of the lungs, heart, or other organs. The immune response itself—which can bring fever, pain, swelling, and fatigue—often is the major cause of the sick feelings an infected person gets.

Do Infections Always Cause Illness?

No, often they do not. Of people infected with tuberculosis bacteria, for instance, only about one in ten will ever get sick. Some viruses and parasites, too, can remain in the body a lifetime without causing illness. In such cases, called latent infection, people usually get sick only if the immune system weakens.

How Do Infections Spread?

The organisms that cause infections may spread through water, soil, food, or air; through contact with an infected person's blood, skin, or mucus; through sexual contact; or through insect bites. Most germs spread by a couple of these routes; no one microbe spreads in all these ways. In addition, many disease-causing microbes can spread from a pregnant woman to her fetus. When this happens, we say the baby is born with a congenital infection.

What Are the Symptoms of Infection?

The symptoms vary greatly depending on the part of the body and type of organism involved. The first sign of bacterial infection is often inflammation: fever, pain, swelling, redness, and pus. By contrast, viral infections less commonly cause inflammation but may cause a variety of other symptoms, from a runny nose or sore throat to a rash or swollen lymph nodes*.

* **lymph nodes** are round masses of tissue that contain immune cells to filter out harmful microorganisms. During infections, lymph nodes may become enlarged.

What Is the Treatment for Infection?

The main treatment is usually medication: antibiotics for bacterial infections; antiviral drugs for some viruses (for most there is no treatment); antifungal medications for fungus infections; and antihelmintic drugs for worms. In some cases of localized infection, as when an abscess or collection of pus forms, surgery may be necessary to drain the infected area.

How Are Infections Prevented?

Disinfecting wounds When a wound occurs, infection may be prevented by washing and covering the wound, using antibacterial ointment or spray, and getting medical attention if the wound is serious.

Immunization Many systemic infectious diseases can be prevented by immunization. Among them are chickenpox, cholera, diphtheria, hepatitis A and hepatitis B, influenza, Lyme disease, measles, mumps, pertussis (whooping cough), pneumococcal pneumonia, polio, rabies, rubella (German measles), tetanus, typhoid fever, and yellow fever.

Hygiene, sanitation, and public health Many other systemic infections can be prevented by having a clean public water supply and a sanitary system for disposing of human wastes; by washing hands before handling food; by cooking meats thoroughly; by abstaining from sexual contact; and by controlling or avoiding ticks and mosquitos.

Resources

U.S. National Institute of Allergy and Infectious Diseases (NIAID), NIAID Office of Communications and Public Liaison, Building 31, Room 7A-50, 31 Center Drive MSC 2520, Bethesda, MD 20892-2520. NIAID publishes pamphlets about infectious diseases and posts fact sheets and newsletters at its website.
http://www.niaid.nih.gov/publications/

The World Health Organization posts fact sheets at its website, covering communicable/infectious diseases, tropical diseases, vaccine preventable diseases, and many other health topics.
http://www.who.org/home/map_ht.html

KidsHealth.org, the website created by the Nemours Foundation, has information on dozens of infections.
http://KidsHealth.org

► *See also*
Bacterial Infections
Fungal Infections
Immunodeficiency
Parasitic Diseases
Viral Infections
Worms

Infertility

Infertility (in-fer-TIL-i-tee) means that a couple has difficulty conceiving a child after approximately a year of trying. The man, woman, or both may have problems with their reproductive system that causes them to be infertile.

KEYWORDS
for searching the Internet and other reference sources

Artificial insemination

Assisted reproductive technology

Gynecology

In vitro fertilization

Reproductive medicine

What Is Infertility?

Infertility is defined as the failure to become pregnant after about a year of trying many times without using contraception*. Infertility problems increase as a person gets older, and they are becoming more widespread as many women are waiting to have babies until they are in their thirties and forties. Currently, fertility problems affect at least 6.1 million couples in the United States. For people who cannot imagine their lives without children and are not considering adoption, the condition may be heartbreaking.

Doctors can find no medical cause for up to 20 percent of infertility cases. In 15 to 20 percent of infertility cases, both the man and the woman have fertility problems. The rest of the time, infertility is caused by problems with either the male or the female reproductive system. Some doctors believe that smoking, drinking a lot of alcohol, poor eating habits, stress, excess weight, and generally poor health can make the physical problems causing infertility even worse.

Male factor infertility Roughly 35 to 40 percent of infertile couples are unable to conceive because of a problem with the male reproductive system. Infertility can result when a man does not produce enough sperm*, or when the sperm have too short a life span, they do not move properly, or they cannot penetrate the egg to fertilize it. These problems can be caused by many factors, including abnormalities of reproductive organs, a varicose vein* in the scrotum*, inflammation* in the male genitals, and sexually transmitted diseases, such as chlamydial (kla-MID-e-al) infections, gonorrhea (gon-o-REE-a), and syphilis (SIF-i-lis). Some men have trouble ejaculating (discharging sperm), which also can cause infertility. In rare cases, the immune system* of the man or woman may produce antibodies* that kill sperm.

Infertility in women Another 35 to 40 percent of couples are infertile because of a problem with the female reproductive tract. Problems can occur in any part of the system:

- **Ovaries:** The ovaries (O-va-reez) are a pair of organs where egg cells develop and mature. About 25 percent of female infertility is caused by the failure of a mature egg to leave the ovary (a process called ovulation).
- **Hormones:** Problems with hormone* production can prevent pregnancy.

* **contraception** (kon-tra-SEP-shun) is the deliberate prevention of conception or impregnation.

* **sperm** are the tiny, tadpole-like cells in the fluid males produce in their testicles (TES-ti-kulz) that can unite with a female's egg to result eventually in the birth of a child.

* **varicose vein** (VAR-i-kose VAYN) is an abnormally swollen or dilated vein.

* **scrotum** (SKRO-tum) is the pouch on a male body that contains the testes (TES-teez) and their accessory organs.

* **inflammation** (in-fla-MAY-shun) is the body's response to infection or irritation.

* **immune system** is the body system that fights disease.

* **antibodies** (AN-te-bod-eez) are proteins produced by the immune system to fight specific infections. In certain disorders, antibodies attack some of the body's own proteins and cells.

* **hormone** is a chemical that is produced by different glands in the body. A hormone is like the body's ambassador: it is created in one place but is sent through the body to have specific regulatory effects in different places.

- **Fallopian tubes**: A woman has two fallopian (fa-LO-pe-an) tubes (one associated with each ovary), which carry eggs from the ovaries to the uterus (YOO-ter-us). Infertility can occur when one or both of the fallopian tubes are blocked, scarred, or collapsed.
- **Pelvic inflammatory disease (PID)**: Infertility also is common in women with PID, which is an infection of the female reproductive organs (especially the fallopian tubes).
- **Uterus**: The uterus is the muscular organ in which a fertilized egg develops into a fetus (FEE-tus; developing baby). If the uterus contains scar tissue or a piece of tissue dividing it in half, the fertilized egg might not be able to implant and grow.
- **Endometriosis**: Women also can have infertility problems because of conditions such as endometriosis (en-do-me-tree-O-sis), which occurs when pieces of the lining of the uterus grow outside of the uterus.
- **Fibroids**: Fibroids (FY-broidz) are noncancerous tumors* that also can cause infertility.
- **Cervix**: The cervix (SER-viks) is the opening between the uterus and the vagina. Infertility can occur if the cervix does not produce enough mucus* to allow sperm to pass into the uterus.
- **Vaginal infections**: The vagina (va-JY-na) is the tubular canal that runs from the cervix to the outside of the body. Certain vaginal infections that spread to the uterus and fallopian tubes can cause infertility.

*__tumors__ (TOO-morz) usually refer to abnormal growths of body tissue that have no known cause or physiologic purpose. Tumors may or may not be cancerous.

*__mucus__ (MU-kus) is a kind of body slime. It is thick and slippery, and it lines the inside of many parts of the body.

How Is Infertility Diagnosed?

The first step in treating infertility is finding out the cause. Both the man and the woman require a complete physical examination to determine if a physical disorder is causing infertility.

The first test for male infertility is an analysis of the sperm for shape, movement, and number. The first test for a woman is to find out if she is ovulating. Home ovulation* kits are available for this purpose, as are body temperature charts (the body temperature fluctuates during the menstrual cycle*). Tests of a woman's blood and urine also help doctors to determine if a woman is having normal menstrual cycles. An x-ray of the uterus and fallopian tubes can reveal any blockage that might prevent the egg from being fertilized. In some cases, the doctor may look inside the body with a laparoscope*, which is a viewing tube that is inserted into the abdomen* through a small incision.

*__ovulation__ (ov-yoo-LAY-shun) is the release of a mature egg from the ovary.

*__menstrual cycle__ (MEN-stroo-al SY-kul) culminates in menstruation (men-stroo-AY-shun), the discharging through the vagina of blood, secretions, and tissue debris from the uterus that recurs at approximately monthly intervals in females of breeding age.

*__laparoscope__ (LAP-a-ro-skope) is a fiber-optic instrument inserted into an incision in the abdominal wall to perform a visual examination.

*__abdomen__ (AB-do-men), commonly called the belly, is the portion of the body between the thorax (THOR-aks) and the pelvis.

How Is Infertility Treated?

Difficulty conceiving a baby may not be a permanent condition, and many couples with fertility problems eventually have a child without medical intervention. However, some couples need medical help to become pregnant, and the treatment depends on the cause of infertility. If a hormone deficiency causes infertility, treatment may involve taking

Multiple Births

One of the major problems facing couples undergoing fertility treatment is that of multiple births. Fertility drugs may result in multiple births, because they can stimulate release of multiple eggs. For example, as many as 10 percent of women who become pregnant with the help of the drug Clomid (KLO-mid), or clomiphene citrate (KLO-mi-feen SY-trayt), have twins, and 1 in 400 women have triplets.

Assisted reproductive technologies such as in vitro fertilization usually place two to five eggs inside the woman's reproductive tract, because not all are expected to survive—but sometimes they all do. In the 1990s, several women who underwent fertility treatment had as many as eight babies at once.

The more embryos that develop at one time in the uterus, the more likely they are to be born prematurely, to be small, and to have serious health problems such as cerebral palsy (se-REE-bral PAWL-zee) and brain damage. Because of such health problems, and because of ethical and financial issues associated with multiple births, fertility treatment can be controversial.

hormones prescribed by a doctor. If there is damage or an abnormality in the female organs, they sometimes can be repaired surgically. For other couples, treatment can range from taking fertility drugs to using assisted reproductive technology (ART). Many treatments for infertility exist; only a few are described in the following.

Artificial insemination Artificial insemination (in-sem-i-NAY-shun) is the introduction of a man's sperm into the opening of a woman's uterus with a tube called a catheter (CATH-e-ter). Before insemination, antibodies and unhealthy sperm are removed from the semen (SEE-men), the fluid containing sperm. The sperm used in artificial insemination ideally comes from the woman's male partner. However, in cases where the man is infertile or carries a genetic disorder, sperm from a donor may be used.

Fertility drugs Fertility drugs can be used to treat problems with ovulation. A number of different medications have been developed that help to stimulate the maturation and release of ova (eggs).

In vitro fertilization (IVF) "In vitro" literally means "in glass" (as in a test tube) and therefore refers to a procedure performed outside the body. In vitro fertilization (IVF) occurs when eggs are removed from the woman and mixed with sperm in the laboratory. Fertilized eggs, or embryos, then are placed in the woman's uterus. This procedure bypasses the fallopian tubes.

Before IVF, women usually take fertility drugs in order to produce multiple eggs. Eggs are taken from a woman's ovaries using a needle inserted through the vagina. The male partner provides a sperm sample, which is mixed with the eggs in a dish in the laboratory. After several days, if the eggs have been fertilized and have developed into embryos, two to five embryos (usually) are placed into the uterus (not all are expected to develop into fetuses). About two weeks later, the woman takes a pregnancy test to see if the procedure was successful.

Coping with Infertility: Jim and Sarah's Story

Jim and Sarah Albertson are among the 10 to 20 percent of the reproductive-aged population in the United States who have difficulty having a baby. Even though pregnancy is possible in more than half of couples pursuing fertility treatment, it does not seem possible for them.

Jim and Sarah began trying to have a baby on their honeymoon, when they were both 34. Five years later, they still have no children. Sarah has had surgery to remove fibroids, and she has taken hormones and fertility pills. Jim has done everything possible to increase his sperm count. They have tried artificial insemination. It seems their whole lives revolve around trying to get pregnant, but nothing is working.

As Jim and Sarah watch one friend after another have a baby, their own home begins to feel empty. They try not to blame each other, but it is hard not to. Even though their health plan does not cover in vitro fertilization, they decided to spend their own money to try to get pregnant that way. Three tries and $30,000 later, they still have no baby. With the help of mari-

A couple with a fertility problem discuss their treatment options with a doctor. *© 1989 Custom Medical Stock Photo.*

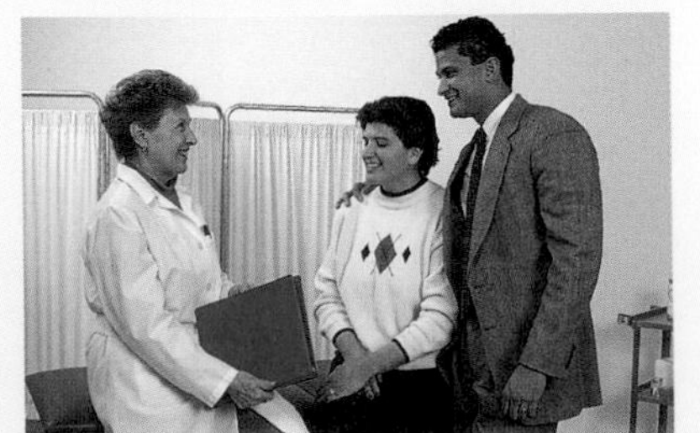

tal counseling and the support of other couples with the same problem, Jim and Sarah are learning to accept that they may not have biological children.

Resources

Books

Cooper, Susan, and Ellen Sarasohn Glazer. *Choosing Assisted Reproduction: Social, Emotional, and Ethical Considerations.* Indianapolis, IN: Perspectives Press, 1999.

Turiel, Judith Steinberg.*Beyond Second Opinions: Making Choices about Fertility Treatment.* Berkeley, CA: University of California Press, 1998.

Organizations

American Society for Reproductive Medicine, 1209 Montgomery Highway, Birmingham, AL 35216-2809.
Telephone 205-978-5000
http://www.asrm.org

InterNational Council on Infertility Information Dissemination, Inc. (INCIID), P.O. Box 6836, Arlington, VA 22206.
Telephone 703-379-9178
http://www.inciid.org

RESOLVE, The National Infertility Association, 1310 Broadway, Somerville, MA 02144.
Telephone 617-623-0744
http://www.resolve.org

▶

See also

Chlamydial Infections

Endometriosis

Gonorrhea

Menstrual Disorders

Pelvic Inflammatory Disease (PID)

Pregnancy, Complications of

Prematurity

Sexually Transmitted Diseases

Syphilis

Varicose Veins

Inflammatory Bowel Disease

Inflammatory bowel disease (IBD) involves inflammation of the intestines and is a chronic (long-lasting) illness. The two major types of IBD are ulcerative colitis and Crohn's disease. Ulcerative colitis affects the lining of the large intestine (colon) and/or the rectum. Crohn's disease affects deeper layers of tissue and can occur in any part of the digestive system, although it occurs most commonly in the lower part of the small intestine (ileum).

KEYWORDS
for searching the Internet and other reference sources

Colitis

Digestive system

Enteritis

Gastroenterology

Gastrointestinal system

Ileitis

Inflammation

Proctitis

What Is Inflammatory Bowel Disease?

Inflammatory Bowel Disease (IBD) encompasses several diseases caused by inflammation* of the intestinal tract. The different types of IBD have many symptoms in common, including abdominal pain, frequent diarrhea

* **inflammation** (in-fla-MAY-shun) is the body's reaction to irritation, infection, or injury that often involves swelling, pain, redness, and warmth.

When inflammation occurs in the large intestine (colon) or in the lower part of the small intestine (ileum), it causes pain and swelling and may lead to diarrhea, weight loss, fatigue, and fever. ▶

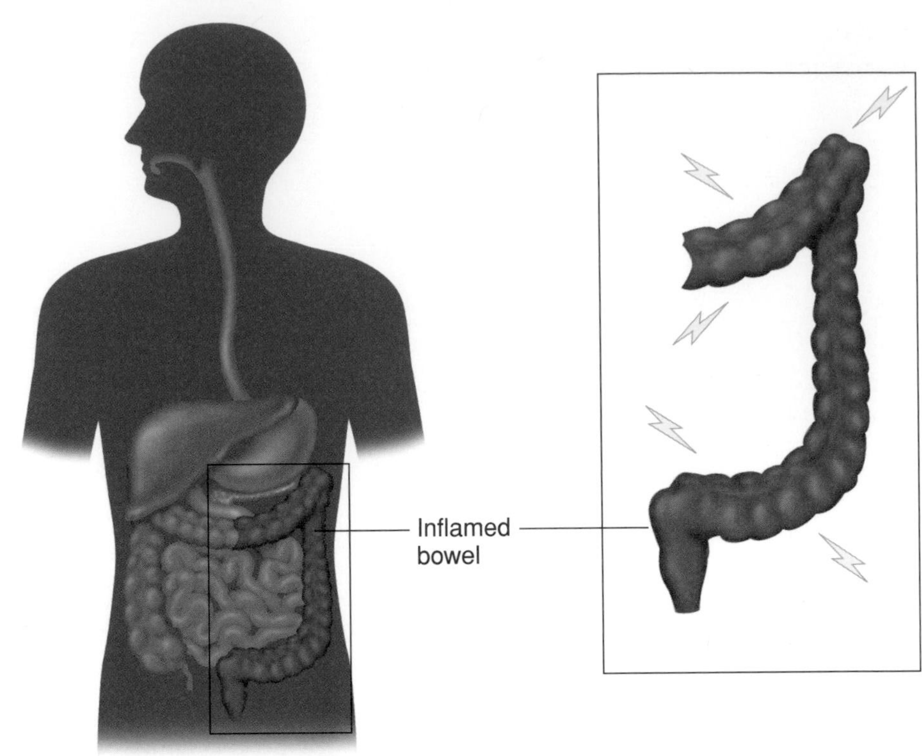

(sometimes with blood and mucus), constipation, weight loss, fatigue, and fever.

Why some people get IBD is not clear. What is known is that IBD is not passed from person to person. However, up to 25 percent of people with IBD have a relative with the disease, suggesting that genetic factors play a role in its development. Some researchers believe that IBD occurs because a virus or bacterium triggers an inappropriate response from the immune system in people who have a genetic tendency for the disease. This response causes the digestive tract to become inflamed.

What Are the Different Types of IBD?

The two major types of inflammatory bowel disease are ulcerative colitis and Crohn's disease.

Ulcerative Colitis Ulcerative colitis is sometimes referred to as colitis or proctitis. Ulcerative colitis is a disease that occurs when the lining of the large intestine and/or rectum become inflamed. Usually tiny open sores, or ulcers, develop on the intestine or rectum wall. These sores often result in bloody diarrhea. Substantial blood loss can occur. People with ulcerative colitis often have symptoms that affect other areas of the body. These may include inflammation of the joints (arthritis) or the eye, skin rashes and mouth ulcers, liver disease, osteoporosis*, and anemia* caused by blood loss.

Most people who develop ulcerative colitis are between the ages of 15 and 40. The severity of the disease varies from person to person.

* **osteoporosis** (os-te-o-por-O-sis) is the loss of material from the bone. This makes the bones weak and brittle.

* **anemia** (an-E-me-ah) is the condition of having too few red blood cells. People with anemia often feel tired and weak.

Some people seldom have an attack of symptoms. Others have almost continuous attacks that interfere with their daily activities.

Experts agree that having ulcerative colitis increases the risk of getting colon cancer. The longer a person has ulcerative colitis and the larger the part of the digestive system involved, the greater the risk of developing colon cancer.

Crohn's Disease Crohn's disease is sometimes referred to as ileitis or enteritis. Crohn's disease is an inflammation that extends deep into the tissues of the digestive system. Although this inflammation can be found anywhere in the digestive tract, most often it is found in the lower end of the small intestine where the small intestine connects to the large intestine. Ulcers often appear in patches separated by stretches of normal tissue.

There are many conflicting theories about what causes Crohn's disease. Men and women seem to get Crohn's disease in equal numbers, and about 20 percent of people with the disease have a relative who also has it. Many people with Crohn's disease have abnormalities in their immune system, but it is not known if these abnormalities are the cause of the disease or the result of it.

Crohn's disease is a chronic condition that varies from person to person in severity. In severe cases, the disease can cause major loss of blood, and it can interfere with food intake and absorption of nutrients* from the intestine. Children with Crohn's disease may develop slowly and not reach their full growth potential because their bodies do not get enough nourishment for normal growth. Adults also may have problems with getting adequate nutrition because of the disease.

* **nutrients** are the components of food (protein, carbohydrate, fat, vitamins, and minerals) needed for growth and maintenance of the body.

The most common complication of Crohn's disease is a blockage of the intestine. Crohn's disease causes the intestinal walls to swell and thicken with scar tissue that may eventually prevent the movement of materials through the intestine. In some people, the ulcers expand into the tissues that surround the digestive system, creating a high risk of additional infection. As with ulcerative colitis, Crohn's disease can affect other parts of the body with symptoms such as arthritis, skin rashes, mouth sores, eye problems, kidney stones, anemia, or liver diseases.

How Is IBD Diagnosed?

A medical history, physical examination, and diagnostic tests are problems required to diagnose IBD. Blood samples may be taken to look for evidence of anemia and infection. Examination of stool samples for the presence of blood also may help the doctor make a diagnosis.

Often the colon is examined through a procedure called a colonoscopy. An endoscope (a lighted flexible tube and camera attached to a television monitor) is inserted through the anus. This allows the doctor to see the inside lining of colon and rectum. Sometimes during the colonoscopy a tissue sample (called a biopsy) is taken from the intestine lining for further examination under a microscope.

Another diagnostic procedure a physician can use is a barium study. A person drinks a mixture of barium that is flavored with another liquid, and then the person is x-rayed. Because barium shows up on x-rays, the doctor can detect abnormalities as the mixture flows through the person's intestines. CT scans* may be useful in evaluating the progress of the disease once it has been diagnosed.

* **CT scans** or CAT scans are the shortened names for computerized axial tomography (to-MOG-ra-fee), which uses x-rays and computers to view structures inside the body.

How Is IBD Treated?

Medication and diet are the two primary approaches to controlling IBD. They do not cure the disease, but are effective in reducing symptoms in the majority of people. In severe cases of IBD, surgery may be necessary. Anti-inflammatory drugs often are used to help control the inflammation caused by the disease. In some cases, immunosuppressant drugs may be helpful in controlling symptoms that do not respond to anti-inflammatory drugs. Antibiotics often are used to treat Crohn's disease. In addition, several experimental drug therapies are under investigation.

Many of the drugs used to treat IBD are powerful and may have undesirable side effects. The physician must balance the undesirable side effects against the positive benefits of the drugs, sometimes trying several different drug combinations before a successful balance is reached.

Diet In addition to drug therapy, a special diet may be prescribed by the physician. Since IBD interferes with the absorption of nutrients from the intestines, people with the disease often must increase the amount of calories, vitamins, and minerals they consume. Some individuals find that they must avoid specific foods that aggravate their symptoms. Other people find a bland, low-fiber diet offers some relief. Because there is no cure for IBD, people with any form of the disease should receive regular medical examinations that include a review of their treatment and diet.

Surgery In severe cases of IBD, when damage has occurred to parts of the intestinal tract, a person may need surgery to remove damaged sections of the intestines. About 20 percent of people with ulcerative colitis require surgery at some point in their lives. If necessary, ulcerative colitis may be treated by surgery that removes the entire colon and rectum. After this procedure, normal bowel movements are not possible, so the small intestine is given a surgically created opening (ostomy) through the lower abdomen. This opening is covered with a bag that collects waste and must be emptied several times a day.

About 70 percent of people with Crohn's disease eventually need to have damaged areas of the colon removed. Removing the damaged parts does not cure Crohn's disease, because the inflammation may return in other places in the colon. Many people with Crohn's disease need additional surgery because the symptoms reappear.

Endoscopy

The word endoscopy means "peering within." Endoscopes allow a physician to see inside the human body.

An endoscope is a long, flexible, viewing instrument that contains lenses and a light source. It is called a fiberoptic instrument because it contains thousands of thin glass fibers that carry light into body cavities and reflect an image back to the viewer by way of a video screen. This system makes it possible for the physician to examine the inside of the body in the area of interest.

Endoscopes also contain an opening through which the doctor can maneuver tiny surgical tools, such as scissors, forceps, and suction devices. This enables the doctor to do surgery or to take tissue samples without cutting through the wall of the abdomen or chest.

In 1957, at the University of Michigan, Dr. Basil Hirschowitz figured out how to light the interior of the body for examination using a fiberoptic tube. This was the first fiberoptic endoscope. Today, endoscopes are used routinely in examinations and surgical procedures.

Living with IBD

There is no cure for inflammatory bowel disease, but people with IBD often go for substantial periods of time when they feel well and have few symptoms. During these times they are able to hold jobs, raise families, and participate in normal daily activities. Throughout the United States, there are support groups for people with IBD that help them learn to cope with their illness and maintain a normal, happy life.

Resources

U.S. National Digestive Diseases Information Clearinghouse, 2 Information Way, Bethesda, MD 20892-3570. The National Digestive Diseases Information Clearinghouse is a service of the National Institute of Diabetes and Digestive and Kidney Diseases (NIDDK). It publishes brochures and posts fact sheets about Crohn's disease and ulcerative colitis at its website.
http://www.niddk.nih.gov/health/digest/pubs/colitis/colitis.htm
http://www.niddk.nih.gov/health/digest/pubs/crohns/crohns.htm

Crohn's and Colitis Foundation of America, 386 Park Avenue South, 17th floor, New York, NY 10016-8804.
Telephone 800-932-2433
http://www.ccfa.org

Pediatric Crohn's and Colitis Association, P.O. Box 188, Newton, MA 02468.
Telephone 617-489-5854
http://pcca.hypermart.net

United Ostomy Association, 19772 MacArthur Boulevard, Irvine, CA 92612-2405.
Telephone 800-826-0826
http://www.uoa.org

See also
Anemia
Colitis
Colorectal Cancer
Constipation
Diarrhea
Diverticulitis/Diverticulosis
Irritable Bowel Syndrome

Influenza

Influenza is a highly contagious viral infection that causes fever, headache, body aches, extreme fatigue, sore throat, and other symptoms.

KEYWORDS
for searching the Internet and other reference sources

Flu

Immune system

Vaccination

Viral infection

Joseph's Story

Joseph is not feeling well, but he goes to school anyway. He is coughing, sneezing, and starting to feel very tired. During lunch, several of Joseph's friends ask how he is doing.

As Joseph starts to answer, he suddenly sneezes. It happens so quickly that Joseph cannot get his hand up to cover his nose. None of his friends sees or feels the microscopic droplets that come out of Joseph's nose at more than 100 miles per hour. They are unaware of the virus in the droplets as they inhale the air.

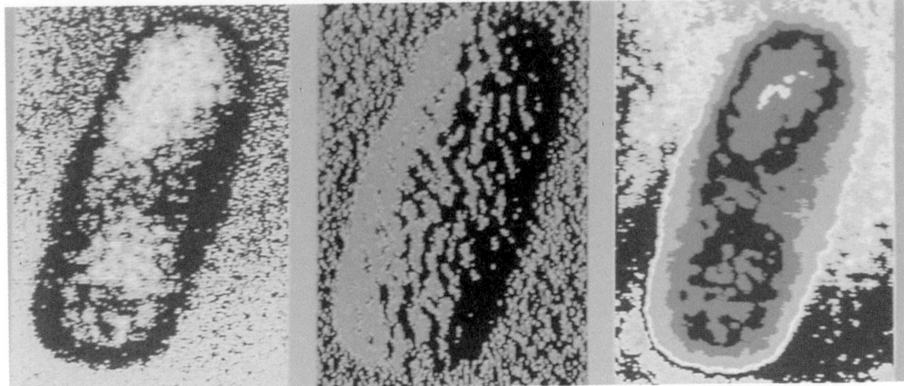

Three digitized views of Type A influenza virus. © *1993 J. L. Carson, Custom Medical Stock Photo*

The next morning, Joseph is not in school. The teacher says that he has influenza, commonly called the flu.

For a couple of days, all of Joseph's friends feel fine. But the virus they inhaled is spreading through their bodies, latching onto the surface of healthy cells and infecting them. Then one morning, each of Joseph's friends wakes up with a fever and fits of coughing. Within a few hours, they feel as if they have no energy. They, too, have the flu.

More Than a Bad Cold

Influenza is a viral infection of the respiratory tract, which includes the nose, mouth, throat, and lungs. Although some people call any bad cold "the flu," influenza is different from the common cold (see sidebar).

The flu virus spreads through the air and is easy to catch. Although most healthy people who catch the flu recover fully, sometimes the flu can be deadly, especially if patients develop pneumonia or have an underlying medical problem. A flu vaccination can prevent infection most of the time. As many as 20,000 Americans, however, die each year from the flu or its complications.

Most people catch the flu during the winter and early spring, when they spend more time indoors in closer contact with other people. It affects all ages but is a special problem for the elderly and those with certain chronic medical problems.

Types of Flu

There are three types of flu virus, labeled Type A, Type B, and Type C. Type A influenza virus is the most threatening to humans, because every few years it can mutate, or change into new strains that can infect people. Humans develop the ability to fight off the viruses they encounter, especially after they have developed an infectious disease such as the flu. But when a new strain of Type A develops, the body's immune system is less prepared than usual to fight the virus. This can cause epidemics, like the one in 1918–1919 that killed 500,000 Americans and 20 million people worldwide (see sidebar).

Type B also can cause serious cases of the flu, but it does not change its structure as drastically as Type A does. Type C causes milder cases of the flu and is much less common than Types A and B.

Planetary Influence?

The word "influenza" derives from the word "influence," because people who lived during the 16th century believed that flu epidemics struck only when people were under the influence of certain constellations of planets and stars.

Spreading the Infection

The virus that causes the flu is contained in the respiratory excretions (the phlegm and mucus) of an infected person and is spread when people sneeze or cough. Even exhaled breath can contain microscopic droplets of the virus. Infection can happen in many ways: when someone like Joseph sneezes near others or when the air is recirculated by heating and cooling systems in classrooms, offices, and airplanes. Even touching an object such as a doorknob that an infected person has used—and later touching one's own mouth, nose, or eyes—can spread the virus.

When people inhale the virus, it enters the bloodstream and begins to attack healthy cells. The virus uses the cells' protein-making capacity to make more of the virus, which attacks surrounding cells. These attacks trigger the body's immune system, which sends white blood cells to fight the virus. By this point—a day or two after exposure to the virus—people are beginning to show the signs of influenza.

EPIDEMIC

More than 20 million people died in the worldwide influenza epidemic of 1918–1919. Influenza viruses mutate frequently. Samples of the 1918 strain are no longer available for study, so the reason for its virulence (deadliness) remains a mystery.

Volunteers in Cincinnati, Ohio, wear gauze masks during the great influenza epidemic. *Corbis-Bettman.*

The Flu Can Be Deadlier than War

More than 8 million soldiers and almost 7 million civilians died during World War I. But as the war was ending in 1918, another killer was rising: influenza. There have been other epidemics of influenza throughout history, but none compares with the one that circled the planet in 1918 and 1919. More than 20 million people died, including almost 500,000 Americans.

The flu began to spread in the spring of 1918, at first in military camps in the United States and France. Later, an epidemic in Spain received much publicity, which is why the event is sometimes called the Spanish flu. As soldiers from many countries came into contact with one another and civilians throughout Europe and the Far East, the flu epidemic spread worldwide. Such large-scale epidemics are called pandemics.

Many people took to wearing masks over their noses and mouths in the hope that they would not catch the flu. Sometimes individuals were not allowed into offices or on public transportation unless they wore masks. Some cities even hired people to spread disinfectant in the air to try to kill the virus.

The pandemic accelerated research into influenza and the search for a vaccine. By the 1930s, doctors were able to isolate the virus and grow it in fertilized chicken eggs. This eventually led to the development of vaccines, which are still created using eggs.

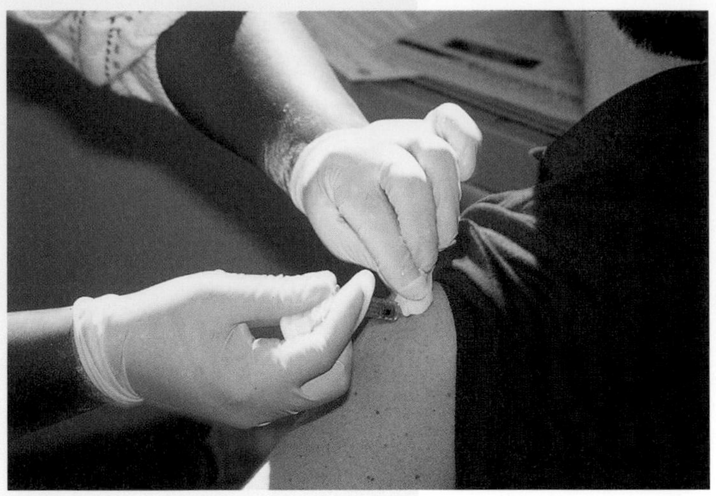

▲
Vaccination: A medic gives a flu shot at a community health fair in New Jersey.
© Jeff Greenberg/Visuals Unlimited

Signs and Symptoms

The day after Joseph felt the first symptoms of flu at school, he woke up and felt that he could not get out of bed. He had a high fever—about 102 to 104 degrees Fahrenheit—and felt chilled, and his head, muscles, and whole body ached. His chest felt congested, as if there were a few heavy bricks resting on it. His throat was sore, and he coughed and sneezed occasionally.

The flu virus overwhelms the body's ability to fight it. The fever and aches result from the body's struggle to control and destroy the virus. White blood cells produce a protein called interleukin (in-ter-LOO-kin) that leads to aches, fever, and fatigue until the virus is eliminated.

The fever often drops within 5 days. Other symptoms start to subside in a week, but the fatigue can last 2 or 3 weeks.

Influenza can develop into pneumonia or bronchitis. Pneumonia (noo-MO-nya) is an infection of the lungs that causes them to become inflamed and fill with fluid. This interferes with the ability of oxygen to reach the blood and can sometimes cause death. With bronchitis, the larger air passages in the lungs become inflamed.

Diagnosis and Treatment

Doctors diagnose the flu based on the symptoms. Many cold viruses can cause symptoms similar to those of the flu, but the symptoms usually are not as severe and do not last as long.

Is It a Cold or the Flu?

Doctors say that more than 200 different viruses can cause symptoms of the common cold. In fact, many people say that they have the flu when they really have only a common cold. How can people tell the difference? Here is a chart comparing the symptoms of a cold with those of influenza:

COLD SYMPTOMS VS. FLU SYMPTOMS

Symptoms	Cold	Influenza
High fever	Rare	Often
Headache	Sometimes	Often
Aches/pains	Slight	Often severe
Fatigue	Mild	Usually, may last weeks
Sneezing	Common	Sometimes
Running nose	Usually	Sometimes
Sore throat	Common	Sometimes
Chest discomfort	Moderate	Usually severe
Coughing	Yes	Yes

Treatment involves bed rest and drinking lots of liquids to prevent dehydration*. Over-the-counter medications can help the fever, aches, and cough, but aspirin should be avoided during the flu or other viral infections because of its relationship to Reye's syndrome.

**dehydration* (dee-hy-DRAY-shun) is loss of fluid from the body.

A Shot of Prevention

Some strains of the flu can be prevented with a flu vaccination in the fall. The vaccine contains inactive versions of the flu viruses that researchers suspect will be most likely to cause influenza during the coming winter and early spring. Because the virus is inactive, people cannot catch the flu from a flu vaccine. The inactive virus causes the human body to create antibodies. When a live virus enters the body, the antibodies are ready to prevent it from attaching to cells and causing an infection.

The vaccine does not ensure that people will not get the flu, but it is effective 70 to 90 percent of the time when the vaccine matches the strain of the flu going around. Flu shots are especially recommended for people in high-risk groups, such as the elderly and people with certain heart and lung diseases. Children can receive the vaccine but seldom do unless they have medical problems such as diabetes, HIV infection, heart conditions, or lung conditions such as asthma. Occasionally, people exposed to the flu may be given antiviral medications such as amantadine (a-MAN-ta-deen).

Other ways to lower the risk of catching the flu include avoiding contact with people who have it and frequently washing hands thoroughly to avoid transmission of the virus.

Resources

Organizations

American Lung Association, (800) LUNG-USA (800-586-4872). This is a leading support organization that promotes flu education campaigns. Its website contains a great deal of useful information.
http://www.lungusa.org

Centers for Disease Control and Prevention, 1600 Clifton Road, N.E., Atlanta, GA 30333, (800) 311-3435. An agency of the U.S. Department of Health and Human Services, the CDC is a good place to get information on influenza and many other diseases.
http://www.cdc.gov

KidsHealth.org, created by the Nemours Foundation, has information on influenza and dozens of other infections.
http://KidsHealth.org

▶ *See also*
Pneumonia
Reye's Syndrome

Ingrown Toenail

An ingrown toenail is a toenail that cuts into the skin of the toe.

KEYWORDS
for searching the Internet and other reference sources

Infection

Inflammation

Onychocryptosis

Paronychia

An ingrown toenail is a common condition in which the corners or sides of the toenail cut into the skin of the toe. This usually happens to the big toe, and can affect people of all ages. An ingrown toenail is a serious condition for people with impaired blood circulation or diabetes.

What Happens When People Have Ingrown Toenails?

Ingrown toenails tend to run in families, although they also may be caused by:

- wearing shoes that are too tight or that do not fit properly
- trimming toenails improperly or too closely
- repeated trauma to the toenail from everyday activities such as work and sports.

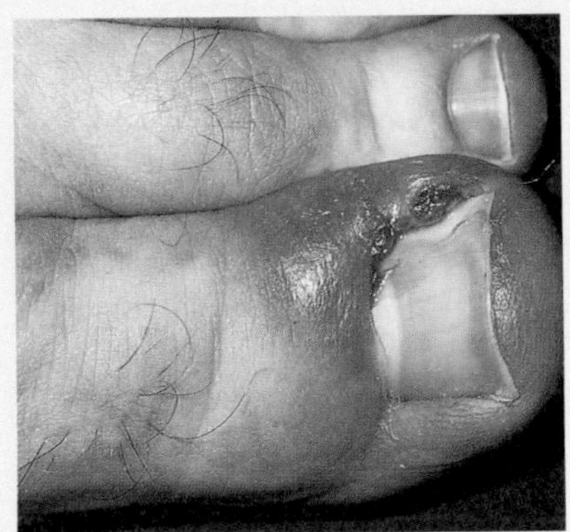

▲ Ingrown toenails that have become infected may be treated with antibiotics. People with diabetes or circulatory system problems should receive regular foot care from a medical doctor or podiatrist.
Dr. P. Marazzi, Science Photo Library/ Photo Researchers, Inc.

Pain and swelling are the first signs of an ingrown toenail. The area around the ingrown toenail also can become infected. A doctor will diagnose an ingrown toenail through a physical examination.

Treatment Treatment depends upon the type and amount of pain present. Ingrown toenails that are not infected may be treated by putting a cotton pad coated with a medicine called collodion (ko-LO-de-on) under the nail's edge. This relieves the pain and allows the nail to grow properly. Ingrown toenails that are infected may be treated with antibiotics or warm soaks. Sometimes, part of the toenail must be removed. An ingrown toenail is a serious condition for people with impaired blood circulation or diabetes. People with these conditions should have their feet cared for by medical doctors or by podiatrists, doctors who specialize in the care of the feet.

Prevention Ingrown toenails can be prevented by wearing shoes that fit properly and by trimming toenails properly. This means cutting nails straight across with a nail clipper, not rounding off the corners, and filing to smooth the nails.

Resource

American Podiatric Medical Association, 9312 Old Georgetown Road, Bethesda, MD 20814-1698. This association's website has consumer information about footcare.
Telephone 301-571-9200
http://www.apma.org

▶ *See also*
Infection

Insect Bites *See* Bites and Stings

Insomnia

Insomnia (in-SOM-nee-a) is a disorder in which people have trouble sleeping or getting enough rest.

KEYWORDS
for searching the Internet and other reference sources

Sleep disorders

Sleeplessness

Why Can't I Sleep?

Humans, like all earth's creatures, have cycles of activity and rest, which perhaps evolved partly as a response to the cycles of night and day. Many of the body's hormones* and processes are related closely to such daily cycles. Sleep provides the opportunity to rest, to restore certain essential neurotransmitters,* and even to avoid certain predators. Sleep, in short, is necessary to health and even to life.

Millions of Americans have insomnia. They may have difficulty falling asleep or staying asleep through the night, or they may wake up too early or sleep so restlessly that the body and mind are not refreshed. Insomnia is not defined by how long it takes to fall asleep or by how many hours a person sleeps, because these characteristics vary greatly from person to person. Babies may sleep 16 to 20 hours a day, and school-age children need between 8 and 10 hours a night. Some adults need 7 to 8 hours of sleep a night, whereas others function perfectly well with just 3 to 4 hours. Instead, people are diagnosed with insomnia when sleep problems begin to interfere with daily living—when they can no longer function normally during the day because of being tired or cranky, having no energy, and being unable to concentrate.

Everyone has trouble sleeping sometimes. Young people who are excited about a holiday or stressed about an exam might have trouble falling asleep. Adults who are worried about a sick relative or stressed at work might wake up in the middle of the night and not be able to fall back asleep. These are examples of short-term, or transient, insomnia, which are sleep problems that last for one night or even for a few weeks and then disappear. In other cases, episodes of short-term insomnia come and go; this is considered intermittent insomnia. But half of all people with insomnia have chronic* insomnia, which is a sleep problem that occurs on most nights for a month or longer.

Insomnia affects people of all ages, but it is most common in older people, especially women. When people travel, start a new job, or move to a new home or school, all of which are changes in routine, they can have trouble sleeping. Physical conditions such as pregnancy, arthritis, the need to urinate frequently, and leg cramps also seem to cause sleep problems. But the most common cause of insomnia is psychological*;

* **hormones** are chemicals that are produced by different glands in the body. Hormones are like the body's ambassadors: they are created in one place but are sent through the body to have specific regulatory effects in different places.

* **neurotransmitters** (NOOR-o-TRANS-mit-urz) are brain chemicals that let brain cells communicate with each other and therefore allow the brain to function normally.

* **chronic** (KRON-ik) means continuing for a long period of time.

* **psychological** (sy-ko-LOJ-i-kal) refers to mental processes, including thoughts, feelings, and emotions.

* **depression** (de-PRESH-un) is a mental state characterized by feelings of sadness, despair, and discouragement.

emotions such as anger, anxiety, depression*, and stress keep many people from sleeping well.

What to Do about Insomnia

If insomnia is transient, it should go away when the stress that triggered it eases, such as when that worrisome exam is over. For underlying psychological or physical issues, seeing a doctor can help improve sleep. Dealing with insomnia, however, is often a matter of lifestyle changes. Things that may contribute to insomnia include:

- Reading, eating, or watching television in bed (use a bed only for sleeping)
- Taking afternoon naps
- Smoking
- Drinking alcohol
- Drinking coffee, tea, cocoa, colas, or other drinks that contain caffeine late in the day
- Taking sleeping pills not prescribed by a doctor

Things that may contribute to a better night's sleep include:

- Keeping to a sleep schedule, which means going to sleep and getting up at the same time every day
- Exercising during the day (but not after dinner)
- Taking a warm bath before bedtime
- Drinking warm milk before bedtime

See also
Anxiety Disorders
Depressive Disorders
Jet Lag
Sleep Apnea
Sleep Disorders
Stress-Related Illness
Sudden Infant Death Syndrome (SIDS)

Irritable Bowel Syndrome

Irritable bowel syndrome (IBS) is a chronic (long-lasting) disorder that occurs when the intestines do not function correctly. A person with IBD may experience abdominal pain that often is accompanied by alternating episodes of constipation and diarrhea.

KEYWORDS
for searching the Internet and other reference sources

Functional bowel disease

Gastrointestinal system

Spastic colon

Georgia Goes Solo

Playing the flute was Georgia's favorite activity. When she got to college, Georgia majored in music and performed regularly with the college orchestra. Until her senior year, Georgia always was healthy and able to make it to concerts, but then she began to have problems with her bowel movements. Either she was running to the bathroom constantly because she had diarrhea, or she suffered from constipation. Her symptoms began to interfere with rehearsals and concerts, so she went to the college health center. The doctor was able to rule out inflammatory bowel disease, but did diagnose irritable bowel syndrome. The doctor prescribed medication for Georgia and referred her to a nutritionist and a stress management program. By graduation, Georgia was able to play a flute solo without having to worry about rushing off to the bathroom.

What Is Irritable Bowel Syndrome?

Irritable Bowel Syndrome is a disorder in which the nerves that control the muscles of the intestine are unusually sensitive, causing the bowels to function improperly. The result is abdominal discomfort and an altered pattern of bowel movements (either diarrhea or constipation). IBS also is called spastic colon or spastic bowel.

IBS is not a disease, and it cannot be caught from another person. Although a person with IBS may experience considerable distress and discomfort from abdominal cramping, gas, constipation, and/or diarrhea, IBS is not medically serious and does not lead to other intestinal diseases such as cancer or ulcerative colitis.

The cause of IBS is unknown. Symptoms may be triggered by diet, by drugs, by stress, or by emotional factors. Triggers vary from person to person. The syndrome is about twice as common in women as men and usually begins in early adulthood.

How Is IBS Diagnosed and Treated?

Diagnosis To diagnose a person as having IBS, the doctor must determine through medical history, physical examination, and diagnostic tests that the patient does not have a disease such as Crohn's disease, ulcerative colitis, or an infection that might be causing the symptoms. Typically, a person with IBS will report some or all of the following symptoms to the doctor:

- abdominal pain or cramping
- constipation*
- diarrhea (may alternate with constipation)
- a feeling that the bowel movement is incomplete
- mucus in the stool
- bloated feeling in the abdomen
- a lot of gas

*__constipation__ is the sluggish movement of the bowels, usually resulting in infrequent, hard stools.

Treatment While there is no cure for IBS, the symptoms often can be controlled. Medications may be prescribed to relieve diarrhea and constipation. Changes in diet help many people control their symptoms. People with IBS often benefit from practicing stress reduction techniques, since stress triggers symptoms in some people. Other people with IBS help manage their condition by seeking supportive psychological counseling.

Resources

U.S. National Digestive Diseases Information Clearinghouse, 2 Information Way, Bethesda, MD 20892-3570. The National Digestive Diseases Information Clearinghouse is a service of the National Institute of Diabetes and Digestive and Kidney Diseases (NIDDK). It publishes brochures and posts the fact sheets *Irritable Bowel Syndrome* and *Irritable Bowel Syndrome in Children* at its website.
http://www.niddk.nih.gov/health/digest/pubs/irrbowel/irrbowel.htm
http://www.niddk.nih.gov/health/digest/summary/ibskids/index.htm

International Foundation for Functional Gastrointestinal Disorders, P.O. Box 17864, Milwaukee, WI 53217.
Telephone 414-241-9479
http://www.execpc.com/iffgd

▶ *See also*
Colitis
Constipation
Diarrhea
Gastroenteritis
Inflammatory Bowel Disease

Jaundice

KEYWORDS
for searching the Internet and other reference sources

Bilirubin

Hemolysis

Hepatic function

Hepatitis

Jaundice (JAWN-dis) is a yellowish discoloration of the skin and of the whites of the eyes. It is caused by accumulation in the body of a bile pigment called bilirubin (bil-e-ROO-bin). Jaundice is not itself a disease, but it is a sign of several disorders that affect the liver, the blood, the gallbladder, or bile, which is a fluid secreted by the liver to aid in the digestion of fats. The medical term for jaundice is icterus (IK-ter-us).

What Are Bilirubin and Bile?

When a person is in good health, the bile pigment* bilirubin is formed from the normal breakdown of hemoglobin (HE-mo-glo-bin), which is the oxygen-carrying substance in red blood cells. This process occurs naturally as old red blood cells wear out and are replaced in the body. Bilirubin is then carried in the bloodstream to the liver, where it is combined with bile.

* **pigment** is a substance that imparts color to another substance.

Bile, which is also called gall, gets its greenish-yellow color from bilirubin. Bile is a fluid secreted by the liver to aid in the digestion of dietary fat. Bile is stored in the gallbladder. When it is needed for digestion, the gallbladder pushes it out into the small intestine through a tube called a bile duct. Much of the dark color of stool is the result of bile pigments.

What Causes Jaundice?

There are different kinds of jaundice, but they all occur when the process described above is disrupted and causes buildup of too much bilirubin in the blood.

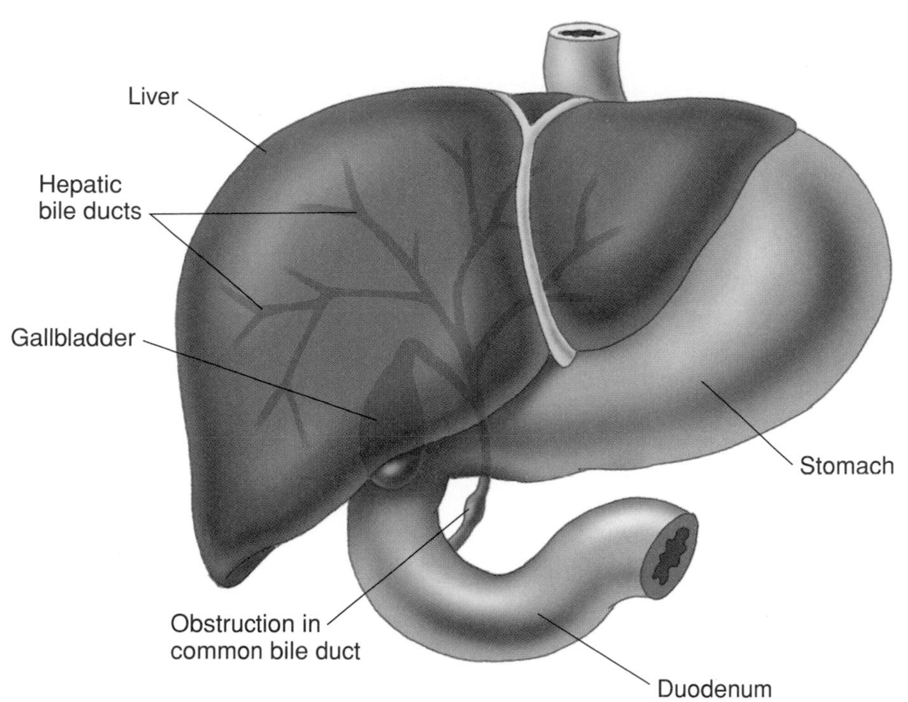

Anatomy of the liver. An obstruction in the bile duct may lead to jaundice.

Hemolytic jaundice Hemolytic* jaundice occurs when the rapid breakdown of too many red blood cells results in the overproduction of bilirubin. This may occur in such diseases as malaria, sickle-cell anemia, and septicemia (sep-ti-SEE-me-a), or blood poisoning.

* **hemolytic** (he-mo-LIT-ik) refers to destruction of red blood cells with the release of hemoglobin into the bloodstream.

Hepatocellular jaundice Hepatocelluar* (liver) jaundice occurs when damage to the liver lessens its ability to remove bilirubin from the blood. Hepatocellular jaundice commonly occurs in hepatitis, cirrhosis of the liver, and liver cancer. Swallowing or inhaling poisonous chemicals and advanced alcoholism can also produce jaundice from liver damage.

* **hepatocellular** (hep-a-to-SEL-u-lar) refers to the cells of the liver.

Obstructive jaundice This is a common form of jaundice. Obstructive jaundice occurs when the bile duct from the gallbladder to the small intestine narrows or becomes blocked, causing bilirubin to back up and accumulate in the blood. Obstructive jaundice may result from gallstones, injuries, tumors, or inflammation that affects the bile ducts.

Physiologic jaundice of the newborn Physiologic* jaundice sometimes occurs when newborn babies have too much bilirubin in the blood. This form of jaundice usually disappears within a few days as the infant's liver matures in its ability to handle bilirubin.

* **physiologic** (fiz-ee-o-LOJ-ik) refers to an organism's healthy and normal functioning.

Is Jaundice a Disease?

Jaundice is not itself a disease, but it is a sign of several disorders that affect the liver, the blood, the gallbladder, or bile. Other signs and symptoms of disease may occur along with jaundice. For example, the urine may be dark brown owing to the excretion of bilirubin, or the stool may be

BILE, GALL, AND "THE JAUNDICED EYE"

The words "bile," "gall," and "jaundice" have all been associated with negative emotions: bile with anger, gall with insolence and audacity, and jaundice with distaste or hostility, as when one views someone or something with "a jaundiced eye." These usages all derive from medieval medicine, when it was believed that different states of the body and mind were caused by "humors," or body fluids, one of which was bile. Bile is quite bitter-tasting. Thus, the term "good humored" came to mean having a pleasant disposition, while "ill humored" came to mean surly or irritable.

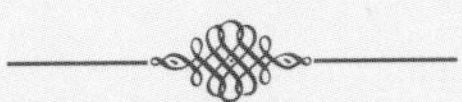

nearly white owing to lack of bilirubin, which produces the normal brown color. Blockage of the bile ducts may also cause intense itching as bile products accumulate in the skin. In hepatitis and other liver diseases, jaundice may be only one among many signs and symptoms.

How Is Jaundice Diagnosed and Treated?

Anyone whose skin becomes abnormally yellow needs to see a doctor to find out why. Part of making the diagnosis may include special blood tests to determine whether the liver is diseased or whether too many red blood cells are being destroyed. A urine sample may be taken to test for bilirubin. A liver biopsy, in which a tiny tissue sample is removed for analysis, may be performed. Ultrasound scanning, which uses sound waves to look inside the body, may be used if the doctor is looking for gallstones or other causes of obstruction. After the doctor completes the diagnostic testing, an appropriate treatment plan is chosen according to the disorder identified as the cause of the jaundice.

Resources

The website of the U.S. National Institutes of Health has a search engine that locates information about diseases that cause jaundice. http://www.nih.gov

American Liver Foundation, 75 Maiden Lane, Suite 603, New York, NY 10038. This website addresses frequently asked questions about liver disease and jaundice. http://liverfoundation.org

See also
Alcoholism
Gallstones
Hepatitis
Malaria
Pancreatitis
Sickle-cell Anemia

Jet Lag

Jet lag is a disruption of the body's internal biological clock that occurs when people cross time zones.

KEYWORDS
for searching the Internet and other reference sources

Biological clock

Circadian rhythm

Jet lag is a common affliction that has surfaced in recent years. The body's internal clock is "set" for the time zone in which a person lives. The light and dark schedule regulates many body functions, including when the body feels hungry and sleepy. In the past, when people traveled by train, ship, horse, or wagon, long-distance trips took months—more than enough time for the body to continually adjust its clock. Air travel changed all that. Now it is possible to cross 8 or 10 time zones in several hours. This means that the body becomes confused: a person may want to sleep even though it is early morning, or be ready to start the day in the middle of the night.

A contributing factor to jet lag is the stress that air travel places on the body. Flights may have cramped, uncomfortable seating. Even though the cabin is pressurized, it is still like being at 8,000 to 10,000 feet in elevation. The lower air pressure causes minor effects such as headache, body aches, and insomnia. The air aboard airplanes is usually dry, which causes minor dehydration. These stresses and the change in time zones result in jet lag.

Although there is no cure for jet lag, there are things that can help minimize it. During long flights, drink plenty of water, get up and walk around the plane occasionally, and before the trip, begin to adjust eating and sleeping schedules to the hours of the destination.

Jock Itch *See* Fungal Infections; Ringworm

K

K

Kaposi's Sarcoma *See* AIDS and HIV

Kidney Cancer

Kidney cancer occurs when cells in the kidney divide without control or order, forming a growth called a tumor and sometimes spreading to other parts of the body.

KEYWORDS
for searching the Internet and other reference sources

Oncology

Nephrology

Renal cell carcinoma

Urology

Wilms' tumor

The kidneys are two bean-shaped organs located near the spine whose main function is to filter salts, excess water, and impurities from the blood, producing the liquid waste called urine. Urine drains from the kidneys to the bladder through a tube called the ureter. It is stored in the bladder until it leaves the body through another tube called the urethra. The kidneys also help produce red blood cells and help maintain healthy blood pressure.

If cancer develops in the kidneys, it may affect not only the kidneys but nearby organs as well, including the liver, pancreas, and large intestine. Or kidney cancer cells may spread through the bloodstream or lymphatic system to other parts of the body. The most common form of kidney cancer in children is Wilms' tumor, and the most common form of kidney cancer in adults is renal cell cancer.

Wilms' Tumor

Wilms' tumor, the most common cause of kidney cancer in children, begins to develop even before a child is born. As the fetus grows in the womb, the kidney cells develop into the netlike structures of blood vessels and tissues that are needed to filter the blood. When these cells do not mature as they should, the baby is born with some underdeveloped cells. Usually these cells mature by the time a child is three or four. But sometimes they start to grow out of control, forming the jumbled mixture of small cells called a Wilms' tumor, after the German doctor Max Wilms (1867–1918), who first wrote about it in 1899.

Doctors find the tumor when a mass is felt while examining a baby's belly. There are usually few, if any, symptoms. If the tumor has not spread out of the kidney, the outlook for the child's recovery is excellent. Most children with Wilms' tumor are treated with surgery or chemotherapy.* If the cancer has spread beyond the kidney, doctors might also prescribe radiation therapy, which uses focused, high-energy rays to destroy cancer cells.

* **chemotherapy** (kee-mo-THER-a-pee) is the treatment of cancer with powerful drugs that kill cancer cells.

Adult Kidney Cancer

Kidney cancer in adults is much more common than in children, affecting about 30,000 people each year. In four out of five cases, the tumor forms in the tissue responsible for filtering the blood, but it also can affect the renal pelvis, the structure that collects the urine after filtration. Unlike Wilms' tumor, kidney cancer in adults often spreads to nearby organs and to other parts of the body.

Kidney cancer is more common in people who smoke cigarettes. Exposure to certain harsh chemicals and to medications containing the pain-reliever phenacetin appears to increase risk for the disease. Heredity can play a role too. However, many cases of kidney cancer develop without apparent cause. The most common early symptoms include:

- Blood in the urine.
- Pain in the lower back.
- Unexplained weight loss.
- Recurring fevers.
- High blood pressure.

How Do Doctors Diagnose and Treat Kidney Cancer?

Diagnosis Doctors start with a medical history, physical examination, and laboratory tests of blood and urine samples. Based on their findings, they may order tests that produce pictures of the kidneys and nearby organs. Additional tests may be ordered, including:

- Intravenous pyelogram (IVP) (in-tra-VEN-us PY-e-lo-gram), which is a series of x-rays of the kidneys, ureters, and bladder after dye is injected.
- Arteriogram (ar-TER-ee-o-gram), which is a similar test that creates images of the network of blood vessels in and around the kidney.
- Imaging tests, such as CT scans*, MRIs*, and ultrasound*.

* **CT scans** or CAT scans are the shortened names for computerized axial tomography (to-MOG-ra-fee), which uses computers to view structures inside the body.

* **MRI,** which is short for magnetic resonance imaging, produces computerized images of internal body tissues based on the magnetic properties of atoms within the body.

* **ultrasound** is a painless procedure in which sound waves passing through the body create images on a computer screen.

If kidney cancer is suspected, a surgeon will perform a biopsy by inserting a thin needle into the tumor and removing a sample of tissue to be examined under the microscope. If these cells turn out to be cancerous, doctors need to find out whether or not the cancer has spread beyond the kidney. Kidney cancer cells often spread through the bloodstream or the lymph nodes, which filter the infection-fighting fluid called lymph. Doctors may order more imaging tests to examine nearby organs and to check for swollen lymph nodes in the chest and abdomen. They also may order chest x-rays and bone scans, because the cancer most often spreads to the lungs or the bones. If the cancer is found to have spread to the lungs or other organs, it still will be kidney cancer because those are the cancer cells that have spread.

Treatment How the disease is treated depends on whether it has spread beyond the kidney. If it has not, the most common treatments are surgery and radiation therapy. Surgery involves removing part or all of the kidney, a procedure called nephrectomy (nef-REK-tom-ee). The remaining kidney generally is able to perform the work of both kidneys.

Kidney cancer that has spread to other parts of the body is very difficult to treat. Doctors can use biological therapy, chemotherapy, and hormone therapy. Biological therapy, also called immunotherapy, attempts to boost the body's own natural defenses against the cancer. Interleukin-2 and interferon are two examples of substances that are used as "immune boosters." Chemotherapy delivers anti-cancer drugs into the person's bloodstream through a needle or in pill form. Hormone therapy involves blocking or increasing the body's own chemical messengers (hormones) to try to control the growth of cancer cells.

These treatments have helped only a small percentage of people with advanced kidney cancer. That is why researchers are conducting clinical trials, which are research studies with volunteer patients, to test new treatment approaches. People with advanced kidney cancer and their caregivers also find support groups a valuable resource.

Resources

U.S. National Cancer Institute, National Institutes of Health, Bethesda, MD. NCI posts a fact sheet called *What You Need to Know about Kidney Cancer* at its website. Its CancerTrials website posts information about clinical trials.
Telephone 800-4-CANCER
http://cancernet.nci.nih.gov/wyntk_pubs/kidney.htm
http://cancertrials.nci.nih.gov

U.S. National Kidney and Urologic Diseases Information Clearinghouse, 3 Information Way, Bethesda, MD 20892-3580. This division of the National Institute of Diabetes and Digestive and Kidney Diseases (NIDDK) posts many different fact sheets about the kidney at its website.
Telephone 301-654-4415
http://www.niddk.nih.gov/health/kidney

American Cancer Society Cancer Resource Center. The ACS posts information about Wilms' tumor and adult kidney cancer at its website.
Telephone 800-ACS-2345
http://www3.cancer.org/cancerinfo/specific.asp

Kidney Cancer Association, 1234 Sherman Avenue, Suite 203, Evanston, IL 60202-1378.
Telephone 800-850-9132
http://www.nkca.org

See also
Anemia
Bladder Cancer
Cancer
Hypertension
Tumor

Kidney Disease

Kidney disease refers to any condition affecting how well the kidneys work. Kidney diseases range from mild infections that can be treated with antibiotics to chronic (long-lasting) diseases that cause the kidneys to deteriorate and ultimately to stop working.

KEYWORDS
for searching the Internet and other reference sources

Diabetes

Glomerulonephritis

Nephrology

Renal diseases

What Are the Kidneys?

The kidneys are a pair of bean-shaped organs located in the back of the abdominal cavity right above the waist. There is one on each side of the spinal column. The kidneys perform a number of functions, chiefly filtering the blood, removing wastes to create urine, adjusting the chemical and fluid balance in the body by controlling the concentration of urine, and participating in the control of blood pressure. The kidneys also are involved in regulating the effects of vitamin D on the body and in stimulating bone marrow to create new red blood cells. When the kidneys are damaged by disease, some or all of these functions can be impaired. When the kidneys do not function properly, a person can become very ill; when they fail to function at all, a person will die without treatment.

Is Kidney Disease a Common Health Problem?

Kidney disease is a major health problem in the United States. Over 3.5 million Americans are affected by some form of kidney disease. Over 300,000 Americans have end-stage renal disease (ESRD), the most severe form of kidney disease. In 1996 over 12,000 people received kidney transplants. Billions of dollars are spent each year treating kidney disease.

What Are the Different Types of Kidney Disease?

There are three main categories of kidney diseases:

- Congenital disorder are genetic or begin very early in life.
- Chronic disorders are long-lasting and may develop gradually over many years.
- Acute disorders occur suddenly, for example from a blockage of the kidney drainage system.

Congenital Disorders People can be born with a kidney disorder, in which case it is called a congenital disease. For example, the two kidneys may be connected at their base to form a single horseshoe-shaped kidney. Some people have one kidney missing from birth, or two on one side, or two ureters (the tubes that carry urine from the kidney to the bladder) for one kidney. A person's body usually can adjust to these problems because people can function with one kidney.

Mild Conditions Can Become Serious Chronic, or long-lasting, kidney diseases are very serious conditions because they cause the

What Is Dialysis?

When the kidneys stop filtering blood properly because of injury or disease, hemodialysis (hemo means blood) is the most common treatment. A dialysis machine acts as an artificial kidney. People undergoing dialysis are hooked up to the machine via needles and tubes so that the blood is pumped out of the body and through the filters in the machine. The machine does the job of the kidney in removing wastes and excess water before the blood is returned to the body through a vein. Some people need dialysis temporarily while their kidneys heal, but many more depend on it permanently to stay alive. The only alternative to dialysis for these people is a kidney transplant. In 1996 more than 180,000 people in the United States relied on dialysis.

kidneys to deteriorate over time. Glomerulonephritis (glom-er-u-lo-ne-FRY-tis) is a condition in which the filtering units of the kidneys called the glomeruli (glom-ER-you-li) become inflamed. It often accompanies other diseases such as diabetes* and high blood pressure, or it can develop as the result of a bacterial infection or immunologic disease.

The immune system makes proteins called antibodies to fight infection. In glomerulonephritis these antibodies become trapped in the glomeruli causing them to become inflamed. Glomerulonephritis may be treatable, or it may progress and cause severe kidney damage. Cancer, or tumors in the kidneys, also over time can stop the kidneys from functioning properly. Eventually, many of these diseases lead to end-stage renal disease (ESRD), a condition in which the kidneys shut down.

Acute Kidney Failure Acute, or sudden, kidney failure can be caused by many things, including injury that severely reduces blood flow, severe dehydration, exposure to chemicals and drugs that are poisonous to the kidneys, infections, tumors, and kidney stones.

Pyelonephritis (PY-el-o-ne-FRY-tis), or infection of the kidney, is a common type of acute kidney disease. Its symptoms can include pain in the back or abdomen, fever, and frequent or painful urination. It can be treated effectively with antibiotics. Another well known condition is kidney stones. Kidney stones are hard crystals made of chemicals that separate from the urine and build up in the kidney. Small kidney stones can pass out of the body on their own, but larger stones require a procedure that breaks them into smaller pieces so that they can leave the body in the urine. People may recover from these kidney diseases without permanent damage to the kidneys. However, if left untreated, these diseases can cause permanent damage and kidney failure.

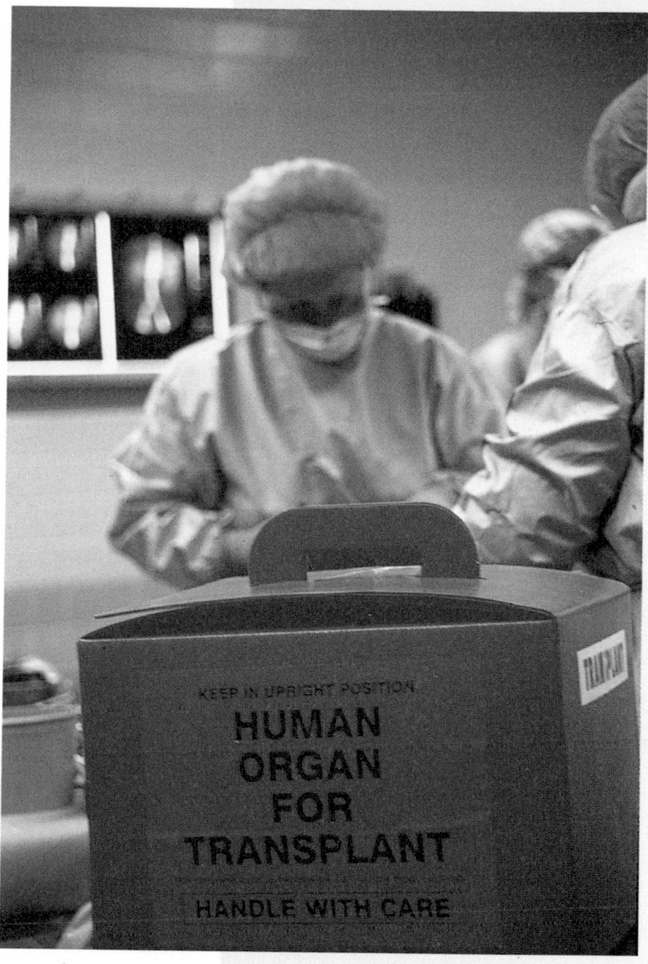

▲

Organ for transplant. If kidney disease leads to kidney failure, dialysis or kidney transplant may be necessary. © *1996 Michelle Del Suercio/Custom Medical Stock Photo.*

diabetes (di-a-BEE-teez) is a disease in which the body cannot produce sufficient amounts of the hormone insulin to properly regulate the amount of sugar (glucose) in the blood.

How is Kidney Disease Diagnosed and Treated?

Disorders that affect the proper functioning of the kidneys may be diagnosed by a number of methods: blood tests, urinalysis, kidney imaging (such as x rays and MRI scans*), and renal (kidney) biopsy (taking a sample of tissues). These tests are used to determine the type and extent of kidney disease.

How kidney disease is treated depends on the underlying cause. For example, an infection might require antibiotics, but a tumor would require surgical removal. Chronic conditions can be treated with drugs to reduce symptoms when the disease cannot be cured. A restricted diet also may help alleviate symptoms. Complete kidney failure requires dialysis two or three times a week or a kidney transplant.

MRI means magnetic resonance imaging, which uses magnets to view inside the body.

The kidneys are located on both sides of the spinal column just above the waist.

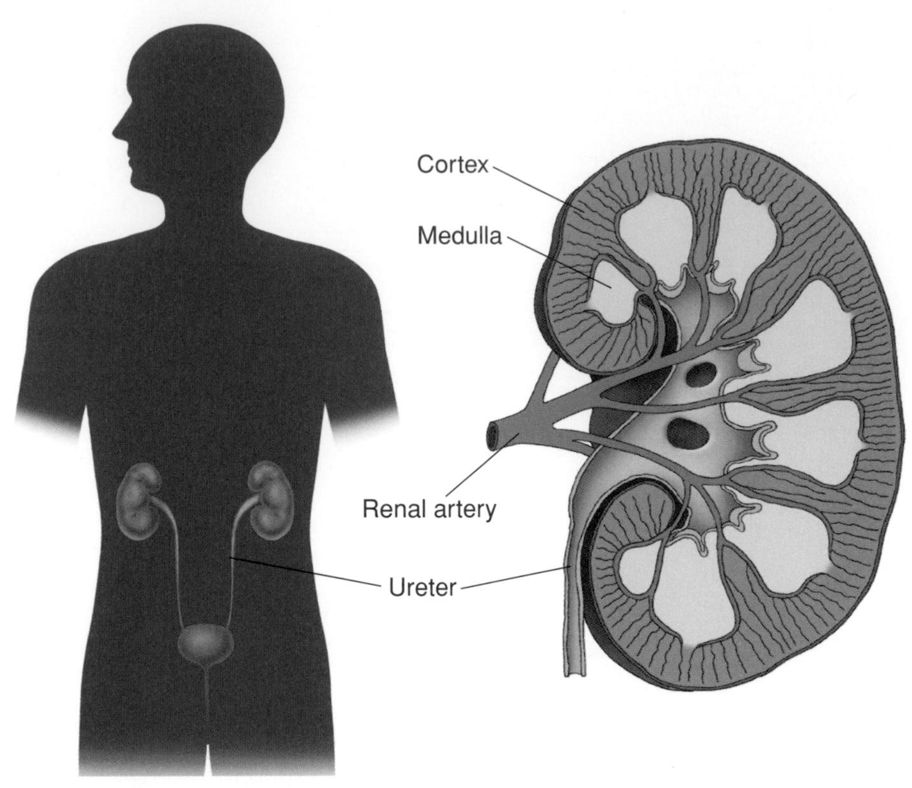

Resources

Books

Bock, Glenn H. *A Parent's Guide to Kidney Disorders.* Minneapolis: University of Minnesota Press, 1993.

Cameron, J. Stewart. *Kidney Failure: The Facts.* New York: Oxford University Press, 1996.

Organization

U.S. National Kidney and Urologic Diseases Information Clearinghouse, 3 Information Way, Bethesda, MD 20892-3580. http://www.niddk.nih.gov/health/kidney

See also
Diabetes
Hypertension
Kidney Stones
Nephritis
Nephrosis

Kidney Infection *See* Urinary Tract Infection

Kidney Stones

Kidney stones are composed of crystals formed by chemicals that separate from the urine and that build up in the kidney. Most kidney stones pass out of the body without treatment, but in severe cases surgery may be required.

KEYWORDS
for searching the Internet and other reference sources

Lithotripsy

Nephrolithiasis

Nephrology

Renal disorders

Urolithiasis

What Is a Kidney Stone?

The kidneys are bean-shaped organs about the size of a juice-box that are located on either side of the spine toward the back of the abdomen. They filter water, salts, and waste products out of the blood to make urine, and they maintain the body's water and ion* balance. When the ratio of water and ions in the urine is out of balance, kidney stones can form.

*__ions__ are positively or negatively charged elements or compounds, like hydrogen, sodium, potassium, and phosphate, which are necessary for cellular metabolism.

Kidney stones can be made of various chemicals, but the most common (80 percent) are made of calcium plus oxalate (OX-al-late) or phosphate. Stones also can be formed from uric (YUR-ik) acid and from cystine (SIS-teen). Stones can be as small as a grain of sand or as big as a golf ball.

The causes of kidney stones often are unknown. However, a family history of stones, urinary tract infections, and several metabolic disorders may make a person more likely to develop kidney stones.

What Happens When People Have Kidney Stones?

Symptoms Although the smallest kidney stones can pass out of the body in the urine without the person even knowing it, the passing of stones can cause severe pain. People have described passing a kidney stone as the worst pain they have ever experienced. The pain occurs when the stone passes from the kidney through the ureter, a tiny urine collection tube, into the bladder. In addition to sharp pain in the back and side, nausea, vomiting, fever, chills, and blood in urine often occur. Large kidney stones can be life threatening if they block the urinary tract and cause the kidney to shut down.

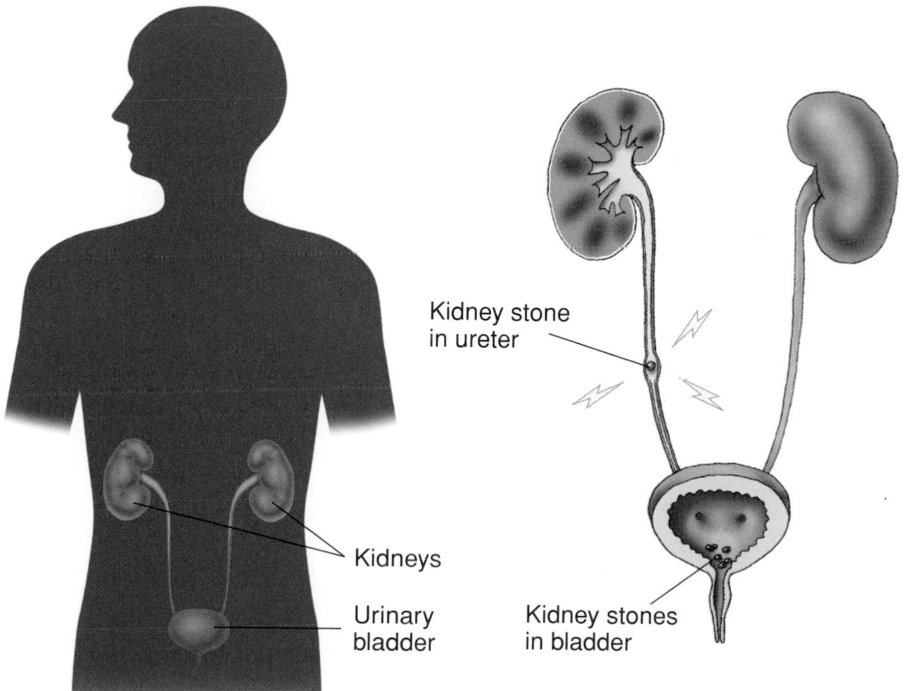

Kidney stones may develop in the kidneys or in the urinary tract if crystals of calcium phosphate or calcium oxalate that have separated out from urine grow too large to pass out of the body.

*** sonograms** (SON-o-gramz) are images or records made on a computer using sound waves passing through the body.

Diagnosis Doctors use x-rays and sonograms*, along with analyses of blood and urine to determine if a person has kidney stones.

Treatment Most kidney stones pass through the urinary tract on their own, with the help of lots of water and pain medication. If the stones are very large (more than one half inch in diameter), doctors can use various techniques to break the stones up inside the kidney or ureter so that the smaller pieces can pass out on their own. Ultrasonic shock waves (lithotripsy), for example, can pass through the body without harm to the place where the stone is located. They break the stone into tiny particles, which then can be passed without pain in the urine. Surgery (nephrolithotomy) is rarely necessary.

Did You Know?

- Kidney stones are mentioned in the Hippocratic (hip-o-KRAT-ik) Oath taken by doctors when they begin their medical careers.
- Scientists have found what they think is a kidney stone in a 7,000-year-old Egyptian mummy.
- Approximately 10 percent of all people will have a kidney stone during their lifetime.
- Kidney stones occur in men more often than in women.
- Kidney stones usually affect people who are between 20 and 40 years old.
- Doctors sometimes ask people with kidney stones to cut back on foods and drinks that contain calcium and oxalate, including some fruits and vegetables, some dairy products, coffee, chocolate, tea, and cola drinks.

How Are Kidney Stones Prevented?

Kidney stones usually affect people between the ages of 20 and 40. Approximately 10 percent of people will have one in their lifetime, and once a person has had one kidney stone, he or she has a 70 to 80 percent chance of developing another. Therefore, once a person has passed a stone, it is important to find out what kind it is. This information may help the doctor determine why the person is developing the stones, and the doctor often will ask people who have passed stones at home to bring them in for laboratory analysis. Often, changing diet, drinking more water, and taking certain kinds of medication can help reduce a person's chance of developing more stones.

Resources

U.S. National Kidney and Urologic Diseases Information Clearinghouse, 3 Information Way, Bethesda, MD 20892-3580. This division of the National Institute of Diabetes and Digestive and Kidney Diseases (NIDDK) publishes brochures and posts fact sheets at its website.
Telephone 301-654-4415
http://www.niddk.nih.gov/health/kidney/pubs

National Kidney Foundation, 30 East 33 Street, New York, NY 10016.
Telephone 800-622-9010
http://www.kidney.org

See also
Gout
Kidney Disease
Metabolic Diseases

Kuru

KEYWORDS
for searching the Internet and other reference sources

Cannibalism
Neuromuscular system
Prions
Spongiform encephalopathies

Kuru is a disease of the nervous system that is extremely rare today, but that once was common among people in certain tribes in Papua, New Guinea, who practiced cannibalism.

Mystery in New Guinea

In the 1950s, a strange disease of the nervous system was killing people in certain tribes in the highlands of New Guinea, an island north of Australia in the Pacific Ocean. An American scientist named Daniel Carleton Gajdusek traveled to New Guinea to study the disease, which the people there called kuru. Eventually, he traced the problem to cannibalism, the eating of human flesh by another human. In this case, cannibalism took the form of a ritual in which people ate the uncooked brains of relatives who had died. Today, those New Guinea tribes no longer practice this ritual, and kuru has almost vanished.

Gajdusek thought that kuru was passed from a dead person's brain to a living person by a slow virus, a virus that takes years to cause symptoms. Most scientists no longer believe this theory, however. Instead, most now think that kuru is caused by a prion, a type of protein that can cause infection. Kuru belongs to a group of human and animal diseases of the brain, known as transmissible spongiform (SPUN-ji-form) encephalopathies (en-sef-a-LOP-a-theez), that may be caused by prions. The word "spongiform" refers to the way infected brains become filled with holes until they look like sponges under a microscope. The most common such disease in humans is Creutzfeldt-Jakob disease.

What Are the Symptoms?

People with kuru have trouble controlling their movements, and this problem gets worse over time. Their arms and legs may appear stiff, or they may have rapid muscle spasms. Occasionally, their muscles may twitch or jerk uncontrollably, or their fingers, hands, toes, and feet may move in a slow, writhing motion. As the disease gets worse, people with kuru may start to lose their mental abilities, such as thought, memory, and concentration. Death usually occurs within 3 to 12 months. Kuru is extremely rare today, but it still fascinates scientists who are studying related diseases.

▶ *See also*

Creutzfeldt-Jakob Disease

Kwashiorkor

Kwashiorkor (kwash-e-OR-kor) is a form of severe malnutrition that affects children living in poverty in tropical and subtropical parts of the world. It is caused by a lack of protein in the diet. Kwashiorkor stunts growth and causes children to have bloated bellies and thin arms and legs.

KEYWORDS
for searching the Internet and other reference sources

Malnutrition

Marasmus

Protein energy malnutrition

Tanya's Story

Tanya lived outside of Tubmanburg in Liberia with her parents and four older brothers and sisters. Her family was poor, and her parents had a

Many children in this West African village show signs of kwashiorkor. Their stomachs are bloated, their arms and legs are thin, and their skin is flaky. © *Charles Cecil/Visuals Unlimited*

hard time feeding all of the children. Nevertheless, Tanya was a healthy infant because she was breastfed; breast milk contains all of the protein and other nutrients a baby needs. But when Tanya was just over a year old, her mother had another baby and Tanya could no longer breastfeed. Instead, she had to eat the only food available: white rice, cassava, and yams. These foods contain mostly carbohydrates and have almost no protein. Because of the lack of protein in Tanya's diet, she developed kwashiorkor: her stomach was bloated, her arms and legs grew very thin, her skin flaked, and she was very weak. Tanya is typical of children from all around the world whose families are too poor to feed their children the nourishing food they need.

What Is Kwashiorkor?

Kwashiorkor is a disease caused by the lack of protein in a child's diet. Kwashiorkor is a type of protein energy malnutrition (PEM) that is widespread throughout the developing world. Infants and children growing up in tropical or subtropical areas (such as Africa, Asia, and South America) where there is much poverty are at risk for kwashiorkor.

The term "kwashiorkor" comes from a word used in Ghana that means a "disease of a baby deposed from the breast when the next one is born." Kwashiorkor usually happens when a baby is weaned from protein-rich breast milk (for any reason) and switched to protein-poor foods. In impoverished countries, protein-rich foods are difficult to acquire.

What Are the Symptoms of Kwashiorkor?

Children with kwashiorkor have edema (excess water retention in body tissues), which makes them look puffy and bloated. They are weak and irritable, and in many cases their skin flakes, and their hair loses its curliness and color. If left untreated, kwashiorkor causes enlargement of the liver, loss of fluids (dehydration) from the bloodstream even when the child has edema, stunted growth, and severe infection due to a weakened immune system. It also can result in jaundice, drowsiness, and a lowered body temperature.

How Is Kwashiorkor Treated?

An international team of medical workers traveling in Liberia saw Tanya sitting on the ground too tired to play and realized how sick she was. They took her to the hospital in Tubmanburg, where she was kept warm and given fluids to replace those she had lost. Initially, she was given small amounts of milk and vitamin and mineral supplements. Zinc supplements helped stop her skin from flaking. After the edema went away, the doctors gave her a high-calorie diet rich in protein.

Of the children who are hospitalized and treated for kwashiorkor, 85 percent survive. Most children properly treated for kwashiorkor early enough recover completely. However, children who develop kwashiorkor before the age of two, like Tanya, usually experience stunted growth.

Can Kwashiorkor Be Prevented?

Because kwashiorkor is a dietary deficiency disease, it can be prevented by eating a well-balanced diet. However, in many parts of the world, people are too poor to provide their families with protein-rich foods, or such foods are not available. International efforts to provide food and to teach people about growing different kinds of foods, eating the right foods, and ways to limit family size are helpful in the fight against malnutrition, but it remains an ongoing problem in developing countries.

Resource

Tamberlane, William. *Yale Guide to Children's Nutrition.* New Haven: Yale University Press, 1997.

▶ *See also*
Dietary Deficiencies
Jaundice

L

L

Lactose Intolerance

Lactose intolerance is the inability to digest lactose, the main sugar contained in milk products.

KEYWORDS
for searching the Internet and other reference sources

Galactose

Glucose

Lactase

Metabolism

Erin's Story

Erin's favorite food had been ice cream since her first birthday. On her thirteenth birthday, the rocky road sundae with hot fudge went down without a hitch, but an hour later she felt awful. She had cramps and diarrhea*, and, even more embarrassing, gas. Erin's friend, whose mother had the same reaction to milk products, explained that she probably was becoming lactose intolerant, meaning that she could not digest all of the natural sugar in the ice cream.

* **diarrhea** (dy-a-RE-a) is abnormally frequent and watery bowel movements.

* **enzyme** (EN-zim) is a natural substance that speeds up a specific chemical reaction in the body.

What Is Lactose Intolerance?

Lactose intolerance refers to the inability of the small intestine to break down the sugar lactose (LAK-tos) because of a lack of or too little of the enzyme* lactase (LAK-tays). Lactose is a complex sugar found in milk products. Normally, when lactose reaches the small intestine, it is broken down into the simple sugars glucose (GLOO-kose) and galactose (ga-LAK-toz) by a protein, or enzyme, called lactase. Simple sugars can be absorbed easily through the wall of the small intestine into the bloodstream, but larger, more complex sugars like lactose cannot. If someone is lactose intolerant, that person's intestine does not make enough lactase, or the lactase it does make does not work properly.

If lactose is not broken down, it absorbs water, so that the water cannot pass through the intestinal wall into the bloodstream. This extra fluid remaining in the bowel causes diarrhea. Also, bacteria (microorganisms) in the digestive tract convert lactose to lactic (LAK-tik) acid in a process called fermentation (fur-men-TAY-shun). Fermentation causes bowel movements to be acidic and burn, and it also causes gas, bloating, and cramps. Lactose intolerance is not dangerous, but it is uncomfortable.

The Nutrition Facts panel on a carton of lactose-free milk shows lactase enzyme as the second ingredient after milk.
© *Leonard Lessin, Peter Arnold, Inc.*

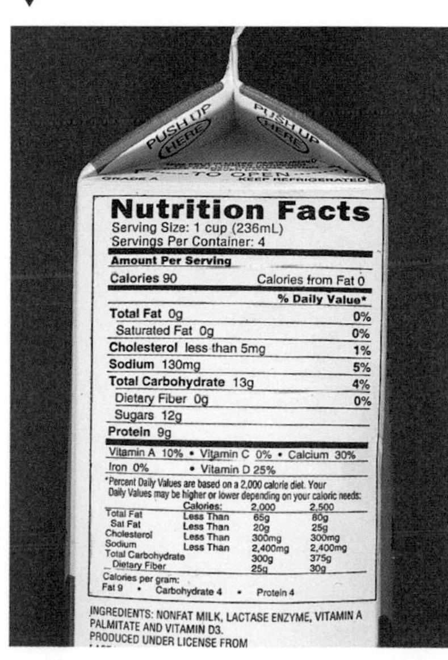

Who Becomes Lactose Intolerant?

Doctors estimate that 30 to 50 million people in the United States are lactose intolerant. Up to 75 percent of people of African, Mexican, and Native American ancestry develop lactose intolerance, as do 90 percent of people of Asian ancestry. People of other ancestry are affected less by the problem.

Nondairy Sources of Lactose

Milk, cheese, butter, and ice cream are obvious sources of lactose, but did you know that lactose often is added to the following items?

- Baked goods, including bread, and mixes for baked goods
- Instant breakfast drinks, potatoes, and soups
- Lunch meats
- Margarine
- Nonfat dry milk powder
- Powdered coffee creamer
- Many prescription drugs
- Processed breakfast cereal
- Salad dressing
- Many snack foods
- Whey
- Whipped toppings

▶ See also
Diarrhea
Metabolic Disease

Many people develop lactose intolerance as they get older, because the ability to make lactase decreases with aging. Digestive diseases and injuries to the small intestine also can cause lactose intolerance. Occasionally, children are born without the ability to make lactase.

How Is Lactose Intolerance Diagnosed?

Doctors use three tests to diagnose lactose intolerance. After a person eats or drinks something containing lactose, the doctor can:

- Test for a low level of glucose in the bloodstream, which would show that lactose was not broken down properly and absorbed (lactose intolerance test)
- Test for a lot of hydrogen in exhaled breath, a sign that bacteria are fermenting lactose (hydrogen breath test)
- Test for acidic bowel movements, also a sign that fermentation is occurring (stool acidity test); usually used to test infants and small children

Living with Lactose Intolerance

Symptoms vary from person to person and depend on the amount of lactose eaten. Trial and error helps people learn what not to eat or how much they can eat without becoming ill. Avoiding milk products should eliminate symptoms of lactose intolerance, but people on such a diet must get calcium and vitamin D from other sources. Nonprescription products containing lactase are available that can be taken along with milk products and help the body break down lactose.

Lactose intolerance usually can be managed by following simple strategies:

- Drink milk in small servings: 1 cup or less per serving.
- Eat cheeses that are low in lactose, such as cheddar.
- Only drink milk with meals or other foods.
- Eat active-culture yogurts, which contain less lactose than other dairy products.
- Use low-lactose or lactose-free milk.
- Take lactase enzyme tablets before consuming dairy products, or add lactase enzyme drops to regular milk.

KEYWORDS
for searching the Internet and other reference sources

Hyperfunctional voice disorders
Inflammation
Larynx
Otolaryngology
Voice

Laryngitis

Laryngitis is an inflammation or irritation of the vocal cords that makes the voice hoarse, or too soft to be heard.

An Unspoken Problem

During Bill Clinton's first campaign to become president of the United States, he kept losing his voice. He had developed laryngitis (lar-in-JY-tis), an inflammation or irritation of the vocal cords that makes the voice hoarse, or too soft to be heard. In President Clinton's case, doctors said his voice problem was due to a combination of overuse and allergies. The laryngitis got so bad that a speech therapist* was hired to travel with President Clinton.

*__speech therapists__ are health professionals who assess and treat voice, speech, and language disorders.

How Are Sound and Speech Created?

The human voice is produced by the back and forth movement of the vocal cords. These are two bands of smooth muscle tissue that lie across from each other in the larynx (LAR-inks), or voice box. The larynx is located between the base of the tongue and the top of the windpipe*. When at rest, the vocal cords are open to let air move past freely. When the person speaks, however, the cords close in a firm but relaxed way. As air from the lungs forces its way between them, they move back and forth rapidly (vibrate), and this produces sound. When the vocal cords become inflamed or irritated, they swell. This keeps them from moving as they should, which affects the sounds they make.

*__windpipe__ (or trachea) is the tube that carries air from the throat toward the lungs.

What Causes Laryngitis?

There are several things that can cause a short-term case of laryngitis. One common cause is speaking or singing too loudly or too long. Another is a common cold or other infections of the upper respiratory tract, such as flu. Other things that can irritate the vocal cords include an allergic reaction or the breathing of harsh chemicals.

Constant irritation of the vocal cords can lead to long-term problems with laryngitis. Two common causes of long-term problems are heavy drinking of alcohol and smoking. Another cause is frequent heartburn, in which acid from the stomach comes back up into the throat and spills over into the larynx, irritating the vocal cords.

Parts of the body involved in the creation of sound and speech include the larynx, epiglottis, trachea, vocal cords, tongue, and palate.

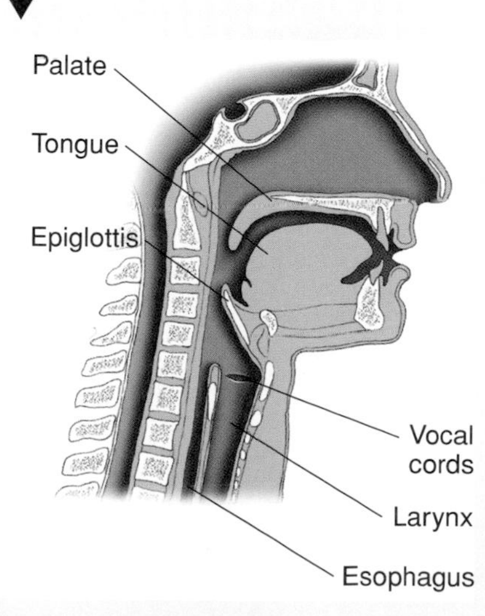

What Happens When People Get Laryngitis?

Symptoms The main symptom of laryngitis is hoarseness, ranging from slight hoarseness to deep raspiness to an almost total loss of the voice. The throat may tickle or feel raw, too, and people with laryngitis may feel as if they need to clear the throat. When these symptoms are caused by a short-term illness or mild irritation, they usually go away after a few days. If the hoarseness lasts for two weeks or longer, then it is time to see a doctor. Although lasting hoarseness is often caused by long-term overuse or irritation, it sometimes signals a more serious medical condition.

Diagnosis To find the cause of laryngitis, the doctor asks about symptoms and performs an exam. As part of the exam, the doctor may look directly at the vocal cords using a tiny mirror held inside the mouth at the back of the throat. In more complex cases, the doctor may look at the vocal cords using a thin tube with a tiny camera and light attached.

The tube can be passed through the mouth or nose and into the throat. This method lets the doctor view the movement of the vocal cords during speech. In some cases, the doctor may refer the person for further testing by a speech therapist.

Treatment A person with laryngitis should rest the voice as much as possible, since talking or even whispering irritates the vocal cords further. In addition, it may help to drink warm liquids and to use a home humidifier, a machine that puts moisture into the air. For brief attacks of laryngitis caused by overuse, a minor infection, or an irritating chemical that was breathed, these steps may be all that are needed. If the laryngitis is due to an infection caused by bacteria, the doctor also may prescribe an antibiotic, a drug that fights bacteria. If the laryngitis is due to allergies, the doctor may prescribe an antihistamine (an-tee-HISS-ta-meen), a drug that counteracts the allergic reaction.

In cases of long-lasting hoarseness, the continuing source of irritation must be removed. If the laryngitis is caused by heavy drinking of alcohol or smoking, the person should give up these harmful habits. If it is caused by frequent heartburn, the person should seek medical care for the condition.

Long-term overuse of the voice can lead to the development of small growths or sores on the vocal cords. These problems often occur in professional singers and speakers. People with such problems may have to rest their voice for several weeks before the vocal cords get back to normal. In some cases, an operation also may be needed to remove the growths. In other cases, speech therapy may help the person learn how to put less strain on the vocal cords.

Speaking of Prevention

People can help maintain healthy voices by avoiding overuse of the voice, by keeping the vocal cords moist, and by avoiding things that irritate or dry out the throat. Tips include:

- avoiding talking or singing too loudly or for too long
- drinking plenty of water and using a humidifier if the air is dry
- gargling with saltwater, sucking on lozenges, or chewing gum
- avoiding drinks that contain caffeine (coffee, tea, and cola), as caffeine may dry out the throat
- avoiding alcoholic beverages, as alcohol may dry out the throat
- avoiding smoking or breathing smoke from other people's cigarettes, as cigarette smoke is irritating.

Resources

U.S. National Institute on Deafness and Other Communication Disorders (NIDCD) Information Clearinghouse, 1 Communication

Avenue, Bethesda, MD 20892-3456. The NIDCD posts a fact sheet about laryngitis and other disorders of the vocal cords at its website. Telephone 800-241-1044
http://www.nih.gov/nidcd/health/pubs_vsl/vocalabuse.htm

The American Speech-Language-Hearing Association posts a fact sheet about laryngitis called *Conserve Your Voice* at its website.
http://www.asha.org/professionals/governmental%5Faffairs/conserve.htm

▶ *See also*
Allergies
Cold
Croup
Heartburn (Dyspepsia)
Influenza

Lassa Fever

Lassa fever is a highly infectious and sometimes fatal viral disease that occurs in western Africa.

KEYWORD
for searching the Internet and other reference sources

Hemorrhagic fevers

What Is Lassa Fever?

Lassa fever is an infectious illness caused by a virus. It is named after the town in Nigeria where it was discovered. Most people infected with the virus have only mild symptoms. But one out of five people with Lassa fever becomes very ill. Lassa virus affects approximately 100,000 to 300,000 people in western Africa each year.

Lassa virus is spread to humans by the Mastomys rodent, which is found in the grasslands and forests of tropical Africa, as well as in human homes. A person can catch the virus by touching objects that have been contaminated with the urine and droppings of the rodents. It is also possible to catch Lassa virus by breathing air near rat droppings, or by eating the rats for food. In addition, person-to-person transmission is common in village settings and in hospitals.

Symptoms of Lassa fever may include fever, pain in the chest, sore throat, cough, vomiting, and diarrhea. The virus is so infectious that medical personnel diagnosing the disease must take special precautions. One-third of people with Lassa fever will develop deafness that is sometimes permanent. One percent of people infected with the virus will die from it.

How Is Lassa Fever Treated and Prevented?

Lassa fever can often be successfully treated with an antiviral drug called ribavirin when it is given within the first six days of illness. Because Mastomys rodents are found all over western Africa, however, it is unlikely that the virus can be prevented by getting rid of the rats. More promising methods of prevention include educating people about how to keep their homes free of rodents and developing a vaccine for Lassa fever.

The U.S. and the World

Lassa fever was first identified in 1969.

- Since 1969, Lassa fever has been killing about 5,000 people a year and infecting as many as 300,000 in West Africa, the only region where it is found. Those numbers may underestimate the extent of the disease, because of poor reporting in some countries.
- About 15 to 20 percent of people who are hospitalized with Lassa fever die. In some areas with high rates of Lassa fever, like Sierra Leone and Liberia, approximately 15 percent of all hospital admissions involve people with Lassa fever.

Resources

Book

Garrett, Laurie. *The Coming Plague: Newly Emerging Diseases in a World Out of Balance*. New York: Farrar, Straus, and Giroux, 1994.

Organizations

The World Health Organization's Communicable Disease Surveillance and Response division posts a fact sheet about Lassa Fever at its website. http://www.who.int/inf-fs/en/fact179.html

The U.S. National Institute of Allergy and Infectious Diseases posts a fact sheet about emerging infectious diseases at its website. http://www.niaid.nih.gov/factsheets/eid.htm

▶ *See also*
Viral Infections

Lazy Eye *See* Strabismus

Lead Poisoning

Lead poisoning occurs when a person swallows or breathes lead, which can damage many parts of the body, especially in young children.

KEYWORDS
for searching the Internet and other reference sources

Heavy metal

Plumbism

Timmy's Story

The year Josh turned 12, his parents bought a bigger house so that they would have a bedroom for his little brother, Timmy, who had just started to crawl. Everyone in the family was excited about the move to the house, which was in an older neighborhood with giant trees in the yards.

Josh spent many Saturday afternoons helping his dad fix up the 50-year-old house. Josh's dad knew that chips of paint from homes this age often contain lead, which could be poisonous to Timmy if he put them in his mouth. One of his first projects, then, was to scrape off the old paint and replace it with new, lead-free paint.

A few months later, Timmy's doctor tested his blood during a routine checkup and found a high level of lead. His parents had not known that Timmy could get lead poisoning from lead dust as well as paint chips. Luckily, the problem was caught and treated early.

What Is Lead Poisoning?

Lead is a metal that has been mined for thousands of years. In the past, it was used to make many everyday items found in or near homes, such as paint, gasoline, water pipes, and food cans. When a person swallows or breathes lead, however, it can be highly poisonous. It is especially dangerous to children ages 6 years and younger. This is partly because the bodies of such young children are changing rapidly and partly because children in this age group tend to put things in their mouths.

Lead is poisonous because it interferes with some of the body's basic activities. To some extent, the body cannot tell the difference between lead and calcium, a mineral that helps build strong bones. Like calcium, lead stays in the bloodstream for a few weeks. Then it is deposited into the bones, where it can stay for a lifetime. Even small amounts of lead can permanently harm children over time, leading to learning disabilities, behavior problems, decreased intelligence, and other damage. Large amounts of lead can cause seizures, unconsciousness, or even death.

What Causes Lead Poisoning?

There are many familiar items that are in our everyday environment that can cause lead poisoning.

Manufacturers used to put lead in paint to make it last longer and cling better to surfaces. Since 1978, the sale of lead-based paint for use in homes has been banned in the United States. It also has become illegal to paint children's toys and household furniture with lead-based paint. However, lead-based paint is still found in more than four out of five homes built before the time of the ban. Old paint that is peeling, chipped, or chalky is a hazard. Because lead has a sweet taste, children may eat chips of lead paint. Even lead-based paint in good condition can pose a risk if it is on surfaces that children chew or that get a lot of wear and tear. Lead-based paint can also be found on old children's toys and household furniture.

The most common way to get lead poisoning is through contact with lead in the form of dust. Lead can get into dust when old paint is scraped or sanded, or when painted surfaces bump or rub together. This dust can then settle on objects that people touch or children put into their mouths.

Oil companies used to add lead to gasoline to improve performance. This let lead particles escape into the air through car exhaust systems. In 1978, the amount of lead allowed in gasoline in the United States was cut, and cars today use lead-free gasoline. However, the soil around roads may still contain leftover lead from the old gasoline. Lead also can get into soil when the outside paint on old buildings flakes or peels.

Lead was once widely used in household plumbing. This lead can get into water that flows through the pipes. In 1986 and 1988, the use of lead in public water systems and plumbing was limited in the United States. However, the lead in old faucets, pipes, and solder used to connect pipes is still a problem. The amount of lead in water depends on the water's temperature (warm or hot water can contain more lead), the minerals and acid it contains, how long the water sits in the pipes, and the condition of the pipes.

Lead solder was once used to seal food cans. This lead could mix with the food inside the can. In 1995, the United States banned this use of lead solder, but it still may be found in some imported cans.

Some other sources of lead are:

- Lead-glazed pottery or leaded crystal can leach lead into foods and drinks.
- Lead smelters and other industries can release lead into the air.
- Jobs that involve working with lead can get lead dust on the clothes, skin, and hair.
- Hobbies such as making pottery and refinishing furniture use lead.
- Folk medicines and homemade cosmetics sometimes contain lead.

Who Is at High Risk?

Anyone of any age can be poisoned by lead. However, the risk is greatest to young children. In the United States, about 900,000 children ages 1 to 5 years have a dangerously high level of lead in their blood. These are some situations linked to increased risk in young children:

- Living in or regularly visiting a home built before 1950.
- Living in or regularly visiting a home built before 1978 that has chipped or peeling paint or that has been remodeled recently.
- Living with an adult whose job or hobby involves contact with lead.
- Having a brother, sister, or playmate who has had lead poisoning.

What Are the Symptoms?

Lead poisoning is not easy to detect. Sometimes no symptoms occur, and at other times the symptoms look like those of other illnesses. Some of the possible early signs of lead poisoning in children are constant tiredness or overactivity, irritability, loss of appetite, weight loss, decreased attention span, trouble sleeping, and constipation.

High levels of lead can cause seizures, unconsciousness, or even death in children. However, most cases of lead poisoning involve much lower levels of lead. Over time, though, even low levels of lead may cause permanent damage. At low levels, lead can cause problems like learning disabilities, behavior problems, decreased intelligence, speech problems, decreased attention span, brain or nerve damage, poor coordination, kidney damage, decreased growth, and hearing loss.

Contact with lead is especially dangerous for children. However, it can be harmful for teenagers and adults as well. If a pregnant woman comes into contact with lead, it can raise her risk of illness during pregnancy. It can also cause problems, including brain damage or death, in her unborn baby. At high levels, lead in adults can cause problems such as infertility, high blood pressure, digestion problems, nerve disorders, memory problems, decreased attention span, and muscle and joint pain.

Lead's Role in History

Lead lasts a long time and has a low melting temperature. In ancient Rome, wealthy families had indoor plumbing with lead pipes. (The chemical symbol for lead is Pb, from the Latin word plumbum for a lead weight. This also is the root for the word "plumber.") The Romans also lined their outside pipes and water tanks with lead, and they made lead plates and eating utensils. Roman wine makers even sweetened sour wine by adding a syrup containing powdered lead. Modern historians have suggested that lead poisoning may explain the strange behavior of several Roman emperors, including Caligula (A.D. 12–41), who wasted a fortune on public entertainment, banished and murdered relatives, made his favorite horse a public official, and declared himself a god. The decline and fall of the Roman Empire may have been due, at least in part, to lead.

How Is Lead Poisoning Diagnosed?

Often lead poisoning has few symptoms. The only way to know whether a person has lead poisoning is to get a blood test that measures the amount of lead in the blood. Children who are not at high risk are usually tested at ages 1 and 2 years. Children who are at high risk are usually tested every 6 months between the ages of 6 months and 2 years, then once a year until age 6. A blood test can also be done at any time on anyone who has symptoms or may have had exposure to lead.

How Is Lead Poisoning Treated?

The first step in treatment is to avoid more contact with lead. This means finding and removing any sources of lead in the home. The next step is to make any needed changes in diet. Children should eat at least three meals a day, because they absorb less lead when they have food in their systems. Children also should eat plenty of foods high in iron and calcium, such as milk, cheese, fish, peanut butter, and raisins. When they do not get enough iron and calcium, their bodies mistake lead for these minerals and more lead is absorbed and deposited in their tissues.

If blood levels of lead are high enough, the doctor may prescribe a drug that chelates (KEE-lates), or binds to, lead in the body. Once lead is bound up in this way, the body can remove it through urine or bowel movements. Depending on the drug used, it may be given in a vein, by shot, or by mouth.

Getting the Lead Out

These tips can help prevent lead poisoning:

- Wash the hands often, especially after spending time outside and before eating.

- Wash the floors, windowsills, and other surfaces in the home weekly.
- Use a sponge or mop with a solution of water and all-purpose cleaner to clean up dust.
- Rinse the sponge or mop thoroughly after cleaning dirty or dusty areas.
- Keep younger children from chewing on painted surfaces, such as windowsills or cribs.
- Do not let younger children put toys and other objects with painted surfaces in their mouths.
- Have younger children play in grassy areas instead of soil, which may have lead in it.
- Wash a younger child's bottles, pacifiers, toys, and stuffed animals often.
- Use cold tap water for drinking or cooking, because lead is more likely to leach into hot water taken from the tap.
- Eat a well-balanced diet that is low in fat and high in iron and calcium.

Resources

Book

Kessel, Irene, and John T. O'Connor. *Getting the Lead Out: The Complete Resource on How to Prevent and Cope with Lead Poisoning.* New York: Plenum Publishing, 1997.

Booklet

Environmental Protection Agency, Office of Pollution Prevention and Toxics. "Lead in Your Home: A Parent's Reference Guide." To order, contact the National Lead Information Center.
http://www.epa.gov/lead

Organizations

Centers for Disease Control and Prevention, Lead Poisoning Prevention Branch, Mailstop F42, 4770 Buford Highway, Atlanta, GA 30341, (888) 232-6789. A federal agency that aims to prevent childhood lead poisoning.
http://www.cdc.gov/nceh/pubcatns/97fsheet/leadfcts/leadfcts.htm

National Lead Information Center, 8601 Georgia Avenue, Suite 503, Silver Spring, MD 20910, (800) 424-LEAD. A federal clearinghouse for lead information.
http://www.epa.gov/lead/nlic.htm

See also
Environmental Diseases

Legionnaires' Disease

Legionnaires' disease, also called Legionellosis, is a serious infection caused by the Legionella pneumophila *bacterium. This infection leads to inflammation of the lungs (pneumonia) and to other health problems.*

KEYWORDS
for searching the Internet and other reference sources

Infection

Legionella pneumophila

Legionellosis

Pontiac fever

When Problems Are Legion

In 1976, a mysterious illness affecting the lungs suddenly struck more than 200 people attending an American Legion convention at the Bellevue Stratford Hotel in Philadelphia. The illness, dubbed Legionnaires' disease, killed 34 people in this outbreak. Eventually, the cause of the disease was identified as a previously unknown type of bacteria, named *Legionella pneumophila*, which were thriving in the warm still water of the hotel's air-conditioning system. It now is estimated that 10,000 to 15,000 cases of Legionnaires' disease occur in the United States each year.

The bacteria that cause Legionnaires' disease can live in many water sources, including hot water tanks, large air conditioners, and whirlpool spas. When these bacteria get into the air from the water, people can breathe them and become infected. For example, people might breathe bacteria that have been sprayed from a public air-conditioning system through cooling vents or from a hot water heater through a faucet. The disease cannot be passed from one person to another.

Anyone can catch Legionnaires' disease, although older adults and those who smoke cigarettes or have chronic* lung conditions seem to be at higher risk. People also are more likely to get the disease if their immune system (the body system that fights off infection) has been weakened by other conditions, such as cancer or AIDS, or by certain medications.

* **chronic** (KRON-ik) means continuing for a long period of time.

What Happens When People Get Legionnaires' Disease?

Symptoms The symptoms of Legionnaires' disease start 2 to 10 days after a person is infected. They usually include high fever, chills, and coughing. The person also may have muscle aches, headache, tiredness, loss of appetite, and diarrhea. These symptoms get worse over a period of days. As part of the disease, the person develops pneumonia (noo-MO-nee-a), a serious inflammation* of the lungs. The person also may develop serious kidney problems.

* **Inflammation** is the body's reaction to infection, irritation, or injury that often involves swelling, pain, redness, and warmth.

Diagnosis As with most medical conditions, the doctor usually begins by giving the person a thorough exam and by asking about his or her medical history. A chest x-ray may show signs of pneumonia, and other lab tests may show signs of kidney failure. To check whether these problems are caused by Legionnaires' disease, the doctor must order special tests. These tests look for signs of the infection in the person's blood, urine, or sputum (mucus that is coughed up).

Pontiac Fever

Pontiac fever is a milder illness caused by the same bacteria that cause Legionnaires' disease. It usually strikes people who are otherwise healthy. The symptoms, including fever and muscle aches, start within hours after the person is infected.

Unlike Legionnaires' disease, Pontiac fever does not cause pneumonia. People with this disease usually recover in 2 to 5 days without treatment.

▶ *See also*
Bacterial Infections
Infection
Pneumonia

Treatment Legionnaires' disease is treated with an antibiotic, or bacteria-fighting drug, such as erythromycin (e-rith-ro-MY-sin). People with Legionnaires' disease often need to go to the hospital to receive extra fluids, to replace fluids lost due to high fever, and to receive oxygen to help treat the symptoms of pneumonia.

Resource

The U.S. Centers for Disease Control and Prevention (CDC), National Center for Infectious Diseases, Division of Bacterial and Mycotic Diseases, 1600 Clifton Road, Atlanta, GA 30333. CDC posts a fact sheet about Legionnaires' disease and Pontiac fever at its website.
Telephone 800-311-3435
http://www.cdc.gov/ncidod/diseases/bacter.htm

Leprosy

KEYWORD
for searching the Internet and other reference sources

Skin disease

Leprosy (LEP-ro-see) is an infectious disease that damages the nerves, skin, and mucous membranes. It is caused by the bacterium* Mycobacterium leprae. *It is slowly progessive, which means that it slowly becomes worse and worse. The disorder also is called Hansen's disease, after the Norwegian physician who discovered its cause in 1874.

What Is Leprosy?

A disease that can cause extreme disfigurement and disability, leprosy has been among the most dreaded of diseases throughout human history. It was known to the ancient Babylonians, Hebrews, Greeks, and Romans, and is mentioned frequently in the Bible. Until comparatively recent times, leprosy was incurable, and people with leprosy were sent away from the communities in which they had lived.

Leprosy became widespread in Europe in the Middle Ages, probably aided by the large movement of populations during the time of the Crusades. By the 13th century, there were more than 2,000 institutions for people with leprosy in France alone, and hundreds more in Germany, England, and Scotland. Although the disease had almost disappeared from Europe by the 1500s, outbreaks occurred in Scandinavia and the Hawaiian Islands in the 1800s.

Leprosy Today

Leprosy is uncommon in most countries today, but it causes massive suffering in the areas where it is still found. These areas are largely confined to tropical and subtropical regions of Africa, Asia, and Central and South America. The disease rarely is seen in North America and Europe.

In the United States, most cases occur among people who came from other countries.

Children are more susceptible to leprosy than are adults, and men are more likely to get the disease than women. In terms of living conditions, the incidence of leprosy is greatest in areas of dense population that have poor nutrition and sanitation, and lack of adequate medical care.

▲ Balakot Leprosy Hospital in Pakistan. A man who has lost his fingers from leprosy is shown with his healthy grandson. *© 1973 Bernard Pierre Wolff/Photo Researchers, Inc.*

How Does a Person Get Leprosy?

Contrary to what most people believe, leprosy is not highly contagious. In fact, it is very difficult for one person to catch it from another. There are two reasons why this is so: the bacterium itself does not easily cause disease, and, in any case, almost everyone's immune system can ward it off. Only close contact for a long period of time with a person whose disease is in an advanced stage is likely to cause infection. It is believed that the bacterium travels from person to person by way of the respiratory tract, through discharges from the nose or mouth, such as sneezing or coughing.

The incubation period, from the time of infection until the disease sets in, is very long, usually from 1 to 10 years or more.

What Are the Symptoms of Leprosy?

Leprosy does not cause fingers and toes to fall off; this is another myth connected with the disease. Leprosy can lead to severe damage to such peripheral parts of the body (such as hands and feet), however.

There are two main types of leprosy, called the tuberculoid (too-BER-ku-loid) and the lepromatous (lep-RO-ma-tos). The tuberculoid is the milder form, and it mainly involves the skin and the nerves that supply the skin and other surface parts of the body. Lepromatous leprosy mainly affects the skin, but the infection tends to progress and become more widespread. It is the more severe form.

Tuberculoid leprosy begins as an infection at the nerve endings. Gradually, there is a loss of feeling around them, and pale areas develop on the skin. Over a period of years, these lesions* widen and thicken. Muscular paralysis often develops in the hands and feet. Accidental injuries may not be noticed in areas where sensation has been lost, so that fingers and toes can easily be damaged and scarred. In some cases of tuberculoid leprosy, healing may occur by itself.

* **lesion** (LEE-zhun) is damaged tissue

In the lepromatous form, large soft nodules, or lumps (lepromas), develop over the body. Facial features may become greatly enlarged, producing a characteristic lion-like appearance. The mucous membranes of the nose, mouth, and throat may be invaded by the infection. When the eyes are affected, blindness often results. The progression of leprosy is highly variable, and symptoms may come and go in some individuals.

The Gifts of Father Damien

Father Damien (DAHM-yan) was the religious name of Joseph de Veuster, born in the village of Tremeloo in Belgium on January 3, 1840. De Veuster knew when he was a young boy that he was meant to be a priest. He soon became a missionary and left Belgium to work in the Hawaiian Islands. There, in the course of his work, he became an accomplished carpenter and builder, and even had a basic stock of medicines to help the sick.

In the meantime, leprosy had reached the islands and had begun to spread among the native populations. To isolate the disease, a colony was established on the island of Molokai, and those affected were brought there and abandoned.

Father Damien chose to work in this lonely, sad, and lawless settlement, beginning in 1873. He not only attended to the spiritual needs of the diseased, but also bandaged their sores, provided food, built shelters, and buried the dead. In time, his efforts and achievements attracted the support of doctors and hospitals, and he began to receive distinguished visitors at what had become his model colony. He eventually developed leprosy himself and died from the disease on April 15, 1889.

How Is Leprosy Diagnosed and Treated?

The signs and symptoms of leprosy can resemble those of some other conditions that affect the skin and nerves, especially when the disease is in its early stages. Diagnosis must therefore be made by doing a biopsy, in which a small piece of skin is taken to analyze for the leprosy bacterium. Early diagnosis is very important because it can prevent permanent deformities and disability.

Treatment of leprosy today is with a prescription drug that kills the bacteria. Other drugs have lately been added to treatment because of the growing resistance of the bacteria to the original drug in recent years. To prevent leprosy from coming back, drug treatment is usually continued for at least 2 years. Various operations can be performed to help patients who have become disfigured or have developed physical handicaps. In the United States, the Public Health Service makes treatment available for patients with leprosy, and there are specialized hospitals and clinics in different areas.

Because leprosy is much less contagious than once believed, it is no longer considered necessary to prevent the spread of the disease by isolating patients from other people.

See also
Bacterial Infections
Skin Conditions

Resource

Information concerning leprosy is provided by the World Health Organization at its website
http://www.who.int/lep/

Leukemia

Leukemia (loo-KEY-me-a) is a type of cancer in which the body produces a large number of immature, abnormally shaped blood cells. It usually affects the white blood cells, or leukocytes (LOO-ko-sites), which help the body fight infections and other diseases.

KEYWORDS
for searching the Internet and other reference sources

Acute lymphocytic leukemia

Bone marrow transplantation

Neoplasms

Oncology

Sam's Story

Sam had been looking forward to the basketball season for weeks. Now that it had actually started, though, he was having trouble keeping up during practice and in games. He just did not have the energy that he usually had, and he felt pain in his joints like never before. He found that he always needed to ask the coach to give him breaks during games. His teammates accused him of being out of shape, but Sam knew that it was more than that. His mother noticed that, even though he was playing less, he had more bruises than he did last season. Eventually, Sam was forced to sit out for a few weeks with a bad case of what appeared to be the flu. He felt constantly weak and tired, and he kept getting fevers. His mother decided that it was time to see the doctor and figure out what was going on.

After hearing about Sam's symptoms, the doctor ran some blood tests. These showed that Sam had leukemia, and further testing indicated that it was a type called acute lymphocytic (lim-fo-SIT-ik) leukemia, or ALL. This is the most common type of leukemia in children.

Overall, leukemia accounts for about one third of cancer cases in children. However, like most other types of cancer, it is much more common in adults. Each year, roughly 27,000 adults and 2,000 children in the United States are diagnosed with leukemia.

What Is Leukemia?

Leukemia is a type of cancer that affects the bone marrow, the soft, spongy center of the bone that produces blood cells. White blood cells, or leukocytes, help the body fight infections and other diseases. Red blood cells, or erythrocytes (e-RITH-ro-sites), carry oxygen from the lungs to the body's tissues and take carbon dioxide from the tissues back to the lungs. Platelets help form blood clots that control bleeding.

These cells are normally produced in an orderly, controlled way as the body needs them, but with leukemia, the process gets out of control. In most cases, the marrow produces too many immature white blood cells (called blasts), that are abnormally shaped and cannot carry out their usual duties. This explains why the disease is called "leukemia," which literally means "white blood." As these blasts multiply and crowd the bone marrow, they interfere with the production of other types of blood cells. When the blasts move into the body, they can collect in different places, causing swelling or pain.

Different types of leukemia are described according to how quickly the disease develops and what type of blood cell is affected:

- Acute (a-KUTE) leukemia gets worse quickly, with fast multiplication of abnormal, immature blasts.
- Chronic (KRON-ik) leukemia worsens gradually. Abnormal blasts are present, but they are more mature and can carry out some of their functions.
- Lymphocytic leukemia affects certain white blood cells called lymphocytes (LIM-fo-sites), which control the body's immune response by finding and destroying foreign substances.
- Myelogenous (my-e-LOJ-e-nus) leukemia affects other types of white blood cells in the bone marrow.

In all, there are four main forms of the disease: acute lymphocytic leukemia (ALL), acute myelogenous leukemia (AML), chronic lymphocytic leukemia (CLL), and chronic myelogenous leukemia (CML). Another less common form is called hairy cell leukemia, a chronic condition in which the cells develop projections that look like tiny hairs.

What Causes Leukemia?

In most cases of leukemia, doctors cannot pinpoint a specific cause. However, researchers have identified a few possible risk factors*. Studies have shown that people who are exposed to high or repeated doses of radiation*, such as Japanese survivors of the atomic bomb dropped at Hiroshima, and people with other types of cancer who have been treated with radiation therapy*, are more likely to develop leukemia. Workers who are exposed to certain chemicals, such as the benzene found in gasoline, also develop leukemia more frequently. In addition, certain viruses may play a role in the disease, although this is still under investigation.

Researchers also are studying how a person's genes* may be involved in causing leukemia. In studying the cells of people who have the disease, researchers have found that they often share certain genetic abnormalities.

Some people have suggested a possible connection between childhood leukemia and the low-energy waves given off by high-voltage electric power lines. However, recent studies have not shown a relationship.

What Are the Symptoms of Leukemia?

When someone has leukemia, the abnormal, immature white blood cells that form cannot help the body fight off infections. As a result, the person may have frequent infections and develop flu-like symptoms, such as fever and chills. As these cells keep multiplying and move out into the body, they tend to collect in the lymph nodes* or in organs such as the liver* or spleen*. This may cause pain and swelling. If the cells collect in the central nervous system (the brain and spinal cord), they may cause headaches, vomiting, confusion, loss of muscle control, or seizures.

The oversupply of white blood cells also interferes with the normal production of red blood cells and platelets, causing bleeding problems and a disorder called anemia (a-NEE-me-a). The person may look pale or feel

Understanding Leukemia Lingo

Many of the terms associated with leukemia, including the name of the disease itself, are derived from the Greek language. Breaking down the words into their Greek roots makes them easier to understand.

- **Leuk-** or **leuko-** means white or colorless and is used to form the words "leukemia" and "leukocyte."
- **-emia** means blood and is found in the words "leukemia" and "anemia."
- **-cyte** means cell and is used to form the words "leukocyte," "erythrocyte," and "lymphocyte."
- **Erythr-** or **erythro-** means red. "Erythrocytes" are red blood cells.
- **Chron-** or **chrono-** means time. "Chronic" leukemia develops over a long period of time.

* **risk factors** are anything that increases the chance of developing a disease.

* **radiation** is energy that is transmitted in the form of rays, waves, or particles. Only high-energy radiation, such as that found in x-rays and the sun's ultraviolet rays, has been proven to cause human cancer.

* **radiation therapy** is a treatment that uses high-energy radiation from x-rays and other sources to kill cancer cells and shrink cancerous growths.

* **genes** are chemicals in the body that help determine a person's characteristics, such as hair or eye color. They are inherited from a person's parents and are contained in the chromosomes found in the cells of the body.

weak and tired. They also may bleed or bruise easily, or find that their gums are swollen or bleeding. Other possible symptoms of leukemia include loss of appetite and/or weight; tiny red spots under the skin; sweating, especially at night; and bone or joint pain.

How Is Leukemia Diagnosed?

Doctors who see patients with these symptoms usually start by doing a full physical exam and feeling for swelling in the liver, the spleen, and the lymph nodes under the arms, in the groin, and in the neck. They also may take a sample of blood and examine it under a microscope to see what the cells look like and to determine the number of mature cells versus immature cells. Although blood tests may reveal that a patient has leukemia, they may not show what type it is. Another test called bone marrow aspiration may be necessary to check further for leukemia cells or to tell what type of leukemia a patient has. In this test, the doctor inserts a needle into a large bone, usually the hip, and removes a small sample of bone marrow. The sample then is examined under a microscope for leukemia cells.

If leukemia is present, the doctor may order additional tests to look for abnormal cells in other parts of the body. A spinal tap involves taking a sample of the fluid that fills the spaces in and around the brain and spinal cord, so that it can be checked for leukemia cells. Chest x-rays and special scans can reveal signs of the disease elsewhere in the body.

How Is Leukemia Treated?

Once acute leukemia is diagnosed, doctors start treating it right away, because it tends to worsen quickly. The goal is to bring about a complete remission, which means that there is no evidence of leukemia in the bone marrow or blood. Then doctors can give further treatment to help prevent a relapse, which means a return of the signs and symptoms of the disease after a period of improvement. Many people with acute forms of leukemia can be cured today. Just a few decades ago, ALL was considered incurable, but now it is one of the most curable forms of cancer.

Chronic leukemia sometimes is detected through a routine blood test before symptoms appear. People with chronic leukemia may not need treatment right away if they are not having symptoms yet. Doctors monitor the disease until treatment is needed. It usually can not be cured, but it can be controlled.

Chemotherapy The most common treatments for leukemia are chemotherapy (kee-mo-THER-a-pee), radiation therapy, and/or bone marrow transplantation. In chemotherapy, patients take one or more anticancer drugs by mouth or intravenously, through a tube in one of the veins. In certain cases, doctors need to inject the drugs directly into the fluid that surrounds the brain and spinal cord. Chemotherapy can cause side effects, such as hair loss, nausea, fatigue, or easy bruising, depending on the drugs used. Most side effects go away gradually between treatments or after treatment stops.

* **lymph nodes** are round masses of tissue that contain immune cells that filter out harmful microorganisms.

* **liver** is a large organ located in the upper abdomen that cleanses the blood and aids in digestion by secreting a substance called bile.

* **spleen** is an organ near the stomach that helps the body fight infections and use red blood cells effectively.

Radiation therapy In radiation therapy, doctors use a special machine to deliver high-energy rays that damage cancer cells and stop them from growing. The rays may be directed to one specific area of the body where leukemia cells have collected, such as the spleen, or to the whole body. Like chemotherapy, radiation therapy can cause temporary side effects, such as fatigue, hair loss, nausea, or red, dry, itchy skin.

Bone marrow transplantation In bone marrow transplantation, doctors give high doses of chemotherapy and radiation to destroy all of the patient's bone marrow, in order to kill the cells that are the source of the cancer. Then they give the patient healthy bone marrow from a donor whose tissue is similar, ideally from an identical twin or sibling. They also might give bone marrow that was removed from the patient earlier and specially treated to remove any leukemia cells. A patient who has a bone marrow transplant usually stays in the hospital for several weeks. The risk of infection is high until the transplanted bone marrow begins to produce enough white blood cells.

Biological therapy The newest form of treatment under investigation is called biological therapy, which uses substances produced by the body to increase its ability to fight off leukemia. Scientists have identified several substances that are involved in the immune response, which is the body's way of protecting itself from infections and other diseases. Today scientists can produce some of these substances in the lab and use them to help the body defend itself against leukemia and other forms of cancer.

Living with Leukemia

Living with leukemia can be difficult. Not only can the disease make someone feel sick, but the treatments can, too. Fortunately, though, these treatments often make the disease go into remission. Once this happens, patients still need to see their doctors often for follow-up visits and tests. That way, if the leukemia comes back, it will be detected as quickly as possible.

Having leukemia can be difficult emotionally, too. It is scary for patients to find out that they have a form of cancer and to worry about what the future may hold. Some people withdraw, get angry, or get depressed when they are diagnosed with leukemia. However, with the support of family, friends, support groups, and health professionals, a spirit of realistic optimism can win out.

Resources

Books

Keene, Nancy. *Childhood Leukemia: A Guide for Family, Friends, and Caregivers*. Sebastopol, CA: O'Reilly and Associates, 1997. This book is written mainly for parents, but it offers a wealth of practical advice on coping with childhood leukemia.

Organizations

American Cancer Society, 1599 Clifton Road Northeast, Atlanta, GA 30329-4251. This large nonprofit organization provides information about leukemia in both children and adults.
Telephone 800-ACS-2345
http://www.cancer.org

Leukemia Society of America, 600 Third Avenue, New York, NY 10016. This nonprofit organization provides extensive information about leukemia to the public.
Telephone 800-955-4572
http://www.leukemia.org

National Bone Marrow Transplant Link, 29209 Northwestern Highway, Number 624, Southfield, MI 48034. A support organization for bone marrow transplant patients.
Telephone 800-LINK-BMT
http://comnet.org/nbmtlink

U.S. National Cancer Institute, Building 31, Room 10A03, 31 Center Drive, Bethesda, MD 20892-2580. This U.S. government agency provides detailed information about leukemia and posts a fact sheet *What You Need to Know About Leukemia* at its website.
Telephone 800-4-CANCER
http://rex.nci.nih.gov
http://cancernet.nci.gov/wyntk_pubs/index.html

▶ *See also*
Anemia
Cancer
Immunodeficiency
Radiation Exposure Conditions

Lice

Lice are tiny insects that can be found on the scalp, body, pubic area, or clothing and whose bites may lead to severe itching.

KEYWORDS
for searching the Internet and other reference sources

Parasites

Pediculosis

Sexually transmitted diseases

A Lousy Deal

Lice are tiny insects that are found on the hairy parts of the body or in clothing. A single one of these insects is known as a louse, and the eggs of a louse are known as nits. The bites of these insects can cause severe itching. Judging from the way people talk, lice are not too popular. When people have an awful day, they say it was lousy. When they make a mess of things, they say they have loused up. When they are overly critical, they are said to be nit-picking.

What Are Lice?

The medical term for having lice is pediculosis (pe-dik-yoo-LO-sis). Lice are parasites* (PAIR-a-sites) that feed on human blood. There are three types of lice that live on humans:

* **parasites** are organisms that live on other organisms and usually cause harm or disease.

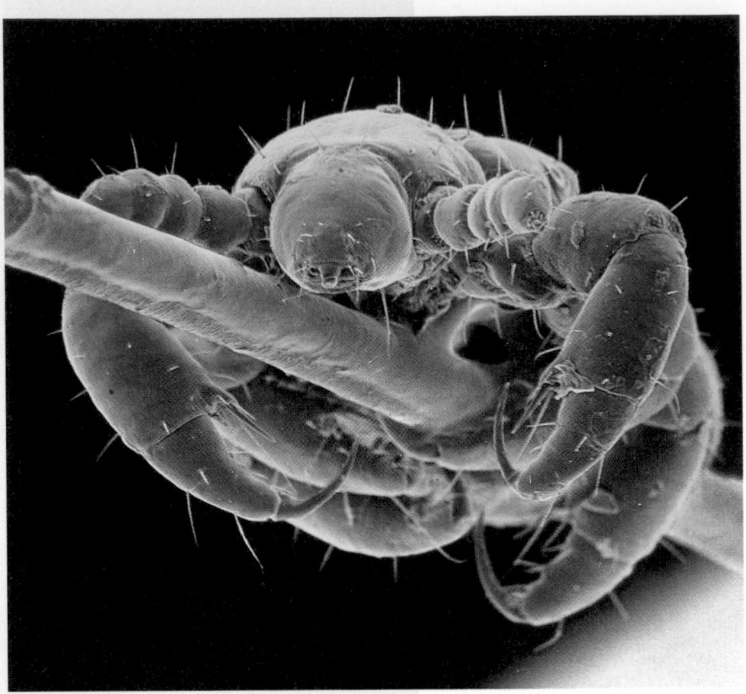

▲

Under an electron microscope, a head louse clings to a human hair. *CNRI/Science Photo Library, Photo Researchers, Inc.*

- **Head lice** (*Pediculus humanus capitus*). These lice are usually found on the scalp.
- **Body lice** (*Pediculus humanus corporis*). These lice are found in clothing, from which they travel to the skin to feed.
- **Pubic** (PYOO-bik) **lice** (*Phthirus pubis*). These lice, also known as crab lice, are found in the pubic area, surrounding the genitals.

Who Gets Lice, and How?

Lice are a very common problem. Anyone can get lice, which are easily spread from person to person. Head lice are spread by close contact with a person who already has them. They also can be passed by sharing combs, brushes, hats, barrettes, pillows, headphones, and the like. Head lice are especially common in young children and their families. They may spread quickly among children in school or camp. They are not a sign of dirtiness or poor hygiene.

Body lice usually are passed along on clothing and bedding. They are sometimes found in people who live in crowded conditions where clothes are not changed or washed very often. Pubic lice usually are spread by close physical contact involving the genital area, such as sexual contact, so typically they are found in people who are sexually active. In a few cases, they may be picked up from bedding or clothing.

What Are the Symptoms?

Head lice do not cause serious medical problems. However, they can be very annoying. The first sign of trouble usually is severe itching on the part of the body where the lice are biting. However, it may take as long as 2 or 3 weeks for the itching to start. Although it may be hard, a person with lice should try not to scratch, because this can spread the lice to other parts of the body. It also can lead to infection if germs are allowed to get into sores caused by scratching. Another possible sign of lice is a tickling feeling of something moving in the hair.

Although lice are tiny, they can be seen with the naked eye if a person looks closely. The nits, or eggs, are tiny yellow or white ovals attached to the hair near the scalp. They can be confused with dandruff or drops of hair spray. Nits take about a week to hatch into baby lice, known as nymphs. These babies turn into adults in another 7 days or so. Adult lice have six legs and are about the size of a sesame seed. They can live for up to 30 days on a person.

Head lice usually are found on the scalp. Often they are seen at the back of the neck and around the ears. In a few cases, head lice are found on the eyelashes or eyebrows. Body lice are hard to see on the body, because they burrow into the skin. They are usually easiest to see in the seams of clothing, from which they travel to the skin to feed. Pubic lice are found on the skin and hair of the pubic area. This is the area where hair grows around the genitals.

How Are Lice Treated?

Lice usually can be identified by sight. If the lice themselves are not seen, finding nits close to the scalp shows that a person has lice. The treatment for lice involves using a shampoo, cream rinse, or lotion that contains a medicine that kills lice. Such medicines are known as pediculicides (pe-DIK-yoo-li-sides). Some are sold over the counter, but others are sold only with a doctor's prescription. Home remedies that do not include a lice-killing medicine may not always work.

When using a lice-killing medicine, read the label and follow the instructions carefully. These medicines may be harmful if not used correctly and should be used with adult supervision, as follows:

- Remove all clothing before the treatment.
- Apply the product according to instructions.
- Do not use a regular cream rinse or combination shampoo-conditioner first.
- Do not wash the hair again for a couple of days.
- Put on clean clothing after the treatment.

Special combs are sold to help remove any leftover nits from the hair. The lice-killing medicine may need to be used again in 7 to 10 days to make sure that no nits have survived. If the treatment does not work, talk to a doctor. Do not use extra amounts of medicine or more treatments than suggested.

Removing nits with a fine-toothed comb. *National Pediculosis Association, Inc.*

What Else Can Be Done?

These steps must be followed along with the use of lice-killing shampoos, rinses or creams to help prevent the spread of lice to others:

- Machine wash in hot water all clothing and bedding that the person with lice touched during the 2 days before treatment.
- Then put the clothes and bedding in a dryer on the hot cycle for at least 20 minutes.
- Dry clean any clothes that cannot be washed.

- Store any clothing, bedding, or stuffed animals that cannot be washed or dry cleaned in a sealed plastic bag for at least 2 weeks.
- Soak combs and brushes for about an hour in rubbing alcohol or Lysol, or wash them in soap and hot water.
- Vacuum the floors and furniture.
- Let the school know about the lice. Stay home until 24 hours after treatment, or as long as the school requires.
- Check other people who have had close contact with a person with lice for signs that they may have caught lice, too.
- In the case of a person with pubic lice, any sex partners from the month before treatment should be treated as well.

How Can Head Lice Be Prevented?

These steps can help prevent the spread of head lice:

- Never share combs and brushes.
- Always bring your own sleeping bag and pillow to a sleep-over.
- Do not try on a friend's hat or headphones.
- If your head itches, tell an adult right away; do not wait.

Resources

Fact Sheets

National Center for Infectious Diseases. "Head Lice Infestation" and "Treating Head Lice." To order, contact the Centers for Disease Control and Prevention, NCID, 1600 Clifton Road, N.E., Atlanta, GA 30333, (888) 232-3228.
http://www.cdc.gov/ncidod

National Institute of Allergy and Infectious Diseases. "Other Important STDs." To order, contact the NIAID Office of Communications and Public Liaison, 31 Center Drive, Building 31, Room 7A50, Bethesda, MD 20892-2520, (301) 496-5717.
http://www.niaid.nih.gov

Organization

National Pediculosis Association, P.O. Box 610189, Newton, MA 02461, (781) 449-NITS. A group concerned with head lice.
http://www.headlice.org

See also
Parasitic Diseases
Sexually Transmitted Diseases

Lou Gehrig's Disease *See* Amyotrophic Lateral Sclerosis

Lung Cancer

Lung cancer is an abnormal growth of cells in the lungs, usually caused by smoking cigarettes, that frequently spreads to other parts of the body and often is fatal.

KEYWORDS
for searching the Internet and other reference sources

Carcinoma

Neoplasms

Oncology

Pulmonary disorders

Respiratory system

Tobacco

Even the Marlboro Man Was Not Immune

In the 1960s, actor David McLean was hired to portray the Marlboro Man, a macho, cigarette-smoking cowboy, in television and print advertising for the tobacco company Philip Morris. McLean smoked many packs of cigarettes to get the right, ruggedly handsome look for each ad, and later he continued to receive boxes of cigarettes as gifts from the company. McLean had begun smoking at age 12, and he never was able to quit. In 1985, he began to suffer from a lung condition called emphysema* due to smoking, and in 1993, he was diagnosed with cancer of the right lung. By 1995, the cancer had spread to his brain and spine. McLean died that year at age 73.

* **emphysema** (em-fi-ZEE-ma) is a lung condition in which the air sacs of the lungs are enlarged, which makes the lungs work less well and leads to shortness of breath.

How Do the Lungs Work?

The lungs allow people to breathe by bringing air in and out. They take in oxygen and get rid of carbon dioxide, a gas that is a waste product of the body. The lungs are two sponge-like organs in the chest. The right lung has three sections, called lobes, and the left lung has two. A lining, called the pleura (PLOOR-a), surrounds the lungs and helps protect them. Air travels into the lungs through the trachea (TRAY-kee-a) (also called the windpipe), which divides into two tubes called bronchi (BRONK-eye), which in turn divide into small branches called bronchioles (BRON-kee-oles). At the distant tips of these branches are millions of tiny air sacs called alveoli (al-VEE-o-lye), which look like little buds. These structures together make up the lungs.

How Does Lung Cancer Start?

Lung cancer usually starts in the lining of the bronchi. However, it can begin in any other part of the lungs. The disease takes a long time to develop. Lung tissue, like other kinds of body tissue, contains DNA. This is material that people get from their parents that contains the instructions, or genes*, for everything the cells do. Gene changes, called mutations, can cause normal cells in the lungs to do abnormal things and to form cancers. Some genes tell cells when to grow, and others tell them when to stop growing. Mutations in these genes may tell cells to grow too much, or they may fail to tell them to stop growing. In either case, the result is cells that are out of control. The cells have repair mechanisms to correct the faulty signals, but when a cell is growing very fast, errors may slip past.

* **genes** are chemicals in the body that help determine a person's characteristics, such as hair or eye color. They are inherited from a person's parents and are contained in the chromosomes found in the cells of the body.

Most of the mutations that occur in lung cancer are not believed to be changes that are inherited from a person's parents. Instead, the mutations seem to occur during the person's lifetime. However, it is possible for a

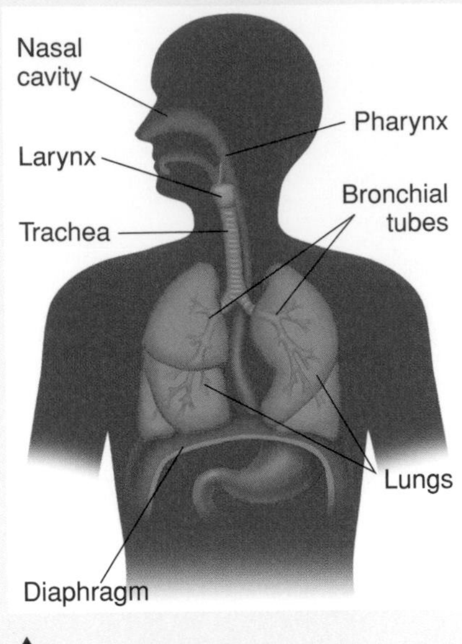

▲

Anatomy of the respiratory system.

person to inherit a reduced ability to break down certain kinds of cancer-causing chemicals. Scientists cannot tell yet which people have these reduced abilities.

Who gets lung cancer? In the United States, more men and women die from lung cancer than from any other kind of cancer. The American Cancer Society estimates that, every year in the United States, about 178,000 people will find out that they have lung cancer, and more than 160,000 people will die from the disease. Lung cancer is rare in people under age 40, because it takes years to develop. The number of cases increases with age, particularly after age 65.

What causes lung cancer? Up to 90 percent of lung cancer is caused by smoking. Tobacco smoke damages cells in the lungs of smokers in ways that can lead to cancer. Although most smokers do not get lung cancer, the longer a person has been smoking, the greater the risk.

People who have worked with asbestos, a substance once widely used as an insulating material that is now banned in the workplace and in home products, also have a higher risk of getting lung cancer. Other risk factors* for the disease include cancer-causing chemicals in the workplace.

* **risk factors** are anything that increases the chance of developing a disease.

What Happens When People Have Lung Cancer?

Symptoms Symptoms of lung cancer often do not appear until the disease is advanced. Many times, the cancer is discovered when a person gets a chest x-ray for an unrelated reason. When symptoms do occur, they are so general that many conditions could cause them. Possible symptoms include a cough that does not go away, chest pain, hoarseness, bloody sputum*, and shortness of breath. The only way to find out for sure whether cancer is causing these symptoms is to see a doctor.

* **sputum** (SPYOO-tum) is mucus that is coughed up from the lungs.

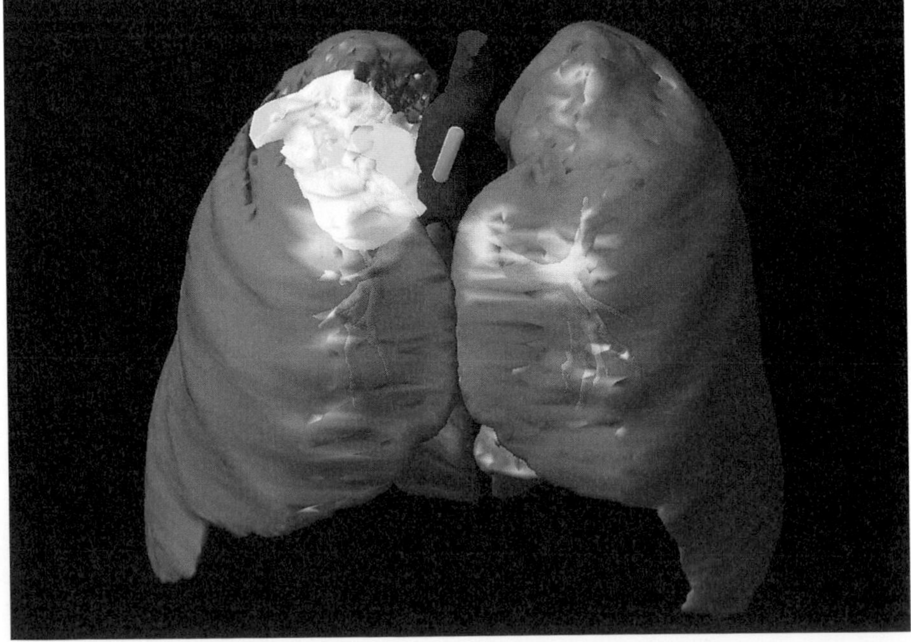

▶

This color-enhanced CT scan shows what lung cancer looks like inside the body. Healthy lung tissue is shown in blue, and the major air passages are in red. The cancerous lung tumor is yellow, and the green rod is the tube (endoscope) that the doctor uses to view the tumor and to plan surgery to remove it. *Volker Steger/Siemens, Science Photo Library/Photo Researchers, Inc.*

Diagnosis If lung cancer is suspected, the doctor may perform a physical exam and a chest x-ray. The doctor also may take a sample of sputum to be examined for abnormal or cancerous cells. In addition, if a tumor* is found on the x-ray, the doctor can do a biopsy* of the lung tissue. This procedure uses special instruments to remove a small sample of abnormal tissue from the lung for examination under a microscope.

*__tumor__ (TOO-mer) usually refers to an abnormal growth of body tissue. Some tumors are cancerous, but others are not.

*__biopsy__ (BY-op-see) is the removal and examination of a sample of tissue from a living body for the purpose of diagnosis.

How Is Lung Cancer Treated?

Staging First tests are done to find out how far the cancer has spread. Based on these tests, the cancer usually is assigned a Roman numeral from I to IV. This process is called staging. The smaller the number, the less the cancer has spread. In contrast, a stage IV cancer means a more serious stage of the disease. This system is used for most types of lung cancer, including the types called squamous cell cancer, large cell cancer, and adenocarcinoma. One-fourth of lung cancers are a type called small cell lung cancer. Instead of getting a Roman numeral, this type is rated either limited (not widespread) or extensive (in both lungs, for example, and spread to distant organs).

The best treatment for lung cancer depends on the type of cancer, the stage, and the person's overall health. Treatment usually consists of a combination of surgery, chemotherapy (kee-mo-THER-a-pee), and radiation therapy.

Surgery For cancer that has not spread, surgery offers the chance of a cure by removing the diseased part of the lung. However, some tumors can not be removed by surgery because of their size or location, and some patients can not have surgery for other health reasons.

Chemotherapy Chemotherapy is the use of anticancer drugs to kill cancer cells. The drugs are given into a vein in the arm or as pills. Because these drugs enter the bloodstream and can reach all areas of the body, they may be useful for treating cancer that has spread beyond the lungs. Chemotherapy can have side effects, including nausea (a feeling of wanting to throw up) and hair loss. Not everyone reacts to chemotherapy in the same way. Usually, the side effects disappear and hair begins to grow back when the treatment is over.

Radiation therapy Radiation therapy is the use of high-energy x-rays to kill or shrink a tumor. In lung cancer patients who are not healthy enough for surgery, radiation may be the main treatment. For other patients, radiation may be used after surgery to kill small areas of cancer cells too tiny to be seen during surgery. Radiation can make a person feel tired, and the skin in the treated area may look first sunburned, then tan. The skin eventually will return to normal.

So Long, Joe Camel

For a long time, cigarette advertising on billboards was a familiar feature of the American landscape. One of the most famous signs was a 72-foot-high billboard in New York's Times Square that showed Joe Camel puffing out smoke rings for 25 years.

During the 1980s, one in three billboards advertised tobacco. However, in 1999, as part of a $206 billion agreement between tobacco producers and 46 states to settle lawsuits related to smoking, cigarette makers and outdoor advertising companies removed tobacco billboards all over the United States.

Can Lung Cancer Be Prevented?

No smoking The best way to prevent lung cancer is by not smoking. People who do not smoke should not start, and people who do smoke should quit. Because the nicotine in cigarettes is so addicting, it is not easy to quit, but it is well worth the effort. Simply switching to "low tar" or filtered cigarettes does not prevent cancer. Everyone also should avoid breathing in other people's smoke. In addition, people can find out whether cancer-causing chemicals are used in their workplace and take steps to protect themselves.

Advances on the horizon Right now, prevention seems to offer the greatest chance for fighting lung cancer. Research is continuing into ways to prevent lung cancer in people at high risk by using vitamins, foods, and medications, but the results so far have not been very helpful. Researchers also are looking into ways of detecting lung cancer earlier.

Studies of treatments for lung cancer are looking at new chemotherapy drugs or new combinations of old drugs. Treatments that help the patient's immune system* fight lung cancer more effectively also are being tested. In addition, gene therapy* may one day be able to repair the genetic mutations that lead to lung cancer.

* **immune system** is the body system made up of organs and cells that defend the body against infection or disease.

* **gene therapy** is a treatment that works by altering genes.

Living with Lung Cancer

Some people recover from lung cancer, but even in the least severe cases, only 50 percent of people with lung cancer are alive five years after their diagnosis. When all cases of lung cancer are taken together, including both most severe and least severe cases, the survival rate at five years drops to 14 percent. This is one reason that it is so important not to start smoking or to quit if a person does smoke.

Because of the low rate of cure, lung cancer patients typically have concerns about whether the cancer will come back after treatment and how long they will live. People need their lungs to breathe, so in advanced cases, as the cancer takes up more and more of the space usually occupied by air, breathing may become difficult. In addition, growth of the cancer around certain nerves may cause severe pain. Medications can relieve this pain, and patients should not hesitate to ask for them.

Young People and Smoking

A study published in the *Journal of the National Cancer Institute* in 1999 showed that lung cancer patients who had started smoking before age 15 had twice as many DNA changes in their lung tissue as those who started after age 20. The message from this study is that smoking at a very young age may be especially likely to cause lung damage that lasts a lifetime.

Resources

American Cancer Society, 1599 Clifton Road Northeast, Atlanta, GA 30329-4251. A national, nonprofit organization that provides accurate, up-to-date information about lung cancer.
Telephone 800-ACS-2345
http://www.cancer.org

American Lung Association, 1740 Broadway, New York, NY 10019. Another large, nonprofit organization that provides detailed information about lung cancer.
Telephone 800-LUNG-USA
http://www.lungusa.org

U.S. National Cancer Institute, Building 31, Room 10A03, 31 Center Drive, Bethesda, MD 20892-2580. This U.S. government agency offers

information about lung cancer to patients and the public, and a posts a fact sheet *What You Need to Know About Lung Cancer* at its website.
Telephone 800-4-CANCER
http://rex.nci.nih.gov
http://cancernet.nci.nih.gov/wyntk_pubs/index.html

▶ *See also*
Cancer
Emphysema
Tobacco-Related Diseases
Tumor

Lupus

Lupus (LOO-pus) is a chronic (long-lasting) disease that causes inflammation of connective tissue, the material that holds in place the various structures of the body.

KEYWORDS
for searching the Internet and other reference sources

Autoimmune disorders

Rheumatology

"Oh, not again!" shouted 18-year-old Julia, her toothbrush falling into the sink with a clatter. It was the fifth morning this week that it had slipped from her hands. She had been waking up with achy, puffy hands, and she was finding it hard to grip things with her stiff fingers. A few weeks later, when filling out a form for a back-to-school physical, she wrote about her stiff hands and also mentioned that she had been feeling really tired all summer. Her doctor suggested she get some blood tests and called Julia's mother a few days later with a referral to a rheumatologist*. He suspected that Julia had lupus.

*__rheumatologist__ (roo-ma-TOL-o-jist) is a doctor who specializes in disorders involving the connective tissue structures of the body.

What Is Lupus?

Lupus causes inflammation of connective tissues in the body. Connective tissue is the material that holds the various structures of the body in place. The cause or causes of lupus are uncertain. However, it is believed to be an autoimmune disorder, which is a reaction of the immune system against one's own body. The medical name for lupus is lupus erythematosus (er-i-thee-ma-TO-sus).

There are two main types of lupus. These are discoid lupus erythematosus (DLE), which mostly causes reddened patches on the skin, and systemic lupus erythematosus (SLE), which affects the skin but also involves other tissues and organs.

A third condition, called lupus vulgaris, is unrelated to lupus erythematosus. It is a rare form of tuberculosis that typically produces nodules, or small lumps, on the skin.

Who Gets Lupus?

Lupus is a disorder that occurs in people of all ages worldwide. In the United States, it has been estimated that there are half a million lupus patients, or about one person in every 600.

Although members of both sexes can get lupus, the great majority of people affected by the disease are women (at least 9 out of 10 in the case of

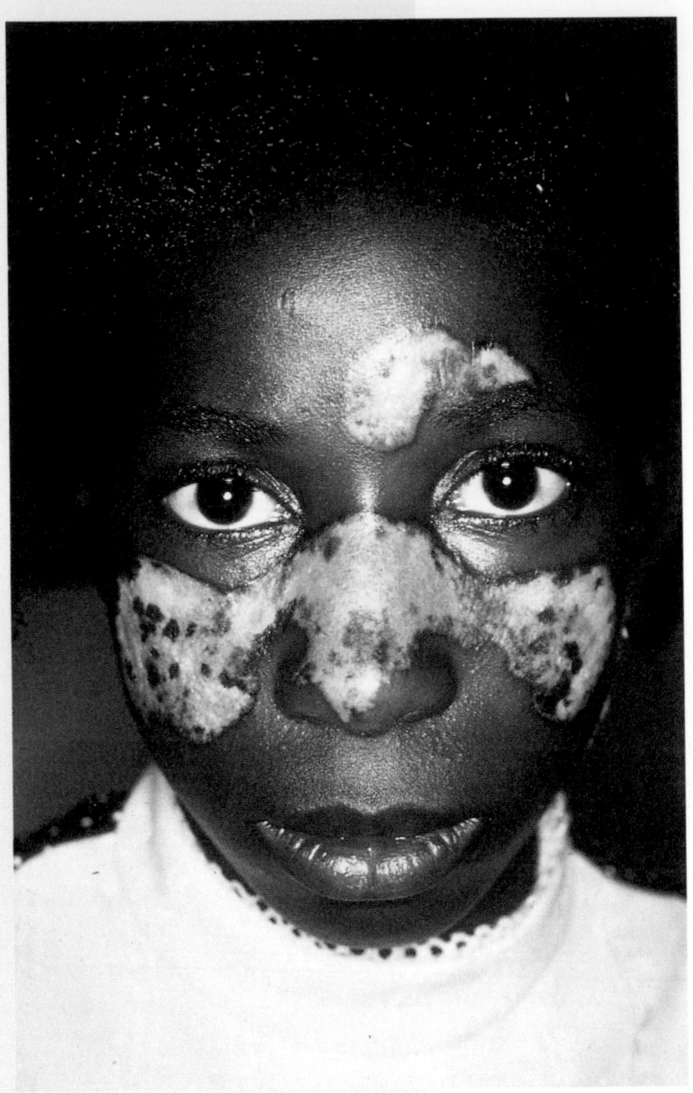

▲ Butterfly facial rash. © *Ken Greer, Visuals Unlimited*

SLE, and approximately 7 out of 10 in the case of DLE). The majority of women affected are young to middle-aged. Like Julia, about half of SLE patients show their first signs of the disorder between the ages of 15 and 25.

In the United States, lupus is about three times more prevalent in people of African ancestry than in people of European ancestry. It also appears to be more prevalent in people of American Indian and Asian origin.

What Causes Lupus?

Lupus is not a contagious disease. One person cannot catch it from another, and there is no need to avoid being near someone who has lupus.

In about 10 percent of cases, certain prescription drugs, such as those used for irregular heartbeat or high blood pressure, can cause symptoms of SLE. (The symptoms usually go away when the drugs are discontinued.) This effect is noted most often in elderly patients and is referred to as drug-induced lupus. In the other 90 percent of SLE cases and in all instances of DLE, the cause or causes of the disorder are not known with certainty.

Although most people who have studied lupus agree that it is an autoimmune disorder, this knowledge provides only a part of the explanation of its cause. The reason is that the causes of immune disorders are not themselves very well understood. There are, however, some things that doctors believe can play a role in the development of lupus.

Heredity is assumed to play a part, although it is not known exactly what its role is. It has been determined that a person with a close relative who has SLE is slightly more likely to develop the disease (by about 10 percent) than someone who does not. The likelihood increases if one has an identical twin with SLE.

Its higher prevalence in some racial groups also suggests that heredity plays a role. However, no gene (hereditary factor) has been specifically linked to the development of lupus.

The fact that women are much more likely to get lupus than men suggests that hormones also may be associated with the disorder.

Certain environmental influences are believed to play a part in the onset of lupus. It is believed that autoimmune responses in some individuals may be triggered by bacteria, viruses, extreme stress, sunlight, certain antibiotics, or food additives. But not everyone gets lupus because they caught a particular virus or bacteria, are stressed about something in their lives, took a certain antibiotic, or ate a certain food.

The antibodies involved in the autoimmune response are called "autoantibodies." They are thought to react specifically with certain chemical constituents of the cells in the body, producing inflammation and damage to organs and tissues.

What Are the Symptoms of Lupus?

The signs and symptoms of lupus vary greatly in different individuals, both in the parts of the body involved and the degree of severity. The symptoms may also come and go, and may go away for weeks or months. Although lupus occurs much more frequently in women than in men, the symptoms in males are no less severe than in females.

Discoid Lupus Erythematosus The mildest and most common form of lupus, DLE usually involves only the skin. It produces a rash of thickened, scaly reddish patches on the face and sometimes other parts of the body. Often the rash spreads in a characteristic butterfly-shaped pattern over the cheeks and bridge of the nose. After a few weeks or months, when healing has taken place, dark-colored or pale scars may remain. If the condition extends to the scalp, the person may lose some of his or her hair.

Sunlight tends to trigger and worsen the rash of lupus. In DLE, the patches sometimes nearly disappear during the winter months. Most people who have DLE are otherwise in good health. The condition only rarely progresses to SLE.

Systemic Lupus Erythematosus People with SLE may have the same type of rash as those with DLE, and they may lose hair as well. In SLE, however, the skin lesions may spread and cause damage to the mucous membranes and other tissues. In some SLE patients the skin is not affected.

Arthritis may be the first symptom in some people with SLE. In fact, SLE is medically classified in the same family of diseases as rheumatoid arthritis, a disorder that causes painful inflammation in the joints. Other early symptoms may include weakness, extreme fatigue, fever, sensitivity to sunlight, and loss of weight.

Internal organs also may be affected by SLE, often causing serious disorders. Problems with kidney function are common in SLE patients, and uremia (yoo-REE-me-a), or the buildup of toxic substances in the blood due to kidney failure, can be fatal. The nervous system may be affected, causing psychological problems, seizures, or other symptoms. The lungs, heart, liver, and blood cells may also be involved.

In the blood, the presence of certain antibodies called anti-phospholipid (AN-ti-fos-fo-LIP-id) antibodies interferes with the normal function of the blood vessels, and can bring on a stroke or heart attack. In pregnant women, the presence of these antibodies can cause a miscarriage.

How Is Lupus Diagnosed?

Lupus can be hard to diagnose, especially if there are just a few symptoms. There is no one sign or symptom that definitely means someone

Did You Know?

- The name "lupus erythematosus" comes from lupus, which is Latin for "wolf," and "erythema," which refers to reddened skin. In the past, people thought that patients with the facial rash looked as though they had been bitten or scratched by a wolf.
- The large majority of lupus patients are women.
- Lupus is not contagious.
- There is no one symptom or test that means someone has lupus.
- Many lupus patients develop arthritis.
- Many people with lupus have to stay out of the sun.
- Most lupus patients can lead nearly normal lives.

What Is an Autoimmune Disorder?

Nearly everyone is familiar with allergies such as hay fever and asthma, either in their own experience or that of friends or family. An autoimmune disorder might best be understood as a kind of allergy, except that the immune system attacks parts of one's own body instead of outside substances such as dust and pollen.

The normal function of the immune system is to protect the body from invading microorganisms or toxic substances. In order to perform this function, it produces antibodies and special white blood cells (lymphocytes) that will recognize and destroy the intruders.

In autoimmune disorders, these responses (for reasons that are as yet not fully understood) occur against the body's own cells, tissues, and organs. This reaction can produce a number of illnesses, including rheumatoid arthritis, a type of diabetes, and lupus.

has lupus, and there is no single laboratory test that will diagnose it either. For this reason, a combination of observations and tests is always necessary.

Diagnostic tests for SLE include blood tests for certain antibodies that attack the nucleus of cells, and for LE cells. LE (lupus erythematosus) cells are white blood cells that destroy other blood cells and are an indication of lupus. Sometimes a skin biopsy (removal of a small sample) is performed to examine for antibodies active in lupus.

Early diagnosis is important so that treatment can be started as soon as possible.

How Is Lupus Treated?

Various types of treatment may be chosen depending upon the particular needs and symptoms of lupus patients. A variety of drugs are prescribed to counteract pain, inflammation, and related problems.

NSAIDs (nonsteroidal anti-inflammatory drugs), such as aspirin, ibuprofen, and naproxen, are used to lessen pain and inflammation in the joints and muscles. Another group of medications, called corticosteroids (kor-ti-ko-STEER-oids), is prescribed to reduce inflammation and activity of the immune system. A third group, called anti-malarials because they also are used to treat malaria, is often prescribed for skin and joint symptoms. Skin eruptions are treated with ointments and creams that contain corticosteroids and sunscreens.

Drugs prescribed to treat lupus can often cause unwanted side effects. For this reason, and because symptoms may change, ongoing medical advice with regular checkups is needed.

Is There a Cure for Lupus?

There is no cure for lupus, but effective treatment can maintain normal body function and control symptoms in the great majority of patients. Nonetheless, SLE can be a life-threatening disease, particularly when the kidneys are involved. The most common causes of death are kidney failure, bacterial infection, and heart failure.

Living with Lupus

There is no specific preventive measure, like vaccination, that one can take to keep from getting lupus. If one is diagnosed with lupus, however, there are ways to reduce the likelihood of "flares," or sudden worsening of symptoms. Patients who are sensitive to sunlight can help prevent rashes by avoiding excessive exposure to the sun, using sunscreens, or wearing broad-brimmed hats. Although there is no vaccination for lupus itself, immunization against other infections is recommended.

Lifestyle changes can help patients with lupus avoid or control symptoms as well. Regular exercise can prevent some muscle weakness and fatigue. Smoking and excessive alcohol intake can be harmful, as they are to anyone. Changing such negative habits can bring about general improvement in one's health. Joining support groups and talking with family, friends, and physicians can ease the effects of stress.

Resources

Lahita, Robert G., and Robert H. Phillips. *Lupus: Everything You Need to Know.* Garden City, NY: Avery Publishing Group, 1998. A nontechnical guide written in a question-and-answer format.

Blau, Sheldon Paul, and Dodi Schultz. *Living with Lupus: All the Knowledge You Need to Help Yourself.* Reading, MA: Perseus Books, 1993. A comprehensive guide to coping with lupus medically and in daily life.

The National Institutes of Health posts information about lupus on its website.
http://www.nih.gov/niams/healthinfo/slehandout

Further information may be obtained from the website of the Lupus Foundation of America.
http://internet-plaza.net/lupus/

See also
Arthritis
Kidney Disease

Lyme Disease

Lyme (LIME) disease is a bacterial infection that is spread to humans by bites from infected ticks. Lyme disease can cause a number of symptoms, some of which may be severe.

KEYWORDS
for searching the Internet and other reference sources

Arthropod-borne infections

Borreliosis

Jill's Story

Jill lives in a small town in Delaware that is bordered by green woods filled with deer and other wildlife. In the summer, Jill likes to spend many of her days in these woods, playing with her dog, reading, staring at the trees, and daydreaming. It is peaceful there, and she enjoys feeling close to nature. When she was 13, though, Jill was bitten by a tiny tick that carried a nasty infection. Soon a red spot formed at the site of the tick bite, then spread into a circular rash. At the same time, Jill came down with a flu-like illness. She ran a fever, felt tired, and had a headache and stiff neck. Her mother took her to see her doctor, who recognized the telltale signs of Lyme disease. Thanks to quick treatment with the right medicine, Jill never became very ill.

Mike's Story

Just up the road, Jill's friend Mike was not as lucky. He never noticed the tick, small as a pinhead, and he never saw the doctor for what seemed like a mild case of flu. Several months later, he started having repeated attacks of pain and swelling in his knees. By this time, Mike's Lyme disease was at a more serious stage. Even with treatment, it was a few months before the attacks stopped.

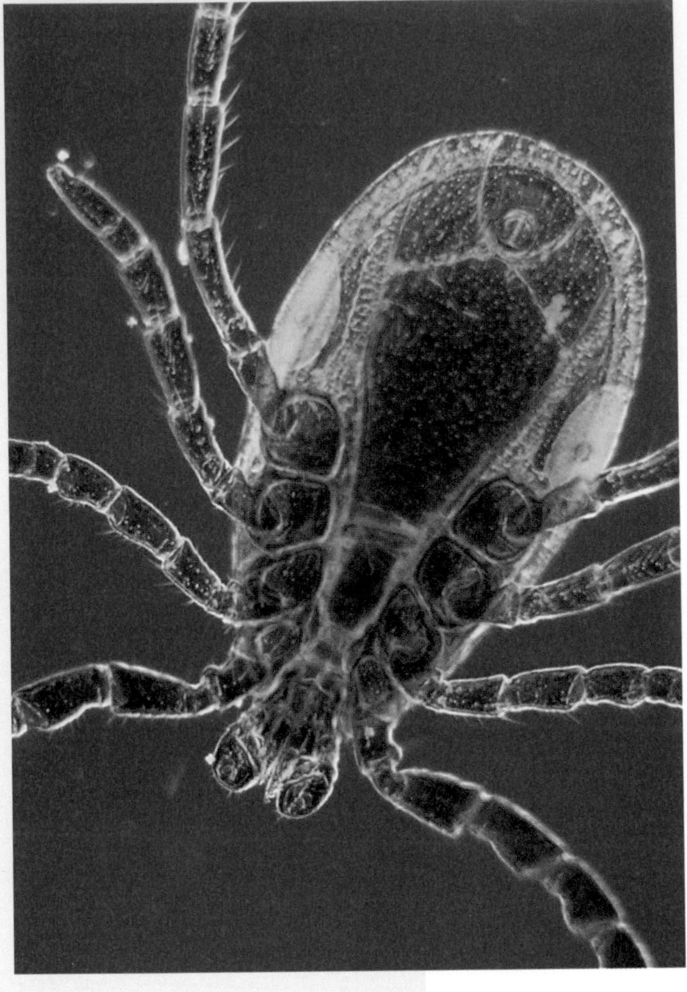

▲

Magnified photograph of a deer tick, adult male, *Ixodes dammini.* © *Kent Wood, Photo Researchers, Inc.*

What Is Lyme Disease?

Lyme disease is an infection that is passed to humans by the bite of tiny ticks. The ticks that spread Lyme disease to humans are much smaller than ordinary dog ticks. In fact, they may be little larger than the period at the end of this sentence. These tiny ticks belong to a group of species named *Ixodes* (iks-O-deez).

These ticks are infected with slender, spiral-shaped bacteria. The bacterium that causes Lyme disease is known as *Borrelia burgdorferi* (bo-REE-lee-a burg-DOR-fe-ry). The ticks that most commonly become infected with these bacteria often feed and mate on deer during the adult part of the tick's life cycle. In recent years, the number of deer living in the northeastern United States has grown rapidly. In addition, more and more people have moved into what were once rural areas, where deer ticks are found. These factors may have played a role in the fast rise of Lyme disease.

Lyme disease can cause a number of symptoms, some of which may be severe. Early signs of infection include a skin rash and a flu-like illness. Treatment is quicker and easier at this stage. If left untreated, Lyme disease may lead to arthritis. It may also lead to serious heart or nerve problems.

Which Ticks Carry It?

One type of *Ixodes* tick, commonly known as the deer tick or black-legged tick, is the source of Lyme disease in the Northeast, Midwest, and certain other parts of the United States. Such ticks feed not only on deer, but also on the white-footed mouse, other mammals, and birds. Another type of *Ixodes* tick, commonly known as the western black-legged tick, spreads the disease in the West.

Although Lyme disease has been reported in nearly every state of the United States, it is most common along the northeastern coast from Massachusetts to Maryland and in Wisconsin, Minnesota, northern California, and Oregon. It also occurs in Europe, China, and Japan. People are most likely to run into the ticks that carry Lyme disease in the woods or underbrush. However, the ticks can also be carried by animals into lawns and gardens. Ticks can bite year-round. In the Northeast, though, the peak season for tick bites runs from April through September. On the West Coast, it runs from November through April.

Tick Attack

- More than 103,000 cases of Lyme disease have been reported since 1982 in the United States.
- In 1997 alone, there were over 12,500 cases of Lyme disease reported in 48 states.
- The yearly total of reported cases was 25 times greater in 1997 than in 1982.

Who Gets Lyme Disease?

Anyone can get Lyme disease. However, it often strikes children and young adults who live in or visit rural areas, because of their high risk of coming into contact with infected ticks. Campers, hikers, and outdoor workers who spend time in woodsy, brushy, or grassy places may also come across the ticks.

What Are the Symptoms?

The symptoms of Lyme disease depend on its stage.

Early Stage In most people, the first symptom of Lyme disease is a red skin rash, known as erythema migrans (er-i-THEE-ma MY-granz). It starts as a small spot at the site of the tick bite. Over days or weeks, this spot expands into a circular rash. Sometimes the rash looks like a bull's-eye, with a red ring surrounding a clear area with a red center. This rash can range from the size of a dime to the width of a person's back. As the infection spreads, rashes can appear at other places on the body. Along with a rash, people may have signs of a flu-like illness. Unlike the common flu, however, the symptoms tend to last and may come and go.

These are early signs of Lyme disease:

- Skin rash
- Fever
- Chills
- Headache
- Stiff neck
- Body aches
- Tiredness
- Swollen lymph nodes ("glands")

Late Stage If Lyme disease is not treated early, the illness may get worse. It can affect many parts of the body, including the joints, heart, and nervous system. These symptoms may not appear until weeks, months, or even years after the tick bite:

- **Arthritis.** This usually shows up as repeated, brief attacks of pain and swelling in the large joints, especially the knees. These symptoms can come and go for several years. More than half of people who are not treated early in the course of Lyme disease with the right medicines go on to get arthritis.
- **Nervous System Problems.** Up to 15 percent of people with untreated Lyme disease develop nervous system problems, which can include numbness, pain, weakness, stiff neck, severe headache, poor coordination, and temporary loss of control of the face muscles. Other symptoms, such as memory loss, poor concentration, sleep problems, and mood changes, have also been linked to Lyme disease. Such symptoms often last for weeks or months. Usually they go away, but they may come back.

Ehrlichiosis

Ehrlichiosis (er-lik-e-O-sis) is another disease that can be transmitted by ticks. In ehrlichiosis, the brown dog tick carries the *Ehrlichia canis* bacterium. People with ehrlichiosis experience low-grade fever, muscle aches, and headaches beginning 1 to 2 weeks after being bitten by an infected tick. The disease usually goes away on its own.

Ehrlichiosis occurs in the United States, Europe, and in a few Asian countries. Diagnosis may be difficult, because people sometimes get more than one disease from the same infected tick.

In areas with ticks, it is important to take precautions against tick bites, and to remove ticks found on the body as soon as possible.

The telltale circular rash at the site of the tick bite. © *CDC, Peter Arnold, Inc.*

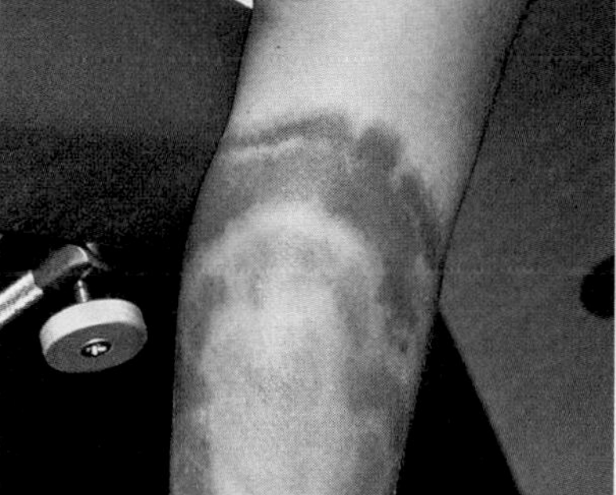

Connecticut Connection

Lyme disease was first recognized in 1975. An unusually large number of children in the town of Lyme, Connecticut, as well as two nearby towns had come down with the joint condition known as arthritis. When scientists tried to find out why, they discovered that most of the children lived near woods, which were the home to ticks. They also found that the children's illness usually started in summer, which was the height of tick season. The final clue fell into place when several of the children said they remembered having a skin rash just before the arthritis, and many said they recalled being bitten by a tick at the place where the rash appeared. Today Connecticut still leads the nation in reported new cases of the disease.

- **Heart Problems.** Less than a tenth of people with untreated Lyme disease develop an irregular heartbeat, which can lead to dizziness or shortness of breath. Such symptoms rarely last for more than a few days or weeks.

How Is Lyme Disease Diagnosed?

Lyme disease can be tricky to diagnose, because it may look like many other illnesses, including the flu and other types of arthritis. To diagnose Lyme disease, the doctor will ask about the person's symptoms. However, the unusual rash is the only symptom unique to Lyme disease, and 10 to 25 percent of people with the disease never seem to get the rash. The doctor also will ask about possible contact with ticks. However, many people with Lyme disease cannot recall being bitten by a tick. This is not surprising, because the tick is so tiny, and the tick's bite is usually painless.

In addition, the doctor may do blood tests. Such tests look for antibodies (substances made in the blood to fight bacteria or other harmful things) against the bacteria that cause Lyme disease. Blood tests often give false results if done within the first month after a person gets the infection. After that time, the tests are more accurate, but some false results still occur. For this reason, the doctor still needs to rely on clues such as the person's outdoor activities in an area where Lyme disease occurs and the time of year when the symptoms began.

How Is Lyme Disease Treated?

In general, the sooner treatment for Lyme disease starts, the better. The disease is treated with antibiotics. Such drugs are usually taken by mouth, although they may be given in a vein in severe cases. In early Lyme disease, antibiotics usually work quickly and completely. In late Lyme disease, antibiotics still work for most people, although recovery may

New Disease or Old News?

Doctors first recognized Lyme disease as a distinct illness in the mid-1970s. However, it may have been around much longer than that. In Europe, a skin rash similar to that of Lyme disease was described in medical articles dating back to the 1800s. Lyme disease may have spread to the United States by the early 1900s. Throughout the twentieth century, doctors noted a link between various symptoms of Lyme disease. It was not until 1977, however, that an article was published that described a "new" disease, causing skin rashes and joint pain, which was called Lyme arthritis. Today we know that arthritis is just one possible symptom of what is now called Lyme disease.

take longer. For a few people, symptoms may last or come back, making it necessary for them to take antibiotics again.

Arthritis due to Lyme disease usually goes away within a few weeks or months after antibiotic treatment starts. It may take years to disappear completely in some people, though. If the arthritis had gone on long enough before being treated successfully, there may be permanent joint damage. A few people with nervous-system problems due to Lyme disease may also have long-term damage. Once cured of Lyme disease, people can get it again if bitten by another infected tick.

Can It Be Prevented?

One way to prevent Lyme disease is to avoid the ticks that carry it. Check with the local health department or county agricultural extension service in an area for information about where infected ticks have been found.

In December, 1998, the first Lyme disease vaccine was approved for use by the U.S. Food and Drug Administration. In studies so far, this vaccine seems generally to be safe and work well at preventing Lyme disease in people ages 15 and older who do not yet have the illness. People in this age group may want to talk to a doctor about the vaccine if they live, vacation, work, or play in areas where Lyme disease is widespread. The vaccine is given as a series of three shots over a period of one year. It is not yet known whether booster shots will be needed in later years. The vaccine is not approved at this time for children younger than age 15.

Top Ten Tick Tricks

- Stay away from areas with lots of ticks, such as thick woods or underbrush.
- Walk in the center of trails to avoid overhanging brush or grass.
- Wear light-colored clothing, which makes it easier to spot ticks.
- Cover up by wearing a hat, a long-sleeved shirt, long pants, socks, and boots or shoes.
- Tuck shirt into pants, and the legs of pants into socks or boots.
- Tape the area where pants and socks meet, so ticks cannot crawl under clothing.
- Shower and wash clothing after being outdoors in an area with lots of ticks.
- Use tick sprays with care; some should not touch the skin.
- Check your skin and check your pets thoroughly for ticks each day.
- Remove any attached ticks carefully: Tug gently but firmly with blunt tweezers near the head of the tick until it lets go of

the skin. To avoid contact with bacteria, do not crush the tick's body or touch the tick with bare hands. Wipe the skin around the bite with an antiseptic (a substance that kills bacteria).

Resources

Book

Veggeberg, Scott. *Lyme Disease.* Springfield, NJ: Enslow Publishers, 1998.

Pamphlets

Arthritis Foundation. "Lyme Disease." To order, contact the Arthritis Foundation, P.O. Box 7669, Atlanta, GA 30357-0669, (800) 283-7800. http://www.arthritis.org

National Institute of Allergy and Infectious Diseases. "Lyme Disease: The Facts, The Challenge." To order, contact the NIAID Office of Communications and Public Liaison, 31 Center Drive, Building 31, Room 7A50, Bethesda, MD 20892-2520, (301) 496-5717. http://www.niaid.nih.gov

Organizations

American Lyme Disease Foundation, Mill Pond Offices, 293 Route 100, Somers, NY 10589, (914) 277-6970. A group that supports research and informs the public about Lyme disease. http://www.aldf.com

The National Institutes of Health posts information about Lyme disease on its website. http://www.nih.gov/publications/lyme/default.htm

The U.S. Centers for Disease Control and Prevention, Division of Vector-Borne Infectious Diseases, 1300 Rampart Road, Colorado State University Foothills Research Campus, P.O. Box 2087, Fort Collins, CO 80522, (970) 221-6400. A federal agency that studies Lyme disease.
http://www.cdc.gov/ncidod/dvbid/dvbid.htm
http://cdc.gov/ncidod/dvbid/lymeinfo.htm

KidsHealth.org has web-based information on Lyme disease. http://KidsHealth.org

▶ *See also*
Arthritis
Bell's Palsy

Lymphoma

Lymphoma (lim-FO-ma) is the name for a group of cancers that arise in the lymph nodes, which are part of the immune system. These cancers include Hodgkin's disease and non-Hodgkin's lymphoma.

KEYWORDS
for searching the Internet and other reference sources

Cancer

Hodgkin's disease

Neoplasms

Non-Hodgkin's lymphoma

What Is Lymphoma?

Lymphoma is a general term for a group of cancers that begin in the lymphatic system, the body system that includes the tissues and organs that make, store, and carry the white blood cells that fight infections and other diseases. This system includes the bone marrow*, spleen*, and hundreds of bean-sized lymph nodes* throughout the body. Lymphoma results when white blood cells, or lymphocytes (LIM-fo-sites), undergo changes and start to multiply out of control. Eventually, the cells crowd out healthy cells and create tumors*. Lymphoma can occur in a single lymph node, a group of lymph nodes, or in other parts of the lymphatic system, such as the spleen or bone marrow. Eventually, it may spread to almost any part of the body.

Lymphoma is divided into two main types: Hodgkin's disease, named after Dr. Thomas Hodgkin, who discovered it in 1832, and non-Hodgkin's lymphoma. The cancer cells in Hodgkin's disease look different under a microscope than do the cells in non-Hodgkin's lymphoma. However, both cancers make a person sick in the same way. Some types of lymphoma are among the most common childhood cancers. Nevertheless, most cases of lymphoma occur in adults.

What Causes Lymphoma?

No one knows exactly what causes lymphoma. It is not contagious, like a cold or chickenpox. People with other kinds of cancer sometimes have what are known as risk factors. A risk factor is anything that increases a person's chances of getting a disease. Having AIDS* or an autoimmune disease* increases the risk for lymphoma. However, most people with lymphoma have no known risk factors.

Scientists recently have made great progress in understanding how certain changes in DNA may cause normal lymphocytes to become lymphomas. DNA is material that people inherit from their parents that carries the instructions for everything the cells do. Just as people get bumps and scrapes during their lifetimes, the genes*, which are part of DNA, also suffer different kinds of damage or malfunction. When that happens, a cell may receive wrong signals that cause it to grow out of control and form a tumor.

In addition, certain viruses appear to cause changes in genes that can lead to lymphoma. Epstein-Barr virus* can cause lymphoma in people with weakened immune systems*. In people with healthy immune systems, the same virus has been linked to a form of the disease called Burkitt's lymphoma. This illness occurs in children and adults in Central Africa, but is rare in the United States. A virus called HTLV-1* causes a kind of lymphoma seen almost only in certain geographical areas, particularly Japan, the Caribbean, and the southeast United States. In most cases, however, doctors simply have no idea why lymphoma develops.

What Are the Symptoms of Lymphoma?

Some people with lymphoma have early symptoms that cause them to go to the doctor. Others, however, may have no symptoms at all, or they

* **bone marrow** is the soft, spongy center of large bones that produces blood cells.

* **spleen** is an organ near the stomach that helps the body fight infection.

* **lymph nodes** are round or oval masses of immune system tissue that filter bodily fluids before they enter the bloodstream, helping to keep out bacteria and other undesirable substances.

* **tumors** (TOO-morz) are abnormal growths of body tissue.

* **AIDS,** short for acquired immunodeficiency (im-yoo-no-de-FISH-un-see) syndrome, is the disease caused by the human immunodeficiency virus (HIV). In severe cases, it is characterized by the profound weakening of the body's immune system.

* **autoimmune disease** (aw-to-im-YOON disease) is a disease resulting from an immune system reaction against the body's own tissues or proteins.

* **genes** are chemicals in the body that help determine a person's characteristics, such as hair or eye color. They are inherited from a person's parents and are contained in the chromosomes found in the cells of the body.

* **Epstein-Barr virus** (EP-stine-BAHR VI-rus) is a common virus that causes infectious mononucleosis.

* **immune system** (im-YOON SIS-tem) is the body's defense system, fighting off attacks by viruses, bacteria, fungi, and other foreign substances that can cause illness or hurt the body.

* **HTLV-1,** short for human T-cell lymphotropic virus type 1, is a virus that is associated with certain kinds of adult leukemia and lymphoma.

This drawing shows the lymphatic system, which includes a network of tiny tubes that branch, like blood vessels, into tissues throughout the body. Lymph nodes are located along this network.

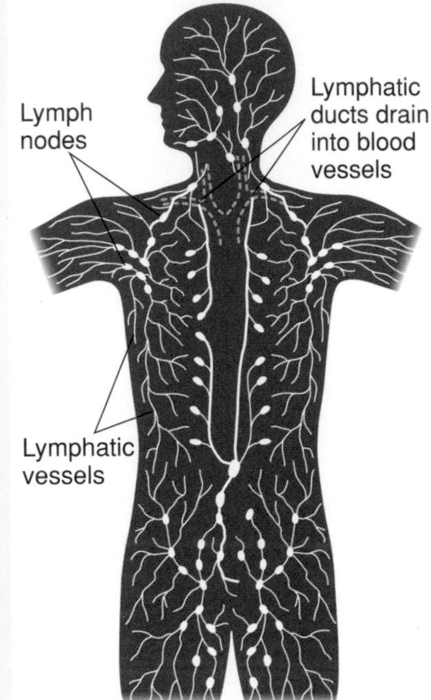

may mistake their symptoms for the flu or another ordinary illness. This is because the body responds to lymphoma as though it were an infection. For example, Jacqueline Kennedy Onassis, the widow of President John F. Kennedy, was diagnosed with lymphoma after she went to the doctor thinking she had the flu. John Cullen, a hockey player for the Tampa Bay Lightning, experienced his first symptom as a pain in his chest after a game. Other common symptoms of lymphoma are painless swellings in the neck, armpit, or groin; night sweats; and tiredness. In addition, the same physical reaction that causes itchiness in allergic reactions can cause widespread itching in lymphoma.

How Is Lymphoma Diagnosed?

If lymphoma is suspected, the doctor can order various medical tests, including imaging studies to allow the doctor to see inside the body. Because many of the symptoms of lymphoma can be caused by noncancerous problems such as infections, the only way to be sure that a person has lymphoma is to do a biopsy (BY-op-see). This procedure involves removing a sample of tissue from a lymph node, or sometimes even an entire node, for examination under a microscope.

How Is Lymphoma Treated?

Once the doctor knows for sure that a patient has lymphoma, the next step is to do something called staging. This means seeing whether the cancer has spread, and if so, how far. Staging is the most important step in deciding what kind of treatment a person with lymphoma will get and what the outlook for survival is. The systems used to stage Hodgkin's disease and non-Hodgkin's lymphoma are different, but the goal of both is to decide the best treatment for the patient.

Early stage non-Hodgkin's lymphoma that has not spread is usually treated with radiation therapy, which uses high-energy waves to damage and destroy cancer cells. If the disease is widespread, it will probably require chemotherapy (kee-mo-THER-a-pee), which uses anticancer drugs that can reach everywhere in the body to fight cancer cells. Chemotherapy drugs are given either through a vein in the arm or as pills. Sometimes chemotherapy is combined with radiation. Hodgkin's disease also is treated with radiation, chemotherapy, or both.

Both chemotherapy and radiation can have side effects, because treatments that kill cancer cells can affect healthy cells, too. The most common side effects of chemotherapy are nausea (feeling sick to the stomach), vomiting, hair loss, and tiredness. Nausea and vomiting can be prevented with medication, and, fortunately, most of these side effects go away after the treatment is completed.

Is It Possible to Prevent Lymphoma?

Unlike many other kinds of cancer, there are no known factors related to lifestyle, such as exposure to sunlight or specific eating habits, that a person could change in the hope of lowering the risk of getting lymphoma.

However, preventing HIV (AIDS virus) infection would prevent many cases of non-Hodgkin's lymphoma.

Will Treatment for Lymphoma Change in the Future?

Today researchers are studying how normal lymphocytes develop into cancer cells. This information may be used one day in gene therapy* to replace abnormal genes with normal ones and allow cells to grow normally again. This same knowledge also is being used to try to detect lymphoma earlier and to test how completely lymphoma has been destroyed by treatment.

Lymphoma cells sometimes become resistant to chemotherapy. This means that the cancer cells are able to change so that the drugs are no longer effective. Drugs are being studied that can interfere with this resistance, thus making chemotherapy more effective. Treatments that help the patient's immune system recognize and destroy the lymphoma cells also are being investigated.

Living with Lymphoma

Because treatment of both non-Hodgkin's lymphoma and Hodgkin's disease usually involves chemotherapy and radiation, one of the hardest parts of living with lymphoma is coping with treatment. Many side effects of chemotherapy and radiation are short-term and will go away when treatment stops. However, other side effects are long-term. For example, treatment may affect a person's ability to have children, or it may trigger the development of a different lymphoma many years later.

Follow-up care may continue for years or even decades. Aside from doctor's visits, though, once all signs of cancer are gone, people can go back to doing whatever they did before they got lymphoma. Most children with childhood lymphoma will survive it, and they can expect to lead normal lives as adults.

Resources

Books

Hobbie, Douglas. *Being Brett: Chronicle of a Daughter's Death*. New York: Henry Holt, 1998. A father's account of his young adult daughter's struggle with Hodgkin's disease.

Hurwin, Davida Wills. *A Time for Dancing*. Boston: Little, Brown, 1995. A novel about the friendship of two teenage girls, one of whom is diagnosed with lymphoma.

Organizations

American Cancer Society, 1599 Clifton Road Northeast, Atlanta, GA 30329-4251. A national, nonprofit organization that provides accurate, up-to-date information about lymphoma.

A Poison That Saves Lives

Near the end of World War II, an Allied ship loaded with sulfur mustard, a poisonous gas used by the Germans during World War I, blew up in an Italian port. Doctors treating the injured soldiers noticed that the gas had an effect on the soldiers' immune systems. Because certain cancers form in the immune system, the doctors wondered whether a related gas called nitrogen mustard could be used to treat the cancers. They discovered that it could. Today nitrogen mustard is one of about 30 anticancer drugs that have helped to save or prolong the lives of people with lymphoma and other cancers.

* **gene therapy** is a treatment that works by altering genes.

Telephone 800-ACS-2345
http://www.cancer.org

Lymphoma Research Foundation of America, 8800 Venice Boulevard, Number 207, Los Angeles, CA 90034. A foundation that supports research and provides information on lymphoma.
http://lymphoma.org

National Cancer Institute, Building 31, Room 10A03, 31 Center Drive, Bethesda, MD 20892-2580. This U.S. government agency offers information about lymphoma to patients and the public.
Telephone 800-4-CANCER
http://rex.nci.nih.gov

See also
Cancer
Radiation Exposure Conditions
Tumor

M

Mad Cow Disease *See* Creutzfeldt-Jakob Disease

Malaria

Malaria is a disease caused by a parasite called Plasmodium *that is spread to humans by the bite of an infected* Anopheles *mosquito.*

KEYWORDS
for searching the Internet and other reference sources

Anopheles mosquitoes

Chloroquine

Infection

Parasites

Plasmodia

Quinine

Staging a Comeback

Malaria is a serious disease that once seemed to be headed for the history books. From the 1940s through about 1970, it was disappearing. Insecticides, or insect-killing chemicals, had been developed for killing the mosquitoes that carry malaria before they could spread the disease. In addition, an inexpensive medicine called chloroquine had been developed for killing the malaria parasite after humans had been infected.

Then things took a turn for the worse. Most species of the mosquitoes that carry malaria developed resistance to at least one insecticide. This means that they could no longer be killed by it. In addition, many strains of the malaria parasite developed resistance to chloroquine and other drugs. At the same time, there was a rise in global travel and trade that spread these drug-resistant parasites around the world. The result is that malaria has made a comeback. In many countries, especially in Africa, it takes a huge toll in health, money, and lives.

What Is Malaria?

Malaria is a disease that is caused by a parasite, a living thing that lives and feeds on another living thing without helping its host in any way. The parasites that cause malaria are tiny, single-celled creatures known as protozoa. The four types of protozoa that cause malaria all belong to a category known as *Plasmodium*. Of these, *Plasmodium falciparum* is the most common and the deadliest.

Malaria parasites are spread to humans by the bite of an infected *Anopheles* mosquito. Such mosquitoes are found in almost all countries in the tropics (region around the equator) and subtropics (region just beyond the tropics).

In fact, malaria is a public health problem in more than 90 countries, where two out of every five people in the world live. There are 300 to 500 million cases of malaria each year, and more than 1 million of these cases

▲
There are about 2,700 species of mosquitoes, including more than 90 species of *Anopheles* mosquitoes, many of which carry malaria. *Anopheles* mosquitoes typically bite between dusk and dawn. Only female mosquitoes suck blood and, thus, spread malaria. This is the female *Anopheles gambiae* mosquito seen up close and personal under an electron microscope. © *1998 SPL/Dr. Tony Brain, Science Photo Library/Custom Medical Stock Photo.*

lead to death. Although malaria is found around the world, more than 9 out of 10 cases occur in Africa south of the Sahara Desert. Most of the deaths there occur among young children, especially in rural areas where the people cannot reach good medical care. This is especially unfortunate because malaria can be cured if it is diagnosed early and treated promptly.

How Does the Malaria Parasite Cause Disease?

The *Plasmodium* parasite that causes malaria is carried by the *Anopheles* mosquito. When an infected mosquito bites a person, it can pass tiny, immature forms of the parasite into the person's body. The immature parasites travel through the person's bloodstream to the liver, where they develop and multiply.

The parasites then reenter the bloodstream and invade the red blood cells, which carry oxygen from the lungs throughout the body. Some of the parasites reach a sexual stage. If these are sucked up by another mosquito drinking its next blood meal, they can meet in the mosquito's gut. There, they can start a whole new generation of malaria parasites.

While in the red blood cells, the parasites continue to multiply. After 48 to 72 hours, the red blood cells break open and release more parasites into the bloodstream. The person then has symptoms such as chills, fever, and headache. The fever lasts for several hours. Then the person starts sweating and his body temperature falls. This cycle of symptoms comes and goes every 48 to 72 hours, following the life cycle of the parasites. Each cycle worsens the person's anemia, or lack of red blood cells. As a result, less and less oxygen reaches the brain and other organs.

Who Is at Risk?

Malaria is mainly a problem in poor countries. Rural areas in such countries are hit particularly hard. Mosquitoes are most likely to spread malaria during the rainy season, when families in these areas are busy farming. Illness then makes it tougher for them to survive. There are about 1,000 cases of malaria a year in the United States, mostly among travelers returning from such areas.

Malaria is a special threat to young children in places where it is common. Worldwide, about 3,000 children under age five die of the disease each day. Malaria is also particularly dangerous for women who are pregnant. It may increase the risk of the baby being born early or dying before or at birth.

What Are the Symptoms?

The symptoms of malaria include chills, fever, sweating, headache, muscle aches, and tiredness. Other possible symptoms include vomiting, diarrhea, and coughing. In its early stage, the disease may be mild, resembling the flu. If it is not treated, however, malaria caused by the *Plasmodium falciparum* parasite may get much worse, leading to liver and kidney failure, seizures, coma, and sometimes death.

Although the symptoms caused by other *Plasmodium* parasites are less severe, the parasites can remain in an inactive state in the liver for long periods. Later, the parasites can become active again, and the symptoms can reappear after months or even years.

The first symptoms of malaria usually start within one to three weeks after a person is bitten by an infected mosquito. However, the time can stretch to several months in some cases. Travelers who come down with a fever or flu-like illness during or after a trip to an area where malaria is a problem should see a doctor right away.

How Is Malaria Treated and Prevented?

To test for malaria, a doctor checks a blood sample for malaria parasites. If they are found, prompt treatment is critical. There are several drugs that can treat malaria effectively in its early stage. Even better, travelers can take these drugs before visiting risky areas to help prevent the disease.

Chloroquine is still used in parts of the world where the parasites have not yet developed resistance to this drug. In other parts of the world, the U.S. Centers for Disease Control and Prevention (CDC) now recommends that travelers take a drug called mefloquine.

Other choices are available for people who cannot use mefloquine, such as those who are allergic to it. Drugs to prevent malaria are started a week

Global Warming and Mosquitoes

The *Anopheles* mosquitoes that carry the *Plasmodium* parasite do not like places where temperatures fall below 16°C (61°F).

Temperatures are increasing all over the world, however, because of increased heat-trapping gases such as carbon dioxide in the atmosphere. Climate change as a result of global warming is likely to increase the number of areas where *Anopheles* mosquitoes can live and spread malaria.

In the 1990s, unusually hot and humid weather was believed to be responsible for outbreaks of malaria in California, New Jersey, New York, Texas, Georgia, Florida, Michigan, Virginia, and Ontario, Canada.

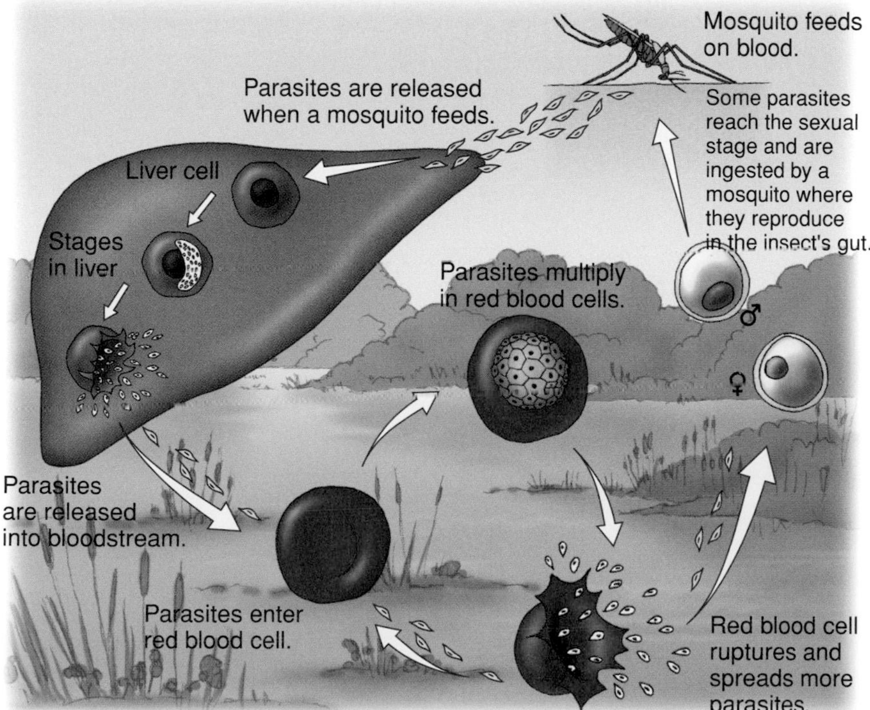

Cycle of malaria infection. *Plasmodium* parasites can reproduce inside the *Anopheles* mosquito and be transmitted to people through mosquito bites. In people, the parasites can multiply in the liver and in the red blood cells.

before visiting a risky area. They are taken weekly while there and for four weeks after returning. Travelers should take such drugs exactly as prescribed.

What Else Helps Prevent Malaria?

People also can take steps to protect themselves from the mosquitoes that carry malaria. To reduce bites, people should wear clothes that cover most of the body, apply insect repellent to clothes and uncovered skin, and stay in well-screened areas when possible. Since these mosquitoes typically bite at night, people should hang mosquito netting over their beds. For extra protection, these nets can be soaked in insect repellent, and people also can spray repellent in their bedrooms.

Resources

U.S. National Institute of Allergy and Infectious Diseases (NIAID), Office of Communications and Public Liaison, Building 31, Room 7A-50, 31 Center Drive, MSC 2520, Bethesda, MD 20892-2520. The website for this government institute, part of the U.S. National Institutes of Health, has information on malaria research.
Telephone 301-496-5717
http://www.niaid.nih.gov

Quick Take on Quinine

Long before doctors understood malaria, they knew they could treat it with quinine, a natural chemical compound. Quinine is found in the bark of the cinchona tree, which is native to Peru. For years, malaria patients put quinine into the body by chewing on cinchona bark. From about 1600 until the 1940s, this was the only way to treat malaria.

Today, scientists still are not sure how quinine kills the parasites that cause this disease. The best guess is that it keeps them from turning glucose, a sugar found in the human bloodstream, into energy. What is known is that soon after a person is given quinine, the parasites disappear from the bloodstream and the malaria symptoms go away.

The problem with quinine is that it can only kill malaria parasites that are in red blood cells. Once the patient stops taking quinine, parasites that have been lying in wait elsewhere in the body can become active, and the patient can become ill again.

To solve this problem, scientists searched for years for a way to make a drug in the laboratory that could kill malaria parasites in all cells of the body, not just red blood cells. In the 1940s, they developed several such drugs, among them chloroquine, chloroguanide, primaquine, and pyrimethamine.

Blackwater Fever

Blackwater fever is a rare but deadly form of malaria. In some cases, it can kill a person within a few hours of being infected.

In Blackwater fever, *Plasmodium falciparum* parasites cause the breakdown of a huge number of red blood cells at the same time. Hemoglobin from these broken-down cells is passed from the body mostly in the urine, so that the victim's urine turns such a deep red that it is almost black. This is how the disease got its name.

The effects of Blackwater fever come on so fast that drug therapy may not be effective. Instead, people with Blackwater fever are given exchange blood transfusions in an effort to get rid of infected red blood cells and replace them with healthy cells.

For the Record Books

Just how long can malaria last within the human body? In 1998, doctors reported the longest known malaria infection. It occurred in a 74-year-old Greek woman, who may have been infected as long as 70 years before. The parasite that caused her infection was *Plasmodium malariae*, which can lead to symptoms that reappear after being inactive for decades.

In countries where malaria is common, people often sleep under mosquito netting. © *Glenn M. Oliver/Visuals Unlimited.*

U.S. Centers for Disease Control and Prevention (CDC), 1600 Clifton Road N.E., Atlanta, GA 30333. The website for this government agency has information about malaria for travelers.
Telephone 800-311-3435
http://www.cdc.gov/travel/rx_malar.htm

World Health Organization, 525 23rd Street N.W., Washington, DC 20037. WHO posts a fact sheet about malaria at its website.
Telephone 202-974-3000
http://www.who.int/inf-fs/en/fact094.html

See also
Infection
Parasitic Diseases

Nobel Prize Winners

The symptoms of malaria had been known for millennia, but the cause of the disease was not well understood until the late nineteenth century. Previously, miasma (bad air) emanating from decaying organic matter had been thought to cause malaria.

In 1880, the French physician Charles Louis Alphonse Laveran (1845–1922) announced that he had discovered the malaria parasite *Plasmodium*, although his finding was regarded with skepticism by those who believed that bacteria caused malaria.

In 1897, the British physician Sir Ronald Ross (1857–1932) described the complete life cycle of *Plasmodium* and of the *Anopheles* mosquito that transmitted it to humans.

Both Laveran and Ross were awarded the Nobel Prize for medicine for their discoveries: Laveran in 1907 and Ross in 1902.

Manic Depression *See* Depressive Disorders

Marfan Syndrome

Marfan syndrome involves the body's connective tissue and is characterized by abnormalities in the skeleton, heart, and eyes. It is caused by an abnormal gene that usually is inherited. People with Marfan syndrome are generally taller than average, have little body fat, and have long, thin fingers.*

KEYWORDS
for searching the Internet and other reference sources

Circulation

Heredity

Myopia

Skeletal disorders

* **genes** are chemicals in the body that help determine a person's characteristics, such as hair or eye color. They are inherited from a person's parents and are contained in the chromosomes found in the cells of the body.

What Is Marfan Syndrome?

Marfan syndrome was first described in 1896 by the French physician Antonine Marfan. Some famous people of the past, such as Abraham Lincoln, who was very tall and lanky, and the brilliant violinist Niccolo Paganini, who had very long fingers, are believed by some to have had Marfan syndrome. Today, the disorder has received attention in the media largely as a result of health problems and deaths among very tall athletes, such as some basketball and volleyball players. Still, the disorder is rare.

Marfan syndrome affects only about 1 to 2 persons of every 10,000. In the United States, it has been estimated that 40,000 or more people have the disorder. It affects men and women in equal numbers, as well as people of all racial and ethnic groups. Marfan syndrome can affect the heart and aorta*, the eyes, and the skeleton.

* **aorta** is the main artery that carries blood from the heart to the body.

What Causes Marfan Syndrome?

For many years, it had been known that Marfan syndrome was inherited. It had been observed that if someone had the disorder, each of his or her children would have about a 50 percent chance of developing it as well. However, it was not known what gene or genes were responsible for the disorder.

Then, in the early 1990s, researchers found that the condition is caused by a single abnormal gene. This gene is involved in the production of a type of protein, called fibrillin, which gives connective tissue its strength. Connective tissue is the material that holds in place all the structures of the body. When the gene is defective, it causes critical changes in fibrillin that may weaken and loosen the connective tissue. This effect, in turn, causes the wide range of features, such as tall stature and loose joints, that are found in Marfan syndrome. It is not as yet known just how alterations in the genes produce these features.

Although anyone born to a parent with Marfan syndrome has a 50-50 chance of inheriting the disorder, an estimated 25 percent of people with Marfan syndrome do not have a parent who has it. This is because a person can have the defective gene owing to a spontaneous mutation, or change, in the normal gene.

What Are the Signs and Symptoms of Marfan Syndrome?

The characteristic signs and symptoms of Marfan syndrome usually do not begin to become apparent until about age 10. When they do emerge, they may involve any or all of three parts of the body: the skeleton, the circulatory system (heart and blood vessels), and the eyes.

The Skeleton A person who has Marfan syndrome usually (but not always) grows to be very tall and thin. The fingers also tend to be long and thin, or "spidery." The head is sometimes elongated too, and the chest may have a caved-in look. The joints tend to be supple and loose, and are prone to becoming dislocated. Sometimes there may be scoliosis (sko-lee-O-sis), a side-to-side curvature of the spine.

The Circulatory System The most serious features of Marfan syndrome involve the heart and aorta, the main artery that carries blood directly from the heart to the body. A characteristic defect in one of the valves of the heart (mitral valve) can cause irregular heart rhythm. Weakness in the aorta can allow it to widen, eventually leading to the development of an aneurysm (AN-yoo-riz-um), a weakness or bulge. If undiscovered or untreated, the weak spot in the aorta can rupture, causing severe internal hemorrhage and death, without warning.

The Eyes A common symptom of Marfan syndrome is myopia (my-O-pee-uh), or nearsightedness. In addition, in about half of individuals with the disorder, there is dislocation of the lens of the eye, which can make cataracts (clouding of the lens of the eye) more likely to develop.

How Is Marfan Syndrome Diagnosed?

Marfan syndrome can be difficult to diagnose. As yet no single laboratory test can identify it. Some people with the condition do not have all of its characteristic signs. Conversely, most people who are tall, lanky, and nearsighted do not have Marfan syndrome. (Again, the disorder is rare.)

Accurate diagnosis is made from a combination of one's family history and a complete physical examination that focuses on the skeleton, heart and aorta, and the eyes. An echocardiogram (ek-o-KAR-de-o-gram), a picture of the heart produced by using sound waves, can detect abnormalities in the heart and aorta. Eye doctors can look for possible lens dislocations.

The recent identification of the gene that causes Marfan syndrome, and of fibrillin as the component of connective tissue affected by the gene, will likely aid in future diagnosis.

How Is Marfan Syndrome Treated and Prevented?

Treatment and prevention of complications depend upon the individual symptoms of the person affected by the syndrome. Main aspects include annual echocardiograms to watch for enlargement of the aorta and to monitor heart function, and continuing eye examinations to detect lens dislocation. Medications called beta-blockers may be prescribed to lower blood pressure to help prevent aneurysms from developing in the aorta. Braces can be used to correct spinal curvature.

ABRAHAM LINCOLN

Abraham Lincoln had elongated fingers and was very tall (6 feet, 4 inches), which are attributes that are among the most visible and easily recognized signs of Marfan syndrome. For this reason, some experts believe that he may have had the disorder. However, because the syndrome was not medically known in his day, and because many others with these characteristics do not have it, no one knows for sure. Today, people growing up with Marfan syndrome might find encouragement in knowing that Abraham Lincoln may have had some of the difficulties that they have experienced, and that he overcame them.

In terms of lifestyle, strenuous sports may have to be avoided to reduce the risk of damage to the aorta. Genetic counseling is advisable for anyone thinking about having children, because of the risk that children will inherit the condition. Although there is no cure for Marfan syndrome, working closely with one's doctor in an ongoing monitoring and treatment program can greatly improve the outlook for long life.

Resources

The National Marfan Foundation website has links to support groups and other resources.
http://www.marfan.org/

The National Institutes of Health posts information about Marfan syndrome on its website.
http://www.nih.gov/niams/healthinfo/marfan.htm

See also
Aneurysm
Cataracts
Genetic Diseases
Nearsightedness
Scoliosis

Mastoiditis *See* Ear Infections

Measles

Measles, also called rubeola, is a highly contagious* disease of childhood that causes fever and a rash.

KEYWORDS
for searching the Internet and other reference sources

Infectious diseases

Vaccination

* **contagious** means transmittable from one person to another.

Daniel's Story

Daniel overheard his mother telling a neighbor that one of Daniel's classmates had come down with measles. The classmate, Bianca, had recently moved from Bangladesh to the United States with her family. "What's measles, Mom?" Daniel asked later. His mother explained that measles is sort of like having the flu and a bad rash at the same time. She said that a long time ago, everybody used to get the disease, and sometimes people died of it. But now most children get shots to protect them against measles, and it is very rare. What Daniel's mother told him is right. Measles is rare in the United States and other wealthier countries that can provide immunization for children. But in poorer countries, like Bangladesh, where many children do not get the shots, measles is still a disease that people fear.

What Is Measles?

Measles is caused by a virus that is spread directly from person to person. Animals do not spread measles. Once the virus finds its way into a person's body, it attaches to the lining of the respiratory tract, which consists of organs like the nose and throat that carry air into the lungs. In the respiratory tract, measles causes cough and a runny nose. It also spreads to other parts of the body. As the body senses the invading virus, it responds by raising body temperature, causing a fever. Measles also causes a sore throat, tiny white blisters with red rings around them that appear inside the cheeks, and a red skin rash. A person who has measles may find that his eyes become red and very sensitive to light, and the rash may become slightly itchy.

Is Measles Serious?

Measles can make a person feel very sick, and it can become serious and involve a number of the body's organ systems. When that happens, we say a person has developed complications. The complications of measles

Measles Throughout History

Because measles needs people to spread, it probably first became a menace with the building of large cities. It was already established around the Mediterranean during the time of the Roman republic. European explorers brought measles to the Americas about 500 years ago, and along with smallpox and other infectious diseases, measles was responsible for destroying a large part of the Native American population. Before a vaccine was developed for measles in 1963, between 7 and 8 million children around the world died of the disease every year. It still kills around 1 million children annually, mostly in Africa. For this reason, the World Health Organization has called for a worldwide effort to eradicate measles by 2005.

▲

Teenaged girls line up for inoculation against measles. © *Zeva Oelbaum/Peter Arnold, Inc.*

include ear infections and pneumonia (noo-MO-nya), an inflammation of the lungs. Inflammation of the brain, called encephalitis (en-sef-a-LY-tis), is another complication that can be life-threatening. Measles is most dangerous to infants, very young children, pregnant women, and people whose immune systems are weak, for example, from malnutrition or from other diseases.

How Does a Person Get Measles?

Measles is probably one of the most infectious* diseases known. It occurs mostly among children, and mostly in crowded areas, like cities. A person catches measles by breathing in infected droplets that someone with the disease has coughed or sneezed out. It is possible to catch measles simply by being in a room where another person who has the disease has been. For this reason, measles often spreads quickly in a family or in a classroom. People who have measles are infectious from about 5 days after they have been exposed to the virus until 5 days after the rash appears.

* **infectious** means able to spread to others.

Recognizing Measles

Daniel's classmate Bianca began to feel sick in school. When her mother came to pick her up, Bianca was hot and flushed. Her throat felt scratchy, her nose was running, and when she and her mother went out to the car, the light hurt her eyes. Back at home, Bianca's mother called the doctor. The nurse told her that Bianca probably had measles and that she should stay at home to avoid spreading the disease. Sure enough, a day or so later, a blotchy red rash appeared on Bianca's forehead and behind her ears and gradually spread from her head to her toes. Bianca stayed in bed, feeling sick and too uncomfortable to read or to watch television. Four or five days later, her temperature was back to normal, and the red spots were fading. She was herself again.

It used to be easy for the doctor to tell that a person had measles, but today fewer doctors have actually seen a case of measles since the widespread use of the measles vaccine. If there is any doubt about what is making a child sick, there are several tests that a doctor can order to be sure that a person has measles.

What Is the Treatment for Measles?

Most of the time measles gets better by itself, and there is no treatment for it. Drinking a lot of water and fruit juice will help to replace fluids lost through the skin due to the high fever. Complications like ear infections and pneumonia usually are treated with antibiotics, which are medications that destroy the bacteria that cause these infections. Once measles has gone away, people can do all the things they did before they got sick. Children can usually go back to school about 5 days after the rash and fever are gone.

What Is the Best Way of Preventing Measles?

The best way to prevent measles is to be vaccinated against it. Vaccination is a way of introducing the body to a harmless form of a disease-causing organism, so that when the body encounters the organism in the future, it will be able to recognize it and fight against it. Once people have had measles, they will never get it again. But because complications can occur, it is safer to be vaccinated than to catch measles. Measles vaccine is an injection that is usually given twice: first to infants between 12 and 15 months of age, and again before the child starts kindergarten or the seventh grade. People who have not been vaccinated and know they have been around someone who has measles can be given a shot of immune globulin, which contains antibodies from the blood of other humans that can help fight infection. This treatment also helps to protect people who cannot be vaccinated, for example, pregnant women, or people who have serious allergies to eggs, which are used to produce the vaccine. Doctors and other health professionals can answer questions about who should or should not be vaccinated.

Resources

The U.S. Centers for Disease Control and Prevention (CDC), located in Atlanta, Georgia, posts a fact sheet about measles at its website.
http://cdc.gov/nip/vaccine/nip-mmr.htm

The World Health Organization (WHO) posts a fact sheet about measles at its website.
http://www.who.int/gpv-dvacc/research/virus/htm

KidsHealth.org posts a tutorial called Childhood Infections: Rubeola (Measles). Helpful information for parents about measles from The Nemours Foundation.
http://kidshealth.org/parent/common/measles.html

▶ *See also*
Ear Infections
Encephalitis
German Measles (Rubella)
Pneumonia
Viral Infections

Melanoma *See* Skin Cancer

Meningitis

Meningitis is an inflammation of the membranes that surround the brain and the spinal cord.

KEYWORDS
for searching the Internet and other reference sources

Cerebellum
Enteroviruses
Infection
Inflammation
Meninges
Vaccination

What Is Meningitis?

In Greek, the word for membrane is "menix." This is the source of the word "meningitis," which means an inflammation of the membranes (the thin covering layers) that surround the brain and the spinal cord. These membranes are known as the meninges, and inflammation (swelling) is the body's reaction to infection or injury.

The most common form of the disease is viral meningitis. In 9 out of 10 cases, the cause of viral meningitis is one of a large group of viruses known as enteroviruses. These viruses infect the digestive tract, but they easily spread to other parts of the body.

The second most common form of the disease is bacterial meningitis, which is caused by bacteria. Before the 1990s, *Haemophilus influenzae* type b (Hib) was the leading cause of bacterial meningitis. However, new vaccines for children have reduced this problem. Today, *Streptococcus pneumoniae* and *Neisseria meningitidis* are the chief causes.

Meningitis also can be caused by fungi such as *Cryptococcus neoformans*, or things other than infection, such as a drug reaction or cancer involving the meninges.

It is important to know the cause of meningitis, because this determines how severe the disease may be and its treatment. Viral meningitis usually is less severe than bacterial meningitis. Most people recover in 7 to 10 days. In contrast, bacterial meningitis can be very serious. If not treated promptly, it can lead to permanent hearing loss, brain damage, learning disorders, or even death.

How Do People Catch Meningitis?

Some, but not all, types of viral and bacterial meningitis are contagious. People infected by a virus that causes meningitis may not always develop the disease, but they can pass on the virus to others, who may get meningitis. Fewer than 1 in 1,000 people infected with viruses that cause meningitis actually get meningitis. Most infected people do not get sick, or they become only mildly ill with a cold, rash, or low-grade fever.

Enteroviruses, the most common cause of viral meningitis, are very common in the summer and early fall, and many people catch them. Enteroviruses usually are spread through contact with saliva or mucus. This typically happens when people are exposed to the virus on the hands of, or on objects touched by, people with enteroviruses, then rub their own eyes, nose, or mouth.

The virus also is found in the stool (bowel movement) of people who are infected with enteroviruses. It is spread this way mainly by young children who are not toilet trained, or by adults who change the diapers of infected babies. Good hand washing (thoroughly and often) is important to prevent the spread of the viruses that cause meningitis.

Some forms of bacterial meningitis are contagious. The bacteria are spread through coughing, kissing, and other breath and throat secretions. They are not spread by casual contact. However, people who are in close contact with an infected person may catch the infection. This includes those who live in the same house as the infected person or children who go to the same daycare center as infected children. It also may include girlfriends or boyfriends who kiss infected people. Outbreaks may occur in places like dormitories, military barracks, and prisons.

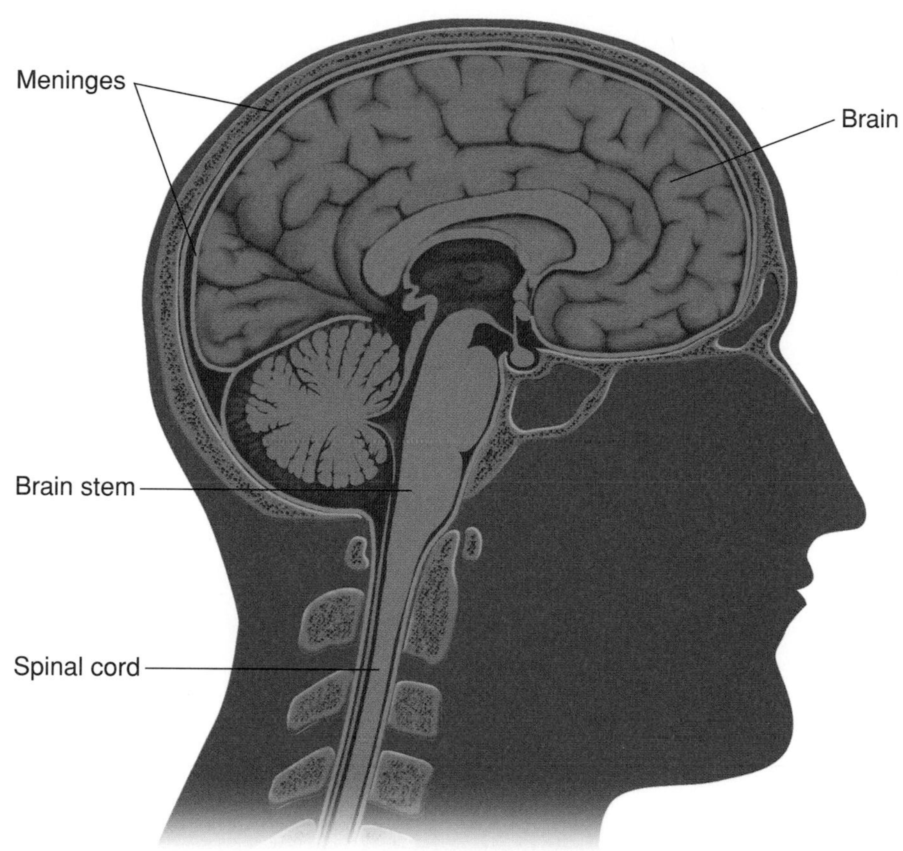

Anatomy of the brain. In meningitis, the meninges that line the brain become swollen and inflamed.

Most cases of both viral and bacterial meningitis occur in babies and children under the age of five. Most cases of meningitis caused by a fungus occur in people with an immune system* that has been weakened by other diseases (such as AIDS) or by taking certain medications.

* **immune system** is the system that defends the body against disease.

What Are the Symptoms of Meningitis?

The symptoms of meningitis vary from person to person but common symptoms in people over the age of two are:

- fever
- severe headache
- stiff neck
- eyes that are sensitive to bright light
- sleepiness
- confusion
- nausea
- vomiting

In babies, the classic symptoms of fever, headache, and a stiff neck may not be present, or they may be hard for other people to notice. Possible symptoms in babies include fever (sometimes), crankiness, lack of activity, vomiting, refusing to eat, and being hard to wake up. As meningitis gets worse, people of any age may have seizures. In severe cases, the disease can lead to coma or even death.

The symptoms of both viral and bacterial meningitis may develop over a period of several hours or several days. With bacterial meningitis, adults may get very sick within 24 hours and children even sooner. In contrast, meningitis caused by a fungus, cancer, or other noninfectious disease may take weeks to develop. A few types of bacteria and viruses also lead to slow-developing meningitis. These include the bacteria that cause tuberculosis, Lyme disease, and syphilis, and the virus that causes AIDS.

How Is Meningitis Diagnosed and Treated?

Diagnosis The symptoms of viral and bacterial meningitis often are the same. Therefore, it is important to see a doctor right away if these symptoms appear, because early diagnosis and treatment are critical for bacterial meningitis. A diagnosis usually is made by testing a sample of the fluid that surrounds the spinal cord. This sample is obtained by a spinal tap, a procedure in which a thin hollow needle is inserted into an area of the spine at the lower back and a small amount of fluid is withdrawn. This fluid is tested in a laboratory for signs of meningitis and to identify which type of bacteria, if any, is causing the disease, because this affects the kind of antibiotics that will be used to treat it.

Treatment The treatment for meningitis depends on the cause. People with most types of viral meningitis usually get better on their own. To help them feel better, doctors may advise them to rest and to take non-prescription medication to relieve headache and fever. People with bacterial meningitis can be treated with a number of effective antibiotics, depending on the type of bacteria involved. People with meningitis caused by a fungus can be treated with antifungal medication. For the best results, treatment should be started as early as possible.

How Can Meningitis Be Prevented?

It is difficult to avoid the enteroviruses that cause most cases of viral meningitis. However, it helps to wash the hands thoroughly and often. People who are close to others who have bacterial meningitis caused by *N. meningitidis* may receive antibiotics to prevent spread of the disease.

Vaccination There are vaccines against several bacteria that cause bacterial meningitis, including *Haemophilis influenzae* type b (Hib), some strains of *Neisseria meningitidis*, and many types of *Streptococcus pneumoniae*.

The vaccines against Hib are safe and very effective. It is now standard for all children in the United States to receive Hib vaccine. The vaccine against *N. meningitidis* is not routinely given as part of childhood immunizations. However, it is sometimes used to control small outbreaks of meningitis in the United States in schools, prisons, and other closed settings.

The U.S. and the World

- There are about 500,000 cases of meningococcal meningitis (*N. meningitidis*) worldwide each year.
- There are about 50,000 deaths worldwide each year.
- The largest outbreaks occur in Africa south of the Sahara desert during the dry season.
- The World Health Organization recommends that travelers to countries affected by meningitis outbreaks get the *N. meningitidis* vaccine.

Large outbreaks of the disease occur in some countries, and travelers to these areas may need to get the *N. meningitidis* vaccine as well. The vaccine against many types of *S. pneumoniae* helps prevent not only meningitis but also pneumonia caused by these bacteria. The vaccine is recommended for everyone over the age of 65 and for younger people with certain ongoing medical problems.

Resources

U.S. Centers for Disease Control and Prevention (CDC), 1600 Clifton Road N.E., Atlanta, GA 30333. CDC posts fact sheets about bacterial meningitis and about viral (aseptic) meningitis at its website.
Telephone 800-311-3435
http://www.cdc.gov/health/diseases.htm

World Health Organization (WHO), Avenue Appia 20, 1211 Geneva 27, Switzerland. WHO posts fact sheets about meningitis and other communicable/infectious diseases worldwide at its website.
http://www.who.org/home/map_ht.html

See also
AIDS and HIV
Bacterial Infections
Cancer
Fever
Fungal Infections
Immunodeficiency
Infection
Lyme Disease
Pneumonia
Seizures
Syphilis
Tuberculosis
Viral Infections

Menstrual Disorders

Menstrual (MEN-stroo-al) disorders result in abnormal menstrual periods. Usually, these disorders occur when the hormones* that control menstruation (men-stroo-AY-shun) are out of balance, but in some cases another medical problem is the cause. Menstrual disorders include pain during periods, changes in the length of the menstrual cycle, and heavy, prolonged, or too frequent periods.

KEYWORDS
for searching the Internet and other reference sources

Abnormal uterine bleeding
Amenorrhea
Gynecology
Ovulation
Reproductive medicine
Uterus

Kim's Story

Kim plays soccer in the fall, plays basketball in the winter, and does gymnastics in the spring and summer. Her friends call her the "lean, mean, fighting machine," because she is almost all muscle and no fat. Kim is proud of her athletic ability, but she wishes her body had a few more curves. She feels self-conscious because she just turned 16 and still has not gotten her period, whereas all of her friends got their first period years ago. Kim is embarrassed and a little bit scared, because her mother made Kim an appointment with a gynecologist* to find out why Kim has not had her period.

The doctor examined Kim and asked her a number of family history and health questions, including questions about sports and how long she has been playing. She told Kim that there was probably nothing wrong with her; some girls just get their period later than others. To be sure, the

* **hormones** are chemicals that are produced by different glands in the body. Hormones are like the body's ambassadors: they are created in one place but are sent through the body to have specific regulatory effects in different places.

* **gynecologist** (gy-ne-KOL-o-jist) is a doctor who specializes in the reproductive system of women.

doctor ordered some blood tests that would show if Kim had a medical condition affecting her menstrual cycle. The tests showed that there was nothing wrong, and three months later Kim got her first period.

What Is Menstruation?

Menstruation, also called menses (MEN-seez), is a normal part of being a healthy female of reproductive age. During menstruation, the lining of a woman's uterus (YOO-ter-us) is shed, resulting in blood and tissue being expelled from the body.

Menstruation is just one part of a cycle that the female reproductive system undergoes each month when a woman is not pregnant. The female reproductive system, located in the abdomen*, consists of two ovaries (O-va-reez), two fallopian (fa-LO-pe-an) tubes, and the uterus, cervix (SER-viks), and vagina (va-JY-na). The almond-sized ovaries contain the female reproductive cells, or eggs. The ovaries also make chemicals called hormones that act as messengers throughout the body. Eggs are carried through the fallopian tubes to the uterus, which is a pear-shaped, muscular organ in which a fertilized egg can grow and develop into a baby. If the egg is not fertilized, the lining of the uterus, which had thickened in preparation for pregnancy, is shed. The blood and tissue fragments exit the uterus through its opening, the cervix, and travel through the vagina to the outside of the body.

* **abdomen** (AB-do-men), commonly called the belly, is the portion of the body between the chest and the pelvis.

The menstrual cycle is controlled by hormones that are in a delicate balance. The hormones interact with each other and with the reproductive organs to either take care of a fertilized egg that will become a baby or cause menstruation to occur.

The hormonal balancing act: a typical menstrual cycle The following are the major events in a typical menstrual cycle.

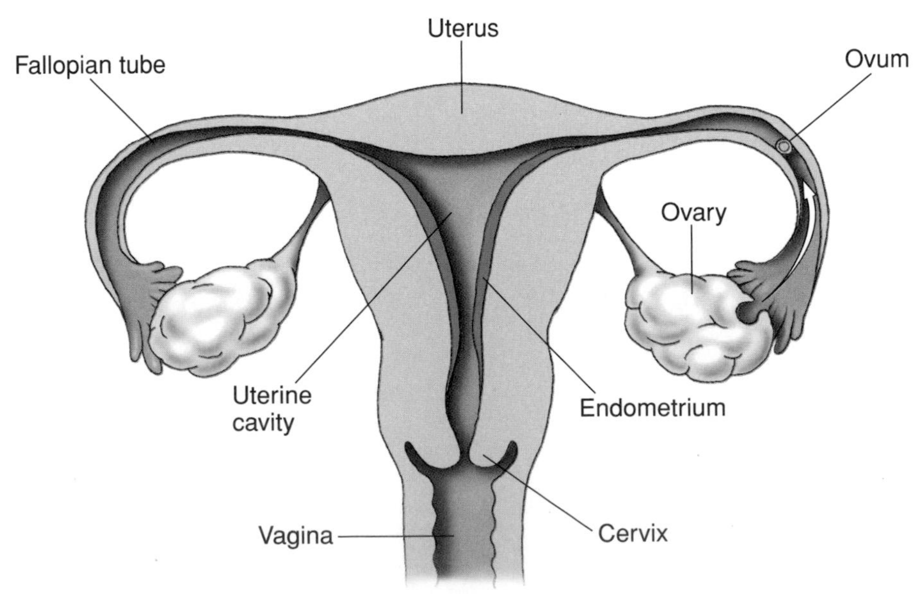

The anatomy of the female reproductive system, including an unfertilized egg in one of the fallopian tubes. ▶

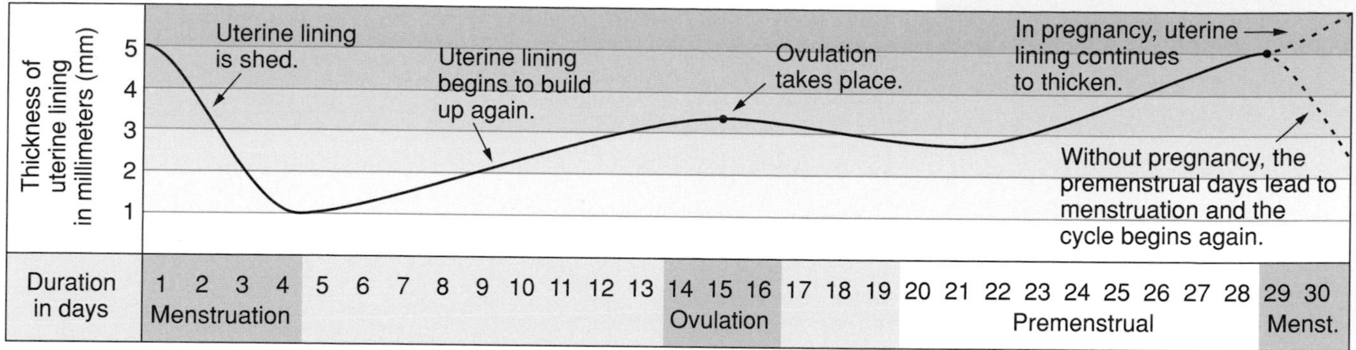

The 28-day menstrual cycle, showing changes in the thickness of the endometrial lining.

- Day 0 to 5: At the very beginning of the cycle, the levels of the hormones estrogen (ES-tro-jen) and progesterone (pro-JES-te-rone) in the body are low. Menstruation begins, and blood and tissue are expelled from the uterus. The ovaries begin making more estrogen, and the lining of uterus, called the endometrium (en-do-ME-tree-um), begins to thicken. Meanwhile, an egg in one of the ovaries begins to mature in a small sac of tissue.
- Day 14: The egg leaves the ovary (which is called ovulation [ov-yoo-LAY-shun]) and travels through the fallopian tube to the uterus. Ovulation is controlled by gonadotropin (gon-a-do-TRO-pin)-releasing hormone (GnRH), follicle (FOL-i-kul)-stimulating hormone (FSH), and luteinizing (LOO-tee-in-eye-zing) hormone (LH). The empty sac in the ovary that once held the egg is now called the corpus luteum (KOR-pus LOO-te-um), and it makes the hormone progesterone. The combination of estrogen and progesterone cause the endometrium to keep growing thicker. A woman can get pregnant just before, during, or right after ovulation. If the egg is fertilized, the thickened endometrium is ready to nourish the developing embryo*.
- Day 17 to 27: If the egg is not fertilized, hormone levels decrease.
- Day 28: The endometrium begins to break down, and menstruation begins. The hormone prostaglandin (pros-ta-GLAN-din) is produced by cells in the uterine lining. Prostaglandin causes blood vessels to narrow, which slows the supply of oxygen to the uterus and causes the muscles of the uterus to contract. This process helps to expel the blood and tissue of the uterine lining.

* **embryo** (EM-bree-o) in humans, an embryo is the developing organism from the end of the second week after fertilization to the end of the eighth week.

What Is Normal?

In a woman who is not pregnant, the menstrual cycle occurs approximately every 28 days. However, the length of the cycle can vary from 21 to 35 days in normal healthy girls and women. Cycle length is calculated from the first day of one period to the first day of the next. Usually, bleeding lasts for a period of several days, hence the term menstrual "period." A woman wears a pad in her panties or a tampon inserted into the vagina to absorb the blood.

The first time a young girl gets her period is called menarche (MEN-ar-kee) and can be a scary thing or a much anticipated event, depending on the girl. In the United States, the average age when menarche occurs is 12, but some girls start menstruating at 10, others at 16. After menarche, a woman usually will get her period for 30 to 40 more years, until she goes through menopause*.

* **menopause** (MEN-o-pawz) is the time in a woman's life when she stops having periods and can no longer become pregnant.

There is huge variation among women in the length and duration of their menstrual cycle and whether they bleed a lot or a little. Some women have a period every 23 days, others every 35. Some periods last 3 days, whereas others last 7. And some women use 3 tampons or pads a day, whereas others need 10. Because of this wide range of "normal," determining if a woman has a menstrual disorder can be difficult. It requires that a woman knows her own body and what is normal for her.

What Are Menstrual Disorders?

Menstrual disorders occur when something goes wrong with the normal monthly menstrual cycle. There are many different types of disorders. Usually, they occur when the hormones controlling menstruation are out of balance for some reason. However, menstrual disorders can be caused by underlying medical conditions. A woman who experiences changes in her menstrual cycle, especially if these changes include heavy bleeding or cause problems with daily living, should see her doctor right away.

Disorders in menstrual cycle length Amenorrhea (a-men-o-REE-a) means "no menstrual periods." Primary amenorrhea means not ever having a first period. Secondary amenorrhea is when a women or girl stops getting her monthly period.

A related problem is oligomenorrhea (OL-i-go-men-o-REE-a), which means having menstrual periods that are more than 35 days apart. Once doctors diagnose problems with menstrual cycle length, they then try to find out what is causing it.

Shelly, a 25-year-old woman who usually gets her periods like clockwork, stopped having her period for 3 months. The first thing her doctor ordered was a pregnancy test; it was a surprise to Shelly and her husband, but she was pregnant. Pregnancy is the most common cause of amenorrhea in women in their reproductive years.

When Anne turned 48, the amount of time between her periods started getting longer and longer. When she did not get her period for 4 months, she went to see her doctor. The doctor examined Anne and did some tests; Anne's amenorrhea was caused by approaching menopause. Menopause is another perfectly natural cause of amenorrhea.

Kim provides a good example of primary amenorrhea, which refers to a girl not getting her first period by the time she is 16. This condition may be caused by a hormonal imbalance or a developmental problem. Young female athletes often experience primary or secondary amenorrhea or both; strenuous exercise seems to lower estrogen levels, thus causing periods to stop. Altered hormone levels can cause anovulation (an-ov-yoo-LAY-shun), when ovulation does not occur, which in turn often causes amenorrhea. Hormones are affected when a woman exercises too much, loses or gains a lot of weight, is stressed, is breast-feeding a baby, or has an eating disorder; all these things can lead to amenorrhea.

Medical problems, such as cysts (fluid-filled sacs) in the ovaries, abnormal growths or tumors* in the reproductive organs, anorexia nervosa*, and diabetes*, can also cause amenorrhea or oligomenorrhea.

Bleeding disorders Sometimes women have menstrual disorders in which they bleed too much, too often, or for too long. For example, Sally has menorrhagia (men-o-RA-jah), which means very heavy periods, and the bleeding goes on for almost 12 days. Sally will not even go to work on the first day of her period; she goes through a tampon and a pad every hour for the first five hours, and every month she ends up with bloodstains on her pants. Barb, on the other hand, gets her period every 19 days, which is far too often for her liking; this condition is called polymenorrhea (pol-ee-men-o-REE-a). These conditions are classified as abnormal uterine bleeding, or AUB. AUB also includes bleeding, or spotting, between periods and bleeding after menopause.

Eighty percent of women with menorrhagia have it because of a hormone imbalance or because they have fibroids (FY-broidz), which are abnormal growths in the uterus. Women with endometrial (en-do-ME-tree-al) cancer, infections of the vagina or cervix, small growths on the cervix or uterine wall (polyps), thyroid* conditions, or diseases of the liver*, kidney*, or bloodstream often experience menorrhagia.

Menorraghia and other bleeding disorders that are caused by hormonal imbalances also are called dysfunctional uterine bleeding (DUB). Often, DUB occurs because of anovulation or when estrogen and progesterone are out of balance. Without proper hormonal cues, normal monthly shedding of the uterine lining does not occur, and the endometrium keeps building up. The abnormally thick endometrium eventually starts to break down and results in heavy and prolonged bleeding. DUB is common in teenagers, whose hormones have not yet been fine-tuned and who often do not ovulate regularly. Anovulation is also common in women about to go through menopause.

Painful periods Linda's teacher was really beginning to get annoyed with her by midsemester. For four months in a row, Linda went home sick each time she started her period. Linda was not faking it; she went home to bed with a backache and severe cramps, only getting up when she thought she might have to throw up.

Linda suffers from dysmenorrhea (dis-men-o-REE-a), or painful periods. Almost every woman has this condition at some time in her life. The symptoms of dysmenorrhea range from mild, uncomfortable cramps to abdominal pain, a sore back, nausea, and vomiting. Linda has primary dysmenorrhea, which means painful periods with no underlying medical disease. This type of dysmenorrhea is very common, especially among teenagers. The symptoms are caused by the hormone prostaglandin, which is released by the cells that are being shed from the uterus.

***tumors** (TOO-morz) usually refer to abnormal growths of body tissue that have no known cause. Tumors may or may not be cancerous.

***anorexia nervosa** (an-o-REK-se-a ner-VO-sa) is an emotional disorder characterized by dread of gaining weight, leading to self-starvation and dangerous loss of weight and malnutrition.

***diabetes** (dy-a-BEE-teez) is an impaired ability to break down carbohydrates, proteins, and fats because the body does not produce enough insulin or cannot use the insulin it makes.

***thyroid** (THY-roid) is a gland located in the lower part of the front of the neck. The thyroid produces hormones that regulate the body's metabolism (me-TAB-o-liz-um), the processes the body uses to convert food into energy.

***liver** is a large organ located in the upper abdomen that has many functions, including storage and filtration of blood, secretion of bile, and participation in various metabolic (met-a-BOLL-ik) processes.

***kidney** is one of the pair of organs that filter blood and get rid of waste products and excess water as urine.

Secondary dysmenorrhea is caused by medical conditions such as polyps*, fibroids, and narrowing of the cervix. One common cause is endometriosis (en-do-me-tree-O-sis). Endometriosis is a condition in which uterine tissue grows outside the uterus, and it affects both young and older women. Even though fragments of endometrial tissue, also called implants, are not in the uterus, they still respond to hormones just as the normal endometrial tissue does. Therefore, in response to estrogen and progesterone, the implants grow, break down, and bleed. Because there is no opening through which the blood can leave the body, the blood irritates the body, which can be very painful. Sometimes, the implants keep growing and form scar tissue or they act as an adhesive and stick organs together. Endometriosis can make it impossible for a woman to get pregnant, because implants may block the fallopian tubes or prevent the eggs from leaving the ovary. Endometriosis is found in 10 to 15 percent of 25- to 33-year-old women who actively are menstruating.

* **polyps** (POL-ips) are protruding growths from a mucous (MU-kus) membrane.

Another type of pain that accompanies menstrual periods is caused by infections of the endometrium. This pain, seen in pelvic inflammatory disease (PID), needs rapid diagnosis and medical treatment.

Premenstrual syndrome Every month, Stacy can tell her period is a week away by a trio of signs: her skin breaks out, her lower back begins to ache, and her breasts feel sore. Her friend Sonya experiences a different set of symptoms: she feels bloated, is incredibly tired, has bad headaches, and is depressed and grumpy.

Stacy and Sonya have premenstrual syndrome, or PMS, which is a set of symptoms that includes both physical and emotional complaints. Most women with PMS have a set of symptoms that occur each month at the same time. Fortunately, the symptoms disappear when the period begins.

PMS is often referred to as a "phenomenon," which indicates that it is still a controversial topic. Part of the problem with PMS is that no one knows for sure what causes it, but most scientists agree that it is linked to hormones. PMS symptoms appear during the second half of the menstrual cycle, after ovulation has taken place, when progesterone levels are highest.

Is There Such a Thing as Too Much Exercise?

How much estrogen a woman's body produces appears to be linked to her level of body fat. Young gymnasts, ballerinas, and other athletes who regularly take part in strenuous exercise typically do not have much body fat and do not make much estrogen. If their hormone production is low enough, they might not get their first period until they are 16 or 17. Other young athletes who have normal periods for a while may develop amenorrhea when they resume strenuous exercise.

Because bone mass is linked to the level of estrogen in the body, some scientists suggest that even a few years of amenorrhea, especially during a girl's teens, can have lasting effects on bone formation or contribute to excessive bone loss. Young athletes should see their doctor if they experience a menstrual disorder; diet and hormone therapy may fix the immediate problem and have a positive effect long into the future.

Treatment for Menstrual Disorders

To determine if a woman has a menstrual disorder, doctors will take a medical history and ask questions about her menstrual cycle. Doctors need to know what has changed from past normal periods. A pelvic exam may also be necessary; doctors will examine the reproductive organs by feeling and pushing on the uterus through the abdomen and by feeling the vagina, cervix, uterus, fallopian tubes, and ovaries through the vaginal opening. This procedure is slightly uncomfortable but not painful, and it takes only 5 to 10 minutes. Blood tests also may be used to measure the levels of hormones in the body. In rare cases, a doctor will use ultrasonography (ul-tra-so-NOG-ra-fee), where sound waves are used to produce images of organs inside the body, and hysteroscopy (his-ter-OS-ko-pee) or laparascopy (lap-a-ROS-ko-pee), where instruments are inserted into the body through a small incision to take a direct look at the internal organs, to find out what is happening in a woman's body.

For all menstrual disorders, treatment depends on the underlying cause. Therefore, it is important to see a doctor if anything seems to be wrong.

Hormonal imbalance When a hormonal imbalance is the cause of a menstrual disorder, hormone therapy often helps menstrual cycles return to normal. Hormone therapy includes taking birth control pills, mixtures of estrogen and progesterone, or just progesterone.

Dysmenorrhea and PMS Products such as ibuprofen (i-bu-PRO-fen) and naproxen (na-PROKS-en) suppress prostaglandin and are helpful in treating dysmenorrhea. Over-the-counter products to relieve menstrual cramps and bloating help some women with PMS. Birth control pills also reduce painful periods in some women, as does exercise.

Endometriosis and other conditions For some women with endometriosis, the doctor can prescribe medicines to relieve symptoms. However, for women with severe endometriosis, surgery to remove implants may be necessary.

Severe menstrual disorders can be eliminated by destroying the endometrial tissue in the uterus or by hysterectomy (his-ter-EK-to-mee), which is the removal of uterus (and sometimes also the ovaries). This treatment is better for older women who are past childbearing years. This is not a treatment for younger women who want to have children.

For medical conditions, such as fibroids, polyps, or cancer, surgery and other treatments may be needed to correct the problem.

Resources

Books

Gillooly, Jessica B. *Before She Gets Her Period: Talking with Your Daughter about Menstruation.* Memphis, TN: Perspective Publishing, 1998.

Gravelle, Karen, Jennifer Gravelle, and Debbie Palen. *The Period Book: Everything You Don't Want to Ask (but Need to Know).* New York: Walker and Co., 1996.

Organizations

American Society for Reproductive Medicine, 1209 Montgomery Highway, Birmingham, AL 35216-2809.
Telephone 205-978-5000
http://www.asrm.org

The U.S. Food and Drug Administration has several websites that present information on menstruation.
http://www.fda.gov/opacom/7teens.html
http://www.fda.gov/opacom/catalog/ots_mens.html

Literal Meanings of Menstrual Terms

Many words used to describe menstruation and menstrual disorders come from Latin ("mensis" means month) and Greek. For example:

- Menarche, a girl's first period, comes from "mensis" + "archaios" (from the beginning).
- Menopause, or the end of monthly periods, comes from "mensis" + "pausis" (to cease).
- Menorrhagia means heavy or prolonged bleeding and is derived from "mensis" + "rhegynein" (to burst forth).
- Menorrhea comes from "mensis" + "rhoia" (to flow) and means the normal flow of blood and tissue from the uterus during a menstrual period (also called menses and menstruation).
- The prefix "a" means not; amenorrhea is the cessation of menses. The prefix "dys" means bad or painful, and dysmenorrhea means painful periods. The prefix "oligo" means little or few; oligomenorrhea is having infrequent periods. "Poly" means many, and so polymenorrhea means periods that come too frequently.

▶ *See also*
Endometriosis
Infertility
Pelvic Inflammatory Disease (PID)
Pregnancy, Complications of

Mental Disorders

Mental disorders cover a wide range of conditions that lead to abnormalities of thought, feeling, and behavior. These abnormalities cause distress or impair a person's ability to function.

KEYWORDS
for searching the Internet and other reference sources

Behavior

Delirium

Dementia

Psychiatry

Psychology

Psychosis

Three Stories

A man in a tattered coat stands on the street corner, yelling at no one in particular. Although the man appears to think that he is arguing logically, his words are jumbled together and make little sense.

In a nearby apartment, a young woman cannot sleep until she is sure that her kitchen stove is turned off. She leaves her bed, checks the stove, and then returns to bed. But can she be sure? Once more, she goes to check the stove, a process she will repeat many times throughout the night.

In a suburban home, an 11-year-old boy wakes in a panic. He dashes to his parents' bedroom to make sure that they are safe, gripped by fear that they have been in mortal danger while he slept.

What do these three people have in common? While their thoughts, feelings, and behaviors are very different, each has a mental disorder that requires careful diagnosis and can be helped with proper treatment.

What Are Mental Disorders and What Causes Them?

Mental disorders is a broad term that includes a wide range of psychological* and behavioral* conditions. Among the conditions included are everything

* **psychological** means related to the way a person thinks and feels.

* **behavioral** means related to the way a person acts.

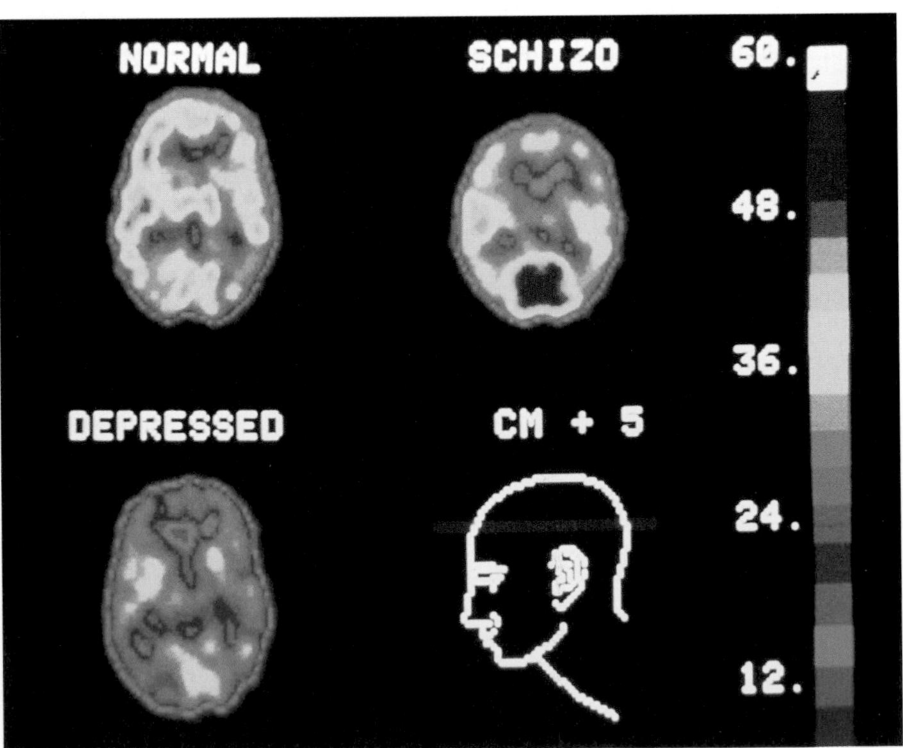

Doctors and researchers use computer-generated positron emission tomography (PET) scans to study how the brain functions. These PET scans compare brain activity in a healthy person (top left), a person with schizophrenia (top right), and a person with depression (lower left). The red line through the diagram at the lower right shows the area of the brain that is depicted in the scans. *NIH/Science Source, Photo Researchers, Inc.*

from disorders first diagnosed during childhood or adolescence, such as the separation anxiety experienced by the 11-year-old above, to disorders often associated with old age or with medical illnesses, including Alzheimer's disease*, AIDS*, Huntington's disease*, and strokes*.

Many mental disorders have been found to stem from changes in the structure or function of the brain. Some disorders also may be related to drug or alcohol abuse. Although the exact cause of most mental disorders is not known, some of these conditions tend to run in families, indicating that inherited or genetic factors may play a role.

Among the more common mental disorders are schizophrenia, depressive disorders, anxiety disorders, eating disorders, and sleep disorders. Phobias, such as claustrophobia (fear of closed spaces) and social phobias (fear of embarrassment in social situations), also are classified as mental disorders.

* **Alzheimer's disease** leads to changes in personality and to a gradually worsening loss of mental abilities, including memory, judgment, and abstract thinking.

* **AIDS** (acquired immune deficiency syndrome) is a viral infection that can lead to damage in many parts of the body, including the brain and nervous system.

* **Huntington's disease** is a genetic condition that leads to involuntary twitching or jerking of the muscles in the face, arms, and legs along with a gradual loss of mental abilities.

* **strokes** are events that occur when a blood vessel bringing oxygen and nutrients to the brain bursts or becomes clogged by a blood clot or other particle. As a result, nerve cells in the affected area of the brain cannot function properly.

Behaviors and Disorders

Psychologists and psychiatrists use many different terms to describe mental disorders and their symptoms:

- **Anxiety disorders** (ang-ZY-e-tee dis-OR-derz) are mental disorders characterized by extreme, unpleasant, and unwanted feelings of apprehension or fear, sometimes accompanied by physical symptoms.
- **Delirium** (de-LEER-e-um) is a mental state in which a person suddenly becomes confused and disoriented, perhaps not knowing what day it is or not recognizing a friend. It often accompanies a physical illness and usually goes away when the illness gets better.
- **Delusions** are false beliefs that a person clings to, despite their lack of basis in reality. For example, delusion of grandeur refers to the false belief that a person has great importance, power, wealth, intelligence, or ability.
- **Dementia** (de-MEN-sha) is a gradually worsening loss of mental abilities, including memory, judgment, and abstract thinking. It is more common in older people.
- **Depressive disorders** (de-PRES-iv dis-OR-derz) are mental disorders associated with feelings of sadness, hopelessness, and loss of self-esteem and enjoyment. Significant levels of depression impair a person's feelings, thoughts, and behaviors.
- **Eating disorders** are mental disorders that lead people to starve themselves or to eat huge amounts of food.
- **Hallucinations** are false perceptions by the senses. People hear voices, see visions, or sense things that are not really there.
- **Mental retardation** is a condition present since childhood in which the person has significantly below-average intelligence. These

individuals may be limited in their ability to learn, work, communicate with others, care for themselves, and live independently.

- **Neurosis** (noo-RO-sis) is a broad term covering many mental disorders that are long-lasting or recurring. People who have a neurosis remain in touch with reality, unlike those who have a psychosis. But the anxiety, depression, and distress common to neurosis can interfere with the quality of life.
- **Obsessive-compulsive disorder** (ob-SES-iv-kom-PUL-siv dis-OR-der) is a mental disorder that causes people to feel trapped by distressing or senseless thoughts and to feel as if they have to repeat actions.
- **Phobias** (FO-be-as) are mental disorders that lead to a lasting, intense, irrational fear of a particular object, activity, or situation.
- **Post-traumatic stress disorder** (post-traw-MAT-ik STRESS dis-OR-der) is a mental disorder that interferes with everyday living and occurs in people who survive a life-threatening event, such as school violence, car accidents, natural disasters (earthquakes, hurricanes, floods), or military combat.
- **Psychosis** (sy-KO-sis) is a broad term covering severe mental disorders that make a person unable to recognize reality, relate to other people, or function in daily life. A disorder like depression could be considered a neurosis or a psychosis depending on how severe it is.
- **Schizophrenia** (skitz-so-FRE-ne-a) is a form of psychosis that causes people to have hallucinations, delusions, and other confusing thoughts that distort their view of reality.
- **Separation anxiety** (sep-a-RAY-shun ang-ZY-e-tee) is a mental disorder in which children worry excessively about leaving their homes, parents, or caregivers.
- **Sleep disorders** are long-lasting disturbances of sleep. Some sleep disorders have mainly psychological causes, while others have mainly physical causes.

How Are Mental Disorders Diagnosed and Treated?

Diagnosis of mental disorders requires careful evaluation by a qualified physician or mental health professional. A variety of tests are used. The physician may assess how severe a person's symptoms are, how long the symptoms have lasted, the person's prior mental and medical history, whether the disorder has a medical basis, and whether the disorder is caused by alcohol or another drug.

Treatment depends on the specific disorder and may include psychotherapy* for the individual or for the family. Often a combination of psychotherapy and medication is prescribed.

* **psychotherapy** is treatment for a mental disorder that usually involves talking with a trained therapist to undercover the roots of a person's behavior or to learn new ways of thinking or behaving.

Resources

U.S. National Institute of Mental Health, 6001 Executive Boulevard, Room 8184, MSC 9663, Bethesda, MD 20892-9663. NIMH is the government institute that oversees research on mental disorders and provides information for professionals and the public.
http://www.nimh.nih.gov

American Psychological Asssociation, 750 First Street NE, Washington, DC 20002-4242. The American Psychological Association publishes books, brochures, and fact sheets about mental health, mental disorders, and psychotherapy. It provides referrals to local psychologists, and its website includes a *KidsPsych* feature.
Telephone 202-336-5500
http://www.apa.org

American Psychiatric Association, 1400 K Street NW, Washington, DC 20005. The American Psychiatric Association publishes the *Diagnostic and Statistical Manual of Mental Disorders* for doctors, and the *Let's Talk Facts About* pamphlet series for the public. Its website also posts a *Psychiatric Medications* fact sheet.
http://www.psych.org

National Alliance for the Mentally Ill, 200 North Glebe Road, Suite 1015, Arlington, VA 22203-3754. A self-help organization for people with serious mental illness, their families, and their friends.
Telephone 800-950-NAMI
http://www.nami.org

National Mental Health Association, 1021 Prince Street, Alexandria, VA 22314-2971. A national organization that offers information to the public about various mental disorders and mental health.
Telephone 800-969-NMHA
http://www.nmha.org

▶ *See also*
AIDS and HIV
Alcoholism
Alzheimer's Disease
Amnesia
Anxiety Disorders
Attention Deficit Hyperactivity Disorder
Autism
Depressive Disorders
Dyslexia
Eating Disorders
Huntington's Disease
Hypochondria
Insomnia
Mental Retardation
Multiple Personality Disorder
Obsessive-Compulsive Disorder
Phobias
Post-Traumatic Stress Disorder
Schizophrenia
Sleep Disorders
Stroke
Substance Abuse

Mental Retardation

Mental retardation is a condition in which people have below average intelligence that limits their ability to function normally. The condition, which is present from birth or childhood, has many different causes. Its effects range from mild to profound.

KEYWORDS
for searching the Internet and other reference sources

Down Syndrome

Fetal alcohol syndrome

Fragile X syndrome

What Is Mental Retardation?

Mental retardation is a condition in which people have significantly below average mental functioning (an intelligence quotient or IQ of 70-75 or less compared to the normal average of 100), causing problems with everyday

A trio of winners celebrate their victories at a Special Olympics meet in North Carolina. The Special Olympics were founded in 1968 to provide children and adults with mental retardation continuing opportunities to train and compete in athletic events. © *B.E. Barnes/PhotoEdit.*

living. People who are mentally retarded may have problems with communication, taking care of themselves, daily living, social skills, community interactions, directing themselves, health and safety, school, leisure activities, and work.

Studies in the 1980s suggest that between 2.5 and 3 percent of all people in the United States are considered mentally retarded. According to the 1990 census, 6.3 and 7.5 million people in the United States have mental retardation.

The condition, which is more common in boys than girls, begins at birth or in childhood. If a person with normal intelligence becomes impaired as an adult, such as in severe mental illness or brain injury, the condition is not called mental retardation.

How Is Mental Retardation Classified?

There are four levels of mental retardation: mild, moderate, severe, and profound. These levels are determined by performance on standardized IQ tests and by the potential to learn adaptive skills such as communication and social interaction.

Mild retardation The vast majority of people with mental retardation have IQ levels of 55 to 69 and are considered mildly retarded. Mildly retarded children often go undiagnosed until they are well into their school years. They are often slower to walk, talk, and feed themselves than most other children. They can learn practical skills, including reading and math, up to about the fourth to sixth grade level. Mildly retarded adults usually build social and job skills and can live on their own.

Moderate retardation A much smaller number of people with mental retardation have IQs ranging from 40 to 54 and are considered moderately retarded. Children who are moderately retarded show noticeable delays in developing speech and motor skills. Although they are unlikely to acquire useful academic skills, they can learn basic communication, some health and safety habits, and other simple skills. They cannot learn to read or do math. Moderately retarded adults usually cannot live alone, but they can do some simple tasks and travel alone in familiar places.

Severe retardation An even smaller percentage of people with mental retardation have IQs ranging from 20 to 39 and are considered severely mentally retarded. Their condition is likely to be diagnosed at birth or soon after. By preschool age, they show delays in motor development and little or no ability to communicate. With training, they may learn some self-help skills, such as how to feed and bathe themselves. They usually learn to walk and gain a basic understanding of speech as they get older. Adults who are severely mentally retarded may be able to follow daily routines and perform simple tasks, but they need to be directed and live in a protected environment.

Profound retardation Only a very few people with mental retardation have IQs of 0 to 24 and are considered severely mentally retarded. Their condition is usually diagnosed at birth, and they may have other medical problems and need nursing care. Children who are profoundly retarded need to be continuously supervised. These children show delays in all aspects of development. With training, they may learn to use their legs, hands, and jaws. Adults who are profoundly retarded usually learn some speech and may learn to walk. They cannot take care of themselves and need complete support in daily living.

What Causes Mental Retardation?

Mental retardation is a complex condition, which may be caused by the interaction of many factors. In about 75 percent of cases, the exact cause is never known. Causes of mental retardation include defects in the genes* or chromosomes*, injuries or conditions that develop while a fetus* is developing in the womb, diseases of early childhood, and environmental influences. The three major causes of mental retardation are Down syndrome, fetal alcohol syndrome, and fragile X.

The role of genetics If one or both parents have mental retardation, there is a much greater chance that their children will also have this condition. There are many genetic (inherited) causes of mental retardation that arise from defects or omissions in the genetic material passed from parent to child.

Sometimes mental retardation is caused by an abnormality in the chromosomes rather than the individual genes. Down syndrome, one of the most common causes of mental retardation, is caused by an extra chromosome in the cells. Another fairly common chromosomal defect called fragile X syndrome causes mental retardation mainly in boys.

Problems during pregnancy Infections in pregnant women such as German measles (rubella) or toxoplasmosis* also are a cause of mental retardation. Even though the mother may not be harmed by the infection,

* **genes** are chemicals in the body that help determine a person's characteristics, such as hair or eye color, and are inherited from a person's parents. They are located on chromosomes found in the cells of the body.

* **chromosomes** (KRO-mo-somes) are threadlike structure inside the nucleus of cells on which the genes are located.

* A **fetus** (FEE-tus) in humans, is the developing offspring from nine weeks after conception until birth.

* **toxoplasmosis** (tok-so-plaz-MO-sis) is a disease caused by a single-celled organism sometimes found in the stool of cats.

Two men with less pronounced levels of mental retardation wash dishes under minimal supervision at an adult day care facility in New Jersey. © *Jeff Greenberg, Peter Arnold, Inc.*

the developing fetus becomes infected through the mother, and shows much more serious effects of the infection.

Pregnant women who drink too much alcohol risk having a mentally retarded child through a condition known as fetal alcohol syndrome (FAS). This is a common, and preventable, cause of mental retardation. Some drugs (for example, cocaine or amphetamines), when taken during pregnancy, may harm the mental development of the unborn child. Maternal malnutrition and exposure to radiation during pregnancy can also cause mental retardation.

Problems during childbirth Babies born prematurely (born before the normal duration of pregnancy has ended) are more likely to be mentally retarded than babies born at full term, especially if the baby is very premature and weighs less than 3.3 pounds (1.5 kg). Problems during childbirth such as an interruption in the supply of oxygen to the baby during the delivery can also cause mental retardation.

Disorders occurring after birth Mental retardation can also be caused by problems after birth such as lead or mercury poisoning, severe malnutrition, accidents that cause severe head injuries, an interruption in the supply of oxygen to the brain (for example, near-drowning), or diseases such as encephalitis, meningitis, and untreated hypothyroidism in infants. Some of these conditions are more likely to occur in children raised in circumstances of severe poverty, neglect, or abuse.

Living with Mental Retardation

There is no cure for mental retardation. Treatment focuses on helping people who have the condition develop to their full potential by building their educational, behavioral, and self-help skills. For children with mental retardation, the support of parents, specially trained educators, and the community helps them reach to their fullest ability. Parents may benefit from ongoing counseling to discuss their options and to help them cope with the changes in their household that arise from living with someone who has mental retardation.

Many children with mental retardation benefit from living at home or in a community residence and going to a regular school. Schools in all states are now required to provide appropriate education for children with mental retardation until they are 21 years old.

Can Mental Retardation Be Prevented?

There is no certain way to prevent mental retardation. Improved health care, prenatal testing, and public health education are making it possible to avoid some cases of mental retardation. People who want to become parents can get genetic counseling to determine the likelihood of mental retardation from an inherited disorder. Medical tests such as amniocentesis*, chorionic villus sampling*, and ultrasonography* can help detect inherited metabolic and chromosomal disorders linked to mental retardation. Vaccinations can prevent pregnant women from getting infections such as German measles that can harm developing fetuses. Preventing toxoplasmois and avoiding drugs and alcohol during pregnancy also help prevent mental retardation. Screening blood tests for newborns can detect some disorders at birth, allowing for earlier treatment. It is also important to protect babies from lead poisoning and head injuries.

* **amniocentesis** (am-nee-o-sen-TEE-sis) is a test in which a long, thin needle is inserted in the mother's uterus to obtain a sample of the amniotic fluid from the sac that surrounds the fetus. The fetal cells in the fluid are then examined for genetic defects.

* **chorionic villus sampling** (KOR-ee-on-ik VIL-lus sampling) is a test in which a small tube is inserted through the cervix and a small piece of the placenta supporting the fetus is removed for genetic testing.

* **ultrasonography** (ul-tra-so-NOG-ra-fee) is a painless test that uses high-frequency sound waves to record and show the shape of the fetus in the mother's uterus.

Resources

Books

Kaufman, Sandra Z. *Retarded Isn't Stupid, Mom!* Baltimore: Brooks Publishing Co., 1988.

Shyer, Marlene. *Welcome Home, Jellybean.* New York: Macmillan, 1988.

Organizations

ARC of the United States (formerly known as the Association for Retarded Citizens), 500 East Border Street, Arlington,TX 76010. This organization provides information, advocacy, and local resources for people with mental retardation.
Telephone 817-261-6003
http://www.thearc.org

U.S. National Institute of Child Health and Human Development (NICHD), 31 Center Drive, Building 31, Room 2A32, Bethesda, MD 20892-2425. NICHD is one of the National Institutes of Health. Its Mental Retardation and Developmental Disabilities Branch (MRDD) supports 15 regional Mental Retardation Research Centers and posts useful fact sheets at its website.
Telephone 301-496-5133
http://www.nichd.nih.gov/publications

▶ *See also*
Autism
Birth Defects
Cerebral Palsy
Down Syndrome
Environmental Diseases
Epilepsy
Fetal Alcohol Syndrome
Genetic Diseases
German Measles
Lead Poisoning
Meningitis
Muscular Dystrophy
Phenylketonuria
Sudden Infant Death Syndrome
Thyroid Disease
Tourette Syndrome
Toxoplasmosis

Metabolic Disease

KEYWORDS
for searching the Internet and other reference sources

Biochemistry

Endocrine system

Energy metabolism

A metabolic (met-a-BOLL-ik) disease is a condition that interferes with the body's chemical processes involved in growth, maintenance of healthy tissues, disposal of waste products, and production of energy to fuel body functions. As a result, a person may have too much or too little of certain substances (such as protein, fat, or carbohydrate) in the body. This imbalance often interferes with the normal function of various body tissues and organs.

"Inborn Errors of Metabolism": A Scientist's Discovery

Nearly 100 years ago, a British scientist named Archibald Garrod suggested that people actually could inherit genetic (je-NE-tik) information that causes problems with the body's metabolism. A gene is the unit of heredity that carries physical characteristics from parent to child. The parents usually do not have the particular metabolic problem themselves; however, they both carry a "hidden" mutant (changed or abnormal) gene for the disorder that is passed on to the child.

Inheriting the mutant gene from both parents creates problems for the child when the child's body needs to metabolize (me-TAB-o-lize), or process, certain nutrients and other substances properly. Garrod's theory was revolutionary at the time, since no one had yet suggested that the body's chemical processes might somehow be related to heredity. Moreover, it generally was believed that diseases were caused only by things from outside the body, such as germs and bacteria.

In lectures delivered in 1908, Garrod described several hereditary diseases that are caused by too little or complete lack of certain enzymes (EN-zimes). An enzyme is a protein that speeds up or controls certain chemical reactions in the body. In three of the diseases Garrod described—alkaptonuria (al-cap-to-NYOOR-ee-a), cystinuria (sis-ti-NYOOR-ee-a), and pentosuria (pen-tos-YOOR-ee-a)—certain forms of acids and sugar were found at abnormally high levels in the urine, showing that the body had not processed them correctly. This suggested that the enzymes needed for processing were absent or not functioning properly. Dr. Garrod called these diseases "inborn errors of metabolism," a name that persists to this day.

It has been nearly a century since Dr. Garrod made his discovery, and in that time scientists have identified more than 200 genetic mutations that cause different metabolic disorders.

How Does Metabolism Normally Work?

Most people eat and drink every day without giving much thought to what happens inside the body afterwards, beyond the fact that the stomach and intestines help digest what they consume. But in reality, digestion is only the beginning. Once food and drink are broken down into substances that the body can use, the process called metabolism begins. Metabolism actually is a series of chemical processes through which the body makes use of the nutrients in food to carry out its functions: growing, maintaining healthy tissues, disposing of wastes, producing the energy needed for moving, running, jumping, playing . . . and the list goes on. The process as a whole is quite complex, with hundreds of different reactions happening one after the other to convert nutrients into materials that the body needs for the functions of life. It might help to think of metabolism as a kind of "domino effect," with each "domino," or chemical reaction, falling into place to create the end result. Metabolism involves two main phases: "building up" (anabolism) and "breaking down" (catabolism).

Anabolism The "building up" phase, also called anabolism (a-NA-bo-liz-um), includes all the processes that occur when the body makes use of nutrients to grow and build new tissues. This involves converting simple substances into more complex substances. For example, during digestion, important compounds called amino (a-MEE-no) acids are released from food. Through anabolism, the body converts these into proteins that are essential to the body's growth, development, and health. Protein is the main building material for all living tissue, including muscles, skin, and internal organs. It also is necessary to form enzymes, hormones*, and antibodies*, all of which are essential to the body's normal function.

Catabolism The "breaking down" phase, or catabolism (ca-TA-bo-liz-um), involves processes that move in the opposite direction: that is, they break down more complex substances into simpler forms, releasing energy that is used for work, movement, or heat production. For instance, the body's tissues store a carbohydrate called glycogen (GLY-ko-jen) in the liver* and the muscles. When the body needs energy, it breaks down the glycogen into glucose, a form of sugar. Glucose is then metabolized, or broken down, in the body's cells to release energy for fueling body functions.

Enzymes "missing in action" None of the processes involved in metabolism would be possible without substances called enzymes. These are proteins that the body's cells produce to speed up or regulate chemical reactions. Each enzyme is made up of smaller amino acids, which are the building blocks of all proteins. The sequence of amino acids in an enzyme is determined by a person's genes. People who are born with metabolic diseases inherit a genetic mutation (a change) in a specific gene. That mutation causes the body to fail to produce an enzyme, or to produce an enzyme that is inactive. As a result, the enzyme's activity in the body decreases or is completely absent.

It might help to think of enzymes as words and amino acids as letters of the alphabet. When a word is misspelled, its letters are ordered incorrectly, and its meaning may be confusing or unclear. When an enzyme is "misspelled," the amino acids are out of order and it cannot function properly. The particular step in metabolism that the enzyme controls does not happen as it should.

* **hormones** are chemical substances produced in one part of the body that regulate the activities of certain organs or groups of cells in other parts of the body.

* **antibodies** are proteins produced by the body's infection-fighting immune system to defend against bacteria, viruses, and other foreign organisms or substances.

* **liver** is the large organ, located in the upper abdomen, that helps cleanse the blood of waste products and toxic substances. It aids in digestion by secreting bile, and serves as a major site of sugar storage in the body.

There are hundreds of such "misspellings" that can cause many different kinds of metabolic disorders. Some are more serious than others. Many can be treated, but some cannot. If the disease is not treated, particular substances that are not being processed properly—whether carbohydrate, sugar, fat, or protein—build up excessively in the body, or too little of a needed substance is produced. In either case, the result is an imbalance that causes problems with the function and growth of many body tissues and organs, including the brain.

Metabolic Diseases

Specific examples of metabolic diseases are helpful in understanding metabolic diseases in general. Describing all of them would fill this entire book. Here are some of the more common ones.

When early detection and special diet are key: Phenylketonuria (PKU) Labels on diet soda and other food products containing the artificial sweetener aspartame feature a special warning: "Phenylketonurics: Contains Phenylalanine." This alerts people with the metabolic disorder phenylketonuria (FEN-il-ke-to-NYOOR-ee-a) that aspartame contains the amino acid called phenylalanine (fen-il-AL-a-neen). People who have PKU lack the enzyme that is needed to convert this amino acid into another substance called tyrosine (TY-ro-seen). In other words, the body cannot process phenylalanine correctly. This amino acid is necessary for normal growth in infants and children and for normal protein production throughout life. However, if too much of it builds up, it poisons the brain tissue and eventually causes mental retardation. It also can cause the skin and urine to give off an unusual musty odor and lead to skin rashes.

Fortunately, doctors can determine whether an infant has PKU almost immediately after birth. In the 1960s, scientists developed a PKU test that is now performed on all newborns in the United States. It involves taking a small blood sample and placing it with a strain of bacterium that cannot grow without phenylalanine. The PKU test is positive if the bacteria reproduce. Only one out of roughly every 10,000 babies born in the U.S. tests positive for PKU, which makes it a rare condition, but this adds up to several hundred babies each year.

When these babies are put on a special diet right away, they can avoid the mental retardation that was the certain result of PKU in the past. This diet cuts out all high-protein foods, which are also high in phenylalanine, such as meat, fish, poultry, milk, eggs, cheese, ice cream, nuts, and many products containing regular flour. However, the particular restrictions will vary from person to person, depending on the severity of the condition. The diet can be difficult to follow, but it is crucial to staying healthy and avoiding retardation. Children with PKU often need to take a special artificial formula that is used as a nutritional substitute for the foods they cannot eat.

Because of early diagnosis and careful dietary restrictions, children with PKU are now growing up normally. They are achieving in school,

75 YEARS AGO: A DISCOVERY THAT CHANGED CHILDREN'S LIVES

Norway, 1934: A mother with two severely mentally retarded children goes to see Dr. Asbjørn Følling. She is desperate for answers about her children's condition, which no doctor has yet explained to her satisfaction. She also wonders about an unusual smell that her children always seem to have. After testing urine samples, Dr. Følling finds that they excrete a substance not found in normal urine. Although he does not have access to the advanced chemical tests that would become available later in the century, eventually he is able to identify the substance as phenylpyruvic acid, a type of amino acid. He immediately wonders whether the buildup of acid has something to do with the children's retardation.

Dr. Følling collects urine samples from hundreds of other mentally retarded patients and finds that eight of them excrete the same acid. He then publishes a paper that draws a connection between the acid levels and retardation in these ten people. He also makes the hypothesis (hi-PO-the-sis) that the acid is present because these patients are unable to metabolize phenylalanine. Eventually, he confirms that hypothesis when he and his colleague figure out a way to use bacteria to test for high levels of phenylalanine in the blood.

Dr. Følling had just discovered phenylketonuria (PKU), and in so doing, he changed the lives of future generations of children who would be born with this condition. He showed that mental retardation could be avoided if the condition was discovered right away and if phenylalanine levels were controlled through dietary changes.

In 1962, President John F. Kennedy awarded Dr. Følling the Joseph P. Kennedy International Award in Mental Retardation for his achievements. At about the same time, a scientist named Dr. Robert Guthrie was using Dr. Følling's discoveries to develop an effective newborn screening test for PKU. The test became available in the early 1960s, and Dr. Guthrie worked diligently to establish screening programs in the United States and many other countries. All babies in the U.S. now are routinely screened for PKU.

attending college, and entering a wide range of challenging professions as adults. With the exception of the special diet they must follow, children with PKU can do anything that children without PKU can do.

When urine smells sweet, like maple syrup (MSUD) PKU is just one example of several metabolic disorders that occur when the body lacks an enzyme needed to process amino acids. Another is Maple Syrup Urine Disease (MSUD), in which the enzyme needed to process three other amino acids—valine (VAYL-een), leucine (LOO-seen), and isoleucine (i-so-LOO-seen)—is lacking. These acids are essential for the

200 Years Ago: The "Madness" of King George

George III (1738–1820) is remembered as the king of England against whom the American colonists rebelled and fought for their independence. He also is remembered as a king who experienced violent fits of madness that eventually made him incapable of ruling. King George was subject to agonizing pain, excited overactivity, paralysis, and delirium at different times in his life. His "nervous spells" came and went during the last three or four decades of his life, which ended in 1820 when he was 81.

Some historians now believe that King George's problem was in his body, not his mind. When psychiatrists studied the king's letters and examined the notes made by his doctors, they discovered that King George's symptoms included not only nervous attacks but a dark red color of the urine, suggesting that he had the metabolic disease called porphyria. In 1967, two British psychiatrists published a scientific paper called *A Clinical Reassessment of the Insanity of George III and Some of Its Historical Implications* that made this very argument. Further historical investigation suggests that other members of the royal family may have had the condition too.

So the history books may be wrong about "mad King George." Medicine at the time was not advanced enough to determine how the body's chemical processes might affect the mind. But we now know that people with porphyria actually have a problem in the blood that, in some cases, interferes with the normal functioning of the brain.

body's normal growth and function. When they are not metabolized properly, they can build up in the body, causing the urine to smell like maple syrup or sweet, burnt sugar. If left untreated, MSUD can cause mental retardation, physical disability, and even death.

About 1 in 225,000 infants are born with MSUD, making it even rarer than PKU. Not only does their urine smell like maple syrup, but they usually have little appetite and are extremely irritable. Some states require that all newborns be tested for MSUD, but some do not as yet. It is important that the condition be diagnosed and treated right away; otherwise, it can cause seizures, unconsciousness, brain damage, and even death. Treatment takes the form of a carefully controlled diet that cuts out certain high-protein foods that contain the three amino acids the body cannot process. Like children with PKU, those with MSUD are often given an artificial formula that supplies the necessary nutrients they miss by excluding certain foods.

Babies who cannot drink milk: Galactosemia For most babies and young children, mother's milk (or a formula like breast milk) and then cow's milk supply nutrients essential to the body's function and growth. But babies born with the metabolic disease galactosemia (ga-lak-to-SEE-me-a) do not have enough of the enzyme that breaks down the sugar in milk called galactose. This enzyme is usually produced by the liver, but if the liver does not produce enough, galactose builds up in the blood and can cause serious health problems if the condition is not diagnosed and treated.

Symptoms usually appear in the first few days of life, as soon as the baby starts drinking breast milk or formula. The baby often starts vomiting, the liver swells up, and the skin and eyes take on a yellow color (a condition called jaundice). Other symptoms might include infections, irritability, failure to gain weight, and diarrhea. If it is not diagnosed quickly, galactosemia can cause severe damage to the liver, eyes, kidney, and brain. For this reason, many states require that all newborns have a blood test that can detect it. About 1 in 20,000 babies are born with the condition, and it is treated by removing all milk and milk-containing products from the diet. This reduces the risk of permanent damage, but there may still be problems with growth, speech, and mental function as the child gets older.

Fructose intolerance Galactosemia is just one example of many metabolic diseases in which the body cannot process sugars properly. Another is fructose intolerance, in which a person cannot metabolize a certain form of sugar found in fruit, fruit juices, powdered and table sugar, honey, corn syrup, and other foods. Like galactosemia, it is treated by excluding certain foods from the diet. Fructose must be limited strictly to avoid possible damage to the liver and kidneys and mental retardation.

Problems with carbohydrate metabolism The body takes a simple sugar called glucose from foods, converts it into a carbohydrate called glycogen, and stores it in the liver and muscles. When the body needs energy to fuel its activities, certain enzymes then break the glycogen back down into sugar. Some people have problems with one or more of these enzymes, resulting in a condition known as glycogen storage disease.

There actually are seven different types of glycogen storage disease, each involving different enzymes. One example is glucose-6-phosphatase (G6PD) deficiency. Glucose-6-phosphatase is an enzyme normally found in the liver that is needed to release glucose from the liver into the bloodstream so that it can be processed by the body to produce energy. Deficiency of the enzyme can cause the levels of sugar in the blood to fall dangerously low if glucose is not taken in from the diet every few hours.

In G6PD deficiency and other glycogen storage diseases, glycogen is stored in too large amounts in various parts of the body, causing problems with the liver, muscles, blood cells, heart, brain, and/or other organs. Treatment for these conditions usually involves changes in diet.

When the blood gets out of balance: Porphyria The body uses a special chemical called porphyrin (POR-fir-in) to make heme, which is the substance in the blood that carries oxygen to the tissues. Eight different enzymes are in charge of the metabolic process that uses porphyrin to make heme. When any of these enzymes are missing or do not function properly, too much porphyrin builds up in the body, and it is eventually released from the body in the urine or stool. As a result, not enough heme is produced to keep the person healthy. This condition is called porphyria (poor-FEER-ee-a).

People who have porphryia can experience symptoms that involve the skin, the nervous system, and/or other internal organs. When porphyria affects the skin, the person may have blisters, itching, swelling, or extreme sensitivity to the sun. When it affects the brain, it can cause hallucinations*, delirium*, seizures, depression, anxiety, and paranoia*. Other physical symptoms may include chest or stomach pain, muscle cramps, weakness, or urine that is dark purple or reddish in color.

* **hallucinations** are perceptions by the senses that are not based on reality, for example, seeing or hearing things that do not exist.

* **delirium** is a serious mental disorder that may be marked by confusion, speech disorders, anxiety, excitement, and/or hallucinations.

* **paranoia** is a mental disorder marked by feelings of self-importance or suspicion that other people are "out to get" the paranoid person.

Doctors can test someone's blood, urine, or stool to diagnose porphyria. A drug called hemin, which is like heme, can be given, along with other medications to relieve symptoms. Sometimes, a high-carbohydrate diet also can help.

What Does It All Mean?

There are many other metabolic diseases besides those described above. However, these few examples illustrate the chain of events that happen in many inherited metabolic diseases:

1. A person inherits a genetic mutation, or abnormality.
2. Because of this, a certain enzyme is not produced or does not work as it should.
3. Consequently, a certain step in metabolism does not occur normally.
4. The substance that should have been metabolized (broken down or changed into another form) builds up in the body, and/or other important substances needed by the body are not produced in adequate amounts.

The person's system gets "out of balance," so to speak, and this can cause damage if the problem is not corrected with diet or medication. In some cases, the imbalance cannot be corrected and may cause permanent damage or even death.

Resources

U.S. National Institute of Diabetes and Digestive and Kidney Diseases (NIDDK), Building 31, Room 9A04, Bethesda, MD 20892. NIDDK is the government institute that oversees research on endocrine and metabolic diseases. Its website posts fact sheets and has links to more than 30 organizations serving patients and their families. http://www.niddk.nih.gov/health/endo/endo.htm

American Association of Clinical Endocrinologists, 1000 Riverside Avenue, Suite 205, Jacksonville, FL 32204. An organization of physicians who specialize in treating metabolic diseases. http://www.aace.com

Endocrine Society, 4350 East West Highway, Suite 500, Bethesda, MD 20814-4410. An organization of scientists and physicians who specialize in research and publications covering metabolic diseases.
http://www.endo-society.org

National Organization for Rare Disorders, P.O. Box 8923,
New Fairfield, CT 06812-8923.
Telephone 800-999-6673
http://www.rarediseases.org

American Porphyria Foundation, P.O. Box 22712,
Houston, TX 77227.
Telephone 713-266-9617
http://www.enterprise.net/apf

National PKU News: News and Information about Phenylketonuria, 6869 Woodlawn Avenue NE, Number 116, Seattle, WA 98115-5469.
http://www.wolfenet.com/~kronmal/index.html

Parents of Galactosemic Children, 2148 Bryton Drive,
Powell, OH 43605.
http://www.galactosemia.org

The Maple Syrup Urine Disease Family Support Group.
http://www.msud-support.org

See also
Atherosclerosis
Birth Defects
Diabetes
Genetic Diseases
Growth Disorders
Hypoglycemia
Jaundice
Mental Retardation
Obesity
Phenylketonuria
Porphyria
Seizures
Thyroid Disease

Migraine *See* Headache

Mononucleosis, Infectious

Infectious mononucleosis (in-FEK-shus mon-o-noo-klee-O-sis) is an illness caused by a virus* that may lead to symptoms such as fever, sore throat, swollen glands in the neck, and tiredness.

KEYWORDS
for searching the Internet and other reference sources

Epstein-Barr virus

Infection

* **virus** (VY-rus) is a tiny infectious agent that lacks an independent metabolism (me-TAB-o-liz-um) and can only reproduce within the cells it infects.

Kim's Story

When Kim came down with a sore throat and headache, she thought maybe she had caught the flu. By the next day, though, she had a fever, and her throat was so swollen that she could hardly swallow. Worse yet, she felt so tired that she could barely drag herself out of bed. Kim's mother took her to the doctor's office, where a physical exam and blood test revealed that she had infectious mononucleosis. This is a common illness, especially in young people, that is caused by a virus. Mononucleosis, or "mono" for short, is often called the "kissing disease," and Kim took some teasing once she got better and went back to school. However, the doctor had explained to Kim that kissing someone with mono is just one way to catch the illness. It can also be spread by sharing a straw or cup, sneezing, or coughing.

▲

Mono is often called the "kissing disease."
Andy Levin, Photo Researchers, Inc.

What Is Infectious Mononucleosis?

Infectious mononucleosis is an illness that may lead to symptoms such as fever, sore throat, swollen glands in the neck, and tiredness. Although there are a number of infections that cause a mononucleosis-like condition, when people say mono they are referring to the infection caused by the Epstein-Barr virus (EBV). This is a common virus that may infect four out of five people by the time they are 40 years old. This virus is related to the ones that cause cold sores and chickenpox. EBV infects the blood cells and salivary (SAL-i-var-ee) glands (the glands that make saliva). Some people who are infected by this virus get mono, while others never develop symptoms. Once a person catches the virus, it stays in the body in a dormant or inactive condition for life, and it may show up in the saliva again from time to time. However, a person probably will not have the symptoms of mono again from the virus.

EBV is spread through contact with infected saliva, by such means as kissing or sharing a straw or cup. It also can be passed by coughing or sneezing. If the symptoms of mono develop, they usually show up 2 to 7 weeks after exposure. Anyone of any age can catch EBV. When it strikes young children, though, it usually does not cause symptoms. EBV is more likely to cause problems in people who do not become infected until the teenage years or later. In fact, up to four out of five cases of full-blown mono occur in people between the ages of 15 and 30. The number of new cases peaks in those 15 to 17 years old. The disease is particularly common in teenagers and people in their twenties who are in high school, college, or the military.

Did You Know?

- When people of all ages are taken into account, only about 50 out of every 100,000 Americans have mononucleosis symptoms each year.
- Mononucleosis is much more common in young people, however, striking as many as 2 out of every 1,000 teenagers and twenty-somethings each year.

What Are the Symptoms of Mononucleosis?

Mononucleosis usually is not a serious illness, and many people with mono have few or no symptoms at all. However, it can slow a person down for weeks or even months, since most people who get mono can feel very tired for several months. In teenagers and young adults, the illness usually starts slowly, and the early symptoms are similar to those of the flu. They may include a general sense of not feeling well, along with tiredness, headache, chilliness, puffy eyelids, and loss of appetite. Other symptoms may develop later:

- Sore throat
- Tiredness
- Fever. A fever of 101 degrees Fahrenheit to 105 degrees Fahrenheit lasts typically for about 5 days, and it sometimes comes and goes for up to 3 weeks.
- Swollen glands. These are common in the neck, but they occur also under the arm and in the groin (the area where the inner thighs join the trunk).
- Other symptoms. These can include swollen tonsils*, difficulty swallowing, bleeding gums, and a skin rash that lasts 1 or 2 days.

* **tonsils** are paired clusters of lymph tissues in the throat. They help protect the body from bacteria that enter through a person's nose or mouth.

Occasionally, a more serious problem arises. Some people with mono have a swollen spleen*. In a few cases, the enlarged spleen may rupture, or break open, causing a sudden, sharp pain in the upper left part of the abdomen*. If this happens, emergency medical help is needed right away. To lower the risk of a ruptured spleen, people with mono often are advised not to lift heavy objects, do strenuous exercise, or take part in contact sports for 2 months after they get sick.

*__spleen__ is a large organ in the upper left part of the abdomen that stores and filters blood and also plays a role in making and breaking down blood cells.

*__abdomen__ (AB-do-men), commonly called the belly, is the portion of the body between the chest and the pelvis.

How Is Mononucleosis Diagnosed and Treated?

If mononucleosis is suspected, doctors will ask about symptoms and perform a physical exam. Many other viruses can cause symptoms similar to mono, however. To be sure of the diagnosis, the doctor may also order a blood test. One common test that can show indirectly the presence of EBV is called the Monospot test. If the results of the Monospot test are not clear, other blood tests may be needed.

There is no cure for mono. Antibiotics (an-ty-by-OT-iks), drugs that work against diseases caused by bacteria*, do not work against EBV. Rest is the only real treatment. In addition, drinking plenty of fluids can help relieve fever and a sore throat. Taking over-the-counter painkillers such as acetaminophen (a-set-a-MEE-no-fen) or ibuprofen (i-bu-PRO-fun), sucking on throat lozenges, or gargling several times a day with warm salt water may also help. The good news is that, even with no other treatment, the disease will almost always go away by itself, usually in 1 to 3 weeks. For some, however, it may take 2 to 3 months to feel totally back to normal.

*__bacteria__ (bak-TEER-ee-a) are round, spiral, or rod-shaped single-celled microorganisms without a distinct nucleus that commonly multiply by cell division. Some types may cause disease in humans, animals, or plants.

Resources

Book

Silverstein, Alvin, Virginia Silverstein, and Robert Silverstein. *Mononucleosis.* Springfield, NJ: Enslow Publishers, 1994.

Organization

U.S. National Institute of Allergy and Infectious Diseases, NIAID Office of Communications and Public Liaison, 31 Center Drive, Building 31, Room 7A-50, Bethesda, MD 20892-2520. Part of the U.S. National Institutes of Health (NIH), NIAID publishes a pamphlet called *Infectious Mononucleosis.*
Telephone 301-496-5717
http://www.niaid.nih.gov/factsheets/infmono.htm

► *See also*
Cytomegalovirus
Fever
Viral Infections

Motion Sickness

KEYWORDS
for searching the Internet and other reference sources

Internal medicine

Motion sickness occurs when people feel dizzy or nauseated because the motion their body senses and the motion their eyes perceive are not synchronized. The conflicting messages sent to the brain make them feel ill.

The Ruined Fishing Trip

Jon and his dad were very excited about their upcoming deep sea-fishing trip off the Florida coast. Dad's friend Bob had a boat and knew the right spots to look for fish. The sun was bright, and the sea was choppy that day. Bob traveled out about four miles from shore. Suddenly, his motor quit, and the boat vigorously bobbed up and down on the waves.

First Jon felt queasy in his stomach, and then he broke out in a cold sweat. He became nauseated and vomited over the side of the boat. When they got back to shore, Jon's queasiness went away fairly rapidly. He felt frustrated that the pleasure of the fishing trip had been ruined by his bout of motion sickness.

What Causes Motion Sickness?

Dizziness, vertigo*, and motion sickness are all related to the sense of balance and equilibrium in the inner ear. Researchers in space and aeronautical medicine call this sense spatial orientation, because it tells the brain where the body is in space.

* **vertigo** (VER-ti-go) is the feeling that either the environment or one's own body is revolving or spinning, even though they are not.

The following sensors work together to maintain a sense of spatial orientation:

- The chamber of the inner ear known as the vestibular labyrinth (ves-TIB-u-lar LAB-e-rinth) consists of fluid-filled, interconnected tubes called semicircular canals that monitor the direction of motion.

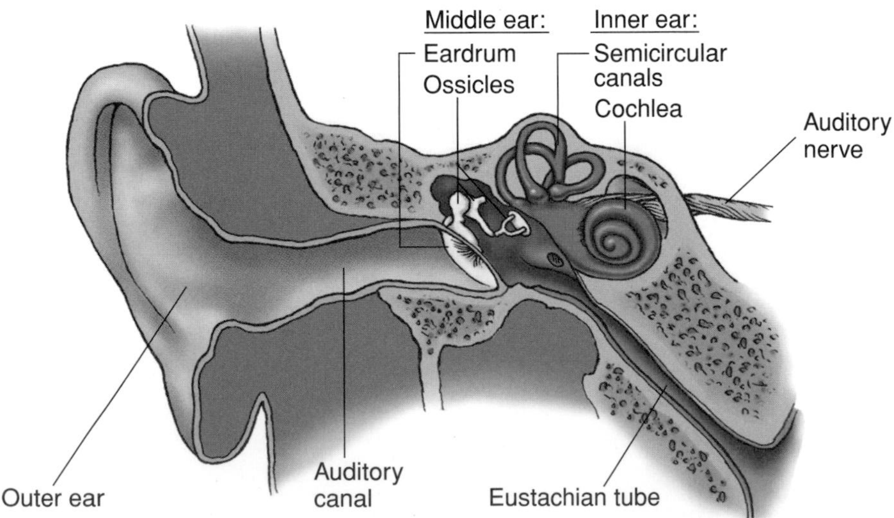

Anatomy of the inner and middle ear. ▶

- The eyes send signals to the brain about where the body is in space.
- Skin pressure receptors tell the brain what part of the body is touching the ground.
- Muscle and joint receptors tell the brain what parts of the body are moving.
- The brain processes all the information from these sensors and puts everything together. When information from the sensors appears to conflict, the brain is confused, and in many people motion sickness occurs. When the boat Jon was in was tossed about on the waves, information from Jon's eyes did not match the information about the boat's movement coming from other parts of his body. This caused him to feel uncomfortable and to vomit. The sensitivity to mixed sensory messages about movement seems to be inherited; motion sickness tends to run in families.

What Are the Symptoms of Motion Sickness?

Almost everyone can get motion sickness at one time or another. Some people, especially children, become queasy when riding in a car or an airplane. Other people get seasick from the rocking motion of a boat on rough water. Some people feel sick from riding a roller coaster or a spinning carnival ride, or even watching a jumpy, fast-moving scene in a movie. Poor ventilation, odors such as gas fumes or smoke, and drinking alcohol make a person more susceptible to motion sickness.

People feeling motion sick may:

- become pale
- yawn
- act restless
- break out in a cold sweat
- feel queasy as if they will have to vomit
- vomit, sometimes repeatedly

How Can Motion Sickness Be Prevented?

Preventing motion sickness is easier than treating it once it has begun.

Travelers should sit wherever there is the least motion. In a car, sitting in the front seat and looking straight ahead may help. In an airplane, passengers feel the least motion in a seat over the wing. On a ship, remaining on the deck and looking at the far horizon rather than nearby objects may help. Eating only a light meal before traveling and avoiding alcohol also help a person avoid motion sickness.

Over-the-counter medications such as meclizine or dimenhydrinate (Dramamine) can be effective in preventing motion sickness. They work best if taken an hour or so before traveling. Although it is not a proven

The Patch

One of the most effective methods of preventing motion sickness is known as "the patch." The patch is a small spot bandage that is usually worn behind the ear. The patch slowly releases scopolamine (sko-PALL-a-meen) through the skin. Scopolamine works by suppressing certain areas of the central nervous system, which decreases motion-induced nausea and vomiting. The patch provides lasting protection against motion sickness for about 3 days. The most common side effect of the patch is dryness of the mouth. Other less common side effects include drowsiness and dilation (widening) of the pupils of the eyes.

medical remedy, some people rely on ginger root, either sliced and chewed or brewed as tea, as a way to prevent motion sickness. In severe or prolonged cases of motion sickness, a doctor may prescribe a scopolamine patch.

Once the symptoms of motion sickness start, they are difficult to treat while the upsetting motion continues. For most people, the symptoms stop soon after the motion stops. If the symptoms persist, the person should consult a physician, because another disorder may be causing the symptoms.

Resource

American Academy of Otolaryngology—Head and Neck Surgery, One Prince Street, Alexandria, VA 22314-3357. This organization's website provides information about the inner ear and how it controls balance.
Telephone 703-836-4444
http://www.entnet.org

▶ *See also*
Vertigo

Mouth Cancer

KEYWORDS
for searching the Internet and other reference sources
Cancer

Mouth cancer, also called oral cancer, occurs when cells in the tissues of the mouth or throat divide without control or order, forming abnormal growths.

What Is Mouth Cancer?

Mouth cancer usually begins in the tissues that make up the lips, tongue, or cheek lining, but it also can affect the gums, the floor or the roof of the mouth, or the salivary glands*. In almost all cases, it is caused by the use of substances that irritate the mucous membranes* in the mouth: spit tobacco (also called chewing tobacco or snuff), cigarettes, cigars, pipes, or alcohol. Over time, this constant irritation takes its toll, and some of the tissue takes on an abnormal appearance and eventually turns cancerous. Mouth cancer most commonly appears in men over the age of 45 who have been longtime users of tobacco and alcohol.

* **salivary glands** (SAL-i-var-ee glands) are the three pairs of glands that produce the liquid called saliva, which aids in the digestion of food.

* **mucous membranes** are thin sheets of tissue that line the inside of the mouth, throat, and other passages within the body.

Many mouth cancers begin as whitish or reddish patches in the mouth, called leukoplakia (loo-ko-PLAY-kee-a) or erythroplakia (e-rith-row-PLAY-kee-a). Other symptoms may include:

- a sore on the lip or in the mouth that does not heal
- a lump on the lip or in the mouth or throat
- unusual bleeding, pain, or numbness in the mouth

- a sore throat that does not go away, or a feeling that something is caught in the throat
- difficulty or pain with chewing or swallowing
- swelling of the jaw
- pain in the ear
- a change in the voice.

Most dentists check for signs of oral cancer as part of the usual dental examination. Early detection is the key to treating it successfully. Otherwise, it can spread throughout the mouth, throat, neck, and even to distant parts of the body through the lymphatic system.*

How Is Mouth Cancer Diagnosed and Treated?

When dentists or doctors find a suspicious-looking area in the mouth, they may order a biopsy. During this procedure, a surgeon removes part or all of the suspect tissue. Examination under a microscope will determine whether cancer cells are present. Once oral cancer is diagnosed, doctors then need to find out whether the cancer has spread.

The first course of treatment is to remove the tumor and any cancerous tissue in the mouth. If there is evidence that the cancer has spread, the surgeon may also remove lymph nodes in the neck as well as part or all of the tongue, cheek, or jaw.

Doctors may also order radiation therapy, either before the surgery to shrink the tumors, or afterward to destroy any remaining cancer cells. In some cases, surgeons may place tiny "seeds" containing radioactive material directly into or near the tumor. Generally, this implant is left in place for several days, and the patient will stay in the hospital.

Chemotherapy is another possible treatment for mouth cancer, especially when it has spread beyond the mouth. It involves taking anticancer drugs by injection or in pill form.

Life after Mouth Cancer

People who are treated for large or widely spread mouth tumors often experience permanent changes that are challenging to deal with, both emotionally and physically. If they lose part of their jaw, tongue, cheek, or palate (the roof of the mouth), they will need reconstructive and plastic surgery. If surgery is not possible, they may need to use an artificial dental or facial part called a prosthesis. In either case, their appearance will be changed permanently.

These people also are likely to have some difficulty chewing and swallowing, and they may lose their sense of taste. For these reasons, weight loss can present a real problem after treatment for mouth cancer.

Many patients have trouble speaking after losing part of their mouth or tongue. Speech therapists will work with them both during and after their hospital stay to help them get back to speaking as normally as possible.

A Major League Fight against Spit Tobacco

For many years, baseball great Joe Garagiola waged a one-man battle against the prevalent use of spit tobacco, also called chewing tobacco, snuff, or chew, by major league baseball players. Himself a former user, Garagiola was concerned both about the players' health and about the effect their behavior was having on young fans. He wanted to convey the message that just because spit tobacco is smokeless does not mean it is safe. To the contrary, it is a major cause of mouth cancer.

In 1996, Garagiola collaborated with a group called Oral Health America to found the National Spit Tobacco Education Program (NSTEP) and get other players involved with the cause. Bill Tuttle, who started using spit tobacco as an outfielder in the 1950s and 1960s, gave talks based on his own experiences with mouth cancer. NSTEP recruited players Lenny Dykstra, Mike Piazza, Tino Martinez, Alex Rodriguez, and Paul Molitor to do anti-tobacco spots that were broadcast during games.

* The **lymphatic system** (lim-FAT-ik system) is a network of vessels, organs, and tissues that produce, store, and carry infection-fighting white blood cells in a colorless, watery fluid called lymph.

A polyp, or mucocele (MU-ko-seel), formed inside the mouth's mucous membrane is a common sign of mouth cancer. © *1991 National Medical Slide/Custom Medical Stock Photo.*

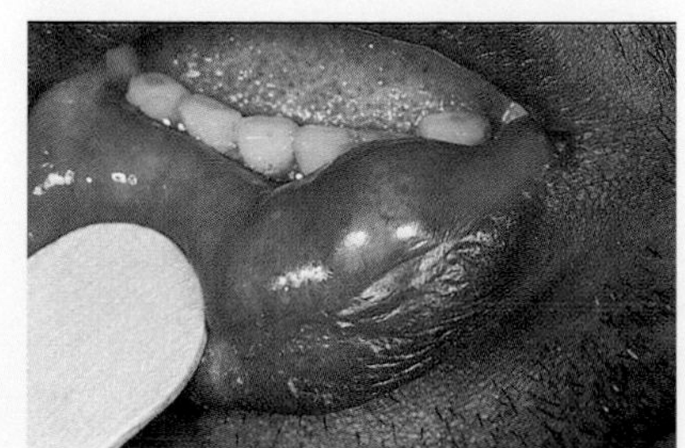

How Is Mouth Cancer Prevented?

People can prevent mouth cancer by not using spit tobacco or smoking cigarettes, cigars, or pipes, or quitting if they already do. If they drink alcohol, they should not have more than one or two drinks per day.

Resources

Book

Koppett, Leonard. *To Improve Health and Health Care, 1998–1999: The Robert Wood Johnson Foundation Anthology.* Edited by Stephen L. Isaacs and James R. Knickman. San Francisco: Jossey-Bass, 1999. See chapter 3, "The National Spit Tobacco Education Program." Available online at
http://www.rwjf.org/library/oldhealth/anthlgyb.htm

Organizations

U.S. National Cancer Institute, National Institutes of Health, Bethesda, MD. This organization has published *Chew or Snuff Is Real Bad Stuff* and *What You Need to Know About Mouth Cancer.*
Telephone 800-4-CANCER
http://rex.nci.nih.gov
See also its fact sheet "What You Need to Know About Oral Cancer"
http://cancernet.nci.nih.gov/wyntk_pubs/index.html

National Oral Health Information Clearinghouse, 1 NOHIC Way, Bethesda, MD 20892-3500. This clearinghouse is a project of the National Institute of Dental Craniofacial Research, National Institutes of Health.
Telephone 301-402-7364
http://www.nidr.nih.gov

Oral Health Education Foundation, P.O. Box 396, Fairburn, GA 30213. This foundation maintains the Oral Cancer Information Center.
Telephone 770-969-7400
http://www.oralcancer.org

Mouth Cancer and Tobacco

Oral Health America, which runs the National Spit Tobacco Education Program, has compiled these statistics about spit tobacco use, which has increased over the past three decades.

- One out of three adolescents in the United States is using some form of tobacco by age 18.
- Spit tobacco use by adolescents is associated with early indicators of gum disease and unusual lesions in the mouth tissue.
- Each year, 10 to 16 million Americans use smokeless or spit tobacco products. Annual sales of these products in 1998 exceeded $1 billion, or more than triple that of 1972.
- Young men ages 17 to 19 are the most frequent users of spit tobacco. The Department of Health and Human Services estimates that 1 million adolescent boys use spit tobacco.
- The risk of developing oral cancer for long-term spit tobacco users is 50 times greater than for non-users.

▶ *See also*
Cancer
Tobacco-Related Diseases

Multiple Personality Disorder (Dissociative Identity Disorder)

Multiple personality disorder is a mental disorder in which a person displays two or more distinct identities that take control of behavior in turn.

KEYWORDS
for searching the Internet and other reference sources

Child abuse
Dissociative disorders
Identity
Memory
Mental disorders
Stress
Violence

The Real-Life Sybil

Sybil Dorsett was a 22-year-old college student who had amnesia*. She also had terrible headaches and sometimes could not see, as if she were blind. Upon turning for help to Dr. Cornelia Wilbur in New York, Sybil soon started to show other personalities. It was as if there were more than one person inside Sybil's body. One personality, who called herself Vicky, said she was from Paris. Another personality, called Peggy Lou, was a tough woman who showed no fear. As time passed, Sybil displayed more personalities: a writer, a flirt, a pianist, a mother, and even an infant and two men.

* **amnesia** (am-NE-zhah) is a loss of memory about one or more past experiences that is more than normal forgetfulness.

Dr. Wilbur noticed that each personality acted and sounded different from the Sybil Dorsett she first had met. Each personality even described his or her physical features in different ways. One said that she had blue eyes, while another said that he had brown. Almost everything, from details about hair color to gestures, changed as Sybil switched from one personality to another. In all, Sybil displayed 16 different identities.

Sybil's case became one of the most famous examples of multiple personality disorder after a book about her experiences appeared in the early 1970s. A movie, starring actress Sally Field, later was made. Sybil's story offers a revealing glimpse of an often-misunderstood mental disorder.

What Is Multiple Personality Disorder?

Multiple personality disorder is a severe mental disorder in which a person displays two or more distinct identities. There can be as many as 100 personalities or more, although most patients display about 10 to 15 different personalities. Each takes control over the patient's behavior for a period of time, usually adopting a unique name, voice, movement style, and life history.

Dissociative identity disorder Descriptions of multiple personality disorder can be found in ancient myths and many other writings through the centuries. However, it was not until the 1800s that it was treated as a mental disorder, and much of what is known about it today was discovered

Actress Sally Field portrayed a woman with multiple personality disorder in the film *Sybil. Photofest.*

only in recent decades. The formal name for the disorder is dissociative identity (di-SO-see-a-tiv i-DEN-ti-tee) disorder. This means that a person's identity is separating into parts, or dissociating, because of the mental disorder.

Schizophrenia Schizophrenia* is another severe mental disorder. Its name comes from the Latin for "split mind." Often, schizophrenia's "split mind" is mistaken for the "split personality" of multiple personality disorder. In reality, however, schizophrenia and multiple personality disorder are two very different mental disorders with different symptoms, causes, and treatments.

* **schizophrenia** (skit-so-FRE-ne-ah) is a serious mental disorder that causes people to have hallucinations, delusions, and other confusing thoughts and behaviors, which distort their view of reality.

What Causes Multiple Personalities?

The exact cause of multiple personality disorder is unknown, but often patients with the disorder have experienced child abuse. This was the case for Sybil, whose mother caused exceptional trauma* for her when she was young. Doctors see multiple personality disorder as an attempt to cope with particularly traumatic events in a person's life. For example, a child might deal with extreme physical or sexual abuse by hiding memories of the abuse and displaying other personalities.

* **trauma** refers to a wound or injury, whether psychological or physical. Psychological trauma refers to an emotional shock that leads to lasting psychological damage.

What Are the Symptoms of Multiple Personalities?

The first symptoms of multiple personality disorder usually involve amnesia. Like Sybil, people with the disorder often start to realize that there are abnormally long periods of time that they cannot remember. For example, they might "wake up" in a different place or in different clothes, and recall nothing that explains the changes. This amnesia can lead them to suspect that something is very wrong.

Patients often are skilled at hiding their multiple personalities from family and friends. A person might be Sam, a shy clerk, at work. However, at night, he might lead life as Jack, an outgoing man who spends time in bars far from his neighborhood.

DR. JEKYLL AND MR. HYDE

Robert Louis Stevenson wrote *The Strange Case of Dr. Jekyll and Mr. Hyde* in three days of frenzied activity in the 1880s. When his wife read the novel, she thought it was so evil that she destroyed it. However, Stevenson simply rewrote it in another three days.

The novel is the account of a good doctor who becomes evil when he drinks a potion. Many people now use the terms Jekyll and Hyde to describe individuals who display a two-sided personality, one side of which is good and the other side of which is evil.

One identity uses the name with which the person was born. This identity often feels depressed, behaves passively, and displays guilt feelings that cannot be explained easily. This primary identity usually is not aware at first of the other identities, although the others might talk about the primary identity in depth. For example, one of Sybil's identities was Vicky, who often commented to Dr. Wilbur about Sybil's life and the lives of the other identities.

Other symptoms include attempted suicide and self-inflicted injuries, such as cuts or burns. Many people with multiple personality disorder also show signs of post-traumatic stress disorder*, a mental disorder that occurs in people who survive a terrifying event. They may have nightmares and startle easily, and they may show signs of depression, anxiety, substance abuse, and eating disorders.

* **post-traumatic stress disorder** (post-traw-MAT-ik STRES dis-OR-der) is a mental disorder that interferes with everyday living and occurs in people who survive a terrifying event, such as school violence, military combat, or a natural disaster.

How Common Are Multiple Personalities?

From 25,000 to 250,000 people in the United States have multiple personality disorder. The estimates vary greatly, because the disorder is difficult to diagnose. People with multiple personalities tend to have a wide range of symptoms that can be confused with other, more common disorders. As a result, it typically takes at least six years for a diagnosis of multiple personality disorder to be made.

In recent years, the number of cases being reported has risen sharply. Some say that this is because doctors are becoming more aware of the disorder's symptoms. Others, however, are concerned that the disorder is being diagnosed in some people who are open to suggestion about memories of childhood trauma.

How Are Multiple Personalities Diagnosed and Treated?

In order for doctors to say that a person has multiple personality disorder, they must see two or more distinct identities. Each identity also must become the dominant personality for a time. In some cases, doctors may talk to the patient for long periods or ask the patient to keep a journal between visits, in hopes of learning more about the different personalities. Doctors sometimes also use hypnosis* to bring out different identities.

* **hypnosis** refers to a trance-like state, usually induced by another person. The person under hypnosis may recall forgotten or suppressed memories and be unusually responsive to suggestions.

The goal of treatment is to bring the separate identities together into one primary identity. Therapy attempts to help the person recall past trauma and deal with emotions without the primary identity being split into parts. Success is possible, but treatment can take many years; it took about 11 years for Sybil's 16 personalities to blend into one.

Resources

Book

Schreiber, Flora Rheta. *Sybil.* New York: Warner Books, reissued 1995. The book about the famous case of Sybil Dorsett has sold more than 6 million copies.

Organizations

National Alliance for the Mentally Ill, 200 North Glebe Road, Suite 1015, Arlington, VA 22203-3754. A self-help organization for people with serious mental illness and their family and friends. The group offers information about multiple personality disorder on its website.
Telephone 800-950-NAMI
http://www.nami.org

American Psychological Association, 750 First Street NE, Washington DC, 20002-4242. The American Psychological Association provides information about psychotherapy and referrals to local psychologists. Its website posts a fact sheet about memories of childhood abuse.
Telephone 202-336-5500
http://www.apa.org/pubinfo/mem.html

See also
▶ **Amnesia**
Mental Disorders
Post-Traumatic Stress Disorder

Multiple Sclerosis

Multiple sclerosis (MS) is an inflammatory disease of the nervous system that disrupts communication between the brain and other parts of the body, resulting in episodes of weakness, paralysis, blindness, and other symptoms.

KEYWORDS
for searching the Internet and other reference sources

Immune system

Nervous system

"She Played Like an Angel"

Jacqueline Du Pré was born in England in 1945. On her fifth birthday, her parents gave her a cello, and she started lessons the next year. At 16, Jacqueline made her debut in London and immediately became a household name. In 1967 she married the pianist and conductor Daniel Barenboim, and together the young, multitalented couple charmed the musical world. Six years later, Jacqueline could no longer feel the strings of her cello. By the mid-1970s, she was unable to dress herself or stand without help. In 1987, at the age of 42, she died of the disease called multiple sclerosis. Many people with MS are mildly affected, but in the most severe cases, like Jacqueline Du Pré's, a person may be unable to write, speak, or walk.

How the Body Communicates Information

Our bodies are able to act and react to the world around us thanks to a network of specialized tissue called the nervous system. This network is divided into two parts, called the central nervous system and the peripheral (pe-RIF-er-al) nervous system, which together process messages to and from all parts of the body. The basic unit of the nervous system is the nerve cell, or neuron, and humans have billions of them. Each neuron looks something like a kite. The top of the kite, or cell body, has many fingerlike extensions called dendrites that receive incoming messages. The tail of the kite, or axon, carries electrical messages from the cell over long distances. Dendrites and axons are called nerve fibers, and a nerve is a bundle of nerve fibers. Nerve cell fibers are wrapped (or sheathed) in a protective fatty substance called myelin (MY-a-lin).

What Is MS?

MS is an inflammation of the nerve fibers in the brain and spinal cord that results in scarred patches called plaques on the myelin sheath that protects the axons and dendrites. When plaques form, the signals passing through the cells may slow down or stop completely. Recent research suggests that, in addition to damaging myelin, MS sometimes slices through the nerve fiber; in other words, it destroys the neuron. About 1 million people worldwide have MS. The disease mostly strikes young adults between 20 and 40, and it affects about twice as many women as men. No one knows what causes MS, but it is believed to be an autoimmune disorder, that is, an attack by the body on its own cells.

When the Body Turns on Itself A healthy body is continually primed to defend itself against disease-causing invaders such as bacteria, viruses, fungi, and parasites. The collection of techniques the body uses to resist disease is called the immune system. Usually the body is able to tell its own cells and foreign cells apart. But sometimes the mechanism for distinguishing self from non-self goes awry. In MS, the body no longer seems to recognize part of the myelin, and begins to attack it.

Are There Different Types of MS? MS can follow several patterns. The most common type is called relapsing-remitting MS, in which symptoms come and go, sometimes with years in between when a person is perfectly fine. In about 50 percent of people with relapsing-remitting MS, the disease eventually will return for good, and when that happens, it is called secondary progressive MS. About 10 percent of people with MS have what is called primary progressive disease, which means that the disease does not go away after the first attack. Patients with primary progressive MS tend to be older (around 40 to 60 years old). A fourth and rare form of MS is called progressive-relapsing disease.

What Causes MS?

Whatever causes the immune system to react in the wrong way in MS is a mystery. Some scientists believe that a virus causes the immune system to attack the myelin sheaths. Others believe that factors in the environment (temperature, for instance) may trigger the disease. Genes* also may play a role in MS. Generally a person's chances of getting MS are very low: less than a tenth of a percent. But if one person in a family has MS, then that person's parents, children, and sisters and brothers have a higher risk of getting the disease. To complicate matters, it seems that more than one gene is involved in a person's susceptibility to MS. In

The U.S. and the World

- Worldwide, about 26,000 people died of multiple sclerosis in 1998 and about 1.5 million people have the disease.
- MS is more common in regions far north or south of the equator, like the northern United States, Canada, Scandinavian countries in Europe, and South America. No one yet knows why.
- As many as 350,000 Americans, or 1.2 percent of the population in 1999, have the disease, according to the Multiple Sclerosis Society. Many live 30 years or more with only mild symptoms. About 25 to 30 percent become disabled to the point where they need a wheelchair.
- Women get MS two to three times more frequently than men.

* **genes** are chemicals in the body that help determine a person's characteristics, such as hair or eye color. They are inherited from a person's parents and are contained in the chromosomes found in the cells of the body.

Word Origin

Sclerosis comes from the Greek word for "scarring" or "hardening."

other words, many different factors are believed to be involved in MS. Research into how genes interact with one another and with the environment may help shed light on what causes MS.

What Are the Signs and Symptoms of MS?

MS may begin very dramatically, or the symptoms may be so mild that a person barely notices them. In the early stages of MS, people may find that simple motions like opening a window or climbing a few stairs tire their arms and legs. Feelings of numbness, or of "pins and needles," are common. Patients often experience blurring and double vision. A person may become uncoordinated. In 70 percent of patients with MS, many of these early symptoms disappear, only to reappear months or years later. Over time, a person may become completely paralyzed. Many patients with MS have frustrating problems related to urination and bowel movements, such as incontinence (in-KON-ti-nens, the inability to control urination) and constipation. A person may become confused or forgetful owing to damage to the part of the brain that processes information. Some people with MS become depressed, or have fits of laughing or crying uncontrollably, for no reason.

Diagnosis

It is not easy for a doctor to establish that a person has MS, because the symptoms are varied and not specific for the disease. Symptoms of MS can be confused with those that follow a viral infection or other diseases. A technique called magnetic resonance imaging, or MRI, is able to visualize the damage that MS causes in the brain. Another technique called magnetic resonance spectroscopy (spek-TROS-ko-pee) provides information about

The First Diagnosis of MS

Jean-Martin Charcot is known as the father of neurology, or the study of the nervous system. Charcot was born in Paris in 1825 and worked at the Salpêtrière Hospital his entire career. In 1868, a young woman came to his clinic with an unusual tremor and other neurological symptoms. The patient subsequently died, and in examining her brain, Charcot found the lesions* that we know today as the plaques caused by MS. Charcot treated patients with similar symptoms using electrical stimulation and strychnine (a nerve stimulant that also is used to poison rodents) in an effort to get the nerves working again. His treatments were unsuccessful, but in writing up the description of the disease and the changes in the brain it brings about, Charcot was the first to diagnose and to name MS. He laid the groundwork for future research, and his definition of the disease still holds today.

* **lesion** (LEE-zhun) is damaged tissue.

the biochemical changes caused in the brain by the disease. These methods, along with other laboratory tests and the typical course of repeated attacks, can help to confirm the diagnosis.

Richard Pryor at an awards ceremony organized by the Congress for Racial Equality. Many people with MS use wheelchairs and other aids to assist in their mobility. *CORBIS/Mitchell Gerber.*

What Is the Treatment for People with MS?

At present there is no cure for MS, and no way to prevent it. Some people do well with no treatment at all. Heat can make the symptoms of MS worse, and swimming or a cool bath may help. Until recently, people suffering severe relapses of MS were offered steroids (drugs with anti-inflammatory properties) as treatment. Steroids can reduce the duration and severity of attacks in some patients, but how they work is not known. Unfortunately, they also can cause acne, weight gain, psychosis, (losing touch with reality), and other serious side effects. These drugs are not recommended for long-term use.

Since 1993, three medications—Betaseron, Copaxone, and Avonex—have been available to treat relapsing-remitting MS. These medications are based on several different forms of a naturally occurring antiviral protein called beta interferon. Interferon reduces the number of MS attacks and may slow the disease down; they also appear to prevent new damage to myelin. A person receives interferon as an injection. Although interferon treatment has side effects, they are much milder than those of steroids, and include flulike symptoms, depression, and mild reactions at the place where the person receives the shot.

What Other Treatments Are under Investigation?

Scientists are working on many new therapies to treat MS. For example, immunotherapy aims to enhance the body's own defense system to fight the disease. Because in MS the message, or electrical signal, that travels along a damaged nerve fiber is weak, researchers are studying ways of making the signals themselves stronger. Other research aims at finding ways of restoring the myelin sheath.

Living with Multiple Sclerosis

Most people with MS can expect to live at least 25 years following their diagnosis. One-third of people with MS will have very mild symptoms and be able to lead relatively normal lives. However, for people who become seriously disabled, life expectancy may be significantly reduced.

The diagnosis of MS is usually devastating because patients are often young adults. Suddenly plans for a career and family must take into account a disease whose course is uncertain. Yet many people with MS will continue to lead productive lives. A woman who has MS may still become pregnant and bear a child safely, although she may be instructed to discontinue her MS medications during pregnancy. And some of the physical limitations of the disease may make it more difficult for a mother with MS to care for her child.

Children whose parents have severe MS may find it hard to accept the changes they see happening in a person they remember as having been able to do everything and whom they still depend upon. They may feel guilty enjoying things like bike rides that their parent can no longer enjoy, or they may get frustrated having to help with simple things like fetching a glass of water or turning the radio up.

MS takes a tremendous emotional and financial toll on the entire family. Support groups and counseling may help MS patients, families, and friends to cope.

Resources

Book

Koplowitz, Zoe, and Mike Celizic. *The Winning Spirit: Lessons Learned in Last Place.* New York: Doubleday, 1997.

Organizations

National Institute of Neurological Disorders and Stroke, National Institutes of Health, Bethesda, MD 20892. The U.S. government's leading supporter of biomedical research on nervous systems disorders, including MS.
http://www.ninds.nih.gov

National Multiple Sclerosis Society, 733 Third Avenue, New York, NY 10017. An organization that since 1946 has been dedicated to helping people with MS and finding a cure for it.
http://www.nmss.org

Tutorials

"Multiple Sclerosis: Hope through Research." An excellent guide to the disease for patients and their families.
http://www.ninds.nih.gov

"How Your Immune System Works." An introduction to the immune system.
http://www.howstuffworks.com/immune-system.htm

▶ *See also*
Paralysis

Mumps

Mumps is an infection caused by a virus*. The main symptoms of mumps are inflammation* and swelling in one or both salivary (SAL-i-var-ee) glands, which produce saliva inside the mouth. In most cases of mumps, there are no complications, and the disease can be prevented by early immunization.

KEYWORDS
for searching the Internet and other reference sources

Parotitis

Vaccination

What Is Mumps?

The mumps virus is spread through the air from an infected person to another person and incubates in the body for 14 to 24 days until symptoms appear. A person who has been infected by the mumps virus can spread the disease to others about a week before any symptoms appear and for about 2 weeks after.

Because of widespread vaccination* against the mumps virus, the number of cases in the United States has dropped sharply since 1967. There were 185,000 cases reported that year. In 1993, only 1,600 cases were reported.

Who Is at Risk for Mumps?

Mumps infects mostly school-age children between 5 and 10 years old in heavily populated areas of countries that do not require immunization against the mumps virus. It is common for the illness to spread to other members of the family as well.

Teenage and adult males who have not been vaccinated are at risk for a complication from mumps. The virus can infect the testicles* of males. They become inflamed and swollen. Usually, only one testicle becomes infected. There have been cases of sterility (the inability to have children) after both testicles became infected. There is a form of vaccination, called passive immunization, that can be given to older males who develop symptoms of mumps.

What Are Some Complications from Mumps?

A serious but not common complication from mumps can be the development of meningitis (men-in-JY-tis). Meningitis is a disease that affects the lining of the spinal column and the brain. Viral meningitis caused by the mumps virus usually is mild. It can cause headache, fever, and a stiff neck.

Another rare complication of the mumps is pancreatitis (pan-kre-a-TY-tis), an infection of the pancreas*. Pancreatitis causes abdominal pain and vomiting.

How Is Mumps Diagnosed and Treated?

Mumps can be diagnosed from saliva or urine samples. Another laboratory test measures the amount of virus antibodies* present in the sample. Usually, treatment involves giving the patient pain relievers, lots of fluids, and soft foods to eat, since chewing is painful. Bed rest is recommended, and the patient should be isolated from other people, especially those who are not immunized against the virus.

Can Mumps Be Prevented?

Mumps can be prevented by receiving a vaccination against the virus. The vaccination for mumps usually is given to children during their second year of life. In most cases, it is combined in a single shot with the measles and rubella vaccinations.

* **virus** (VY-rus) is a tiny infectious agent that lacks an independent metabolism (me-TAB-o-liz-um) and can only reproduce within the cells it infects.

* **inflammation** (in-fla-MAY-shun) is the body's response to infection or irritation.

* **vaccination** (vak-si-NAY-shun) is taking into the body a killed or weakened germ or protein to prevent, lessen, or treat a disease.

* **testicles** (TES-ti-kulz) are the male reproductive organs wherein the sperm are produced.

* **pancreas** (PAN-kree-us) is a gland located behind the stomach that secretes insulin and other hormones and enzymes necessary for digestion and metabolism.

* **antibodies** (AN-te-bod-eez) are proteins produced by the immune system to fight specific infections.

Swelling of the neck and jaw is a sign of the mumps. *Andy Levin, Photo Researchers, Inc.*

Resources

Book

Oldstone, Michael B. A. *Viruses, Plagues, and History.* New York: Oxford University Press, 1998.

Organizations

U.S. Centers for Disease Control and Prevention (CDC), 1600 Clifton Road N.E., Atlanta, GA 30333. The U.S. government authority for information about infectious and other diseases, the CDC posts information about mumps at its website.
http://www.cdc.gov/nip/vaccine/nip-mmr.htm

The World Health Organization (WHO), Avenue Appia 20, 1211 Geneva 27, Switzerland. This group's website posts a fact sheet about mumps.
http://www.who.int/gpv-dvacc/diseases/mumps_disease.htm

See also
Chickenpox
German Measles (Rubella)
Measles
Meningitis
Pancreatitis
Viral Infections

Muscular Dystrophy

Muscular dystrophy (DIS-tro-fee) is a group of inherited disorders in which there is a gradual deterioration and weakening of muscles in the body.

KEYWORDS
for searching the Internet and other reference sources

Duchenne

Muscular disorders

Neurology

What Is Muscular Dystrophy?

The term "muscular dystrophy" actually includes a group of disorders that affect different muscles in the body, and that may range from mild to severe. Although all of the muscular dystrophies are known to be caused by genes*, the way in which the genes produce the disorder is as yet only partly understood.

* **genes** are chemicals in the body that help determine a person's characteristics, such as hair or eye color. They are inherited from a person's parents and are contained in the chromosomes found in the cells of the body.

The muscles that become weakened in muscular dystrophy are mostly the voluntary muscles, those that we can control when we want to move different parts of the body. Another name for voluntary muscle is skeletal muscle. The weakness is usually symmetrical; that is, it occurs more or less equally on both sides of the body. Muscle deterioration is also progressive, or gradually increasing over time. There is no pain connected with the weakening condition, although there may be some cramps and stiffness. Mental retardation sometimes accompanies this condition.

Who Gets Muscular Dystrophy?

All types of muscular dystrophy are uncommon. Still, numbers of individuals affected range in the tens of thousands. Many people have come to know something about muscular dystrophy through the efforts of the famous American comedian and actor Jerry Lewis, who has appeared on television on behalf of the Muscular Dystrophy Association. Similar media appeals, such as the Télethon in France, have raised public awareness about the disease in other countries.

The most common and severe form of the disorder, called Duchenne (du-SHEN) muscular dystrophy, affects about 2 in 1,000 young boys. In the United States, it has been estimated that 40,000 boys and young men are afflicted with this form. In western Europe, an estimated 70,000 are affected. The incidence* is believed to be comparable throughout the world. Muscular dystrophy affects all races, ethnic groups, and social classes equally.

* **incidence** means rate of occurrence.

What Causes Muscular Dystrophy?

Whether or not someone has a form of muscular dystrophy has already been determined through hereditary factors by the time they are born (even though its effects are not apparent at birth). It also means that the disease is not in any way contagious, and that it is not brought on by anything that might happen in one's everyday life.

The defective gene that causes Duchenne muscular dystrophy is located on the X chromosome*. The disorder is therefore said to be sex-linked. It also is recessive, which means that females who inherit the defective gene will not usually develop the disease (because they need to have the defective gene on both X chromosomes) but are carriers of it. They can pass it on to the next generation. Affected males always inherit the gene for Duchenne

* **chromosome** (KRO-mo-som) is a threadlike structure inside cells on which the genes are located. The X chromosome is one of two that determine whether a person is male or female. If you have two X chromosomes, then you are female; if you have one X and one Y chromosome, then you are male.

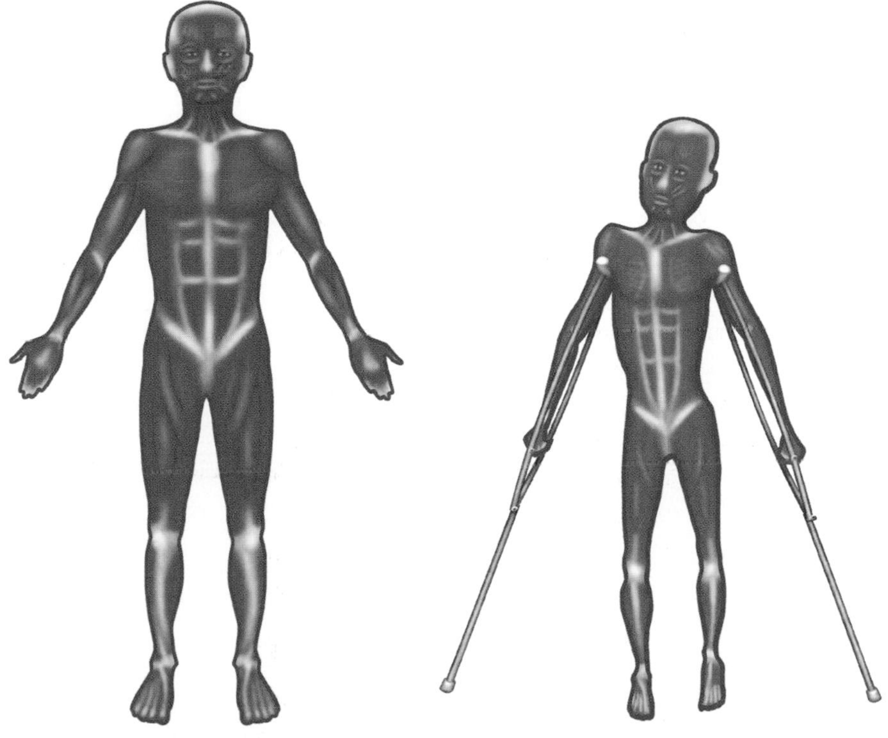

Healthy muscle tissue (left). Muscular dystrophy (right).

▲

Wheelchair racers at International Games for the Disabled. Some of the racers have muscular dystrophy. © *Gerhard Gscheidle, Peter Arnold, Inc.*

muscular dystrophy from their mothers, and each male born to a mother who is a carrier for the disease has a 50-50 chance of inheriting the gene.

Myotonic (mi-o-TON-ik) dystrophy, an adult form of the disorder, is inherited as an autosomal dominant. Autosomal means that the gene that causes the disorder is not located on a sex chromosome. Dominant means that just one defective gene in a pair is able to produce the disease. Males and females are equally affected by the faulty gene, and both can transmit the disease to their children.

Other types of muscular dystrophy follow various different patterns of inheritance, and they can affect both children and adults.

Muscles under a Microscope

The gene responsible for the Duchenne form of muscular dystrophy was discovered in 1986. That was an important breakthrough, but scientists still needed to know how the gene caused muscle weakness. The following year, a protein that was named dystrophin (DIS-tro-fin) was found to be absent in the muscles of Duchenne patients and present in normal tissue. Therefore, the defective Duchenne gene does not produce dystrophin, while the same gene in its normal form does produce this protein. To understand why dystrophin is important in muscle function, a powerful microscope is needed.

Seen under a microscope, muscles are made up of bundles of individual muscle fibers. Under greater magnification, each fiber is seen to have an outer membrane. Dystrophin is believed to be responsible for maintaining the structure of the muscle fiber membrane. Without it, the membrane tends to fall apart and become "leaky." One of the substances that leaks out from inside the muscle fibers is creatine kinase (KREE-a-tin KI-naze), which is needed for the chemical reactions that produce energy for muscle contraction.

In other types of muscular dystrophy, the defect lies in an abnormality in another substance closely associated in function with dystrophin.

What Are the Symptoms of the Dystrophies?

There are several forms of muscular dystrophy. Some experts have listed as many as 20 types. Classification of types is based upon a person's age at the start of the disease, the location of the muscles affected, the rate at which the disorder progresses, and the pattern of inheritance. The following are signs and symptoms of the more common and well-defined forms.

Duchenne Muscular Dystrophy The signs of Duchenne muscular dystrophy may not be noticed until ages 3 to 7, when the young boy is likely to start having difficulty walking. (Because of the way it is inherited, only boys usually have Duchenne muscular dystrophy.) Another characteristic sign is that the calf muscles, although becoming weaker, are enlarged partly because of accumulating deposits of fat in them.

Muscle weakness steadily advances from the lower to the upper body, and a wheelchair is usually needed by about age 12. Complications such as scoliosis (side-to-side curving of the spine) and lung infections commonly occur in the teen years, and the person may not live past his late teens or early twenties.

Becker Muscular Dystrophy In this form, the signs and symptoms are the same as those of Duchenne muscular dystrophy, but begin later in life and progress more slowly. The same gene that causes the Duchenne form is responsible, but its defects are less damaging to muscle. Most affected men must eventually use a wheelchair, but some do not, and many live past middle age.

Myotonic Dystrophy Myotonic dystrophy usually develops in adulthood, but may occur as early as infancy. Males and females are affected equally. The characteristic symptom is myotonia, a delayed relaxation of muscle after it has contracted. Weakness commonly occurs in the muscles of the hands, face, neck, forearms, and lower legs.

Unlike other dystrophies, myotonic dystrophy may involve parts of the body other than the voluntary muscles. For example, the heart rate may be abnormally slowed. Cataracts may develop in the eyes. As in other dystrophies, mental retardation sometimes accompanies the condition. Nonetheless, people with mild forms of myotonic dystrophy may have relatively normal lives and survive beyond middle age.

What's in a Name?

The word "dystrophy" comes originally from the Greek "dys," which means "difficult" or "faulty," and "trophe," meaning "nourishment." This word was chosen many years ago because it was at first believed that poor nourishment of the muscles was in some way to blame for muscular dystrophy. Today we know that muscle wasting in the disorder is caused by defective genes rather than poor nutrition.

The "Duchenne" in Duchenne muscular dystrophy may have been a bit of a misnomer as well. The French neurologist Guillaume Benjamin Amand Duchenne (1806–1875) described the disorder in detail in 1868. However, recent research has shown that the English physician Edward Meryon (1809–1880) had independently described the condition several years before Duchenne.

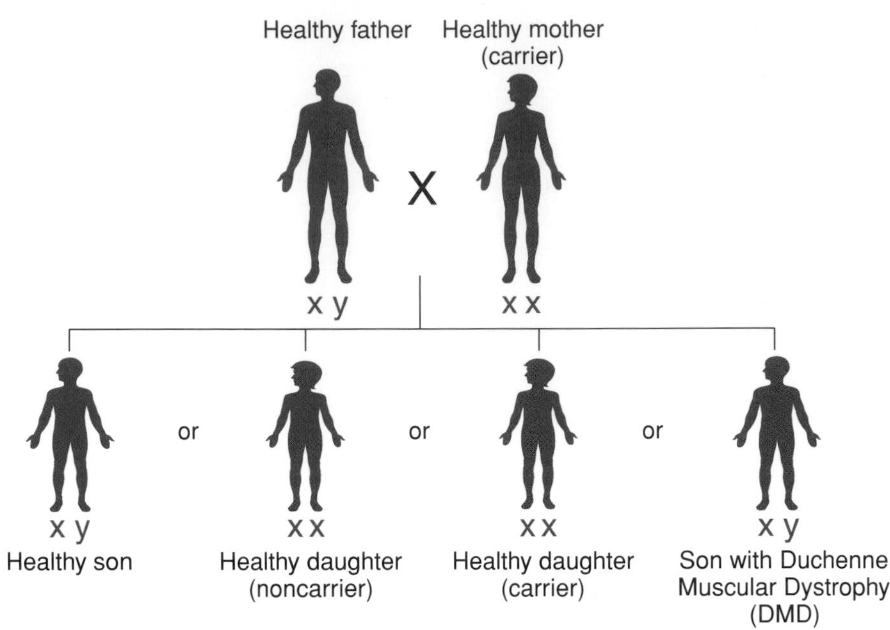

Inheritance pattern of Duchenne muscular dystrophy (DMD). Sons have a 50–50 chance of inheriting the disorder from their mother if she carries the gene for it on one of her X chromosomes.

Facioscapulohumeral Muscular Dystrophy Facioscapulohumeral (fay-she-o-skap-yoo-lo-HU-me-ral) muscular dystrophy gets its long name from the fact that it weakens the muscles of the face, shoulders (the scapula is the shoulder blade), and upper arms (the humerus is the upper arm bone). Facial expression is altered, and the shoulders tend to droop. Both males and females are affected, and the progression of symptoms is usually slow. Symptoms most often begin to appear between the ages of 10 and 40.

Limb Girdle Muscular Dystrophy Muscle weakness in this form occurs mostly around the hips and shoulders (limb girdles). Symptoms may eventually extend to other muscles. Often, however, worsening of the condition is slow. Both sexes are affected, and symptoms may begin in late childhood or early adult life.

How Is Muscular Dystrophy Diagnosed?

A doctor may suspect that someone has muscular dystrophy just by observing certain signs of muscle weakness. If someone in the patient's immediate family is known to have the disorder, the diagnosis becomes clearer.

To confirm the diagnosis, a blood test may be performed to look for high levels of creatine kinase, mentioned earlier as a sign of Duchenne muscular dystrophy. Blood samples may also be analyzed for defective genes, and can help determine the specific type of the disorder. Other tests can measure muscle activity, and a muscle biopsy, in which a tiny sample of muscle tissue is removed to be examined under the microscope, can show specific abnormalities.

How Is Muscular Dystrophy Treated?

At present there is no cure for muscular dystrophy. Sometimes treatment with steroids can slow progress of muscular weakness. Treatment is aimed at maintaining general good health and mobility for as long as possible. An important goal is preventing scoliosis and often fatal lung infection. Moderate exercise, physical therapy, the use of braces, and sometimes surgery can assist walking.

Genetic counselors, using medical tests and family history, can help prospective parents make informed decisions about having children. The disease can be diagnosed in a baby before it is born; this is called prenatal testing.

Meanwhile, medical scientists in the laboratory are working on ways to attack the cause of muscular dystrophy directly, through a technique called gene therapy.

Resources

Emery, Alan E. M. *Muscular Dystrophy: The Facts.* Oxford: Oxford University Press, 1994. This book provides in nontechnical language much helpful information about the disorder for patients and their caregivers.

Muscular Dystrophy Association provides general information on its website.
http://www.mdusa.org/

Muscular Dystrophy Association of Canada also provides information on its website.
http://www.mdac.ca/

▶ *See also*
Genetic Diseases
Scoliosis

Myocardial Infarction *See* Heart Disease

Myopia *See* Nearsightedness

N

N

Narcolepsy *See* Sleep Disorders

Nearsightedness

Nearsightedness is an eye disorder that causes objects that are not close to a person to appear out of focus or blurry.

KEYWORDS
for searching the Internet and other reference sources

Myopia

Ophthalmology

Optometry

Vision

Kate noticed she was squinting when she needed to see the blackboard from the back of her classroom. Squinting helped bring the words into focus. It seemed odd to her, because she did not remember having to squint when she was younger. But now that she was in middle school, Kate started to have trouble seeing things unless they were close.

Kate has a common eye condition known as nearsightedness. It affects more than 60 million people in the United States, and often is not noticed until a child is between 8 and 12 years old. Fortunately, nearsightedness is usually corrected easily with eyeglasses or contact lenses.

What Is Nearsightedness?

Nearsightedness means a person can see things that are close but has trouble seeing distant objects clearly. The condition results when a person's eyeball is not shaped to focus properly when light passes through it. In most cases the eyeball is too long, but in some cases the front of the eye is curved abnormally.

The front of the eyeball, like the lens of a camera, is where the image passes. As it does, the image is bent in order to focus it. The bending is known as refraction (re-FRAK-shun), and it focuses the image on the

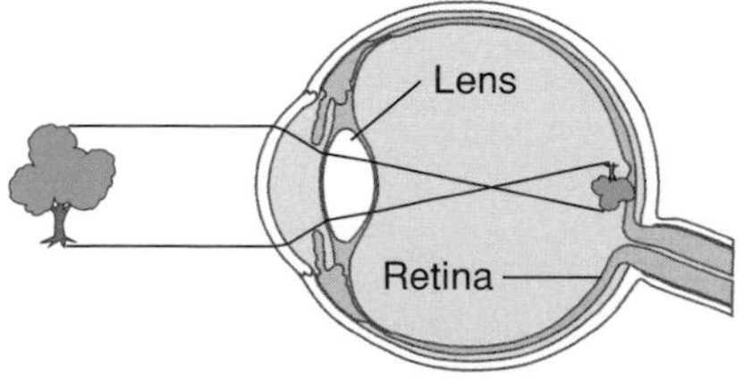

Normal vision: far object is focused on the retina

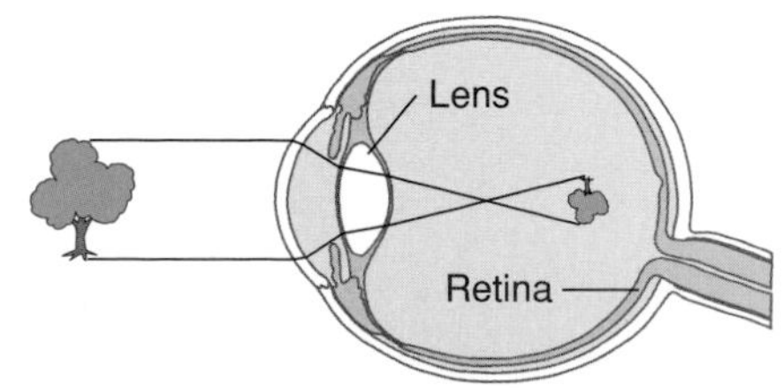

Nearsightedness: far object is focused in front of the retina

Normal vs. nearsighted focus.

retina at the rear inside of the eyeball. The retina is something like the film in a camera. It receives the image. If a person's eyeball is not shaped properly, the light from the image is focused in front of the retina. This results in a blurred image for distant objects.

How Is Nearsightedness Diagnosed?

The first sign that a person is nearsighted usually occurs in childhood between the ages of 8 and 12. It is often a teacher who notices that a student is having trouble seeing the blackboard. The teacher may notice the student squinting, which can help focus distant objects for nearsighted people. Sometimes the condition is discovered during a routine eye examination during childhood. Nearsightedness also is called "myopia," which comes from a Greek word for "closed eyes," perhaps because squinting is common in nearsightedness.

What Are the Treatment Options for Nearsightedness?

Eyeglasses Prescription (pre-SKRIP-shun) eyeglasses are the most common solution for nearsightedness. The glasses change how the light passing through the eye is focused. Contact lenses worn on the eyeball also can help nearsightedness.

As a child passes through the teenage years, nearsightedness often gets worse. This is because as the body grows, the shape of the eyeball changes too. Thus, people with nearsightedness may need to change prescription eyeglasses or contact lenses as they get older. By the time people reach their twenties, however, nearsightedness usually stabilizes and does not get worse.

Surgery Some people with mild or moderate nearsightedness may benefit from refractive surgery. A surgeon cuts small incisions in the surface of the eye, known as the cornea, to flatten it. This allows the image to be focused on the retina. Another type of surgery involves a laser that changes the shape of the cornea to achieve the same result. Many people who have the surgery no longer need glasses at all.

Resources

Book

Cassel, Gary H., M.D., Michael D. Billig, O.D., and Harry G. Randall, M.D. *The Eye Book: A Complete Guide to Eye Disorders and Health*. Baltimore: Johns Hopkins University Press, 1998. A good general reference on eye problems.

Organization

The U.S. National Eye Institute posts a resource list of eye health-related publications and organizations at its website.
http://www.nei.nih.gov/publications/sel-org.htm

See also
Astigmatism
Farsightedness

Nephritis

Nephritis (nef-RY-tis) is an inflammation of one or both kidneys that can result in kidney damage.

KEYWORDS
for searching the Internet and other reference sources

Bright's disease

Glomerulonephritis

Infection

Inflammation

Pyelonephritis

Renal disease

Polly's Sore Throat

Polly will always remember fifth grade because she missed so much of it. She missed one week of school because she had strep throat, a sore throat caused by streptococcal bacteria. Several weeks later, Polly felt very tired, she lost her appetite, her abdomen and back hurt, and her face looked puffy. She rarely had to urinate, and when she did, her urine was dark like cola. Polly's doctor suspected that she had a case of acute (sudden) nephritis that was caused by her strep throat. He explained that her kidneys were not working properly and that waste products from the cells were building up inside her body. Polly's condition got worse. She spent several days in the hospital, then she recovered at home for several weeks.

What Is Nephritis?

The kidneys play an important role in filtering about 400 quarts of blood a day to remove cellular waste products and extra water. Each of the two bean-shaped kidneys is made up of about one million units called nephrons (NEF-rons). Each nephron consists of a collecting tubule that will eventually take wastes to the bladder, and a filtering unit called a glomerulus*.

In a person with nephritis, the glomeruli (plural of glomerulus) do not function properly, often as a result of a bacterial infection like Polly's. Not all the glomeruli are damaged to the same degree, however, so the kidneys can continue to function, but not as well as before. The kidneys may already be affected before the person notices symptoms.

* **glomerulus** (glom-ER-you-lus) is from a Greek word meaning "filter." The glomerulus is a knot of blood vessels that have the job of filtering the blood.

175 Years Ago: Richard Bright

Richard Bright, a British physician who lived from 1789 to 1858, was the first to describe the kidney disorder known today as Bright's disease, or nephritis. Bright studied kidney function and was meticulous in his clinical observations. He worked with kidney patients, studying their symptoms, and then he correlated symptoms with the kidney defects he observed during autopsies (examinations after death). The results of Bright's research first appeared in *Reports of Medical Cases* in 1827. Bright also contributed to the study of lung disease, heart disease, various fevers, and tumors.

Glomerulonephritis (Bright's disease) There are several different types of nephritis. One of the most common is glomerulonephritis (glom-er-u-lo-ne-FRY-tis), also called Bright's disease, a condition in which the glomeruli become inflamed and scarred. Common symptoms of this disease include tiredness, high blood pressure, and swelling of the hands, feet, ankles, and face. This swelling is called edema (e-DEE-ma). The person will pass blood and protein in the urine.

Acute nephritis Another type of nephritis that commonly affects children occurs as a result of infection. Sometimes a bacterial infection can spread from another part of the body, such as the bladder, to the kidney. The body's disease-fighting proteins, or antibodies, can adhere to the glomeruli, causing them to become inflamed. This type of nephritis usually is acute, or sudden, and many affected children recover without long-term kidney damage.

Other causes Nephritis can occur as a side effect of other diseases, such as diabetes*, and of autoimmune disorders such as systemic lupus erythematosus*. Nephritis also can be caused by the overuse of certain common drugs, such as ibuprofen (i-bu-PRO-fen) and acetaminophen (a-set-a-MIN-a-fen), and by sniffing glue or inhaling gasoline.

* **diabetes** (di-a-BEE-teez) is an impaired ability to break down carbohydrates, proteins, and fats because the body does not produce enough insulin or cannot use the insulin it makes.

* **systemic lupus erythematosus** (sis-TEM-ik LOO-pus er-i-them-a-TO-sus), sometimes just called lupus, is a chronic inflammatory disease that can affect the skin, joints, kidneys, nervous system, membranes lining body cavities, and other organs.

What Happens When People Have Nephritis?

Symptoms Acute nephritis is characterized by fatigue, loss of appetite, abdominal and back pain, and edema. People with chronic nephritis might not show any outward symptoms. However, protein and red blood cells can usually be seen when a doctor examines their urine under a microscope. If left untreated, chronic nephritis may cause a drastic reduction in kidney function, and the patient's kidney tissue will deteriorate. The patient may develop high blood pressure and may die either from kidney or heart failure.

Treatment To treat acute nephritis, the doctor may prescribe antibiotics to treat infection, anti-inflammatory drugs to reduce symptoms of inflammation, and diuretics to reduce edema.

Chronic nephritis cannot be cured, but it can be treated. The goal of treatment is to slow the deterioration of the kidneys. Drugs may be used to treat high blood pressure and a special diet may be prescribed to relieve the load on the kidneys. People with an overactive immune system that triggers nephritis may be given immunosuppressant drugs to slow down the attack on the kidneys by the immune system.

Nephritis can lead to kidney failure, in which case dialysis or a kidney transplant is required. Dialysis is a procedure in which blood is passed through a machine to filter out waste products and extra water, then returned to the person's body. A kidney transplant is a procedure in which a diseased kidney is surgically replaced with a healthy kidney from a compatible donor.

Resources

Book

Bock, Glenn H. *A Parent's Guide to Kidney Disorders*. Minneapolis: University of Minnesota Press, 1993.

Organization

U.S. National Kidney and Urologic Disease Information Clearinghouse, 3 Information Way, Bethesda, MD 20892-3580. This division of the National Institute of Diabetes and Digestive and Kidney Diseases (NIDDK) posts fact sheets about hematuria, pyelonephritis, and lupus nephritis at its website.
http://www.niddk.nih.gov/health/kidney/kidney.htm

See also
Bacterial Infections
Diabetes
Infection
Kidney Disease
Lupus
Nephrosis
Substance Abuse

Nephrosis

Nephrosis (nef-RO-sis), or nephrotic syndrome, is a kidney disease that causes the body to lose protein through the urine. Loss of protein results in edema, loss of appetite, and general tiredness. Nephrosis cannot usually be cured, but it can be treated with medication and diet.

KEYWORDS
for searching the Internet and other reference sources

Bright's disease

Proteinuria

Renal disease

Sally's Story

During the summer when Sally was seven years old, she stopped eating much of anything at meals, lay around the house all day, and seemed too tired to do her chores or play with friends. At first Sally's mother thought Sally was just being lazy, but when Sally's whole body began to look puffy, especially her eyes, ankles, and abdomen, her mother began to worry.

The doctor identified Sally's puffiness as edema*, and asked Sally about how often she had been going to the bathroom. When Sally said she was urinating only about twice a day, the doctor suspected a kidney problem. The doctor ran several tests: an analysis of Sally's urine showed that it contained high levels of protein; a blood test showed low levels of protein and high levels of cholesterol. These results made the doctor suspect nephrosis.

** **edema** (e-DEEM-a) occurs when excess fluid collects in tissues causing the hands, feet, and other body parts to swell abnormally.*

The doctor performed several additional tests to eliminate other diseases, then he confirmed the diagnosis with a kidney biopsy. Ultimately, he could not figure out why Sally had developed nephrosis. He explained to Sally and her parents that her condition could not be cured, but that medications and a low-fat, low-salt diet would help relieve the symptoms.

What Is Nephrosis?

The kidneys are a pair of bean-shaped organs located in the abdomen just above the waist. Their chief role is to filter waste and excess water out of the

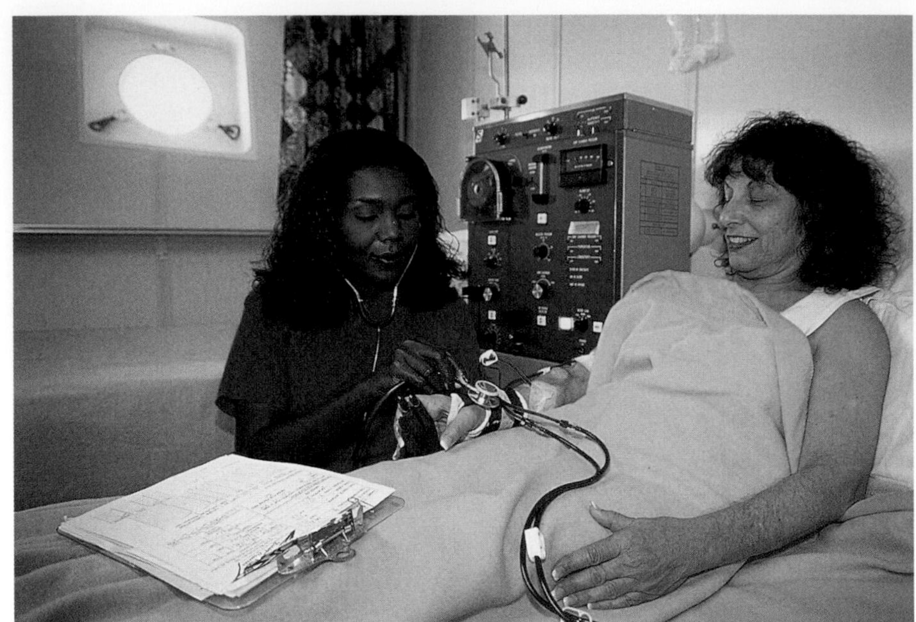

If nephrosis leads to kidney failure, dialysis may be necessary. Here a person on a cruise receives dialysis with the assistance of the ship nurse. © *Jeff Greenberg/Visuals Unlimited.*

blood. The filtering units in the kidney are called glomeruli (glom-ER-you-li). Nephrosis is a kidney disease caused by a defect in the glomeruli.

When the glomeruli are damaged, the filtering mechanism does not work properly. Instead of keeping proteins in the blood, while allowing excess water and wastes to pass through the filter into collecting tubules where they become urine, the glomeruli filters leak. This allows proteins to move out of the bloodstream with the water and wastes, and to be excreted in the urine. Loss of large amounts of protein from the blood allows fluid to leak out of the bloodstream into the body's tissues. The retention of fluid gives the body, especially the face and legs, a puffy and bloated appearance.

What Causes Nephrosis?

Children as well as adults can develop nephrosis. What causes the defect in the glomeruli that results in nephrosis often is unknown. Nephrosis can develop as part of other diseases, however, including:

- Hypertension (high blood pressure).
- Diabetes, when the body cannot produce sufficient amounts of the hormone insulin to regulate the amount of sugar in the blood.
- Systemic lupus erythematosus (sis-TEM-ik LOO-pus er-i-them-a-TO-sus), sometimes just called lupus, which is a chronic inflammatory disease that can affect the kidneys and other organs.
- Amyloidosis (am-i-loy-DO-sis), a condition in which a protein called amyloid collects in the tissues and organs.
- Myeloma (my-e-LO-ma), a tumor derived from bone marrow cells.

- Glomerulonephritis (glom-er-u-lo-ne-FRY-tis), also called Bright's disease, a condition in which the glomeruli become inflamed and scarred.

In addition, overuse of some drugs, exposure to certain chemicals (for example lead or carbon tetrachloride), and in some people, exposure to certain allergens (poison ivy, poison oak, insect stings) can affect the functioning of the kidneys and lead to nephrosis.

What Is the Treatment for Nephrosis?

How nephrosis is treated depends on its cause. If it is caused by another disease, that disease is treated. If the cause of nephrosis is not known, the symptoms may be treated with drugs to reduce inflammation in the kidneys, diuretics* to reduce edema, and antibiotics to stop infection. A diet low in fat and salt might be recommended, and fluid intake might be restricted.

People with nephrosis often recover when the disease causing the nephrosis is treated. People with nephrosis, however, may be at increased risk for other kidney diseases. If the kidneys lose their ability to function, dialysis may be necessary.

* **diuretics** (di-yoo-RET-iks) are drugs that increase the production of urine and help the body get rid of extra water.

Resources

Book

Bock, Glenn H. *A Parent's Guide to Kidney Disorders*. Minneapolis: University of Minnesota Press, 1993.

Organization

U.S. National Kidncy and Urologic Disease Information Clearinghouse, 3 Information Way, Bethesda, MD 20892-3580. This division of the National Institute of Diabetes and Digestive and Kidney Diseases (NIDDK) posts a fact sheet about nephrotic syndrome at its website. http://www.niddk.nih.gov/health/kidney/summary/nephsynd/nephsynd.htm

▶ *See also*
Diabetes
Hypertension
Kidney Disease
Lupus
Nephritis

Neurofibromatosis

Neurofibromatosis (noor-o-fy-bro-ma-TO-sis) is a genetic disorder that causes tumors to grow on nerves and is also characterized by skin changes and deformities in bone.

KEYWORDS
for searching the Internet and other reference sources

Inherited Genetic Disorders

Neurology

What Is Neurofibromatosis?

The most common form, called neurofibromatosis type 1 or NF-1, mainly affects nerves in the skin, producing soft nodules or bumps. Neurofibromatosis type 2 (NF-2) is a very rare disorder that affects the auditory nerves responsible for hearing and balance. Both types are caused by defective genes*.

Neurofibromatosis also is called von Recklinghausen's disease, after the German physician Friedrich von Recklinghausen (1833–1910), who described it in 1882. The tumors he noted, called neurofibromas (noor-o-fy-BRO-mas), arise from the cells that make up the covering sheaths of the nerves.

NF-1 and NF-2 neurofibromatoses occur in both sexes and in all racial and ethnic groups. In the United States, NF-1 occurs in about 1 of 4,000 persons. NF-2 is 10 times less common, occurring in about 1 in 40,000 people.

* **genes** are chemicals in the body that help determine a person's characteristics, such as hair or eye color. They are inherited from a person's parents and are contained in the chromosomes found in the cells of the body.

What Causes Neurofibromatosis?

Although many people who have neurofibromatosis inherited it from one of their parents, between 30 and 50 percent developed it spontaneously from a mutation (change) in their genes before birth.

Neurofibromatosis is inherited as an autosomal (non-sex-linked) dominant disorder. This means that each child born to a parent with neurofibromatosis has a 50 percent chance of inheriting the defective gene and developing the disease.

Genes produce proteins that determine a person's body physical and metabolic characteristics, everything from the color of a person's hair to how fast a person burns fat. Scientists recently have discovered that the neurofibromatosis genes, when normal, produce proteins that suppress tumors. This suggests that when the genes are defective, they may fail to produce enough of these proteins, thus allowing the growth of tumors. Further research is needed to confirm this theory, however.

What Are the Symptoms of Neurofibromatosis?

The signs and symptoms of neurofibromatosis vary greatly among individuals even in the same family. Many people do not know that they

Actor Eric Stolz portrays a high school student with neurofibromatosis in the film *Mask*. *© 1994 Universal City, Photofest.*

have NF-1 until it is diagnosed during a routine physical exam. The disease is usually mild.

NF-1 produces many soft, bumpy or stalk-like tumors under the skin. Another common sign of this disorder is light-brown patches on the skin called cafe-au-lait spots. Although these spots may appear in people who do not have NF-1, people with NF-1 usually have six or more of them. Signs may also include freckles in the armpits or groin areas, growths in the eye or on the optic nerve, deformation of bones, and scoliosis, a side-to-side curvature of the spine.

These signs first appear in infancy or early childhood, and increase as a person grows older. Occasionally, tumors are massive or in rare cases become cancerous. They may also occur inside the body, squeezing or blocking internal organs.

The signs of NF-2 include tumors on the auditory (acoustic) nerves. These growths can cause loss of hearing and may damage nearby nerves and structures in the brain. Tinnitis (ti-NY-tus; a ringing in the ears), balance disturbances, or headache can also occur. People with NF-2 may first notice these symptoms in their teen or early adult years.

The Elephant Man

Neurofibromatosis has long been associated with the "Elephant Man." This was a name given to the Englishman Joseph Carey Merrick (1862-1890), who was exhibited in public as a medical freak because of his grotesque disfigurements. Merrick was, until recently, thought to have had a severe form of neurofibromatosis, but accumulating evidence now indicates that he was suffering from a much rarer disease called Proteus syndrome. Nonetheless, public awareness of neurofibromatosis was greatly increased after the production of a play in 1979 and a film in 1980 on the life of Merrick.

How Is Neurofibromatosis Treated?

The diagnosis of neurofibromatosis is made mainly by noting its outward signs. Internal viewing techniques, such as MRI (magnetic resonance imaging), are sometimes needed as well. Treatment is then based upon controlling symptoms.

Operations and braces may be needed to correct scoliosis. Surgery may also be performed to remove tumors that are exceptionally large, painful, or that press on organs. The tumors often grow back, however.

Various cancer treatments may be used in the rare instances that tumors become malignant.* Recent progress in biomedical research into the causes of neurofibromatosis has raised hopes that someday there will be treatment to slow or halt the growth of its tumors.

*__malignant__ (ma-LIG-nant) refers to cancerous tumors that spread to other places in the body, resulting in a condition that can lead to death.

Some cases of neurofibromatosis can be severely debilitating, and its complications can be fatal. In most instances, however, symptoms are mild, and the person with the disorder can lead a normal, productive life.

Genetic tests and counseling are available for people with neurofibromatosis. It can help them learn more about their condition or that of a family member, and can assist in making decisions about having children of their own.

Resource

Organization

The National Neurofibromatosis Foundation, 95 Pine Street, 16th Floor, New York, NY 10005. This organization provides information for patients and health professionals on neurofibromatosis.
Telephone 800-323-7938
http://www.nf.org

► *See also*
Genetic Diseases

Neurosis *See* Mental Disorders

Night Terrors *See* Sleep Disorders

Nightmares *See* Sleep Disorders

Nosebleeds

KEYWORDS
for searching the Internet and other reference sources

Bleeding

Epistaxis

Bleeding that begins inside the nostrils is referred to as nosebleed. Its medical name is "epistaxis."

What Are Nosebleeds?

Most nosebleeds occur in children and older people and last for a short time. In rare cases, nosebleeds can be associated with other illnesses.

What Causes Nosebleeds?

Nosebleeds usually start after a bump to the nose or when the lining of the nostrils becomes irritated, crusted, or dry. This often happens when someone has a cold, infection, or allergy that affects the amount of mucus secreted from the nose. A high fever can also dry out the lining of the nose and cause nosebleeds. When the crusts are removed, bleeding may occur.

What Is the Treatment for Nosebleeds?

Most nosebleeds can be stopped in a short time by holding the nostrils closed firmly for a few minutes between the thumb and forefinger. A person with a nosebleed should sit down and lean slightly forward and breath through the mouth while holding the nostrils shut. After 10 to 15 minutes, the bleeding should have stopped. The person should avoid blowing the nose for 12 hours after a nosebleed, because this could start the bleeding again. If the nosebleed does not stop after a few attempts at pinching the nostrils for 10 to 15 minutes each time, then a doctor should be contacted. The doctor might put cotton gauze with medication into the nostril to stop the bleeding. Nose drops may also be prescribed for a few days in some cases to help control further bleeding.

Prolonged nose bleeding may be a sign of serious injury to the head or an indication of an illness, like high blood pressure (hypertension) or sinus blockage.

Serious diseases that may rarely be the cause of nosebleeds include leukemia (cancer of the white blood cells), liver disease, atherosclerosis (also called hardening of the arteries), and some hereditary bleeding disorders such as hemophilia, where the blood fails to clot properly.

Can Nosebleeds Be Prevented?

The best way to prevent nosebleeds is to avoid bumping or picking the nose. People involved in contact sports, like football or boxing, are more likely to receive bumps to the head or nose that result in nosebleeds. Appropriate protective gear, such as face guards and masks, should be worn to help prevent these injuries. Humidifying the air indoors in the winter, when the air is very dry because of central heating, will also help.

▶ *See also*
Bleeding Disorders
Hypertension

O

Obesity

Obesity (o-BEE-si-tee) is an excess of body fat.

KEYWORDS
for searching the Internet and other reference sources

Adiposity

Bariatric medicine

Endocrinology

Karen's Story

Karen was a large baby who grew into a very large child. By the time she was 12 years old, Karen was 60 pounds overweight. She was also an after-school couch potato, who spent much of her free time munching chips and cookies in front of the television or chatting with on-line friends at the computer. The more weight Karen gained, the tougher it was to catch her breath when she did try to exercise, and the harder it became to deal with the face-to-face teasing of classmates. Finally, one day Karen decided that a change was in order. Since both of her parents were overweight too, it became a family project. Karen and her parents began going to the local YMCA to exercise almost every day. They also learned how to eat a leaner, healthier diet. Before long, Karen was slimmer, trimmer, and able to enjoy a more active life with her friends.

What Is Obesity?

Obesity is the medical term for an increase in body weight, beyond what doctors usually recommend, as the result of an excess of body fat. It is slightly different from overweight, which is the term for an excess of body weight caused by bone, muscle, and other body tissues and fluids in addition to body fat. In other words, it is possible to be overweight without being obese. For example, body builders might weigh more than normal because they have a large amount of muscle mass. Yet they usually would not have obesity, because the amount of fat on their bodies is not above normal.

It is also possible to be obese without being overweight. For example, a very inactive person with little muscle mass might be of normal weight but still have too much body fat. However, most people with obesity are also overweight.

As a rule, women have more fat on their bodies than men. Women with more than 30 percent body fat and men with more than 25 percent body fat are usually considered to have obesity. The rules are less clearcut for children, as many go through growth spurts in which they may put on weight first, then catch up in height later. A doctor is the best person to judge whether a child weighs more than medical professionals usually recommend.

Body fat (adipose tissue) is made up of fat cells. Obesity results when the body has too many fat cells or when fat cells are overfilled with fat. © *C.P. Hickman/Visuals Unlimited.*

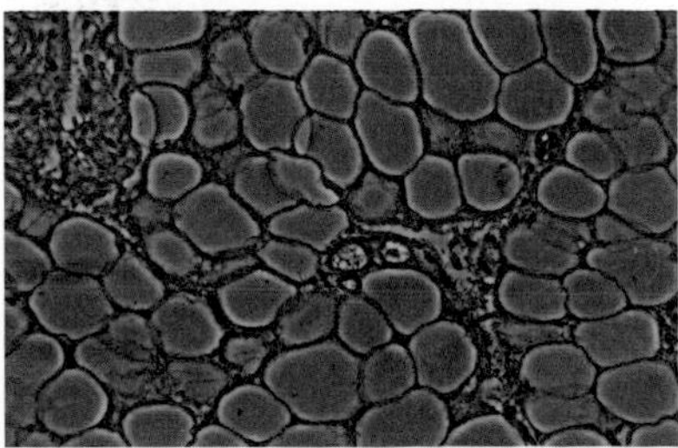

What Are the Health Risks?

Children have fewer health problems from being heavy than adults do. However, such children may suffer stress because they look different from their friends. Some, especially those who are genetically* prone to such conditions, may also have higher blood pressure and higher blood cholesterol*. The greatest health risk faced by overweight children, though, is that they are more likely to be obese when they become adults.

* **genetically** (je-NE-ti-klee) means due to heredity, and stemming from genes, the material in the body that helps determine physical and mental characteristics, such as hair or eye color.

* **cholesterol** (ko-LES-ter-ol) is a fat-like substance found in the bloodstream. Too much cholesterol in the blood has been linked to heart disease.

For adults, obesity is much more than a matter of looks. It is a serious health hazard. The more obese a person is, the more likely that person is to develop health problems. A person who has weighed 40 percent more than doctors recommend for at least 10 years is twice as likely to die early as someone who weighs no more than doctors recommend. Adults with obesity face several health risks:

Heart disease and stroke The leading causes of death and disability in the United States are heart disease and stroke. Stroke is a disorder that occurs when a blood vessel to the brain is blocked or bursts. People who are obese are more likely to have high blood pressure, which raises the risk of heart disease and stroke. Obesity is also linked to having higher levels of cholesterol and fats in the blood, which can lead to heart disease. In addition, obesity is linked to sudden death from heart disease and to stroke and chest pain caused by decreased oxygen reaching the heart muscle.

Diabetes Type 2 diabetes (dy-a-BEE-teez) is the most common form of diabetes, a disorder that reduces the body's ability to control blood sugar. It is a major cause of early death, heart disease, kidney disease, stroke, and blindness. People with obesity are twice as likely as other people to get type 2 diabetes.

Cancer Men who are obese are more likely than other men to get cancer of the colon (main part of the large intestine), rectum (lower part of the large intestine), and prostate (PROS-tate; male gland in front of the rectum). Women with obesity are more likely than other women to get cancer of the colon, uterus (womb), cervix (lower part of the uterus), ovaries (female glands where egg cells develop), gallbladder (small sac under the liver), and breast. For some types of cancer, such as colon and breast, it is not clear whether the greater risk is due to extra body fat or to a high-fat and high-calorie diet.

Gallbladder disease People with obesity are more likely than other people to get gallbladder disease and gallstones, rock-like lumps that form in the gallbladder. Ironically, rapid weight loss itself can also lead to gallstones. Slower weight loss of about one pound a week is less likely to cause this problem.

Osteoarthritis Osteoarthritis (os-te-o-ar-THRY-tis) is a common disease that affects the joints (places where bones meet), especially those in the knees, hips, and lower back. Extra weight seems to promote osteoarthritis by putting extra pressure on these joints and wearing away the tissue that cushions and protects them.

Gout Gout (GOWT) is a joint disease that can lead to problems with the kidneys (organs that filter blood and get rid of waste products and excess water as urine). Gout is more common in people with obesity. Some diets may cause an attack of gout in people who are prone to it. Such people should check with a doctor before dieting.

Sleep apnea Sleep apnea (AP-nee-a) is a serious breathing disorder, which can cause a person to stop breathing for short periods during sleep and to snore heavily. It can lead to daytime sleepiness and sometimes heart failure. The more severe the obesity a person has, the greater the risk of getting sleep apnea.

Just the Facts

- The percentage of young people in the United States who are overweight has more than doubled in the past 30 years.
- About 58 million American adults have obesity.
- At any time in the United States, at least a third of women and a fifth of men are trying to lose weight.
- Poor diet and an inactive lifestyle cause at least 300,000 deaths among American adults each year.

What Causes Obesity?

People with obesity often are the subject of cruel jokes. It is important to remember, however, that obesity is a medical condition, not a character flaw. In the simplest terms, obesity occurs when people take in more calories* than they burn. The reason for this imbalance is still unclear. However, research studies suggest that there may be multiple causes.

* **calories** (KAL-o-reez) are units of energy that are used to measure both the amount of energy in food and the amount of energy the body uses.

Genes Children whose parents, brothers, or sisters have obesity are also more likely to develop obesity. Obesity does tend to run in families. However, not all children with a family history of obesity develop it themselves. Genes* may be one cause for those who do. Shared family behaviors, such as poor eating and exercise habits, also may play a part.

* **genes** are chemicals in the body that help determine a person's characteristics, such as hair or eye color. They are inherited from a person's parents and are contained in the cells of the body.

Lifestyle People's diet and activity level are both important factors affecting their weight. Americans tend to eat high-fat diets and lead inactive lifestyles. This is true of young people as well. More than four out of five young people eat too much fat, and almost half of those between ages 12 and 21 do not get regular vigorous exercise. One reason children are less active today is because of televisions, computers, and video games. The average American child spends many hours a week watching television, time that could be spent being active.

Psychology Many people eat when they feel bored, sad, or angry. In general, though, most people with obesity are as mentally healthy as anyone else. However, about 30 percent of people who are treated for severe obesity have trouble with binge (BINJ) eating. This means that they eat large amounts of food while feeling that they cannot control how much they are eating. Those with the most severe eating problems are said to have binge eating disorder. People with this disorder have more trouble than usual taking weight off and keeping it off.

Scientists use lab mice, like the one shown on the left, for research on the genetic causes of obesity. © *Jackson/Visuals Unlimited.*

Disease In rare cases, obesity is caused by a medical illness, such as a problem with hormones. These are chemicals that

Fad Diets

Fad diets are diets that usually have the goal of helping people lose a lot of weight in a short time. They become fads when they are widely advertised and reported in magazines, newspapers, television, and radio.

Fad diets often revolve around eating a particular food or food group. Fad diets have included the Cabbage Soup Diet, the Grapefruit Diet, the High Fat, High Protein, Low Carbohydrate Diet, and the Fat Burning Diet.

Realistic expectations for a weight-loss diet are the loss of about one half pound (250 grams) of fat over one week. Any more weight lost than that probably will be water.

The best diets recommend exercising and eating a balance of foods from all food groups. It is important to talk with a doctor before trying any diet.

are needed for the body to work normally. Certain drugs also may cause weight gain.

How Is Body Fat Measured?

Measuring a person's body fat is not as easy as it sounds. The most accurate method is to weigh the person underwater. However, this can only be done at laboratories with special equipment. There are two simpler ways for estimating body fat, although they can give faulty results if done by an unskilled person or on someone who has severe obesity. The first involves measuring the thickness of skin folds on various parts of the body. The second involves sending a harmless amount of electric current through the person's body. Both are widely used, but are often inaccurate. Doctors often rely on other ways to diagnose obesity:

Growth charts For children, doctors may use a chart that shows whether a child's weight at a certain height and age is within a healthy range. The doctor also takes the child's growth pattern into account.

Weight-for-height tables For adults, doctors may use a table that shows a range of healthy weights for a person of a given height. Some tables also take the person's sex, age, and frame size into account.

Doctors use charts showing height, weight, and body mass index as guidelines for determining whether people are at a healthy weight or whether they are overweight.

	Body mass index = [weight in kilograms] ÷ [height in meters]^2													
	19	20	21	22	23	24	25	26	27	28	29	30	35	40
Height (inches)	Weight (pounds)													
58	91	96	100	105	110	115	119	124	129	134	138	143	167	191
59	94	99	104	109	114	119	124	128	133	138	143	148	173	198
60	97	102	107	112	118	123	128	133	138	143	148	153	179	204
61	100	106	111	116	122	127	132	137	143	148	153	158	185	211
62	104	109	115	120	126	131	136	142	147	153	158	164	191	218
63	107	113	118	124	130	135	141	146	152	158	163	169	197	225
64	110	116	122	128	134	140	145	151	157	163	169	174	204	232
65	114	120	126	132	138	144	150	156	162	163	174	180	210	240
66	118	124	130	136	142	148	155	161	167	173	179	186	216	247
67	121	127	134	140	146	153	159	166	172	178	185	191	223	255
68	125	131	138	144	151	158	164	171	177	184	190	197	230	262
69	128	135	142	149	155	162	169	176	182	189	196	203	236	270
70	132	139	146	153	160	167	174	181	188	195	202	207	243	278
71	136	143	150	157	165	172	179	186	193	200	208	215	250	286
72	140	147	154	162	169	177	184	191	199	206	213	221	258	294
73	144	151	159	166	174	182	189	197	204	212	219	227	265	302
74	148	155	163	171	179	186	194	202	210	218	225	233	272	311
75	152	160	168	176	184	192	200	208	216	224	232	240	279	319
76	156	164	172	180	189	197	205	213	221	230	238	246	287	328

However, such tables are only rough guidelines. They cannot tell excess fat from muscle, so a very muscular person might appear to be obese using the information from this table when this is not the case.

Body mass index (BMI) Another method doctors use for adults is body mass index (BMI), a mathematical formula that includes a person's height and weight. BMI equals a person's weight in kilograms divided by height in meters squared (BMI = kg/m^2). Like weight-for-height tables, BMI is only a rough estimate that does not tell muscle from fat. In general, though, a BMI of 25 or more can be a sign of obesity in people ages 19 to 34. A BMI of 27 or more can be a sign of obesity in people ages 35 or older. A BMI of more than 30 can be a sign of moderate to severe obesity. BMI should not be used for growing children, pregnant or breast-feeding women, body builders, competitive athletes, or elderly people who are both inactive and frail.

Waist-to-hip ratio Doctors are concerned not only with how much fat an adult has, but also where that fat is located on the body. People whose fat is carried mostly around the belly, rather than on the hips, are more likely to develop many health problems linked to obesity. To find out which people have this body shape, doctors use the waist-to-hip ratio, which equals a person's waist measurement divided by the hip measurement. The health risks of obesity are higher in women with ratios of more than 0.8 and men with ratios of more than 1.0.

How Is Obesity Treated?

Research shows that the best way for people of all ages to control their weight is through regular exercise and a balanced diet. Adults can improve their health by losing as little as 10 to 20 pounds. To lose weight, people must take in fewer calories than they use. They can do this by becoming more active or eating less. The best weight-loss programs combine both of these approaches and also teach people healthy habits that they can follow for the rest of their lives.

Exercise Studies show that regular physical activity, combined with a good diet, is the healthiest and most effective way to control weight. Exercise uses excess calories that would otherwise be stored as fat.

Aerobic (air-O-bik) exercises are any extended activities that make a person breathe harder while using the large muscles at a regular, even pace. Such exercises burn more calories than other activities. They also strengthen the heart and lungs. Examples include brisk walking, jogging, bicycling, lap swimming, aerobic dancing, and using a treadmill or stationary bike. For the best results, aerobic exercise should be done for 20 to 30 minutes at a time, three or more times a week. People who are out of shape should start out exercising slowly.

Muscle strengthening exercises, such as weight training, and stretching exercises should also be part of a balanced exercise program. In addition to burning calories, these activities strengthen the muscles and bones and help prevent injury. Such exercises should be done at least twice a week.

Big Successes

These are just a few of the big names from history who had obesity:

- Louis Armstrong (1900–1971). American jazz musician.
- Sir Winston Churchill (1874–1965). British prime minister.
- Benjamin Franklin (1706–1790). American statesman and author.
- Jackie Gleason (1916–1987). American comedian and actor.
- Alfred Hitchcock (1899–1980). British-born American film director.
- Golda Meir (1898–1978). Israeli prime minister.
- Babe Ruth (1895–1948). American baseball player.
- William Howard Taft (1857–1930). American president.

Diet Children should never go on a diet to lose weight, unless a doctor tells them to do so for medical reasons. Limiting what children eat can interfere with their growth and may be harmful to their health. Instead, children should shift to eating better foods, with most coming from the grain, vegetable, and fruit groups. Some foods from the milk and the meat and bean groups should also be included. Junk foods, which provide few vitamins and minerals but are full of fat and sugar, should be eaten sparingly or avoided altogether. Fat should not be restricted in the diet of very young children. By the time children are five years old, however, they should get no more than 30 percent of their total calories from fat. Simple ways to cut back on fat include eating low-fat or nonfat dairy products, lean meats, and other low-fat or fat-free foods.

Adults who are trying to lose weight often go on low-calorie diets. Such diets typically contain 1,000 to 1,500 calories a day. The exact number of calories that is right depends on a person's size and activity level. The goal should be to lose no more than one pound a week while still eating a varied diet that includes plenty of grains, vegetables, fruits, and other healthful foods.

Other treatments Doctors may also treat severe obesity in other ways:

- **Very low-calorie diets.** These are specially prepared formulas that contain no more than 800 calories a day and replace all other foods. Such diets can lead to faster weight loss than ordinary low-calorie diets. Since they can cause side effects, however, they should only be used under a doctor's guidance.
- **Drugs.** Doctors can prescribe drugs to help adults with obesity who are apt to have health problems caused by their weight. Most drugs work by decreasing appetite or by increasing the feeling of being full. Such drugs are not magic, however. They are usually meant for short-term use over a few weeks or months, and they should always be part of an overall program that stresses long-term changes in exercise and diet. These drugs have the potential for abuse and can be addictive. They can also cause serious side effects, such as high blood pressure and sleep problems.
- **Surgery.** Doctors may advise surgery for people who are extremely overweight. There are two types of weight-loss surgery. One limits the amount of food the stomach can hold by closing off or removing part of the stomach. The other causes food to be poorly digested by bypassing the stomach or part of the intestines. Right after surgery, most people lose weight quickly. Although some weight is often regained later, many people keep much of it off. Unfortunately, surgery itself can cause complications that may lead to medical problems or the need for further operations. In addition, surgical treatment for obesity can reduce the amount of vitamins and minerals in the body and cause gallstones.

Heavy-Hitting Hints

It does not help much for a person to lose lots of weight only to regain it again. Keeping weight off is the toughest part of a weight-loss program for most people. The key to people keeping pounds off after they have been lost or stopping obesity before it starts is to learn healthy habits that last a lifetime. Here are some hints:

- **Get moving.** Turn off the television, computer, and video games in favor of more active things to do. Have fun with friends and family by sharing activities that are good exercise, such as walking, dancing, or bicycling. In addition, look for other ways to become more active throughout the day. For example, walk around during school breaks, and take the stairs instead of the elevator.
- **Eat slowly.** This makes it easier for a person to recognize feelings of hunger and fullness. One way for a person to slow down at meals is to make the meals as pleasant as possible. If meals are stressful, a person is tempted to eat faster in order to leave the table sooner.
- **Snack wisely.** Unplanned snacking often leads to overeating. Planned snacks at particular times of the day can be part of a balanced diet without spoiling the appetite at mealtimes. It is also important to choose healthy snacks, such as fresh fruit, raw vegetables, and low-fat yogurt.
- **Avoid eating in front of the television or computer.** People who are paying attention to a television or a computer are less likely to pay attention to feelings of fullness, and therefore may eat too much.

Resources

Books

Bennett, Cherie. *Life in the Fat Lane.* Laureleaf, 1999. A novel about the high school experiences of a girl from the wrong side of the scales.

Kirby, Jane. *Dieting for Dummies.* Foster City, CA: IDG Books Worldwide, 1998. A book from the American Dietetic Association.

Manheim, Camryn. *Wake Up, I'm Fat!* New York: Broadway Books, 1999. A memoir by a successful actress who wears a size 22 dress.

Organizations

Weight-Control Information Network, 1 WIN Way, Bethesda, MD 20892-3665. A service of the U.S. National Institute of Diabetes and Digestive and Kidney Diseases (NIDDK).
Telephone 800-946-8098
http://www.niddk.nih.gov/health/nutrit/win.htm

The U.S. Centers for Disease Control and Prevention (CDC) posts a fact sheet about obesity at its website.
http://www.cdc.gov/health/obesity.htm

American Dietetic Association, 216 West Jackson Boulevard, Suite 800, Chicago, IL 60606-6995. A group that offers sound advice about healthy eating.
Telephone 800-366-1655
http://www.eatright.org

Shape Up America!, 6707 Democracy Boulevard, Suite 306, Bethesda, MD 20817. A group that offers up-to-date information about healthy weight and increased exercise.
http://www.shapeup.org

TOPS Club, 4575 South Fifth Street, Milwaukee, WI 53207-0360. A club for people of all ages who are trying to Take Off Pounds Sensibly (hence, the name).
Telephone 800-932-8677
http://www.tops.org

Obsessive-Compulsive Disorder

Obsessive-compulsive disorder causes people to feel trapped by distressing and senseless thoughts or to feel as if they have to repeat actions, such as washing their hands or checking locks.

See also
Breast Cancer
Cancer
Colorectal Cancer
Diabetes
Eating Disorders
Gallstones
Gout
Heart Disease
Hypertension
Prostate Cancer
Sleep Apnea
Stroke

KEYWORDS
for searching the Internet and other reference sources

Anxiety disorders

Mental disorders

As Good as It Gets

In the 1997 movie *As Good As It Gets*, actor Jack Nicholson portrays a character who does many things that seem odd. He feels as if he has to eat lunch at the same table each day, and he always brings his own plastic utensils. He follows a complicated procedure to lock his front door. Many of the things he does, from the way he walks around cracks to the way he talks and thinks, are making his life more difficult to live. This character has obsessive-compulsive (ob-SES-iv-kom-PUL-siv) disorder, a mental disorder that affects approximately 4 to 7 million people in the United States.

What Is Obsessive-Compulsive Disorder (OCD)?

Many people have little rituals* that they follow. They might walk the same way to school every day or always touch a particular tree before going into their house. Other people have superstitions*, so they might refuse to walk under a ladder. These rituals and superstitions are generally harmless.

People with obsessive-compulsive disorder go much further. Some have obsessions*, which are repeated thoughts, urges, or images that intrude into a person's mind and seem senseless and distressing. Others have compulsions*, which are repeated behaviors or mental acts that a person feels driven to perform. Such behaviors are aimed at preventing or reducing distress, not providing pleasure. For example, people might have repeated, unnecessary doubts about whether they have performed an important task, such as locking the door. Or they might think that if they do not walk the same route to school every day, something awful will happen to them or to someone they love.

Obsessive thoughts can push aside more important things that the person needs to do and make the person feel compelled to take action. For example, people may follow the same route to school even if it takes them miles out of their way or makes them late for class. Or they may let their doubts about touching the tree cause them to go out and touch it again, only to doubt again whether they took the action. Such people may follow their compulsions because they hope to ease the anxiety* they feel about their obsessions.

The key difference between a harmless ritual or superstition and obsessive-compulsive disorder is that the thoughts and behaviors disrupt the lives of people with the disorder. They cannot resist their obsessions and compulsions, even though they know it makes little sense to think and do the things they do.

Doctors are not sure what causes obsessive-compulsive disorder. However, they suspect that the cause involves neurotransmitters* in the brain that are not sending signals correctly.

What Are the Symptoms of Obsessive-Compulsive Disorder?

The first signs of obsessive-compulsive disorder often appear during the late teenage years. The most common symptom is anxiety over germs. This may lead to washing the hands repeatedly, often with harsh cleansers, or to the fear of catching a disease from shaking hands or eating in restaurants.

Other symptoms include checking rituals, such as returning often to check a door lock, even though each time the person finds it locked. Some people with obsessive-compulsive disorder have violent thoughts. They may fear that they or someone they love will die in a horrible accident or that they will harm someone. One example is drivers who fear that they have run down someone, so they return to the spot to check or give up driving.

How Is Obsessive-Compulsive Disorder Diagnosed and Treated?

Obsessive-compulsive disorder is considered a type of anxiety disorder*. Diagnosis involves looking for symptoms and ruling out other physical and mental conditions, including other anxiety disorders. Many patients respond well to prescription drugs that change how neurotransmitters work in their brain.

Common vs. Uncommon

Here are some of the terms doctors use to describe obsessive-compulsive disorder and its treatment.

- **anxiety** (ang-ZY-e-tee) can be experienced as a troubled feeling, a sense of dread, fear of the future, or distress over a possible threat to a person's physical or mental well-being. It is normal to feel anxiety at times, particularly when a person is reacting to a threat of some kind. However, too much anxiety can interfere with the way the person functions in daily life.
- **anxiety disorder** is a mental disorder characterized by extreme, unpleasant, and unwanted feelings of apprehension or fear, sometimes accompanied by physical symptoms.
- **behavior therapy** is a type of counseling that helps people work to change undesirable behaviors.
- **compulsions** (kom-PUL-shunz) are repeated behaviors or mental acts that a person feels driven to perform. The goal of such behaviors is preventing or reducing distress, not providing pleasure. In many cases, the person feels driven to behave this way to reduce the distress caused by an obsession.
- **neurotransmitters** are chemicals in the nervous system that transmit nerve signals to and from the brain.
- **obsessions** (ob-SESH-unz) are repeated thoughts, urges, or images that intrude into a person's mind and seem senseless and distressing. They are not simply excessive worries about real-life problems. Such thoughts come to the mind despite the person's attempts to ignore or suppress them.
- **rituals** are actions that are repeated in a set way.
- **superstitions** are irrational beliefs resulting from false ideas, fear of the unknown, or trust in magic or chance.

Behavior therapy* to help patients overcome their anxieties also may be useful. One of the most effective types of behavior therapy is known as exposure and response prevention. During treatment sessions, patients are exposed to situations that give rise to their obsessions and compulsions. Patients then learn how to reduce, and eventually stop, their usual responses.

Although there is no way to prevent the disorder, it is important to seek help. Many people with obsessive-compulsive disorder hide their symptoms and withdraw from social contacts. They wait years to seek help, even though treatment is available and quite often successful.

The Boy Who Couldn't Stop Washing

Fourteen-year-old Charles would take showers for three hours or more each day, and then take another two hours to get dressed. His true story is one of many in the book *The Boy Who Couldn't Stop Washing*, by Dr. Judith L. Rapoport.

The book provides many views of obsessive-compulsive disorder as well as information about its causes, diagnosis, and treatment. One of the best things about *The Boy Who Couldn't Stop Washing* is that it encourages patients with obsessive-compulsive disorder and their families to speak out about their situation.

Resources

Book

Rapoport, Judith L. *The Boy Who Couldn't Stop Washing*. New York: Plume, reissued 1990. One of the first books to bring obsessive-compulsive disorder to public attention.

Organizations

U.S. National Institute of Mental Health, 6001 Executive Boulevard, Room 8184, MSC 9663, Bethesda, MD 20892-9663. A government institute that provides information about obsessive-compulsive disorder and other anxiety disorders. Its fact sheets *Step on a Crack* and *Obsessive-Compulsive Disorder* are posted at its website.
Telephone 888-8-ANXIETY
http://www.nimh.nih.gov/publicat/crack.cfm
http://www.nimh.nih.gov/anxiety/library/brochure/ocdbro.htm

American Psychiatric Association, 1400 K Street N.W., Washington, DC 20005. An organization of physicians that provides information about obsessive-compulsive disorder and other anxiety disorders. Its fact sheet *Let's Talk Facts About Obsessive-Compulsive Disorder* is posted at its website.
http://www.psych.org/public_info/ocd.html

Obsessive-Compulsive Foundation, P.O. Box 70, Milford, CT 06460-0070. A support organization for people with obsessive-compulsive disorder and their family and friends.
http://www.ocfoundation.org

See also
Anxiety Disorders
Mental Disorders
Tourette Syndrome

Osgood-Schlatter Disease

Osgood-Schlatter disease is a condition that causes knee pain in some children during their adolescent growth spurt.

KEYWORDS
for searching the Internet and other reference sources
Orthopedics
Osteochondrosis

Danny's Story

Danny's twelfth birthday marked the beginning of soccer season, a 4-inch growth spurt, and a lot of pain in his right knee. When Danny's coach asked him why he was limping, Danny told him that his knee hurt, especially when climbing stairs, kneeling, or jumping. His coach called his parents and suggested they take Danny to the doctor.

Danny's doctor examined the tender, swollen knee. When she pressed the area just below the kneecap gently, Danny grimaced in pain. The rest of the examination was normal. Danny had Osgood-Schlatter (OZ-good SHLAT-er) disease.

This diagnosis scared Danny at first, but quickly the doctor eased his mind by explaining that Osgood-Schlatter disease is a common condition in adolescent boys that almost always goes away on its own. It was named for an American surgeon, Robert Bayley Osgood (1873–1956), and a Swiss surgeon, Carl Schlatter (1864–1934), hence the long, serious-sounding name.

What Is Osgood-Schlatter Disease?

Osgood-Schlatter disease refers to pain that occurs at the bump on the shin bone, or tibia (TIB-e-a), just below the knee. This spot is where a tendon* from the muscles of the thigh attaches to the shin after passing over the kneecap. Sometimes, especially during the adolescent growth spurt, the place where the shin bone is actively growing partially detaches from the rest of the bone, resulting in pain and swelling. This problem most often occurs in children between the ages of 10 and 15, especially those who are active in sports, and it affects more boys than girls.

*__tendon__ (TEN-don) is a fibrous cord of connective tissue that attaches a muscle to a bone or other structure.

Osgood-Schlatter disease usually goes away after the growth spurt ends. To treat the symptoms, doctors suggest taking over-the-counter pain medicine such as ibuprofen (i-bu-PRO-fun) or acetaminophen (a-set-a-MEE-no-fen), stretching well before exercising, and cutting back on sports that require contraction of the quadriceps (KWOD-ri-seps) muscle of the thigh, such as squat thrusts or running. Some doctors will put a cast on the leg to limit a child's activity. Continuing to play sports usually will not make the condition worse, but it can delay the healing process. In a few cases, the problem does not go away on its own, because abnormal bony structures form or small pieces of bone become detached. In these cases, surgery may be required to remove the bone fragments.

Osteomyelitis

Osteomyelitis (os-te-o-my-e-LY-tis) is a bone infection that is caused by bacteria. It can involve any bone in the body, but it most commonly affects the long bones in the arms and legs.

KEYWORDS
for searching the Internet and other reference sources

Infection

Inflammation

Orthopedics

The End of Vacation

Kyle stepped on a nail on his first day of vacation at the lake. It punctured the bottom of his foot and hurt pretty badly. His mother cleaned the wound, put antibiotic ointment on it, and watched him for signs of infection. At first he just limped, but then he developed a fever and chills and complained that the bones in his legs hurt. That ended the vacation: Kyle's family packed up and took him home to see his doctor. Blood tests and x-rays showed that Kyle had a bone infection, a condition the doctor called osteomyelitis. Kyle took antibiotics and recovered fully within a month.

What Is Osteomyelitis?

Osteomyelitis is a bone infection that usually is caused by bacteria such as *Staphylococcus aureus* (staf-i-lo-KOK-us OR-e-us) or *Pseudomonas aeruginosa* (soo-do-MO-nas er-u-ge-NO-sa). Osteomyelitis also may be caused by fungal infections and by tuberculosis, a bacterial infection that most often affects the lungs. An open wound may be the pathway for the bacteria to enter the bloodstream of the body. A very common way that children get it is by stepping on a nail that punctures the shoe and the bottom of the foot. Osteomyelitis-causing fungi and bacteria often live in the soles of gym shoes and can infect the body by contact with wounds on the foot. Other sites of infections may spread into a bone and lead to osteomyelitis. For example, osteomyelitis may occur when a localized infection, such as sinusitis (inflammation of the sinuses in the head), spreads to the nearby bone.

Children get osteomyelitis more often than adults, possibly because children's bones are growing and require more blood circulation (and blood can carry the infection) than the bones of adults. One out of 5,000 children, and twice as many boys as girls, gets osteomyelitis.

What Happens When People Have Osteomyelitis?

The first signs that a person has osteomyelitis are fever, chills, and an overall ill feeling. Tenderness and pain in the infected bone almost always develop, and sometimes the infected area fills with pus. The bone marrow also may become infected.

Osteomyelitis can be either an acute (sudden) or a chronic (long-term) condition. When the bone becomes infected in acute osteomyelitis, the skin that covers the bone usually becomes inflamed and swollen. The condition is diagnosed by a blood culture, by a biopsy (tissue sample), or by an x-ray or bone scan examination. If acute osteomyelitis is confirmed, antibiotic treatment begins immediately, often with an excellent chance of complete recovery.

When osteomyelitis is not treated, or does not respond to treatment, it may become a chronic, or long-term, condition. In its chronic stages, osteomyelitis can be very painful and cause considerable damage to the infected bones. Sometimes this chronic form develops from compound fractures (more than one break in a bone). Antibiotics are used to treat chronic osteomyelitis, but sometimes surgery also is required to remove infected areas of bone.

In rare cases, the lung infection caused by tuberculosis can spread to bones (especially the spine), causing a form of osteomyelitis. When tuberculosis is involved, drugs to combat tuberculosis are used to treat both conditions.

Good hygiene is the best prevention for osteomyelitis. Proper treatment of all breaks in the skin is an important first step in preventing this bone infection. In the United States and other developed countries, osteomyelitis is an uncommon disease. When osteomyelitis does occur, it usually can be treated successfully.

See also
Bacterial Infections
Broken Bones and Fractures
Fungal Infections
Tuberculosis

Osteoporosis

Osteoporosis (os-te-o-po-RO-sis) is a disorder in which there is loss of bone density, which increases the likelihood of fracture.

KEYWORDS
for searching the Internet and other reference sources

Aging

Bones

Menopause

Skeletal system

Bone consists of two layers: a compact outer layer, called cortical bone, and a porous inner layer, called spongy (or cancellous) bone. Osteoporosis weakens mostly bones with a large percentage of spongy bone. These include the vertebrae (bones of the spine), the hips, and the wrists. Bones of this kind are more fragile and are especially prone to fracture when affected by osteoporosis.

Osteoporosis develops gradually over time, although rates vary in different individuals. It results from an imbalance in the normal process in which bone is constantly being broken down and replaced by new bone. In osteoporosis, the rate at which bone tissue is lost exceeds the rate at which it is replaced. This imbalance results in an overall loss of bone.

Prevalence of Osteoporosis

No one can say how many people have osteoporosis, because it develops gradually and merges with the natural process of aging. However, it is known that women are much more likely to develop the disorder than men, and that people of European ancestry have a higher incidence of osteoporosis than people of African ancestry.

Often, a person can have osteoporosis but not be aware of it until she fractures a bone. Typically, this happens in a fall that would not have caused the fracture to occur in a young adult. It has been estimated that in the United States osteoporosis is responsible for more than 1.2 million bone fractures each year. Among women, surveys indicate that at least 10 percent of those over age 50 have bone loss severe enough to increase the risk of fractures of the spine, hip, or long bones.

Types and Causes of Osteoporosis

Osteoporosis is classified as primary or secondary, depending on whether there is some other condition or abnormality causing the bone loss.

Primary osteoporosis Primary osteoporosis is the most common form of the disorder. It has been divided further into age-related osteoporosis, postmenopausal osteoporosis, and idiopathic (of unknown cause) juvenile osteoporosis. Age-related (or senile) osteoporosis occurs mostly in elderly people whose bones have become significantly thinner owing to their advanced age. Postmenopausal osteoporosis results from the acceleration of bone loss in women after they have reached menopause*, when their ovaries have stopped producing estrogen, a hormone that helps maintain bone mass.

* **menopause** (MEN-o-pawz) is the time of life when women stop menstruating (having their monthly period) and can no longer become pregnant.

The amount of bone mass a person has as a young adult when the skeleton is mature is believed to be related to the likelihood of developing osteoporosis after middle life. It is believed that the generally greater incidence* of osteoporosis in women than in men, and in people of European background than in those of African origin, is due largely to their lower skeletal density as young adults. Moreover, the density of bone in a person's skeleton in young adulthood is partly determined by his or her genes* (inherited), and people with lighter skeletons who develop osteoporosis in later life are likely to have relatives with the same condition.

* **incidence** means rate of occurrence.

* **genes** are chemicals in the body that help determine a person's characteristics, such as hair or eye color. They are inherited from a person's parents and are contained in the chromosomes found in the cells of the body.

Juvenile osteoporosis is rare and occurs in boys and girls before they reach their teens. It may last 2 to 4 years until normal bone growth resumes. Another uncommon form occasionally develops in young adults.

Secondary osteoporosis A condition is said to be "secondary" when it is caused by something else not functioning correctly. Secondary osteoporosis may have several causes. Immobility, as in someone with a paralytic disease, can cause the bones to thin and become brittle. This effect also has been observed in astronauts who have undergone prolonged periods of weightlessness in space. (It is difficult to get proper exercise when there is no gravity to work against.)

Additional causes of secondary osteoporosis include hormonal diseases, such as hyperthyroidism, and estrogen loss caused by failure or removal of the ovaries*. Nutritional disorders such as anorexia nervosa can also lead to osteoporosis. Smoking and heavy consumption of alcoholic beverages are thought to be strong contributing factors in some cases of osteoporosis.

* **ovaries** are the sexual glands in which eggs are formed in women and the female hormone estrogen is produced.

Signs and Symptoms

Osteoporosis does not always produce obvious symptoms. That is why an older person may first learn of his or her condition after breaking a bone in a fall. An x-ray then reveals the decreased bone density.

It has been estimated that 70 percent of fractures in people age 45 and older can be attributed to osteoporosis. About one third of women older than age 65 will have fractures of the vertebrae. The ratio of women to men experiencing spinal fractures is about 8 to 1. By the time people reach very advanced age, one third of women and one sixth of men will have broken a bone in the hip. Another common site of fracture is the forearm bone (radius) just above the wrist.

The thinning vertebrae in a person with osteoporosis may collapse spontaneously. Called compression fractures, these breaks can cause severe pain, usually in the mid or lower back. Chronic, or long-lasting, pain may develop after several such fractures have occurred. The person may gradually lose inches of height, and the upper back often curves forward. These signs and symptoms typically develop in women within 20 years after menopause if osteoporosis is not treated.

Diagnosing Osteoporosis

A diagnosis of osteoporosis is usually made by noting the person's physical appearance in general and the spine in particular. X-rays can reveal that the bones are less dense than normal. Special imaging techniques, including photon densitometry (FO-ton den-si-TOM-e-tree), are also used to detect osteoporosis.

In some instances, a blood test and bone biopsy (removal of a tiny sample of bone for examination) may be used to rule out the possibility of osteomalacia (OS-te-o-ma-LAY-she-a), a closely related condition in adults that results from a lack of vitamin D.

Treatment Options

If osteoporosis is not treated, the loss of bone density may continue. The risk of fractures will increase correspondingly as the person ages. Treatment is aimed primarily at stopping the bone loss.

Medications Calcium supplements in tablet form at recommended dosages are safe, inexpensive, and effective. Still more effective is treatment with the hormone estrogen, but this can have harmful side effects. Doctors may or may not prescribe estrogens, depending largely on other health considerations in individual patients. Other drugs such as calcitonin can prevent bone loss and may be given to women who do not take estrogen.

Certain drugs taken to treat other conditions may have the additional effect of causing bone loss. The use of such medications may have to be curtailed or adjusted for people who have osteoporosis. Cortisone, thyroid hormone, and diuretics (used for various disorders to increase the flow of urine) are examples of drugs that can cause loss of bone density.

Men who develop osteoporosis usually are not given hormone treatment but take calcium supplements and can be given some of the newer drugs available.

Lifestyle General measures that can be taken to slow further loss of bone include undertaking a regular program of exercise (including long walks or some equivalent activity), quitting smoking, and drinking alcoholic beverages only in moderation. Good eating habits are important, and a balanced diet should include

False-color x-ray of upper part of femur (thigh bone) with osteoporosis shown in yellow-orange. Fractures are likelier when this amount of osteoporosis occurs because it decreases bone density, which increases brittleness. *Alfred Pasieka/Science Photo Library, Photo Researchers, Inc.*

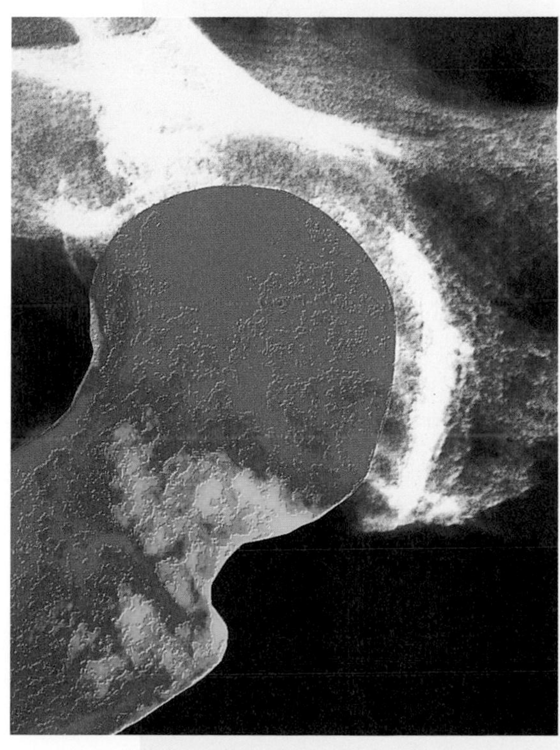

adequate calcium, vitamins, and other nutrients. Elderly people need to take precautionary measures to avoid falls.

Pain Relief Standard pain-relieving drugs, such as aspirin, and heat applications can be used for back pain. Posture training and special exercises for the stomach and back muscles can have long-term benefits in reducing pain and discomfort. Occasionally a back brace may be necessary to provide support.

Early Prevention

The best time to start taking steps to prevent osteoporosis is during the childhood and teen years. This is particularly so for young women with lightweight skeletons and small bones and who have close relatives with osteoporosis. As in older people, getting plenty of regular exercise is important, as is calcium in the diet. It is estimated that more than 70 percent of children and teenagers fail to consume adequate amounts of calcium in their diets. Foods rich in calcium include milk and other dairy products, green leafy vegetables, citrus fruits, fish such as sardines and mackerel, and shellfish. The aim is to achieve full, normal bone density in the skeleton at maturity.

Lifestyle choices such as not smoking and limiting alcohol use are important. Also to be avoided are fad diets that promise rapid weight loss. While exercise, particularly supervised weight training, is important in the prevention of osteoporosis, excessive exercise in teenage girls and young women can have the opposite effect. Extreme amounts of exercise (especially if it is combined with dieting and weight loss) can cause the stopping of menstrual periods and decreased estrogen levels in the body. Significant bone loss can be a result.

Calcium Supplements

Calcium is essential for developing strong bones and teeth and for the proper function of heart, muscles, and the nervous system. Getting enough calcium is especially important for children, adolescent females, and pregnant women. Studies have shown that proper bone development in adolescent females can lessen the effects of osteoporosis later in life. If the diet does not provide enough calcium (for example, when someone is allergic to dairy products), calcium supplements can help make up the difference.

Calcium is usually found in foods and supplements as a salt—that is, the calcium is chemically combined with another element or compound. It is important to read the label of any calcium supplement to find out how much calcium it supplies and in what form of salt it is. Some people's bodies have problems absorbing particular forms of calcium; such persons should avoid calcium supplements with those salts.

Did You Know?

- The thinning of bones due to osteoporosis is believed responsible for more than 1.2 million fractures in the United States each year.
- Someone can have osteoporosis and not know it.
- Spinal curvature in the elderly is a common sign of osteoporosis.
- People can lose several inches of height as a result of osteoporosis.
- The great majority of people with osteoporosis are women.
- Young women in their teens with small bones can take important steps to avoid osteoporosis in later life.

Resources

Books

Bonnick, Sydney Lou. *The Osteoporosis Handbook.* Dallas, TX: Taylor Publishing Company, 1997. Provides further information on the disorder in nontechnical language and is fully illustrated.

Germano, Carl. *The Osteoporosis Solution: New Therapies for Prevention and Treatment.* New York: Kensington Publishing Corporation, 1999. Emphasizes nutrition as it relates to osteoporosis.

Organizations

The National Institutes of Health posts information about osteoporosis on its website.
http://www.nih.gov/niams/healthinfo/opbkgr.htm

The National Osteoporosis Foundation posts relevant information on its website.
http://www.nof.org

Osteoporosis and Related Bone Disorders—National Resource Center also maintains a website with useful information.
http://www.osteo.org

The U.S. Centers for Disease Control and Prevention (CDC), located in Atlanta, Georgia, posts information about osteoporosis at its website.
http://cdc.gov/nceh/

▶ *See also*
Broken Bones and Fractures
Eating Disorders
Rickets
Thyroid Disease

Ovarian Cancer *See* Uterine/Cervical Cancer